PLANNING AND EDUCATIONAL INEQUALITY

A study of the rationale of resource-allocation

This book is dedicated to the memory of the late Phyllis Mary Higgs, former head-mistress of South Park High School for Girls, Lincoln, to whom so many generations of girls owed their equality of educational opportunity during an era of basic inequality.

Planning and educational inequality

A study of the rationale of resource-allocation

Eileen M. Byrne BA PhD

NFER Publishing Company Ltd.

Published by the NFER Publishing Company Ltd.,
Book Division, 2 Jennings Buildings, Thames Avenue,
Windsor, Berks., SL4 1QS
Registered Office, The Mere, Upton Park, Slough, Berks., SL1 2DQ
First Published 1974
© E. M. Byrne 1974
85633 039 6

Printed in Great Britain by
John Gardner (Printers) Limited, Hawthorne Road, Bootle, Merseyside L20 6JX

Distributed in the USA by Humanities Press Inc.,
Hillary House-Fernhill House, Atlantic Highlands, New Jersey, 07716, USA.

CONTENTS

LH
632
.B97

ACKNOWLEDGEMENTS

This work would not have been possible without the practical help and guidance of many people and organizations to whom grateful thanks are due. The *Inner London Education Authority* sponsored and financed the PhD thesis on which this book is based, including a sabbatical year on full pay, and thanks are especially due to that authority for their early faith in the project. At *London University Institute of Education*, Dr George Baron's early support was decisive in establishing the research; but warm acknowledgement is due to Dr Margherita Rendel whose constructive guidance and clear tutorial help over four years partly determined the successful completion of the research. The *Central Research Fund of London University* gave a grant towards the research expenses.

To the Chief Education Officers, Council and Committee members and staffs of *Lincoln, Nottingham* and *Northumberland* local education authorities, thanks are due for unprecedented research facilities and generous practical help. I am especially indebted for the longterm loan of annual reports, epitomes of accounts, published material and data prepared specially; and for the complete freedom of access to staff and records which they trusted to me.

Thanks should also be recorded to the Department of Education and Science, the AEC and the Northern Region of the Central Youth Employment Executive for special data made available for the project.

The writer wishes warmly to acknowledge the contribution of the teaching profession; the heads and principals of schools and colleges visited and representatives of teachers' organizations, who have provided evidence, material and valuable ideas and for whom this work was really undertaken in the hope that the next decade of decision-makers will learn from the last.

Finally, the writer's thanks to Derrick Atkinson, architect in Lincoln, for drawing all diagrams for both thesis and book; to Wendy Lee without whose secretarial help and speed neither thesis nor book would have reached the printers on time; and to Janice Bunn, my current secretary, the value of whose support has been critical in the last year before reorganization of local government.

ABBREVIATIONS AND INTERPRETATIONS

Post-war	After World War II (1939–45)
Pre-war	Before World War II (1939–45)
Form entry	The number of classes admitted to a secondary school at 11+ (thus a four-form entry school admits 4 x approximately 30 or 120 pupils each year)
Ministry of Education	Although the Ministry of Education was renamed the Department of Education and Science in 1964 the term Ministry has been used throughout for simplicity
Members	Councillors or Education Committee members
LEA	Local Education Authority
CEO	Chief Education Officer
AEC	Association of Education Committees
CCA	County Councils Association
HORSA	Hutted Operation for Raising the School Age (1947)
AMC	Association of Municipal Corporations
NUT	National Union of Teachers
Joint Four	The Joint Four Secondary Associations
NAS	National Association of Schoolmasters
GCE	General Certificate of Education
CSE	Certificate of Secondary Education
NCTEC	Northern Counties Technical Examinations Council
(SB)	Secondary boys (school)
(SG)	Secondary girls (school)
(SM)	Secondary mixed (school)

LIST OF DIAGRAMS

CHAPTER I
Introduction and Background

*'It is not the evils which are new; it is the recognition
of them'*

Macaulay (*1800–1859*)

This research project is about the allocation of educational resources
for secondary education. It is therefore fundamentally about
'educational rationing' because the constantly increasing demands
which the education and social services in particular make on limited
public funds regularly outstrip available central and local resources.
And the more so since in times of national economic crises, the public
sector inexorably bears the brunt of constant cut-back. Rationing is
in turn about priorities. Although the research was limited to the
secondary sector, the principles and psychology which have emerged
seem equally relevant to other sectors and services, notably health,
housing and social services whose demands also correlate inversely
to their capital and revenue resources.

The research was undertaken in the period 1968–72, and represents
a detailed analysis of the availability and the allocation of resources
for secondary education in the areas of three local education
authorities, the cities of Lincoln and Nottingham and the county of
Northumberland during the 20 years from 1945 to 1965. It sought to
re-examine some current assumptions about the allocation of
resources in educational administration and in schools. Was there a
rationale of the allocation of resources, based on consistent and
measurable principles? Or were principles subservient to administrative or political accidents in timing, and to controls outside local
government? The research attempted to test how far specific or
dynamic demand affected the release and the allocation of resources;
and how far, conversely, constant lack or limitation of resources
artificially depressed demand. Was it in fact true that political
factors, pressure group tactics, involvement of teachers' organizations
and expressed demands of industry influenced education development through the allocation of resources? Or were other factors
more influential, not to say decisive, such as specific controls direct
from central government; regional and local inherited attitudes;
growth in the proportion of the budget taken by intractable expenditure; widening differentials between richer and poorer
authorities; and unco-ordinated and over-rapid expansion of
expensive curricular innovation for a minority of schools?

It seemed likely that a detailed study of the actual availablity and distribution of resources in some contrasting local authorities would provide at least some answers to these questions. In particular, such an analysis might show the influence or otherwise of *implicit* and *explicit* demand on the allocation of resources, and suggest a relationship between the level and type of resources available on the one hand, and the development of types and standards of education to the educational and vocational needs of secondary school pupils.

In practice, the findings of the inquiry have highlighted on the one hand acute inequality of educational opportunity creating a cycle of deprivation for some groups of pupils in some areas. On the other hand, evidence also emerges of dedicated work by staffs and heads in local education authorities, faced with the task of making bricks without straw (or with ersatz substitutes) in two decades of post-war educational reconstruction.

It might be thought that a survey ending in 1965, nearly a decade ago, has only limited relevance today. Unfortunately many of the tendencies traced in the 20-year period up to 1965 have become more and not less acute since then. Central controls have increased still further. The national failure to match building costs with capital resources based on realistic cost limits has reached and remained at crisis point. The 10-year gap between major recessions (1950–53 and 1960–63, see Chapter V) has narrowed to three (1967, 1970 and 1973), causing drastic slashing of educational building programmes and revenue at a time when the backlog of need identified in this research is still far from wholly met.

How far are the patterns of committee influence, local authority organization and officer involvement still relevant in the light of local government reorganization? Corporate management still remains in 1974 an imperfectly grasped and largely suspect concept in many areas. Very few if any of the new local education authorities have taken the opportunity to build into their establishment educational research officers to monitor and evaluate the many indices of performance and of standards which are now readily available—or of correlations between budget allocation and output. Such monitoring and evaluation are however necessary to prevent a repetition of the Topsy-like quality of growth in the earlier post-war years and to reduce the manifest inequalities which still exist between and within authorities. And local authority education officers are on the whole both too near their problems and increasingly too over-worked to combine constant assessment with the increasingly difficult task of running the service.

The Research: I. Definition of Terms

Resources for the education service are controlled nationally as well as locally. Diagram A on the following page illustrates the actual pattern of the control and allocation of resources in 1965. Resources may be defined as *financial* (capital and revenue), *staffing* (teachers, administrators and other professional staff) and *material* (buildings, major and minor building programmes, books and equipment, etc.)

Financial resources include the capital and revenue budgets available to the county borough and county councils as a whole and not only the total available for education expenditure. Any survey of what is available to meet local needs must also take account of central government grants, that is percentage grants before 1959 and block grants and special grants thereafter, and, where appropriate, Exchequer Equalization or Rate Deficiency Grants. On the other hand, actual *financial need* can be defined as the level of capital and revenue resources which a local education authority needs, for example, in order to build and maintain enough schools to educate all pupils of compulsory school age, and others according to 'age, ability and aptitude'; or to employ enough teachers to meet its quota and keep class sizes to the acceptable national average; or to maintain a viable administrative and advisory establishment for continuity of educational planning and of educational standards. It will need to carry out the increasing mandatory requirements of education legislation. It is distinguished from estimated financial need, or the assessment made by a local Finance Committee based on historical precedent and on an arbitrarily fixed growth rate, which may be lesser or greater than actual need, in practice. Actual need may also differ from the assessment of an authority's needs by central government when awarding equalization grants to raise its rateable resources to the national average.

Staffing resources include teachers, administrators, inspectors and supporting professional staff while *staffing need* is the level of staff required efficiently to carry out the authority's declared policy. Thus an authority may need more than its agreed basic quota of teaching staff in order to develop extended courses in non-grammar schools, remedial work in especially deprived schools, in-service training of teachers or the introduction of new curricular methods which tend to be expensive on staff time. Staffing need may also be the actual number and calibre of educational professional and administrative staff needed to maintain an effective school building programme without falling behind schedule, or to review and assess the education service with a view to the development of certain sectors, as distinct from the staffing establishments with which the Establishment

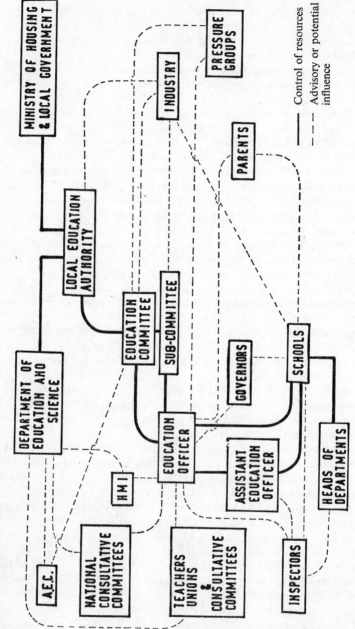

DIAGRAM A: *Control of flow resources—1965*

Control of resources
Advisory or potential influence

Committee estimates a department ought to be able to manage.

Material resources include the inherited capital plant of an authority, its new buildings as they are planned and built, books, equipment and furniture and major specialist aids (for example CCTV). Introduction of new curricular methods (audio-visual language teaching, Nuffield science) is directly correlated with increased allowances for equipment and capitation generally. Maintenance of existing standards is also highly correlated with an increase in resources to match rising costs which will enable outdated texts to be replaced promptly, for example. They also include the national pool of building labour and materials—the period from 1946–53 was one of acute shortage of steel, timber and bricks, a shortage which had a decisive effect on building programmes and on subsequent secondary policy. Even now one of the many reasons advanced by central government for controlling capital building programmes is the limited pool of building resources available regionally and nationally.

Educational need may be interpreted as the level and type of resources required by education officers and by teachers to achieve the kind of educational goals which they consider appropriate for their pupils. Child-centred learning requires, for example, on the whole larger teaching areas, more varied apparatus and more generous allocation of water, gas and power points than the traditional 'chalk and talk' methods. And these will cost more. The type and level of resources needed may vary markedly from the conditions in which teachers have had to manage for the past 25 years and in which some lay Committees might therefore expect them to manage pending the millenium of 'adequate' resources.

Demand on the other hand can be either *explicit* or *implicit*. These terms will be used throughout and should be taken as relating to the definitions which follow. *Explicit demand*, as its name implies, is identifiable influence or pressure by people for the provision of a service or facility or for an improvement in standard which can be clearly defined and which is specifically aimed at those controlling resources (for example Ministers, Committees, Education Officers, heads). Demand may not coincide with need. An area may need new primary school places or extended opportunities for the less able; but the vocal demand may be for more grammar school places. It may need more school transport or more youth clubs; but the articulate demand may be for a sports centre. Explicit demand may come from any or all of the following:

(i) Ministers or Ministries using legislation, nationally imposed standards or financial policies;

(ii) national organizations such as the AEC, AMC, CCA, or the Publishers' Association;

(iii) Committees and Sub-Committees of the Council, seeking to influence either central government departments or their own colleagues;

(iv) chief officers operating in competition or in co-operation with other policy departments;

(v) senior professional and advisory staff who may influence the allocation of resources within their department;

(vi) other local authority departments (for example housing departments create demand for new schools to serve new housing estates);

(vii) teachers and heads, and teachers' organizations (mainly concerned with allocations between and within schools);[1]

(viii) governing bodies;

(ix) industry;

(x) specific pressure groups (for example AASE) and parents.

Explicit demand can be expressed at all levels in the education service. For example, heads of departments make specific and variable demands on head teachers either for more resources generally, or for specific money and equipment for new developments (Project Technology, educational television). Heads will in turn exert pressure on inspectors and on the administration, with or without help from governors. Within the administration, influences are felt which (in theory) affect how much the secondary, as distinct from primary or further education sectors may receive from the basic budget and from the (narrowing) margin for new developments. Chief officers are more or less successful in influencing Committees and Ministries according to their experience, calibre and temperament. All this must be seen in a national framework affected by outside conditions not limited to the education sector—the national economy, competition for skilled man-power (especially, for example, maths and science graduates in the 1950s), other social demands on financial and building resources (urban redevelopment and slum clearance). Pressure alone may be ineffective in the face of the highly individual educational philosophies held by education officers and teachers, leading them to define quite different educational goals towards which they allocate their resources. The addition of judgement is required, particularly on tactics and timing. An accurate and sensitive use of professional judgement can be (and in the survey areas, was) a decisive factor in successfully re-allocating resources to meet educational needs, without which educational progress would be difficult or impossible.

Implicit demand on the other hand is more complex and less easily recognized. It arises from policies or situations rather than from individuals or groups of personalities. A recurrent example is the concealed demand for extra resources resulting from curriculum development. An acceptance in principle for example of new practical methods of teaching languages using audio-visual aids, carries with it an implicit decision to allocate future money from a restricted budget, for the probable provision of language laboratories, more tape recorders, commercial audio-visual programmes and new textbooks, which may accordingly reduce the margin for other curricular development. Similarly acceptance in principle of the Nuffield Science and Project Technology programmes places an extra obligation on the equipment element of future budgets which inevitably competes with demand for money to improve existing science provision. In another sense, a policy decision of the authority (or of its officers by delegated powers) to double its capital programme will create an additional implicit demand of future revenue resources; partly because of increased maintenance costs and partly because of the very substantial proportion of revenue which has to be allocated for loan charges. Nationally for example, loan charges for capital investment in education expressed as a proportion of appropriate annual expenditure on education, increased from 4·19 per cent in 1951–52 to 9·13 per cent in 1961–62.[2] Another major example of implicit demand is the change in the size, distribution and age of the secondary school population over the survey period. Tables II (a) to II (c) of Appendix B give full details of growth in the survey areas over the 20-year period. Thus the demand for extra school places is inherent in the requirement for statutory schooling from 5–15, if the school population within that age group increases. The demand is implicit in the accepted assumption of compulsory schooling; and certainly the demand is not an explicit one on the part of all pupils.

II The Possible Influence of Demand

Are local education authorities sensitive to demand in fact? And if so, what kind of demand? Bleddyn Davies suggests that:

'It seems likely that local authorities are more sensitive to the ethos of a locality and to local pressure groups, than they are to the relative needs of their population for services (as they appear to someone judging all authorities by the same criteria) if only because a local authority lacks machinery for comparing its own relative needs and provisions with those of other authorities.'[3]

There is in fact, however, very little firm evidence about the degree of importance which local communities and citizens attach to the different services provided for them, and their relative importance. It is doubtful how far the computer analysis of *overall* figures and indices, which illustrates many of Davies's conclusions, can do other than indicate very general trends, and how far it can take into account why the facts are as they appear to be in each area; or what administrative or political factors have affected the 'territorial justice' which he defines validly as 'To each area according to the needs of the population of that area' (needs—not demands).

In practice, the distribution of resources tends to remain fairly constant in a static community (such as Lincoln), but in a fast-changing society, the increased competition for resources leads to uneven and inconstant levels of resources. The competitive element (between services, and between sectors) has increased steadily over the past 20 years with a concurrent increase in a complexity of demands from groups attempting to influence decision-making in local authorities. This competitive factor affects decisions relating both to the initial supply of resources (for example capital building programmes) and to issues of major policy. Given this, three hypotheses, two of which are mutually contradictory, emerge. Demand significantly affects the acquisition and allocation of resources. Demand has no effect at all. Demand has only a sporadic or partial effect. But there seems little evidence, based on empirical research as such, available to support, directly or indirectly, an assumption that demand does or does not affect the release of resources for education. The question seems increasingly pertinent. For if explicit demand can release resources (an outstanding or vociferous head of department in a school; a successful chief officer in Council), constant lack of resources does nevertheless depress demand. Assessment of future allocations tends to be calculated on the basis of past needs and on the likely percentage increase that can be negotiated, and not on present or future needs. Most influential is the psychological deterrent, that demands tend to be fixed at a level approaching what is likely to be given. Constant conditioning against 'extravagance' or 'frills', or conversely, conditioning towards the encouragement of innovation and improvement, are important influences on apparent demand.

There are thus two conflicting principles applying here which interact. Which dominates is likely to depend on the basic philosophy of the local education authority, which will tend either to decide on a general policy and to match its aspirations by allocating resources accordingly, or to limit its aspirations to the level of existing resources. Relationships within this framework will be both *imposed* on local education authorities by outside factors (legislation; national limits of resources like the timber and steel shortage in the 1940s and building programme allocations; regional inherited attitudes) and *self-set* (development of audio-visual aids; gradual installation of TV; gradual replacement of obsolete furniture; an agreed annual margin for experimental work).

I have suggested that there is little research evidence so far to confirm or deny the effect of demand on resources. Two major national reports have, however, suggested that its effect is at least measurable. The Crowther report commented in 1959 that:

'The evidence goes to show that good educational facilities, once provided, are not left unused; they discover or create a demand that public opinion in the past has been slow to believe existed. If this is so, then it follows that many boys and girls are at present deprived of educational facilities which they would use well and which they are legally entitled to receive. The translation of this great potential demand into effective demand, by the provision of extended courses manifestly within the reach of every secondary school boy or girl who wants them, seems to us to be an immediate task for the educational system.'[4]

And the Robbins report not only dealt at some length with the increased demand for higher education (which has in fact affected subsequent provision), but also established quite clearly the relevance of secondary resources, especially grammar school places, to the level and type of recruitment to higher education. This research does in fact, therefore, attempt to measure the effect of demand on resources as well as to trace the actual pattern of allocations which have developed.

III Method

This research has been confined to the secondary sector although the problem of resources at the primary stage is as crucial to sound educational development. It was however necessary to limit the project to manageable proportions, and both sectors could not be covered in enough depth as a combined project. It could be argued that the most final influences on a young person's future career and qualifications occur in the secondary years; and that factors affecting educational opportunities in the secondary sector would directly affect adversely or well future employment, training or entry to further and higher education. Moreover, the more varied organization of secondary education both between and within schools demands a greater complexity in the allocation of resources, notably because of the wider curricula and the demands of external examinations; but also because of inherited assumptions leading to differential levels of resources considered appropriate for older and younger, and for able and less able secondary pupils; and even for boys and for girls.

Time-span

To assess with any validity either the influences affecting the use of resources, or trends in their distribution, inquiry over a fairly long time-span is necessary. The period 1945–65 has been chosen for a number of reasons. The development of post-war secondary education in the local authority sector springs directly from the development plans prepared as a result of the 1944 Education Act which was to provide 'secondary education for all' at last. The inquiry therefore stems naturally from these development plans, using them as starting points. The survey period ends, appropriately enough, at the issue of circular 10/65 of the Department of Education and Science[5] which made necessary a complete revision of the existing development plans and the preparation of new schemes for secondary education in each area.

The choice of the survey areas

Given the likely variety of factors affecting the supply and allocation of resources, and the varied effect of demand, it seemed important to look at developments in different areas so as to cover all likely important relevant factors (although no one area would be likely to contain all factors). It was therefore necessary to look at both a county borough and a county council since their responsibilities and financial arrangements differ. Viability was likely to be a factor—it therefore became important to choose one very small and one reasonably large authority. Preferably, the positions of a relatively poor and a relatively rich authority (or one needing and one not qualifying for, equalization grants) should be reviewed. Different social class structures might be relevant, especially in the context of articulate demand. Finally, urban and rural problems differ; it would be helpful to cover both. The main criteria was therefore size, type, financial standing and social background. Less than two would not throw up all factors; more than three would be beyond the resources of a single research worker.

Lincoln and *Nottingham* county boroughs and *Northumberland* county council were chosen and all three authorities agreed to cooperate. Readers not familiar with these areas are advised to read the profiles in Appendix A before the main work. *Lincoln* (77,180 population) was a small county borough in a rural area with low rateable value, qualifying for a reasonably high degree of government grant, with a stable population and a slow rate of growth. Its organization of secondary education was bipartite with a strong grammar sector (25 per cent in 1945) but an under-developed secondary modern sector until 1964. Its inherited local traditions were strong, possibly because of its historical position and its relative isolation from the urban Midlands. As a very small authority its staffing structure was necessarily limited and its financial viability questionable. *Nottingham* (315,050) by contrast was much larger, a regional centre for the East Midlands, with a heavy concentration of major industry and a high rateable value per head. Unlike Lincoln it had had a School Board and had inherited many old buildings from Victorian and Edwardian times. It was initially tripartite (grammar, technical and modern) with only 12 per cent of grammar school places in 1945 but discontinued its technical schools, after the development of bilateral schools in the mid 1950s. Like Lincoln its social background is predominantly working class and lower middle class, the 'higher' social and economic groups tending to live outside the city in the county area. This authority has been sufficiently financially viable not to need any substantial equalization grants from the central authority. One strong local tradition in the earlier postwar years was that of a town dominated by large family businesses.

Northumberland (494,400) was substantially larger than the two other authorities, of average size for a county council. It is an area of sharp contrasts, including urban Tyneside, small market towns and the outlying Cheviot Hills and the Border country. Like most mainly rural counties its financial viability was marginal and it has received very substantial Exchequer equalization grants over the years, to bring its rate resources up to the national average. It inherited a substantial number of all-age schools in 1945, housing over 30 per cent of pupils of secondary age, developed a tripartite system (grammar, technical and modern) until 1959, and had grammar and technical places for only 13 per cent to 15 per cent of the age group for most of the survey period. Few of its secondary modern schools developed extended courses until late in the survey period. Its problems vary from the social and educational ones of deprived areas of Tyneside, to those of the scattered small schools in underpopulated rural areas. Its strongest inheritance is vivid and lingering memories of the depression of the 1920s and 1930s which colour many regional attitudes even today, particularly the vocational aspirations of many school leavers who seek security rather than skilled training in industries at risk.

Appendix D contains further information about method, sources interviews and the 31·5 per cent sample of secondary schools visited in the survey areas, while Appendix B contains full statistical tables for all three authorities. Appendix E gives the actual secondary building programme for each area over the 20 year period.

Although the tables in Appendix B give full details of population changes, school population and financial resources and of their allocation, in all three authorities over the survey period, care must be taken in interpreting these data, which should be read in relation to the description of events in each area and not used necessarily in direct comparison. Financial data in local authority accounts are also not always directly similar, and may be based on different accounting principles. Readers are therefore advised to refer to the tables mainly as check-points, in reading the chapters which follow. The following extract will be a useful initial guide to the relative sizes of the authorities.

Table I (1)

Authority	Population (1945)	Population (1965)	School Population (1965)	Secondary Schools (1965)
Lincoln	65,280	77,180	12,643	12
Nottingham	265,090	315,050	51,643	40
Northumberland	412,080	494,440	78,064	79

Assessment of standards

Certain basic standards have been used as a yardstick where they could be readily applied. The level of grammar school places (or the equivalent provision of advanced courses elsewhere) is generally accepted as one valid index. Another is the Building Code and the Building Bulletins issued by the Department of Education and Science. The 'good average' standards of allowance for books and materials recorded by the IMTA, the AEC and the Publishers' Association are a useful basis for discussion. Davies accepts as indices, if crude, the proportion staying on at school, awards to students and training college entries, and, in common with others, supports the hypothesis that availability of *selective* places affects the level of entry to higher education.

'Variations in the proportions of 13-year-olds in grammar school streams in 1956 is strongly correlated with the proportion of pupils staying on to sit "A" level, and to a lesser extent with the number of pupils going on to further education . . . The past provision of grammar schools, because it affects the proportion of the age group staying on till they are 17, has a very marked effect on the numbers going on to higher education.'[6]

Pupil/teacher ratios and sizes of classes, together with the percentage of grammar places were regarded as valid criteria by the IMTA.[7] Staffing standards are measurable, as is overall cost per pupil. On the other hand, declarations of parity of esteem between types of schools offered opportunities to measure whether the intent was matched by the resources. Thus, national government declared that 'The Modern School will be given parity of conditions with other types of secondary schools',[8] while Lincoln City for example declared its intention that 'Every effort is being made to provide the amenities at these (modern) schools of a standard equivalent to those provided at grammar schools'.[9]

Where possible, assessment has been based on generally accepted standards and these have been referred to where appropriate in the text of later chapters.

It must be stressed however that any attempted measurement is of standards of resources on the one hand and of identifiable output on the other (destinations of school leavers, overall examination successes, takeup of V and VI form courses, etc.) and the correlation of these, if any. There has been no attempt, nor any intention, to measure the quality of education which will, as always, depend on the teaching force, on pupils and on parents, and the measurement of which defies more skilled and numerically larger teams of research workers. That standards of resources are, however, relevant to the quality of education most teachers would support. Indeed, Sir Ronald Gould, speaking to the World Confederation of Organizations of the Teaching Profession, said in his Presidential address in 1963 that there are three prerequisites for quality in education; good physical environment; enough teachers; and good teachers.

'Whenever criticism is directed at shocking school buildings, obsolete equipment or an inadequate supply of books, someone is sure to reply "This is really unimportant. What really matters is the quality of the teacher." No doubt this sounds virtuous, but often such people really wish to economize on both schools and teachers . . . school buildings can increase or limit educational opportunity in the narrower sense . . . Can children be taught to love books when there is no library, explore modern knowledge if all text books are dated, and there is no radio, film or television?'[10]

This research sought also to relate standards of resources to standards of educational opportunity in the three survey areas.

Relevance of the research
The project was ambitious for a single research worker and its

limitations are accepted. It is at least however a useful basepoint, and some of the basic correlations which emerge and the ideas which lie behind, will sponsor further debate. Because, for example, the relationship of supply and demand is examined is not to argue that all demands should be met. But if major and basic demands have a lessening influence on the sharing of resources, the likelihood of 'educational equality' and of real partnership in the education service becomes vulnerable. Because again, forms of discriminal allocation are identified, is not to say that all discrimination in its literal sense is wrong ('to make or constitute a difference between: a distinction or division') but to question the ideologies behind the particular selective practices used. It is not necessarily wrong to have smaller schools but may be debatable how far we should deny them an adequate educational pool of resources to achieve the objectives we still set them, in order to spend money elsewhere. And it is by no means a matter for criticism to register the importance of the personality, calibre and quality of the education leadership, if we wish to preserve a healthy and more autonomous local government—as long as we are pellucidly clear just how and why decisions as basic as allocations of resources, are reached.

That some indices are superficial does not wholly invalidate them in the context of a reorganized local government. The most serious problem now facing teachers and authorities is one of perpetual 'educational rationing' of basic resources between authorities and between schools—buildings and specialist rooms, teachers, books, money, even courses of advanced further education. A widening differential between the haves and the have-nots, declining standards of accommodation, libraries, or material resources, risk accentuating the trend to give in to dynamic demand (often rightly) but thereby further penalizing those still suffering basic need (poorer, older, smaller and rural schools) or those still governed by non-spenders.

We cannot create equality by 'social engineering' in schools; nor should we manipulate curricular development. But we certainly can't produce it by deliberately *planning for inequality* in basic opportunity at the most rudimentary levels.

Chapter II which follows, deals with some aspects of this in relation to curricular resources. Chapter III tells in some detail of the organization and structure of the three local education authorities and the role of the administration, while chapters VI to VIII give fuller accounts of the development of secondary education in Lincoln, Nottingham and Northumberland and of the influence or otherwise of forms of demand. It is impossible however wholly to account for the level of resources, and to a degree for their allocation, without considering how far controls by central government and the balance of central and local financing might have influenced events. The idea that increased government grant necessarily carries *per se* the burden of increased central governmental control is a hypothesis which has rested largely on a coincidence in timing of the two. Chapter IV therefore examines in some detail the financial status and practices of the three survey areas and describes what actually happened to the budget, while Chapter V describes in highly specific terms, the increasing controls exercised by the Ministry (later Department) of Education. Chapter V also illustrates some major influences of central government on educational developments in the secondary sector, and gives examples both of explicit demand arising out of the policies of the central government and of restrictions on capital programmes, depressing the level of demand from local authorities.

Teaching staff are perhaps the crucial resource, and chapter IX therefore deals with the supply and remuneration of teachers. Chapter X describes the results of the schools' survey and some aspects of school design while the penultimate chapter comments on the destination of some of the school leavers from the survey areas.

Notes

1 A study by the World Confederation of Organizations of the Teaching Profession in 1966 examined the contribution apparently made by teachers' organizations to educational planning. The questionnaire used, presupposed a real influence on budget and buildings as well as on educational and social programmes. *The Role of Teachers' Organizations in Educational Planning,* WCOTP. Washington, USA (1966).

2 *Education* (5.7.63) p.11., reporting a written answer by the Minister of Education to a question by Sydney Irving.

3 DAVIES, B. (1968). *Social Needs and Resources in Local Services,* London: Michael Joseph. p.24.

4 15–18, a report of the Central Advisory Council (England) (1959) HMSO: para. 100.

5 Department of Education and Science, Circular 10/65 (12.7.65). 'The organization of secondary education'. This research was begun only three years after its issue. Circular 2/70 was issued in 1970, removing compulsion for local authorities to reorganize but leaving them discretion to do so.

6 DAVIES, B. (1968). *Social Needs and Resources in Local Services.* London: Michael Joseph. pp.266–267.

7 *Local Expenditure and Exchequer Grants,* 1956. IMTA

8 *The New Secondary Education,* 1947, Ministry of Education pamphlet 30, p.30.

9 Lincoln, Annual report on Education, 1945–46, p.8.

10 GOULD, Sir Ronald. Presidential address to WCOTP quoted in *Education* (9.8.63).

CHAPTER II

The Allocation of Curricular Resources

'I call, therefore, a complete and generous education, that which fits a man to perform justly, skilfully and magnanimously, all the offices both private and public, of peace and war.'

John Milton

'He that will not apply new remedies must expect new evils: for time is the greatest innovator.'

Francis Bacon (1561–1626)

The relationship of curricular aims, the allocation of curricular resources and administrative and education ideologies is at best difficult, not to say sensitive. The liberal-educationists eschew manpower planning, the social engineers seek relevance in education and neither seems conscious of the need to monitor and evaluate where the resources actually go and why.

Yet the discriminal patterns of allocating resources in the three survey areas, while predictable in their time, appeared to be based on widespread assumptions bearing little traceable relationship to assessed educational needs according to 'age, ability and aptitude' or to future social and industrial needs. What assumptions?

For example, only the top 12 per cent, 15 per cent or 25 per cent of the ability range respectively in the survey areas could cope with external examinations—until the late 1950s and mid-1960s proved the authorities wrong. But by then scores of schools had been designed and staffed for non-examination syllabuses without extended courses. Small schools are better than large schools for the less able whatever the educational product at 15+; but grammar school children need large, economic and viable schools offering a wider variety of subjects. The education of boys ought to be different from the education of girls. Secondary modern pupils don't want to stay on for a Vth year. Rural children and those in small schools don't need the full range of specialist subjects or resources. Less able pupils need less money, fewer staff, lowerpaid staff than the academically bright. Children in new schools need more money than those in old schools. Children in non-grammar schools don't need or can't profit from Nuffield science projects, Project Technology, audio-visual language courses. They shouldn't even learn modern languages. Girls don't want to do physics; boys don't want to do biology or to cook. Clever pupils don't like or need technical crafts. And above all, teachers in post-war schools, especially non-grammar schools, can offer a full education in schools overcrowded by 10 per cent, 15 per cent or even 20 per cent.

But were any of these assumptions valid? For if they were not, they nevertheless underlay what actually happened to resources in the survey areas. It became evident from both records and from interviews with Council and Committee members, officers, heads and HMIs, that many assumptions were implicit, inherited and un-examined in current social terms. To question the basis of the assumptions caused almost universal surprise.

There may be general agreement that the main aim of education is to offer intellectual and creative educational development to each child to the highest degree of excellence for his age, ability and aptitude. This is a platitude, however, which begs the social question what the child is to do with the excellence once achieved? And excellence in what, if there is a choice, when resources are rationed —as accommodation and staff were for the whole 20 year period?

Opinions are, predictably enough, sharply divided on the further aims of secondary education, but most committee members, education officers and teachers interviewed by the writer in 1968–69 accepted that a second fundamental aim in the secondary years should be to equip a boy or girl for the most highly skilled employ-ment, trade or profession of which they are capable. The findings of the report of the Schools Council in 1968 on young school-leavers give prominence indeed to the great importance which 15-year-old school-leavers attach to the school's role as instrumental in teaching them those things which would enable them 'to get as good jobs or careers as possible'. Eighty-six per cent of boys and 88 per cent of girls rated this as the most important school objective. About the same percentage of parents rated help towards good jobs or careers as a major school objective.[1]

About half of those involved in providing education interviewed by the writer, also accepted as a concurrent aim that the education system should be producing the skilled manpower needed by the country as a whole, by the region or by the locality. This is dangerous ground for an idealistic educationalist; but reform, innovation and development rarely wait upon a secure and uncontroversial path.

The desire of a schoolchild for the best job of which he or she is capable, is a form of *explicit demand;* as is the need of the country for trained labour. Are these two principles mutually exclusive? Should the needs of the individual outweigh the needs of industry, commerce and the public services for a steady flow of appropriately trained personnel? The *reductio ad absurdum* on the one hand might be a plethora of unemployable medieval linguists and social psychologists, while an equally unacceptable converse would be the 'direction' at 18+ of potential commercial managers or scientific research workers into sewage outfall engineering. Somewhere between the two extremes, decisions are in fact now already made by both central and local government agencies and by universities and polytechnics which are aimed at controlling resources for secondary, further and higher education, in an attempt to strike a balance of opportunity while eschewing the ultimate sanction of direction.

There is not space here to develop the arguments for and against the role of education in manpower planning. Readers wishing to pursue this may find interest in the 1964 UNESCO report and the 1967 OECD report, both on educational planning[2], in Parnes' work of 1964 and in articles by Moser and Layard[3] among others.

Floud and Halsey accepted at an early stage that an element of vocational bias and a responsibility to provide trained manpower, were valid educational aims, and concluded in 1956 that

'Education affects the efficiency of the distribution of labour by its influence on both the "ability" and the "opportunity"; the skill of labour at various levels reflects the scale and nature of education provision, which exercises a decisive influence on vocational choice and on movement between occupations, i.e. on the adjustment of the supply to the demand of trained labour.'[4]

Perhaps the most striking illustrations of the basic relationship were given by the 1968 (Swann) Committee on Manpower Resources for Science and Technology which concluded that:

'at present the pattern of supply of highly qualified manpower reflects in large measure the studies pursued by individuals at school and in higher education.'[5]

and there is good reason to accept this view.

It is difficult to avoid the suggestion that in fact such negative factors as lack of rooms, teachers and examinations determines and limits the supply and distribution of skilled manpower quite as strongly as the positive guidance and related developments which many apparently eschew on philosophical or liberal grounds. For the less able moreover, manpower, employment and capacity on leaving school become an essentially *local* and not regional or national equation (See Chapter XI).

Curricular Resources

For the purpose of the argument these are defined here as buildings, staff, books, equipment and money. The demand made by the curriculum on the pool of resources available to a local education authority, can be both implicit and explicit. The addition of extended courses (leading to GCE or CSE for example) to non-grammar schools carries, for example, an *implicit* assumption that extra money and staff will need to be provided. The addition of new subjects to a traditional course, means at the least, new staff, books and materials. Curricular innovation sponsored by, for example, the Schools Council or by local teachers' centres, creates further demand on the limited money for furniture, books and apparatus. *Explicitly,* staff make demands on a head teacher for more money or different equipment for their own department; for more periods on the timetable; even for more accommodation. Pupils and parents may specifically ask for new opportunities, for example a course in electronics or pre-nursing to match local employment outlets; or for a foreign language not hitherto taught.

Discriminal Education by Ability

In all three areas, as indeed elsewhere, two assumptions which might be questioned have been seen consistently to underly educational planning and the consequent resource-allocation for the more able children. First, that these necessarily need longer in school than the non-grammar pupils; and secondly, that they necessarily need more staff, more highly paid staff and more money for equipment and books. The questioning of these basic assumptions was regarded with considerable surprise in all three survey areas.

For authorities had built and staffed grammar schools (or streams) for five full years (plus an extended course to 18 years for about half of each grammar school age group). But local authorities, encouraged by the Ministry of Education, had planned and built schools for non-grammar children for four-year courses only. By the time that belatedly, *Nottingham* and *Northumberland* decided to build for a full Vth year, the Ministry then refused to allow the authorities to do so for a further ten years. The Ministry would, for example, sanction only 17 classrooms out of 20, or 8 out of 10, when approving a capital project for a building programme. Authorities were instructed to build for example, 'a four-form entry school, less 3 classrooms' throughout fifteen of the twenty years. But in practice in all three survey areas, secondary modern children stayed on after 15+ in defiance of the lack of accommodation with the result that over half of the schools surveyed in 1968–69 were still overcrowded. Effectively, accommodation had to be 'rationed'. Either all pupils

were taught less specialist work, because appropriate rooms were
not available; or some were not taught science or crafts at all. The
Ministry considered, it appeared, that the regular economic crises
to which reference is made in Chapter V, meant that we could not
afford to allow authorities to spend as much of their own money, as
would provide fully for non-grammar pupils to remain at school until
they were 16. (Chapter X deals further with the question of school
design, which is not therefore discussed here although it is the major
curricular resource.) One is reminded of the report of the Taunton
Commission in 1868. Children of the labouring classes were to leave
school between 9+ and 13+; of the mercantile classes at 16+; and
of the professional and upper classes at 18+. The differential
narrowed but had clearly not been abolished—in state schools at
least.

Secondly, it had been assumed by the educational administrators
that for all courses and in all subjects, intelligent pupils need more
money per capita for books and equipment than the less able. A
similar assumption is made, that the curricular needs of all older
pupils (over 15) necessarily involve more money than those of all
younger pupils. All three authorities surveyed, in common with most
at that period, operated a differential scheme of school allowances
based on these principles. Head teachers of the schools surveyed were
asked how they would have related a scheme of equipment and
capitation allowances to the needs of their particular pupils; and
whether they agreed with the differential rates for pupils in grammar
schools and streams. Most of the heads of non-grammar schools
produced realistic examples of curricular methods based on IIIrd
and IVth year programmes, for remedial English, integrated studies
in the humanities and basic modern languages costing up to twice
the amount needed for a typical arts-based VIth form course. Four
heads of grammar schools argued strongly for more favourable
allowances for pupils in the remedial and duller streams of non-
grammar schools. Five schools produced schemes for inter-
disciplinary or integrated studies costing substantially more than
traditional history or geography—but could not obtain extra funds
for the new courses because these were not (a) for examination
candidates or (b) suitable to qualify for the Schools Council special
projects allowances. Threequarters of all heads (grammar and non-
grammar) disapproved of a differential allowance for pupils under
16.

Curricular distinctions were widespread. In practice, the more
able pupils tend to have been taught two or three separate sciences,
while those in secondary modern schools have been assumed, for the
most part on little real evidence, to be able to grasp only a diluted

course of the simpler aspects of the three main sciences, presented as 'general science'. This was especially so in the one-, two- and three-form entry schools in the survey areas which had only one multi-purpose laboratory. The deliberate design of 'general laboratories' has hindered the teaching of specialist sciences which in turn in four instances in schools surveyed, hindered pupils from transferring to grammar schools at 15+ or 16+ for lack of the right preparatory work. Conversely, however, one modern school in an area of high unemployment took a difficult decision to force physics on all boys (not girls) after year III because the neighbouring grammar school would not accept VIth form entrants on transfer possessing 'general science' only, as a basis for advanced work. And the head could not tell at 14+ which boys might wish to transfer.

An analysis of the courses offered by the 42 schools surveyed revealed that of the six schools doing Nuffield Science, three were grammar and two were technical schools. The only modern school involved in Nuffield work happened to have a head of science who was also the county organizer for Nuffield physics. All three schools involved in Project Technology, were also grammar schools heavily involved with Nuffield Science. (A recurrent example of 'to him who hath shall be given'.) The average annual allowance for Nuffield Science awarded to the seven schools from the special 'pool' controlled by the local authority inspectors, ranged from £300—£500 per year per science subject. The secondary modern schools not able to afford to use the Nuffield approach, received from £50 to £80 per laboratory from the schools' allowance (and Table D (iv) of Appendix D shows that most of them only had one or two laboratories anyway). At least one grammar and 12 non-grammar schools would have liked to use Nuffield programmes. But typical comments were 'the money goes to the grammar schools' and 'we would need £1,000 grant and about £300 a year to start each subject—and we haven't even the basic laboratories yet'. The special allowance for teaching science using Nuffield syllabuses were awarded to about 10 per cent of secondary schools in the survey areas. The national position is probably not dissimilar. Presumably one aim of the Schools Council in developing new approaches to learning such as these science-based courses is generally to improve our current methods of helping children to learn. There appeared to be widespread agreement however among teachers and inspectors in 1968 that to introduce the Nuffield approach to a school required about £1,000 initial grant and about £300 per annum maintenance allowance, for each science subject. To have applied this curricular method to the remaining 90 per cent of schools in the three survey areas, (even assuming that the schools have adequate laboratories and space for this; which over half do not) would have cost approximately as follows at that time, on the basis of two sciences in each school based on Nuffield syllabuses:

Table II (1)

	Lincoln	Nottingham	Northumberland
	£	£	£
Initial grant	20,000	60,000	140,000
Annual extra allowances	6,000	18,000	42,000

Since furniture, equipment, books, stationery and apparatus combined, accounted in the survey period for slightly less than five per cent of the total secondary education revenue budget (see Table VII (a) to (c) of Appendix B) to have allocated so much money, to two sciences out of nearly 20 subjects would be disproportionate and beyond the economic means of the authorities.

Similar extrapolations for the cost of applying more widely other new curricular approaches for different subjects, in turn make it seem most unlikely that the innovation which currently is supported in about 10 per cent of secondary schools with special project allowances, can be applied even to the majority of schools in the foreseeable future. This must put into question the principles on which the financing of the more expensive schemes of innovation are currently based.

The general position on revenue expenditure was not dissimilar in that the automatic grammar/non-grammar differential was equally marked. The Lincoln accounts were kept in such a way that it has been possible to isolate key sectors of expenditure for grammar and for non-grammar schools, and these figures are used. While it is almost certainly true that in the period 1948–1964 this differentiation accorded with the philosophy of the third Chief Education Officer in Lincoln, it cannot be assumed that the other authorities did not operate a similar differential, and in some respects there is evidence that they did. The Lincoln figures are used here therefore as an example which it is suspected would be mirrored elsewhere if comparable statistics could be isolated.

Tables VI (a) and VIII—X of Appendix B give full details of Lincoln's expenditure on grammar and modern schools over a period of 13 years of which the following extract shows the very substantial advantage enjoyed by grammar school pupils.

Table II (2): Annual gross revenue expenditure per pupil—maintained secondary schools

Year	Grammar	Index	Modern	Index
	£		£	
1949–50	46·57	100	32·7	100
1954–55	62·66	135	42·1	129
1958–59	83·44	179	57·46	175
1962–63	99·94	215	75·48	230

This was not, of course, uncommon in the early post-war years. Florence Horsbrugh gave the following figures in 1952 for schools which, although not directly comparable, distinguished similarly between able and less able children.

National costs per pupil (1950–51)

£

Elementary	26
Secondary	44

Tables II (3) and (4), which follow, illustrate both the different actual costs and the different growth rates for some aspects of expenditure between the two types of school. A number of variations emerge. First, by 1962, secondary modern rolls had increased more sharply than those of grammar schools. Although the expenditure on modern schools also grew faster, thus lending a superficial credence to the theory that the modern schools benefited most from the post-war expansion of educational expenditure, the pupils in non-grammar schools still had proportionately far less actual benefit. For the growth rates throughout for modern schools did not exceed that for grammar schools, by proportionately enough to narrow the differential very markedly. When the actual expenditure (both total and on individual services) is related to pupil numbers, it will be seen that more was spent on the fewer grammar pupils in 1949 than on those in modern schools. The same amount was moreover spent in 1962 for 25 per cent of the 11+ age group and 42 per cent of the total rolls (attending grammar schools) as on the 75 per cent at 11+ entering modern schools, who represented 58 per cent of the total pupils on roll in secondary schools. Expressed as a gross cost per pupil (on the basis used for Table VIII in Appendix B), the differential remained between 25 per cent and 30 per cent. In 1949, the pupils in modern schools received only about 70 per cent of the level of expenditure given to their more able peers; and in 1962, about 75 per cent.

Table II (3): *Total gross revenue expenditure on grammar and modern schools 1949—62**

| Year | SCHOOL ROLLS | | | | TOTAL DIRECT EXPENDITURE | | | |
	Grammar	Index	Modern	Index	Grammar £	Index	Modern £	Index
1949	1471	100	1857	100	69,436	100	58,799	100
1951	1493	102	1894	102	83,310	120	70,321	120
1953	1509	103	1857	100	88,586	127	74,173	126
1955	1562	106	2492	135	102,768	148	95,029	162
1957	1717	117	2954	159	133,674	192	148,908	251
1959	2058	139	3258	175	163,668	232	185,367	316
1961	2208	151	3166	171	195,869	282	207,452	351
1962	2209	151	3019	164	220,760	319	227,888	386

* comparable figures are not available before 1949 or after 1962.

Table II (4): *Comparison of grammar/modern expenditure*

| Year | GROSS COST PER PUPIL* | | | | TEACHERS' SALARIES | | | | FURNITURE, EQUIPMENT, BOOKS, STATIONERY AND APPARATUS | | | |
	Grammar £	Index	Modern £	Index	Grammar £	Index	Modern £	Index	Grammar £	Index	Modern £	Index
1949	46·6	100	32·7	100	47,136	100	41,835	100	5,523	100	5,603	100
1951	56·9	122	37·6	115	58,621	125	50,618	121	6,584	119	6,209	111
1953	59·3	127	38·5	118	62,054	132	52,247	125	7,350	133	6,221	111
1955	67·9	145	48·0	147	74,229	157	67,147	160	6,919	125	8,247	147
1957	81·0	174	54·0	165	95,840	204	102,774	242	8,121	147	11,008	196
1959	79·5	170	57·9	177	117,202	248	128,427	306	11,639	210	13,237	236
1961	88·7	190	65·5	200	140,007	299	144,508	344	12,454	228	12,334	220
1962	99·9	214	75·5	230	159,921	340	159,534	368	12,426	228	13,005	231

* extracted from Table VIII Appendix B. page 347. Please see explanatory footnote to the table.

The overall figures conceal further anomalies. Only rarely did the salaries of teachers of the 60 per cent or so pupils in modern schools exceed in total those of the teachers of the 40 per cent or so in grammar schools (42 per cent of all pupils on roll; 25 per cent of the age group) for the reasons given in Chapter IX. The differential was slightly less marked for educational equipment etc., although the cost per pupil of all educational furniture and equipment was still far higher in the grammar schools. Further analysis of the figures on which Table II (2) is based shows that the grammar schools had proportionately far more money for books, but did less well on stationery and consumable stock.

Even less accountable is the difference which has been traced between expenditure on grammar and modern schools respectively in Lincoln, on other items. The figures per head annually for maintenance of buildings and grounds, for example, could not be held necessarily to be linked directly with courses organized at each group of schools. Yet the grammar schools consistently obtained a larger proportion of the budget. The following years are perhaps the most marked:

Table II (5): Annual expenditure per pupil on maintenance of buildings and grounds

	Grammar	Modern
	£	£
1949–50	2·85	1·35
1950–51	3·72	0·99
1954–55	3·32	0·99
1957–58	3·96	1·66
1958–59	4·34	2·28
1962–63	4·88	2·65

The other surprising fact is that the cost of maintenance rose so little over the years but there is some evidence from interviews that this element of the budget was especially vulnerable to cuts by Finance Committee seeking reductions in rateborne expenditure.

The secondary modern schools fared no better from the capital budget. Of £12,081 capital expenditure on secondary schools from 1946 to 1953 in Lincoln for example, only £1,279 was spent on the six county secondary modern schools, or one tenth; the remaining nine-tenths going to the four grammar schools. Yet from 1947 onwards there were consistently more pupils in the secondary modern schools than in the grammar schools.

This evidence supports the hypothesis that resources were not allocated in relation to demand, but according to (a) the philosophy of the Chief Education Officer and his Committee, (b) outside factors such as the Burnham agreements, and (c) inherited attitudes on the apparent need for preferential staffing and allowances for able pupils. For the secondary modern heads did fight for more resources, supported by their governors; but with no significant success as chapter VI will illustrate. The grammar school heads appeared to exert no direct pressure in financial terms. The assumption was taken for granted by those in leadership, that the grammar schools should receive more and the educational reasons for the assumption do not appear to have been re-examined. It may be argued that this is now history. But generations of pupils educated in this 20-year period are now competing with more fortunate peers in the adult employment market. And despite very substantial developments since the advent of the fourth Chief Education Officer (see Chapter VI) the city is only in 1974 equalizing as all schools become coeducational comprehensive schools.

Breadth of curriculum—the less able

About two-thirds of heads and staffs in non-grammar schools in all three survey areas regretted the limited curriculum which they were constrained to offer. It was limited partly because of lack of appropriate staff, money and accommodation, and partly because of an inherited conception of what was 'suitable' for non-grammar children. In *Nottingham* and *Northumberland* in particular, where only 12 per cent to 15 per cent achieved entry to grammar schools until the late 1950s, the major curricular loss to the children which concerned the teachers, was the learning of modern languages. A typical comment perhaps summarizes the general feeling. 'Languages were regarded as the grammar schools' prerogative; we felt we were "poaching" when we pressed for teachers of French'.

One reason why the teaching of modern languages was mainly limited to the academically gifted in the survey period was the expressed aim of language teaching at the time. On the continent, and especially in countries like Holland whose very trade, not merely its tourism, depended on widespread competence in French, German and English, the aim was to teach pupils to speak and understand foreign languages fluently. So basic an aim has perhaps suffered in England from the pejorative connotation of 'usefulness', apparently alien to those concerned with a liberal (academic) education. Perhaps the dominant concept of the role of language teaching for much of the period from 1945 to the mid-1960s can be summarized by the following almost incredible quotation from a pamphlet issued by the

Classical Association in 1967. Despite the provenance of the statement, it is one which some modern language teachers seem still to
support and which the policy of many external examination Boards
appear to have supported until relatively recently.

'Modern languages courses in schools are not designed solely, or
even principally, to produce the ability to speak fluently the language
concerned. A main object of these courses is precisely the same as that
of classics courses, to stimulate an interest in the literature and
civilization of another country.'[6]

The merits and demerits of such a statement, written at a time
when quite startling advances had been made by teachers of modern
languages in developing audio-visual methods aimed at the apparently
revolutionary idea of teaching children to speak the language well,
might well be debated. It can however be seen that wherever this
academic, literary attitude was held, the only resources regarded as
necessary would be literary texts and a good teacher, and the subject
as such would be regarded as inappropriate for non-academic
children. And in the survey areas, very few non-grammar schools
offered modern languages even when they admitted from 85 per cent
to 88 per cent of the age group. None of the three authorities made
serious efforts generally to staff and equip non-grammar schools for
languages, until towards the end of the survey period. In the context of England's admission to the European Economic Community,
this highlights an urgent need for resources to be specifically allocated
for a special remedial adult education programme of modern
language teaching, based on industry and commerce. It might well
be argued again that resources have been allocated in accordance
with inherited assumptions and not in direct relation to the pupils'
or the country's needs.

Discriminal education by sex
A similar dichotomy is apparent in relation to the education of boys
and the education of girls. If education according to the individual
needs of 'age, ability and aptitude' is desirable, ought there necessarily
to be any difference between the education of boys and of girls? Is
there much objective psychological evidence that boys and girls have
innately different needs or mental capabilities? But in the three
survey areas this was the strongest inherited assumption underlying
the design of schools and the allocation of resources. Boys' and girls'
needs were held to be different. The conception that the 'education
of girls' was or should be identifiably different, was perpetuated by
educationalists like John Newsom[7] and W. P. Alexander (later Sir

William) whose commentary on the need for equal opportunity for boys and girls still assumed that the majority of girls needed homecraft or office skills:

'It will be important to ensure that a girl who has a special aptitude for technical education has provision for her needs. This will probably be most effectively done in most areas by making technical schools mixed, with a main course for girls *centred either in commercial education or in technical education based on domestic science,* but ensuring that individual girls who desire to pursue courses in engineering, whether mechanical or electrical, or subjects in relation to the building industry, will have the opportunity to do so. . . . The experience of the last five years in the engineering world makes it very doubtful whether we can assume too readily that girls are not interested in technical subjects.'[8]

The expectation of different educational goals was first translated into different accommodation standards. Girls' schools and boys' schools have different types and standards of accommodation. No metalwork in girls' and no housecraft in boys' schools—an inherited assumption of limited educational need and demand not matched by Sweden's practice of providing homecrafts and handicrafts for both.[9] Predictable differentiation, but not related to demand. Less defensible was the application of the Building Bulletin 2A which for 20 years specified a lower standard of scientific and technical facilities in girls' than in boys' schools.

But most schools in the survey areas were mixed—88 out of 133. Since most of them were overcrowded during the survey period, however, accommodation had to be rationed (700 pupils into 520 places won't go; fewer periods per subject or some don't study it at all). It was by no means uncommon practice to give laboratory preference to boys (taking physics), teaching biology to girls in classrooms. The tables in Appendix D illustrate greater deficiencies of accommodation in girls' schools and (Table D (v)) a higher level of tprovision for handicrafts than for homecrafts. The findings of he national science teachers' survey of 1960[10] were mirrored in the survey areas both in the period up to 1965 and during the schools' survey in 1968, except that by 1968 the sharp differential in science allowances for boys and for girls had been abolished. Science and technical studies were still female Cinderellas.

In many mixed schools visited in the three survey areas moreover even where laboratories were freely available in theory to both sexes, many heads created quite separate and differently biased courses and options for boys and for girls respectively at 13+ or 14+. Even where CSE and not GCE was offered, heads tended to 'channel' girls to biology and boys to physics. Seventeen schools quite deliberately split boys and girls for science ('girls will want to do nursing of course— they do biology' was a frequent comment). But one mixed grammar school deliberately mixed its science groups— and had an advanced physics group of 22 boys and 17 girls. A bilateral school in Nottingham insisted on all girls doing a minimum of either chemistry or physics. Proportionately more girls a year from that school trained as laboratory technicians or entered technical industries on leaving school.

There were other tacit assumptions in the survey area, underlying 'technical' options in extended courses offered to boys or to girls at 13+ or 14+, as 'interest based courses', in the words of one headmaster. For example, pre-nursing was offered only to girls—except at Hexham after the appointment of a male matron at the local hospital, when the boys developed an interest. Similarly, most of the schools surveyed, offering 'commerce', (which meant elementary shorthand and typing) organized it as a girls' option *cross-set* with technical studies or other 'boys' subjects on the timetable. And every mixed school organized its timetable so that needlework and homecraft were cross-set with woodwork and metalwork, with the result that pupils could not choose any two out of the four. Only two schools either allowed or encouraged boys to take homecrafts and girls to take handicrafts. Three child-care courses were designated for girls only. Even linked courses with local Colleges of Further Education were organized by sex of pupils—girls to the commerce and boys to the engineering departments.

Allocation of revenue resources also appeared to be consistently unequal. Again the illustrations are from *Lincoln* but there was some evidence in both other areas of patterns not dissimilar. Before the 1956–61 period, part of the difference can be accounted for by the lack of equal pay for women teachers but this does not by any means wholly account for the different costs per boy and per girl. Chapter IX (on teachers) gives fuller details of staffing differentials (grammar/modern and boy/girl). Boys' schools appear to have had consistently more money (and better staffing) than girls' schools of comparable size and type, whether grammar or modern, of which the following table gives a typical example. As in Nottingham and Northumberland, schools with a head who has been a senior officer of a teachers' union appear to do consistently better than other schools. Four head teachers attributed this to their additional knowledge and experience of the system and their greater confidence in dealing with 'the administration'. Their explicit demands were more articulate.

Table II (6): Extracts from annual estimates approved by the governors

YEAR	GIRLS' MODERN		BOYS' MODERN	
	Expenditure	*Roll*	*Expenditure*	*Roll*
	£		£	
1951–52	10,700	322	13,845	311
1957–58	21,570	478	23,340	419
1959–60	22,765	475	24,115	431
1962–63	29,225	440	28,280	403
1964–65	31,785	422	32,660	372

An analysis of the detailed composition of the estimates for the two girls' and boys' county grammar schools reveals that consistently over 20 years the boys' school received more favourable treatment under the Burnham reports, and a more favourable allocation of money for special equipment for science and technical subjects, including arrangements for laboratory assistance. The two voluntary aided grammar schools, comparable in type and size, show a similar pattern of apparently preferential treatment for the boys' school.

Extended courses and viable size of school

Here too discriminal assumptions were widespread. Appendix D, gives details of the sizes of schools surveyed. It will become evident in Chapters VI to VIII that all three authorities deliberately planned, designed and built small non-grammar schools of three- or four-form entry for most of the period on the apparent grounds that the less able children needed more pastoral care, and that a school of 450 or 600 was large enough to be viable and small enough to meet the pastoral needs of the children. Viability becomes an important concept only when resources are limited, as they have been in all three areas and as they are likely to remain. In theory, there is no reason why the smallest school should not have a complete range of specialist rooms, specialist staff and equipment allowances. In practice, this would cost more money per pupil and per school than either the Ministry or local authorities have apparently felt able to justify on 'economic' grounds. This is another inherited value judgement since most one- or two-form entry grammar schools (200 or 360 pupils) were in fact provided with the full minimum range of facilities and staff, despite their small size, enabling them to offer a broadly based curriculum (See Chapter X). Yet authorities felt 'they could not afford' an equivalent range of facilities for 300 secondary modern children. Some positive descriminations in their favour were awarded to small non-grammar schools in Northumberland but did not, in heads' views, meet fully even all basic needs though the county undoubtedly did a valiant best under the constraints of the Building Code and its limited revenue.

There is little evidence from the survey areas that conscious assessment of educational viability in relation to the staffing and curricular resources available, took place when the development plans were discussed and new schools were planned. The Ministry had however already declared in 1947 that:

'It is manifest that if a reasonable variety of courses to meet the differing aptitudes and abilities of the pupils is to be provided, there should normally be provision for at least two streams of each type of education that the school is intended to provide. Even where a technical school or side is based on a single branch of technical work (e.g. Engineering or Housecraft) it should have at least two streams.'[11]

Clearly if new courses were to be based on modern (non-grammar) schools from 1945 onwards, the schools would need more specialist accommodation. Equally clearly other resources would need to be levelled up, since

'Money provided for any one component in the capital cost of schools will be wasted unless adequate and balanced provision is made simultaneously for the others.'[12]

But as Chapter V will illustrate, the Ministry consistently refused to authorize capital building to enable authorities to build larger schools or extend existing ones at the rate that their Development plans to provide technical and extended courses, required. And in 1947, only a minority of schools were larger than 501 pupils:

Table II (7): Size of schools in England and Wales 1947

	School Rolls			
	Under 401	*401–501*	*Over 501*	*Total*
Grammar	559	276	372	1,207
Modern	2,765	201	53	3,019
Technical	282	15	20	317
Total	3,606	492	445	4,543

The corollary of larger schools and more extended courses was more V-form accommodation, more specialist rooms and more staff.

And these were not forthcoming in adequate measure. In practice, despite the Ministry's early statement, extended courses in non-grammar schools were actively discouraged by both the Ministry and its HMIs until the late 1950s and was not positively encouraged until the 1960s.[13] The Ministry controlled the teaching quotas of local authorities (see chapter IX), allowing no extra staff for non-grammar courses. It also refused to allow some authorities to build and design for extended courses in the period 1948–58 when capital resources were restricted. Both Nottingham and Northumberland suffered in this way. Notwithstanding, many authorities did develop the principle of extended courses, in non-grammar schools. Some, like Leeds[14] and Southampton[15] were running specialist courses in the mid 1950s but others suffered from the lack of buildings which held back so many developments. For example, the West Riding Authority hoped to experiment with, among others, agricultural courses in secondary modern schools but had to admit in 1954 that its basic resources were so deficient that a first priority was to level up existing standards, and deferred semi-specialist courses.

'there is, however, as yet not enough accommodation to provide a four-year course (in handicraft) in secondary modern schools. . . . At one time more than thirty housecraft rooms were without teachers which meant that some four thousand to five thousand girls of secondary school age were deprived of housecraft instruction.'[16]

Discussion of new approaches to housecraft and handicraft teaching would, of course, be purely academic to heads of schools where the subjects cannot be taught at all.

In 1956 the NUT made a special inquiry into the organization of bias courses, and discovered that in secondary modern schools GCE courses outstripped the rest, followed by commerce, rural science, technical and craft courses.

'In only two replies out of the hundreds we received in making our survey, was it suggested that definite decisions of the authority prevented specific courses in secondary modern schools.'[17]

In the three survey areas the position varied. *Lincoln* set its face firmly against the development of any bias courses or new developments in secondary modern schools beyond 15+ until 1964, and the promise in the early post-war years that:

'for the pupils in the secondary modern schools it is proposed to develop still further the practical side of the curriculum so that they may continue to make and strengthen their contribution to the needs of industry and commerce and the future skilled craftsmen employed thereon'[18]

remained a dead letter in the absence of the provision in the secondary modern schools of workshops, classrooms for Vth-year pupils, extra teachers, head of department posts under the 1956 Burnham report or adequate equipment allowances to replace obsolete apparatus. *Nottingham* established commercial courses (mostly typing) at a girls' school as early as 1945–1946, and declared to the Ministry as a matter of principle that:

'There is the opportunity of organizing in each one of (the new secondary schools) more than one course of a technical or practical type, as for example an engineering course and also a commercial course. The variety of occupations and industries in the city has been stressed as pointing to the need for a large number of schools which would include a technical or commercial bias.'[19]

Northumberland tended to limit its intake to grammar schools to about 15 per cent of the relevant age group, and to plan for technical schools with some boarding provision. It built in fact very few technical schools before altering the basis of its development plan in 1959, by which time technical courses were being based at grammar schools, and not at separate technical schools. The county was on the whole tardy in developing any form of grouped course outside the selective schools, and the figures of V- and VI-form stayers in the county have been well below the national average throughout, but are however consistent with the general trend in the North.

External examinations

If the argument for viability tends often to centre on the size of 'economic' teaching groups for pupils aiming at GCE or CSE, this is not necessarily to assume that these pupils and courses are more important. It is to acknowledge that if teachers and laboratories or equipment are being used (a) intensively for from five—seven periods a week per pupil subject and (b) uneconomically for teaching groups of less than eight or five, then the school is 'subsidizing' the GCE and CSE groups from its staffing quota and from its curricular allowances. This in turn may deprive the less able of some skilled teachers, small teaching groups and extra books and equipment unless compensating extra resources are awarded to the smaller schools to offset this. If the head of a small school does not offer external examinations to his more able pupils, he is depriving them in turn of their future opportunity to enter further and higher education or skilled employment. Viability should also be related to the ability of a school to offer adequate remedial education, a wide range of craft-based courses and education for the less able, relevant to their local situation on leaving school.

Appendix D Table D (ix) also gives details of courses offered by the schools surveyed in 1968–69. Many smaller schools could not offer GCE at all. Some could only offer CSE in two or three subjects. But almost all offered some external examination work and seven very small schools attempted to offer both GCE and CSE. Some offered bias courses based on 'interest-based' work, which as we have seen, led the head teachers to assume that girls would wish to take commerce or pre-nursing and boys engineering or craft courses.

As with accommodation, extended courses create demand for substantial staffing resources. Chapter IX, Tables 11 and 12 illustrate the different entitlements of grammar and non-grammar schools of about 500 pupils, under the Burnham reports. A similar principle of 'weighting' for older pupils underlies the standard method of assessing the quota of teaching staff for a school. A school with substantial numbers of V and VI-form pupils will qualify for many more staff who are then available to help to teach the younger pupils. Schools of four-form entry or below, with only a small V-year and small GCE groups, will on this basis not be entitled to the extra staff who would automatically be available in a grammar school or a larger school.

In almost all secondary modern schools surveyed (some taking over 80 per cent of the age group) teaching groups for GCE or CSE were below eight. It was not uncommon for teachers to have a single pupil for CSE history, science, or maths. All schools of less than four-entry had had therefore to 'select' the limited subjects to be offered in external examinations. The selection would be based on an advance value judgement (that is by deciding to offer French or Biology and therefore advertising for and appointing a teacher) or on the existing accident of what the existing staff could teach. There are from 15 to 20 subjects normally available in an average sized school. One two-form entry school surveyed, however, only qualified for 13 full-time staff including the head and deputy head, if the normal staffing quota were followed. A one-form entry school surveyed had a staffing establishment of head+five full-time staff+four visiting teachers for housecraft, science, music and remedial work. Not only were subject options limited because of the need for economic groups; but these schools could only offer a third or a half of the total range of subjects to examination level, because they did not have the full range of staff. Chapter X discusses destination of school leavers. A high correlation was found between lack of opportunity for external examination work in basic subjects in schools where the ability range including pupils potentially able to take GCE and CSE in small and in rural schools, and a higher proportion of leavers entering unskilled employment.

Schools below four-form entry in size made as strong a case for extra compensatory equipment allowances, as for extra staff. The award of a *per capita* allowance for educational visits for example, penalizes outlying small schools who may use almost a full year's allowance on one visit to an urban industrial area. Eight small schools (from one- to three-form entry) argued for a special 'pool' of money to be allocated by local authority inspectors, to bring resources in small schools up to a minimum standard of viability. All eight, and many other heads, considered that basic standards in smaller schools were 'pegged' to enable money to be allocated for Nuffield science, technical projects and experimental special programmes of innovation in grammar and larger schools. 'We are told it is uneconomic to give us a full range of major equipment for 170 pupils', one head of a small rural school commented, 'but it is economic to give £400 a year for 14 boys to take Advanced level physics using the Nuffield syllabus.'

Other, related patterns will emerge as the different strands in the educational history of the three areas are unwoven, but the pattern of inherent and correlated inequality already begins to emerge. Less able children subjected to limited expectations, had less educational opportunity. Rural schools were at a basic disadvantage as were small schools. Girls' opportunities were more limited than boys'. Older schools suffered more. But a substantial proportion of pupils were either in small, non-grammar schools or small single-sex schools; or both. Many were in small, rural non-grammar schools. Short of substantial positive discrimination, the pattern of planning for distributing resources meant that these groups of pupils had a three- or four-fold chance of educational deprivation in the nature of things. We planned for a kind of educational inequality for nearly 20 years. Chapter XI's brief account of some of the school-leaver patterns, suggests the effect may be longer term than adolescent educational differential achievement.

A dominant influence was the administration of the local education authorities, and Chapter III therefore describes this for each area.

Notes

1   *Enquiry* 1, *the Young School Leavers* (Schools Council), London: HMSO 1968. pp.33–34.

2   PHILLIPS, H. M. (1964). in *Economic and Social Aspects of Educational Planning,* Paris. pp.21–22. and ANDERSON, C. A. (1967). 'Sociological factors in the demand for education' in *Social objectives in educational planning.* Paris: OECD p.47.

3   In BLAUG, M. (Ed.) (1968). *Economics of Education* 1 *and* 2. Harmondsworth: Penguin.

4   FLOUD, J. and HALSEY, A. H. 'Education and Occupation: English Secondary Schools and the supply of labour', *The Year Book of Education,* 1956 p.519.

5   *The flow into employment of Scientists, Engineers and Technologists* CMND 3760, HMSO, 1968. Preface.

6   *Classics in the School Curriculum,* Council of the Classical Association, 1967, p.7. The Schools Council writing in *The Raising of the School leaving age* (HMSO 1968, para. 88) commented that 'there is of course relatively little experience of teaching a foreign language to the pupils who are the concern of this working paper'.

7   NEWSOM, J. (1948). *The Education of Girls,* London: Faber and Faber. No doubt the early post-war administrators could actually remember the extraordinary report of the Central Consultative Committee of the Board of Education in 1923 on *'The Differentiation of Curricula between the Sexes in Secondary Schools'.* This did at least however recommend more maths in girls' schools, handicraft for girls and cookery for boys.

8   *Education* (8.6.45) p.829, where Alexander comments on the Ministry of Education pamphlet 'The Nation's Schools'. Writer's underlining. The last sentence refers to the war years 1939–45.

9   *The Status of Women,* report of Swedish Government to the United Nations, 1968.

10   *Provision and maintenance of laboratories in grammar schools*—a joint report by the Science Masters' Association, Association of Women Science Teachers, NUT and Joint Four, John Murray, 1960.

11   Ministry of Education, Circular 144 (16.6.47).

12   *School Building resources and their effective use,* OECD, Paris 1966, p.87.

13   Interviews with HMIs in 1968 and 1969, and early published reports of the Ministry of Education.

14   *Education* (10.4.53).

15   *Education in Southampton* (1944–64) published by the Education Committee, pp.13–16.

16   *West Riding Education—Ten years of change* published by the Education Committee pp.48 and 100.

17   Address by R. G. K. Hickman to the 1956 *Annual NUT Conference at Blackpool,* published by NUT, page 17. In addition to the more frequently offered courses in commerce and in crafts, the NUT survey lists Seamanship, Building, Catering, Distributive Trades and House Maintenance.

18   Lincoln, annual report 1946, p.4.

19   Nottingham, Secondary Education Sub Committee (8.1.46).

CHAPTER III

The Organization and Political Background of the Local Education Authorities

'The word "responsibility" . . . connotates a state of mind, which weighs the consequences of action and then acts irrespective it may be, of the concurrence or approval of others.'

L. S. Amery (1947)

Amery described thus a concept of public responsibility which transcends the apparent need for advance public approval of a 'wise policy'. In fact in local government, although administrators and officers tend to anticipate, not follow, public opinion, a finer balance needs to be maintained between the views of those carrying the responsibility for the allocation of resources and the views of the public or other clients on how public funds should be used (if and when such views are expressed).

The organization of the three authorities surveyed and the political and personal background of the main protagonists is relevant to the sequence of events and to the standards achieved. If inherited attitudes can affect the structure and content of the curriculum, they may affect even more certain aspects of educational administration which can influence in turn the standards sought and attained in the educational system—for example the staffing and administration of the Education Department and the organization and composition of the Education Committee and of its sub-committees. Diagram A in chapter I illustrates the control of resources by the central and local administration. Influences can be roughly divided into those over whom the local education authority has in theory at least, complete control (administrators, inspectors, heads and teachers), those over whom it has partial control (sub-committees and governors) and those wholly outside its jurisdiction (industry, teachers' unions, Her Majesty's Inspectors, parents, individual pressure groups).The pressures for an increased level of resources or for a different distribution may come from any of these, and the existence or the success of such pressure will depend on the strength and attitude of these sectors. Who were the administrators and councillors, and how did they operate? What was their inheritance in 1945, the beginning of this survey period? For in one sense, the inherited attitudes of the interwar or prewar years became 'institutionalized' and reinforced by the very structures to which they gave rise and which, by a kind of vicious circle, helped to perpetuate the traditional concepts.

The situation which faced the authorities in 1945 conditioned them for many years afterwards. Inherited attitudes influenced certain financial policies and especially policy for staffing the new Education departments. Some firmly entrenched psychological reflexes on the part of administrators and councillors were modified in due course only by determined pressure from their newer colleagues or from local outside sources. The financial climate in 1945 and the development of new financial policies are dealt with in the following chapter. It is perhaps enough to say here that after the Second World War, public opinion on public spending was decidedly variable at local authority level. It must be remembered, however, that not only the electorate, but the older men and women elected to or working for the local education authorities had been conditioned by the impoverished interwar and war years, and would tend to have applied the ideology and standards of the 1930s unless driven to alternative courses by public demand. Demand would come either explicitly from pressure groups or implicitly from newly adopted national educational policies. In this uneven financial climate, having inherited a budget the size of which had been determined by their predecessors or by historical accident, both councillors and administrators were faced with a new Education Act, a rapidly increasing school population and a request for a new Development Plan entailing capital and revenue expenditure which the most sanguine could foresee as unprecedented in its magnitude. At the least, it would mean more staff, new buildings and rising rates.

Among the newly created local education authorities the three with which we are concerned were fortunate in one important respect. None had suffered any significant war damage and only in Nottingham was it even a minor factor to be considered. Apart from deficiencies because of neglected maintenance in the war years the school buildings were as good—or as bad—as in the 1930s.

The two main protagonists in the story of postwar secondary education were the Chief Officer and the Chairman of the Education Committee. They and their staff were to influence events more than any single factor other than the Ministry of Education. Who were the administrators? Who were the committees?

The Administrators

Despite a strong temptation to divorce educational developments from the administrative organization of local education authorities there is in fact a strong correlation between the strength of the department and the speed with which reorganization and educational reform takes place. Administration can be constructive, a means of helping ideas to become concrete reality; or it can become a machine merely for continuing the status quo. Simple perpetuation of past ideas and standards will rarely stimulate future reforms, and may carry with it a tacit and unchallenged implication that past standards of staffing, material resources and educational goals continue to be adequate.

If, however, the leader (the Chairman, the Director or Chief Education Officer) sets a new collection of educational goals to be attained (for example, extended courses for less able pupils, reorganization of all-age schools, development of secondary technical education) the administration will need to create a material and organizational framework within which the new idea can develop. In most cases this will involve an immediate extra work load and an increase therefore in establishment—preferably at senior (leadership) level to help the translation of creative planning into reality. A reasonable definition of this was produced by Mackenzie in the mid-1940s:

'Administration has an important leadership role and can serve as a powerful constructive influence if it is focussed on ways and means of attaining the educational program. This requires much more than management or keeping the machinery operating smoothly. It demands a continuous study of goals to see how they can be most surely attained, and a constant consideration and analysis of the physical facilities, tools, equipment, materials and personnel to determine how all resources can be utilized most completely.'[1]

Administration is, as it were, the history of decision-making, the architecture of organization and the application of informed judgement. Its sequence of events can be interpreted and described differently by each participant, a story of a set of decisions and choices, interpretations of present limitations, and the determination of future attitudes. Present decisions so condition future actions by precedent, that they often form what comes to be known as 'policy', a practical philosophy and a set of rules to be applied.

Administratively the three local education authorities were all in need of further staff in 1945, but they tackled the task of staffing the new departments in very different ways, and here again inherited attitudes may have been a factor.

Lincoln

Lincoln had acquired powers as a local education authority only in 1902 and had therefore inherited no School Board tradition of administration. The first Director of Education served from 1902 to 1930, when he was succeeded by a local primary school headmaster without previous administrative experience. There were no advisers or inspectors before the Second World War. After initial unwillingness by the first Director in the 1920s, the second Director finally gave way to pressure from the teachers' unions in 1937 and set up a Joint Consultative Committee with representatives of both the public elementary and of the secondary (grammar) schools. His other main contribution to pre-war education was the creation of two new single-sex secondary modern schools and the provision of new buildings for the girls' county grammar school, both in 1937. Administratively however the department had not developed at all by 1945, when there were neither Assistant Education Officers nor inspectors—indeed, no professional staff at all other than the Director. He was succeeded in 1949 by the head of the largest local secondary school (a boys' grammar school), also without previous administrative experience. By this time the city's postwar Development Plan, a bipartite plan with grammar and modern schools only, had been drawn up and approved. By then also the authority had agreed to the creation of one post of Assistant Education Officer as from 1 November 1946. The incumbent however was used almost from the first as an organizer and inspector, and the post lapsed in 1951 when the Authority was asked by the Ministry of Education circular 242 on Educational Expenditure (7.12.51) to reduce main grant services by five per cent 'provided that the essential fabric of the service is not impaired'. On the resignation of Lincoln's first Assistant Education Officer, the Chief Education Officer[2] recommended that the post lapse and the duties be transferred to two junior staff who were promoted to Assistant Education Officer but were paid on Soulbury Scale II as organizers and inspectors and used as such, with few executive or administrative powers. One of the two had been a part-time assistant, becoming full-time on promotion, and was replaced in 1955 from a field of five candidates.

The third Chief Education Officer was in turn replaced in 1964 on retirement, at which time there was still no post of Deputy Chief Education Officer, and the two professional staff then in post were working full-time as organizers. The new (fourth) Chief Education Officer immediately reviewed the establishment and as a result of this a Deputy Chief Education Officer was appointed, the two organizers were regraded Assistant Education Officers and redeployed as administrators; eight staff were upgraded and seven new appointments were made. There were in 1965 still only two inspectors (for girls' and boys' physical education). The retired Chief Education Officer responsible for the main period from 1949 to 1964 discussed the organization of the department with the writer (29.5.69) holding the view that even in the 1960s he could quite sincerely see no need for a hierarchy of professional staff—all decisions should be made at Chief Officer level. He was his own Chief Inspector. He could see no role for inspectors as pace-setters for new methods; or as a potential influence on secondary school curriculum and therefore indeed on assessment of schools' needs for special allowances, extra books or equipment or additional staff.

Two potential 'inside' influences on secondary education were therefore missing in Lincoln until 1965—an Assistant Education Officer identified with secondary education as such, and the stimulus of an advisory service with its own special budget to be used for the development of new courses or to stimulate new teaching methods. These came only after 1964 in the van of a 10-year development plan for comprehensive reorganization which will be achieved in September 1974. There is no indication that this lack of staff was for financial reasons, since the former Chief Education Officer, the former chairman of the Finance Committee and two successive chairmen of the Education Committee all held the view that had a case been made for more staff it would have been granted—as indeed it was in 1965. The position was perhaps also influenced by the tendency for staff of the Education Officer to be recruited from the same grammar school of which the Chief Education Officer had been headmaster, including both (Education) Finance Officers in post in the period, the senior administrative assistant, the second Assistant Education Officer and later, one City Treasurer. One contemporary comment referred to a continuation of the headmaster/prefect relationship, not perhaps conducive to independent initiative on the part of middle management staff.[3]

Nottingham

Nottingham, on the other hand, had had a School Board, and had inherited a flourishing administration along with a considerable number of Victorian school buildings. The Director of Education who served from 1924 to 1938 appears, from accounts given by his contemporaries, to have been lively, determined and a fast worker. Nottingham was one of the earliest authorities to start reorganizing all-age schools before, not after, the 1926 Hadow report and by 1939 all county schools in the city had been reorganized into senior and junior schools. The City built lavishly in the 1930s, using the government building grants extensively, but while the Director was

responsible for creating Nottingham's largest girls' grammar school
his main contribution was to create good schools for the less able—
an inheritance in 1945 which was to prove significant in shaping the
Development Plan. When he handed over to his successor in 1938,
there were grammar places for only 12 per cent of the age group
(Lincoln's percentage approached 25 per cent) but a reasonable
legacy of purpose-built new secondary modern schools. The Director
who took responsibility in 1938 served until 1956 when the fourth
Director was appointed.

The prewar Director steadfastly refused to appoint an inspectorate
('I will be my own Inspector of Schools') and, although after a two-
year dispute with the then Board of Education one inspector was
appointed in the 1930s, the city has never had a large inspectorate.
By 1965 for a school population of 51,686 there were only three
general inspectors and a specialist inspector for each of housecraft,
music, boys' and girls' physical education; the same total establishment as in 1945.

Nottingham in 1944 had in post both a Director and Deputy
Director and two senior clerks responsible for elementary and higher
(including secondary grammar) education respectively. The then
Director, described after his retirement as a good administrator by
some who worked with him, called a special meeting of the Education
Committee in 1944 'for the purpose of considering a memorandum
from the Director of Education on the future organization of the
administrative and clerical staff' as a result of which the Committee
approved the appointment of a graduate Assistant Director (£650–
£800), a new Committee clerk at senior level, as well as three new
senior administrative assistants to be responsible for primary,
secondary and further education respectively. In 1947, the Ministry
of Health, (then responsible for the control of local government)
issued circular 96/47 asking for a reduction in local authority staffing,
as an economy measure. Unlike Lincoln, which fairly readily in 1951
chose the administration as the first aspect to be cut back, the
Nottingham Director refused to consider any reduction and, on the
contrary, reported to his Education Committee in such terms that it
endorsed his prophecy that to cope with the expanding education
service, the staff of his Department would have to be increased and
not reduced, in order to carry out the statutory duties alone of the
new Education Act. In 1946 the Committee had already agreed to the
appointment of a new professional assistant (at £800 p.a.) to deal
with developments arising out of the new Act, (there were 374
candidates for the new post) and this was followed in 1949 by the
appointment of another assistant to deal with special developments
in further education.

In 1956 the Director retired and the Assistant Director then in charge of Development and Building in Nottingham was appointed as Director from a field of forty candidates. The establishment of supporting staff at clerical and middle management levels was steadily increased over the survey period as the work continued to grow. In 1959 the then Deputy Director resigned to take a post as Principal of the Nottingham College of Education, his successor holding office from 1959–1964, when an Assistant Director was again appointed internally to the vacant post. The Department was fortunate moreover in having excellent continuity at middle management level. Of the senior members of the administrative staff interviewed in 1969, one had been in post since 1944, another since 1956, a third since 1952, and one Assistant Director still in post in 1969 had taken his first appointment in the mid-1940s. This greatly helped consistency in planning long-term developments in secondary education. The sub-division of the department into three branches (primary, secondary and further education) helped the identification of the senior officers with their fields of interest although (and this was corroborated by all staff including the fourth Director) both major initiative and important decisions rested at Chief Officer level for the most part. 'Cabinet government' at officer level did not take hold in Nottingham under either of the postwar Directors.

Nottingham's structure of senior staff throughout most of the period therefore gave rise to the possibility of pressure points from within the administrative structure, including the inspectorate, albeit the latter was limited in scope.

Northumberland

Northumberland had reviewed its establishment as early as 1943, when the Director of Education reported to the Education Committee suggesting a new administrative structure of two senior assistant directors and one assistant director. The proposals were revised by the Committee which preferred to support the appointment of a new Deputy Director at a salary of £800 p.a. in place of one of the senior assistant director posts, in the light of the rapidly expanding work at senior level[4]. There was also at that time a County Inspector of Senior Assistant Director rank, with 15 full-time and three part-time Inspectors. General staff increases followed gradually and in 1944 the total staff of the department had grown from 47 in 1943 to 59 in 1944 and 67 in 1950. Shortly afterwards (22.6.45) Constance Lambert was appointed as Examinations and Vocational Guidance Officer, dealing with selection for secondary schools at 11+, and as a result of her work the Northumberland Selection Tests began to set a pattern for review and development of new methods of selection which many other local education authorities were to follow.

The Director in office in 1945 had served since 1934, succeeding the previous Director who had been Clerk to the School Board and had served from 1902 to 1934. The second Director had already gained a national reputation as a competent and progressive educationist. He served for example on the national executive committee of the Association of Education Committees; was appointed in 1948 as a representative of the County Councils Association to serve on the Burnham Committee; and served on the executive committee of the National Foundation (later Institute) for Adult Education. He had appointed a new Deputy Director in 1943 following the staffing review, and the latter became Director in 1953, remaining in office until 1970. The second postwar Director in his turn became a national figure in his own right, pioneering Anglo-German exchanges and serving on many national bodies concerned with education. The Chief Inspector in office for most of the survey period served with the county from the early 1940s, and until his appointment as Chief Inspector, served as a co-opted member of the Education Committee as the nominated teacher representative. In 1955 the post of Deputy Chief Inspector was created. Also in 1955 a general review resulted in the creation of a third post of Assistant Director. From then until 1965 there followed a series of regular reviews and regradings of supportive staff as the demands of the work required it, but no increases occurred at senior professional level and in 1965 the authority was still run by a Director, a Deputy Director and three Assistant Directors supported by three senior administrative (graduate) staff.

Although, unlike Lincoln, Northumberland had had senior professional staff from the very early post-war years, they had not as at Nottingham become identified with three clear sub-divisions or branches of the service. Over the years the edges of fields of responsibility had become more blurred. One Assistant Director for example became responsible for primary schools (every aspect) and secondary schools (staffing only) while a second Assistant Director held nominal responsibility for secondary and further education, but had no major responsibility for the secondary building programme since the senior administrative assistant for Development worked almost direct to either the Deputy or the Director. The Assistant Director also had only partial control over further education, especially after 1959 when the post of County Further Education and Youth Organizer was created for non-vocational work. Thus responsibility for coordinated forward planning was diffuse, the important decisions resting firmly and solely with the Director.

On the other hand the tradition of a relatively strong administration derived from the 1930s. The Director appointed in 1934 had inherited an administration which was educationally weak and which was steeped in a clerical tradition. Very little indeed had been done after the 1926 Hadow report and the department was inexperienced and under strength. He held however that energetic and progressive reform was impossible without a strong administration with a team of professional advisers and his first task was to build this up—no easy task in the 1930s. Like Nottingham, the county took full advantage of the special building grants and the 1934–40 building programme was sizeable and energetic, concentrating on post-Hadow reorganization of schools.[5] The Director in post from 1953–1970 had served under the pre-war Director and had acquired many of his livelier attitudes and priorities, including the value of a numerically large and highly trained inspectorate.

Northumberland shared with Lincoln and Nottingham a lack of 'cabinet government' of any kind at officer level. Delegation to individual officers tended to be according to the wishes of the individual Directors, and professional advice more often went direct to the chief officer and back down to other colleagues for comment rather than by group discussion or group decision-making.[6] This increased the tendency for individual pressures for particular projects or priorities to reach the Director straight from his Assistants.

The Borough Education Officer for Wallsend Excepted District was originally seconded to the borough from the County Hall establishment and only subsequently was he appointed as Borough Education Officer by the Wallsend Education Committee. The budget for Wallsend is compiled separately from the County budget by the Borough Education Officer and Wallsend Chairman of the Education Committee. In theory the Wallsend Education Committee has the right of automatic appeal to the County Education Committee: in practice the Borough Education Officer did not support the use of this right as a method of pressure, relying more on his monthly meetings with the Director, and on the professional relationships at officer level.

Although in theory, therefore, Northumberland had a senior administrative structure open to forms of internal pressures for resources for specific branches of the service, in practice the diffuse distribution of responsibility below the level of Director tended to diminish initiative from Assistant Directors towards any closely-defined corporate goal. It also minimized the likelihood of steady overall monitoring of the use of resources.

Inspectors and Advisers
The influence of advisory staff can be threefold. As Diagram 1

illustrates, they are the field link between the education department, schools and individual heads of departments. They should be able to provide 'feedback' from schools on needs arising from the curriculum for new or additional resources, to advise schools on the best use of their existing resources, and to administer their own 'pool' of money and equipment to further curricular innovation. How far they should be or are concerned in policy-making and decision-making appears to be debatable. In the survey period, their influence was probably less marked than in the period since 1965 when both in the country as a whole and in all three survey areas, advisory services have been strengthened with the growth of teachers' centres and the inservice education of teachers. In 1945, Lincoln had no inspectors and a school population of 8,781, Nottingham seven with 37,218 pupils and Northumberland 16·5 for 51,778 pupils.

Since *Lincoln* had no inspectors for the main curricular subjects, there was no impact from this source of innovation in the city during the 20-year period. In *Nottingham* the inspectors saw themselves as very much in the forefront of the conflict between opposing priorities and opposing principles in the allocation of resources.[6] Both of the key inspectors concerned with secondary education were concerned not to encourage teaching staff to introduce new methods and programmes without the extra money and staff needed for success— and the latter often could not be forthcoming for more than a minority of schools. This seemed to apply particularly in Nottingham to the supply and allocation of visual aids on which there was general agreement from those interviewed, including inspectors, that actual explicit demand grossly underestimated real needs because the fixed rate of expansion determined the level of requests in advance. The senior professional staff were obliged because of limited money to gauge the level of expansion likely to receive committee approval, fix this and then stimulate demand up to about that level.

The initiative for new courses (e.g. the introduction of engineering and electronics or advanced science into a bilateral school) which would need special and expensive resources, tended to come partly from inspectors but mostly it appeared from the Director himself who tended to act as Chief Inspector also. (With three general inspectors for 40 secondary schools, their pressure of routine work would presumably hamper regular objective assessment of course-needs.) The inspectorate delayed recommending new courses or approaches until resources were available to equip them—mainly after the early 1960s when an additional annual 'pool' of money for special equipment was allocated to the inspectors for certain subject areas (sciences, physical education, the creative arts, etc.). Very little demand came from schools to inspectors, possibly it was thought by some because the City's teaching force was excessively stable in many schools (it was commonplace for a teacher to remain 25–30 years in one school in the earlier years up to 1960). The Nottingham inspectorate predictably found that innovation seems always more expensive than the status quo both in terms of the replacement of obsolete books and equipment, and in actual comparison Video-tape recorders, overhead projectors and CCTV eat up substantially more funds than the useful but limited older projectors and record players.

In *Northumberland* the inspectorate were much stronger in number and in distribution, working under the direction and guidance of a Chief Inspector. From the early years the pattern in the county was of close involvement of all partners in the service. For example, the inspectors and advisory staff had no right as such to participate in the work of the Teachers' Advisory Committee (described later in this chapter) but were coopted by the teachers to advise on technical education in schools in the 1950s. In the second decade, the quasi-executive work of the inspectorate (staffing, advice on method or organization etc.) tended to be subordinated to advisory work on curricular reform, cross-fertilization of ideas between schools, deliberate introduction of new resources in selected schools (CCTV, integrated craftwork and engineering, audiovisual equipment for languages) and inservice education of teachers. (The in-service training budget rose from £2,000 in 1963 to £20,000 in 1968–69.)

The inspectorate both supported and influenced major policy from the onset of the postwar reconstruction. This worked both positively and negatively. One notable example was the county's insistence on building several small modern schools in an area rather than one large one in phases. Inspectors interviewed[7] considered with hindsight that the county's preoccupation with 'the small school' as an ideal led to timetabling difficulties, limited options and uneconomic use of staff and resources. 'But at the time we would have defended it.' On the other hand the inspectorate helped to press for the removal of the grammar/modern differential on capitation allowances and for the widespread supply of visual aids, especially to small or to rural schools. They created a rolling programme to provide all schools with strip and slide projectors, all secondary schools with cine projectors and small scattered areas with a mobile film unit; and in another context, to develop instrumental music substantially earlier than the other authorities in the survey period. Having set their goals and convinced the Director of need, there is evidence that financial resources were regularly allocated to meet a substantial part of the 'stimulated' demand from schools. It may well be that the fact that the second postwar Director was himself an ex-inspector (with another authority) set a favourable scene for the involvement of inspectors in decision-making and development in Northumberland.

The Education Committee Structure

All three local education authorities had reviewed their committee structure during the late war years when the 1943 Education Bill was being debated. The Government White Paper on Educational Reconstruction issued in 1943 was duly considered by the three Education Committees. *Lincoln* set up a special sub-committee for Planning which remained operative until 1949. *Northumberland* also set up a special sub-committee, while *Nottingham* devoted a number of special sessions of the full Education Committee to considering an early report of its Director anticipating the White Paper, and followed this by increased delegation of planning powers to its strong Sites and Building Sub-Committee.

The committee structures which were in operation in 1945 and later amendments are illustrated in diagrams B, C and D, which follow the text on the next page.

Local authority committee procedure is fairly standardized in practice and differences lie mainly in the number of sub-committees to which an Education Committee is prepared to delegate its power, and the extent to which delegation is practised. It must be remembered that the local education authority is the full Borough or County Council and no decision of a committee is technically valid until it has been ratified by full Council, although in turn, the Council cannot in law reach a decision on a matter of educational policy without first seeking and obtaining the advice of its Education Committee.[8]

Lincoln

Lincoln replaced its several sub-committees in 1945 by three main standing sub-committees of the Education Committee—Finance and General Purposes, Primary and Special Services Sub-Committees respectively. But there was no Sites and Building Sub-Committee, nor one for Secondary Education, and in practice the Finance and GP Sub-Committee tended to act as the main policy committee of the Education Committee, dealing with all major matters (including the Development Plan on which it received the reports of the special [temporary] Planning Committee set up in the mid-1940s). The absence of a special Sub-Committee either for secondary schools or for school building, meant that there was no group of members especially concerned with the development of a coherent secondary

DIAGRAM B: *Lincoln committee structure, 1945–65*

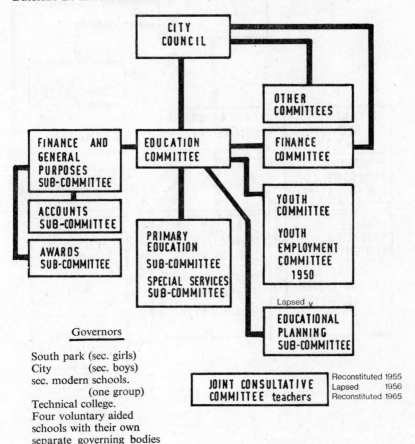

Governors

South park (sec. girls)
City   (sec. boys)
sec. modern schools.
              (one group)
Technical college.
Four voluntary aided
schools with their own
separate governing bodies

DIAGRAM C: *Nottingham committee structure,* 1945–65

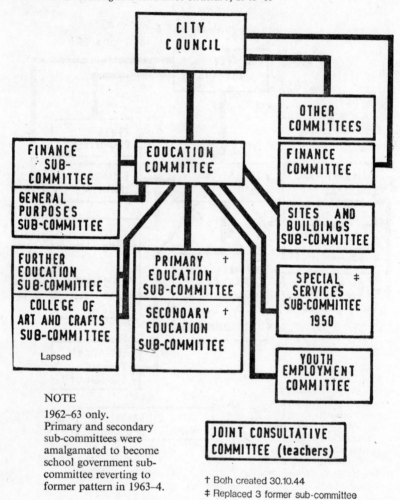

CITY COUNCIL

OTHER COMMITTEES

FINANCE SUB-COMMITTEE

GENERAL PURPOSES SUB-COMMITTEE

EDUCATION COMMITTEE

FINANCE COMMITTEE

SITES AND BUILDINGS SUB-COMMITTEE

FURTHER EDUCATION SUB-COMMITTEE

COLLEGE OF ART AND CRAFTS SUB-COMMITTEE

Lapsed

PRIMARY † EDUCATION SUB-COMMITTEE

SECONDARY † EDUCATION SUB-COMMITTEE

SPECIAL ‡ SERVICES SUB-COMMITTEE 1950

YOUTH EMPLOYMENT COMMITTEE

NOTE

1962–63 only. Primary and secondary sub-committees were amalgamated to become school government sub-committee reverting to former pattern in 1963–4.

JOINT CONSULTATIVE COMMITTEE (teachers)

† Both created 30.10.44
‡ Replaced 3 former sub-committee

DIAGRAM D: *Northumberland committee structure, 1945–65*

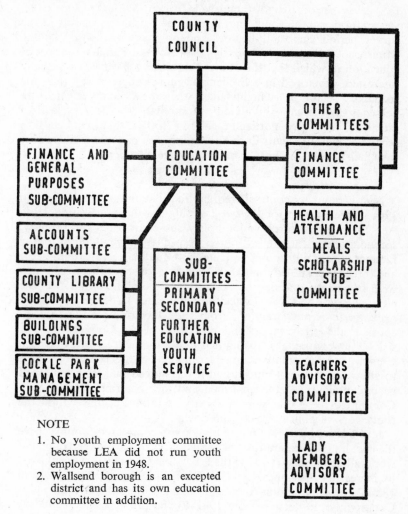

NOTE

1. No youth employment committee because LEA did not run youth employment in 1948.
2. Wallsend borough is an excepted district and has its own education committee in addition.

system or with the design and improvement of schools, who might review progress regularly and assess standards against the declared policy of the parent committee. It is not without significance that there were, however, sub-committees for primary and special education. Although Lincoln's record on secondary development in the survey period is undistinguished, tribute should be paid to the successful design and building of many new primary schools in the survey period against difficulties and obstruction imposed by the Ministry of Education in the early postwar years. Primary and special education in which the third Chief Education Officer was especially interested, developed in a livelier and more coherent way than the secondary sector. It is highly likely that the Committee structure helped to perpetuate this duality of standard by the very lack of members with any particular interest (other than financial) in secondary development. Each Sub-Committee had 10 members plus the Chairman of the Education Committee *ex officio*.

Nottingham

Nottingham, by contrast, reorganized its committee structure in 1944 in preparation for the work arising out of the new Education Act, and created three major policy sub-committees for primary, secondary and further education respectively in addition to the Finance, General Purposes and Sites and Buildings Sub-Committees; and three other sub-committees responsible for special services which were fused into one Special Services Sub-Committee in 1950. The city reviewed the whole Education Committee structure in 1950 in response to a memorandum from the Director of Education 'to consider the organization and procedure of the Committee'. The size of sub-committees was limited to 10, the number of Education Committee representatives on governing bodies was reduced by three to allow for more co-options and it was agreed that 'as a matter of general policy . . . the chairmen and vice chairmen of the Sub-Committees be given more authority to take decisions within the framework of policy already laid down'.[9]

It was also agreed that minor ad hoc sub-committees would relieve the standing sub-committees of special tasks to reduce the volume of work falling on them. In 1953 the Education Committee was enlarged by increasing the number of City Councillors serving thereon from 18 to 24, making a total committee of 28.[10] Under the brief two-year Conservative leadership from 1961–63 the primary and secondary sub-committees were amalgamated to become the School Government sub-committee but the volume of work and the return of a Labour majority in 1963 combined to reinstate the earlier subdivision of function.

Northumberland

Northumberland had an even more complex structure. The main sub-committees affecting secondary education were the Secondary Education, Buildings and Finance and General Purposes Sub-Committees respectively. While in the two county boroughs the Education Committee and Councils met monthly, Northumberland followed the usual county council practice of quarterly meetings and the sub-committee decisions tended to carry accordingly more weight. There is no recorded instance that could be traced of the Northumberland Education Committee's having reversed a sub-committee decision on secondary education during the survey period. The Buildings Sub-Committee in particular was almost autonomous with considerable delegated powers.

Northumberland has one *excepted district,* the borough of Wallsend which has its own Education Committee which meets monthly. In theory the Wallsend Education Committee has the right of direct access to the Department of Education and Science but this was not used in the survey period (the only recorded instance is on secondary reorganization after the issue of circular 10/65 of the Department of Education and Science). Its right of direct access to the County Education Committee in practice made little or no difference to the decisions reached which appeared to be in line with general county policy.

Equally important is the composition of the Education Committee, and the following section gives a brief outline of one or two of the more important factors.

The Education Committees

'The last thing required by a member of the Education Committee was a knowledge of education. All his time was occupied in details of administration, the wages of charwomen, and the grievances of irate parents.'[11]

Some 60 years have passed since Mr Jackson spoke thus to the Fabian Society and some at least of the detailed work has been passed from members to officers of the enlarged education departments. Nevertheless the comment is not inappropriate in postwar England. Relatively few members of the three Education Committees seem to have been appointed because of significant knowledge of or experience in education. The majority were political appointments from the three Councils, and only from a third to one half of co-opted members had had experience in some sectors of education. The balance of power between member and officer moreover remained, as earlier, a fine one.

It is often suggested that women have been more prominent in the Education service than elsewhere—education and child care are regarded as 'women's work'. But the figures in the following table still show a consistent minority of women, despite the fact that traditionally the teaching service includes a majority of women and that women have begun to take their place at middle management level in local authorities. On the whole, more of the women members of the Education Committee in Lincoln and Nottingham were co-opted, while on the contrary, in the county of Northumberland elected women members outnumbered co-opted women members.

Table III (1): *Education Committee members by sex*

	Lincoln				Nottingham		Northumberland	
	M	F			M	F	M	F
1945	20	4	1945		17	1⎱	24	3
			1946		23	3⎰		
1950	18	6			23	3	26	9
1955	19	5			29	5	27	15
1960	20	4			25	5	24	14
1965	21	3			26	5	23	13

Note: Some municipal seats were filled more than once in one year because of incidental vacancies and numbers therefore vary from year to year.

Continuity is also an important factor and the following table shows differences in the overall stability of the Education Committees; which disguises to some extent, however, the fact that the longer serving members tend to be also the leading men and women of some stature who have influenced policy over the years. On the whole, continuity was held by a minority of members and in all three authorities, this minority of strong personalities was more directly influential than groups of changing members.

Table III (2): *Education Committee members by length of service in the period* 1945–65

		Under 5 years	5–9	10–14	15–20
Lincoln	elected	26	12	6	8
	co-opted	9	7	3	3
	(total)	(35)	(19)	(9)	(11)
Nottingham	elected	56	30	10	7
	co-opted	4	2	2	2
	(total)	(60)	(32)	(12)	(9)
Northumberland	elected	38	18	16	9
	co-opted	30	9	4	1
	(total)	(68)	(27)	(20)	(10)

Local authorities took with varying seriousness the recommendation in the new Act of 1944 that persons of relevant experience should be co-opted onto the Education Committee.[12] Both Nottingham and Northumberland co-opted teacher representatives in the mid-1940s but Lincoln resisted this concession until 1959.

Lincoln had eight co-opted members at a time throughout the period, of whom three represented the Anglican, Roman Catholic and Free Churches. The Principal of the Lincoln Diocesan Training College was automatically co-opted, and of the remaining co-options at least one traditionally represented the major local industry of engineering. In 1959 the then Chief Education Officer conceded a 14-year-old battle with the National Union of Teachers and recommended to the Education Committee that one teacher representative, to be nominated by the NUT, be co-opted thereafter.

Nottingham co-opted only four members at a time throughout the period, representing the University of Nottingham and teachers from primary, secondary and further education. It was in response to a request from the Joint Consultative Committee (of members and teachers) in 1946 that Nottingham agreed to co-opt three teachers to represent the three main sectors of the education service.[13]

Northumberland co-opted an average of eight members at a time of whom one represented Durham University, three the main churches (Anglican, Catholic and Free), one the local branch of the NUT. The remainder were appointed for a variety of reasons as 'selected' rather than 'representative' members. Occasionally a former councillor might be co-opted either because of experience or because the Committee considered that a remote part of the county not otherwise represented ought to have a spokesman. In the early 1960s, for example, the very experienced former Councillor for Berwick who had served on the Committee since 1945, became a co-opted member after losing her council seat.

Politics and Educational Development

Political control cannot wholly be divorced from the composition of committees. The background of the councillors tended to reflect their politics—or vice versa. In *Lincoln* the Education Committee in 1945 included a number of councillors who had served throughout the war years and were well established. Their backgrounds varied reasonably well for a small town. On the Conservative bench could be counted lawyer, chemist, engineering director, doctor, supplemented in 1947 by oculist, chemist and grocer. The Labour group included a majority of men from the factory floor, (mostly engineering) with two trade unionists, a publican and a retailer. Conservative councillors tended to come from managerial levels (Insurance manager, master baker, manager of Building Society) while Labour representatives represented the industrial interests or skilled trades.

Nottingham Council reflected the many local industries both at works and managerial levels. Its left-wing councillors varied from one leader from a working class background with 43 years' experience of local government, to men in positions of high responsibility in technical industries. Right-wing opinion was represented by a range of councillors from a former education administrator to the woman director of an old established engineering firm. The longest serving chairman of the Sites and Buildings Sub-Committee in office in the early years of development was an ex-builder.

Northumberland, by contrast included at one time the County families (Viscount Ridley, the Duchess of Northumberland, gentlemen-farmers) and major business interests on the right-wing; while miners, insurance agents, trade unionists and representatives of the county Co-operative societies were consistently represented among Labour councillors.

Political control did not change necessarily at the same points in time in the three survey areas over the 20-year period, and in all three areas there were periods when the ruling Council had no clear majority. There seems no *direct* correlation between changes of control locally and the periods of expansion and cutback in the budget and capital programmes of the three authorities, until 1967.

Table III (3): Changes of political control of the Councils after 1945

Municipal year beginning	Lincoln	Nottingham	Northumberland
1945	Conservative	Labour	Labour
1946	Labour	,,	,,
1948	Conservative	,,	,,
1949	,,	,,	Conservative
1952	,,	,,	Labour
1958	Labour	,,	,,
1961	,,	Conservative	,,
1963	,,	Labour	,,
1965	,,	,,	,,
1967	Conservative	Conservative	Conservative

Lincoln had a fairly evenly balanced council with small majorities over most of the 20-year period but after a period of initial uncertainty settled down to 10 years of Conservative control followed by nine years of Labour rule. *Nottingham* by contrast had a longer initial period of political continuity through the crucial period of postwar planning and again with very narrow majorities. The Education Committee on a number of occasions had to operate with a majority of one while the Town Council's majority varied at one point from one to four. (The Nottingham Playhouse, one of the most important and expensive projects undertaken by the Corporation, was built on a chairman's casting vote.) *Northumberland* had almost uninterrupted Labour control although majorities tended to be narrow, but the Conservatives held the county in the first recession from 1949–52. Party politics, which were rarely obtrusive in any of the survey areas before 1965, were widely regarded as irrelevant by County Council members. Politics were so little a factor in the county indeed that in the brief Conservative rule, the Primary Education Sub-Committee, and the Children's and Health Committees were held by Labour Chairmen, while the Finance and General Purposes Sub-Committee in 1945–47 had been chaired by a Conservative under Labour rule.

Party politics in local authorities can vary in strength according to the local party organization and to the efficient operation or otherwise of the party caucus. If the theory of local democracy is to work however (that is local sensitivity to local needs may differ from national political policy in order of priorities) then party politics must give way more often locally than nationally to applied parochialism or to some independence from the party machine by men and women of any stature. The resources needed to carry out local policy must in theory be related deliberately to local educational needs.

It is however difficult wholly to disassociate the apparently inherited political attitudes of the leaders of the local majority and minority parties from the creation of a definite policy, e.g. the development of secondary education along clear lines. A bad educational environment, a restrictive educational policy can adversely affect the life chances of the next generation. For example, deliberate allocation of technical resources (both staff and equipment) and the provision of extended courses to able children only, will penalize the later opportunities for employment of secondary modern or less able pupils in industries requiring skilled crafts. On the other hand the conscious development of one aspect or branch of the education service with priority of money and staff, may equally consciously penalize other educational aims which conflict in the battle for scarce resources. The priorities applied in this situation will often spring as much as 'political' reflexes as from serious educational judgement of finely balanced needs.

Relatively the least of the potential pressures to be effective was party political pressure. This can be ruled out with two exceptions, both in Nottingham: the building of the Fairham Comprehensive

School and the withdrawal of one further education project from the major building programme.

Politics in Lincoln

Party politics have not been a major issue until after 1965. Individual personalities in this small town have been more influential. In Lincoln the difference between the 'old guard' Labour men of the 1940s and the new left-wing group of the late 1950s was quite marked. The early postwar Labour group were stalwarts who seemed to have been reared on the doctrine of 'a grammar place for every child' almost regardless of ability; Huxley's educational ladder available to all. They were obsessed by the scholarship principle and concentrated therefore for over 10 years on maintaining an expansion of grammar school facilities to match the increase in the school population, although in 1945 Lincoln already had grammar school places for nearly 25 per cent of the age group. The Labour group who took power in 1956 seemed to be of a new style, younger men and women educated in a climate of greater equality, the product of the war years when all of equal ability worked together for a common goal. The war had also proved that women on the one hand and working class recruits on the other could contribute to all levels of technology and management and this partially destroyed the inherited reluctance to admit either group to selective, extended or higher education. The Labour leader who remained chairman from 1958 to 1965 was already talking of reorganizing secondary education on non-selective lines in the late 1950s, and, failing the co-operation of the Chief Education Officer, himself initiated an interim scheme for transfer of secondary modern pupils of 15+ to two of the City's grammar schools. He had, however, difficulty in carrying with him the former Labour leader who regarded any education after 15+ for other than grammar school children as 'a waste of ratepayers' money'. Personalities in Lincoln were stronger than party loyalties. Reorganization therefore had to go into cold storage for a few years until opinion caught up with the new leader. The city being demographically predominantly working class, the group lacked left-wing intellectuals to support the few progressive thinkers.

Thus the Labour group was split, half of its membership agreeing with the Lincoln Conservatives who held that the country's future lay with the able child, and in their terms of office also therefore concentrating on the grammar schools. A dominant right-wing Conservative Councillor, chairman of the powerful city Finance Committee throughout most of the period spoke frankly in interview in 1968 in favour of the ideal government as 'selective despotism by the intelligent few', and discounted even the scholarship ladder principle.[14] Government was, or should be, an inherited faculty. Secondary modern children had therefore no need of technical or extended education for their allotted place in life—a view shared by his Chief Education Officer in office from 1948 to 1964.

The Lincoln Labour attitude of the earlier postwar years contrasted sharply with the Fabian pamphlet then current, which was quite unambiguous in declaring:

'It is important to realize that pupils can now stay on at any secondary school till the age of nineteen. This will enable modern and technical high schools to develop sixth forms and the present shortage of grammar school places offers an excellent opportunity to these schools to provide the longer school life which so far has only been possible in the grammar school.'[15]

With the exception of two who had died before 1968, the main political leaders and some experienced Councillors were interviewed and they and both Chief Education Officers were unanimous that 'party politics' as such had been irrelevant to the postwar developments before 1965. The two factors mostly quoted as influential were strong personalities and tolerable level of rate yield. The Labour chairman however felt the use of his party organization a helpful means of assessing priorities—local priorities, not national ones. The point was made by many that the only formal organizations of any strength in Lincoln were the political parties and the Chamber of Commerce, and discussions often took place in party groups largely because they were the natural social meeting ground. The Labour caucus meeting before each Education Committee was, it was claimed, for example, used largely to smooth over personal differences and rarely for major political theory or tactics. It was therefore important as an exercise in group dynamics rather than as a reflection of the policies and priorities of a national political organization.

The Lincoln officers interviewed, including the senior administrative staff and the former Chief Education Officer, were also unanimous in discounting as a factor before 1965 local party politics identifiably parallel to national party political priorities. They suggested that the individual personalities of three members of the Committee over the period were of more overriding importance.

Politics in Nottingham
Nottingham was in general politically more lively than Lincoln and politics appeared to have been markedly evident on major Council issues like housing. Only one recorded or quoted identifiable instance of party politics can be traced in the education service however, the building of the city's only comprehensive school in the mid-1950s.

The margins on the Education Committee were consistently narrow, especially in the period after the marked swing to Labour in the late 1950s, falling from four to two and in 1960, one.

A strong effort was made, it was claimed by representatives of both parties, to keep politics out of education. The first Labour chairman was a moderate man, the second a man devoted to raising standards by whatever method his Director suggested. The Conservative chairman from 1961–63 was more strongly politically motivated in full council but supported his colleagues in keeping discussion in the Education Committee as neutral as possible. Co-operation between the parties appeared to be good. The vice-chairman of the Education Committee and of all sub-committees was usually of the minority party. The presence of industrial representatives on the Committee probably helped to keep a more neutral balance. It was significant that one of the most politically sensitive of the experienced right-wing councillors, with 20 years' experience of committee work, could not think of a decision other than that to build Fairham Comprehensive School, into which party politics had entered. In theory she considered the parties had different (inherited) priorities but in practice the Committee bowed to the professional advice of its Director and to expediency (for example the need to house extra school children from a rising birthrate, or to meet a new demand from industry or the employment market). The most influential of the sub-committees was the powerful Sites and Buildings Sub-committee which was composed of the 'cream' of the Education Committee, including its chairman and vice-chairman, and on which the leader of the majority party of the Council who was also chairman of the Finance and General Purposes Sub-Committee of the City Council also served. The officer serving this committee for over 17 years could not however recall a second political discussion or decision other than the Fairham Comprehensive School issue.

Politics in Northumberland

Northumberland owes a good deal of its ethos to the tradition and history of the county, and to the involvement of the old 'county' families in county council work. While councillors do stand for election with a political label it has been regarded until relatively recently as undignified, unnecessary or even impolitic to allow party politics to intrude upon matters concerning the Education Committee or county council. Despite marginal political control during many of the postwar years, none of the councillors or officers interviewed in 1969 considered politics even relevant, and certainly could not recall a political issue before the issue of Circular 10/65 in 1965. A very experienced councillor who had been vice-chairman of the

Education Committee for 13 of the 20 years, and chairman of the Children's Committee,[16] found the Labour party organization a useful talking shop to test rank and file opinion on individual issues rather than a political organization as such. One former Assistant Director[17] had seen no party politics but rather disagreements mainly on finance within the party groups which usually met quarterly before Council meetings. All members and officers interviewed agreed that the strong Labour Chairman who died in the mid-1960s after continuous service throughout the postwar years, was concerned with neither politics nor resources, but with what was best for 'his' Northumberland children. He as readily fought his own purse-conscious leader as the councillors of the opposing political party. The Council member for Wallsend (a trade unionist) suggested he had seen more battles on the annual estimates between his two dominant Labour colleagues, than with the Opposition.[18] A veteran in his 80s confirmed the use of party meetings to air local parochial constituency issues (such as bridges over streams to help access to schools) rather than political ones in the sense of nationally agreed political policies.[19] The Conservative leader, a distinguished member of an old family,[20] in his turn could not recall when politics had been an issue in county affairs and commented further that his own group did little group decision-making, as such. These hypotheses were tested in turn on those officers who had held senior office and no trace could be found that decisions on secondary education had been noticeably affected by either a decision of the party organization or of major political interest.

Governors

A commonly held misconception is that governors of secondary schools govern. The duty of providing a governing body is laid down in Sections 17 and 19 of the Education Act 1944, while Section 20 allows for the grouping of schools under one governing body. Local education authorities were however left freedom to frame their own Articles and Instruments of Government although the Minister of Education obligingly provided a model to be followed, constructed noticeably with the example of the former aided grammar schools in mind. All voluntary aided schools would naturally have had their own governing body, since before the postwar introduction of voluntary aided status, the governors of such schools were wholly responsible for the management of voluntary schools. As from the mid-1940s, maintained county schools were to follow suit.

Lincoln accordingly constituted an appropriate body of governors individually for each of its two county grammar schools. The six county secondary modern schools were however grouped under one governing body in 1946, although the schools were geographically dispersed from the extreme south to the extreme north of the City. No official guidelines were laid down by the City Council on the appointment of governors, and in practice the governing bodies were composed of two-thirds local councillors and one-third nominated other persons nominated by the Education Committee.

Nottingham by contrast, saw positive advantages in grouping its 34 secondary schools in groups of 'mixed type'. The Education Committee took advantage of section 20 of the Education Act, 1944 for the grouping of all of its schools for government. In a large city area it would, it was considered, have been impracticable to have separate governing bodies for each of its schools and

'Your Committee have carefully considered the method of grouping, and are in full agreement with the view expressed in the White Paper on Principles of Government in Maintained Secondary Schools to the effect that there are solid advantages in grouping schools on a geographical or regional basis, schools of varying types finding a place in an individual group. . . . At least three of the governors shall be women.'[21]

Six groups of governors were created, all but one containing either a grammar or technical school as well as from three to five secondary modern schools. Two-thirds of the Nottingham governors were also councillors and in practice also members of the Education Committee, which meant that they tended, as in Lincoln, to change as the fortunes of the political parties shifted causing members to be elected to or deposed from the Council.

Northumberland approved new arrangements for governing bodies early in 1945. The grammar schools were to keep their own, separate governing bodies, the only linked schools being the Duke's and Duchess's schools at Alnwick. Northumberland, unlike the two cities, preferred its secondary modern schools to have separate governors but was prepared to group where appropriate. It should be said that in 1945 there were a large number of all-age schools, and less than 30 secondary modern schools. Where schools were grouped they tended to be in the same small town or district, the largest group being in the mining town of Ashington where five small schools were grouped. *Wallsend* was not included in the scheme (and in fact throughout the period its schools were 'governed' direct by the Wallsend Education Committee). In 1945, 12 governing bodies were created for 28 schools,[22] within which six schools had separate governors, and seven groups had only two schools.

As in the cities, some of the governors were councillors appointed by the local education authority but the proportion of councillors in

Northumberland was less, being only half of each governing body. The remainder were nominated from District Councils, local industry and commerce, the University College and, by the late 1950s, parents' associations. Twenty-five per cent at least had to be women.

The 58-page handbook issued for managers and governors in the county specifies numerous matters on which governors should be well informed, but the actual scheme of government makes all resolutions 'subject to the agreement of the Education Committee', thus giving only carefully limited powers to governing bodies.

The administrators and committees of an authority are more likely to be involved with implicit demand, the result of former policies or decisions created either by their own actions or by factors outside their control—a rising birthrate, a decision to create extended courses in non-selective schools. Governors, on the other hand, operate in a kind of hinterland where in theory (as a kind of sub-committee of the authority) they can be caught in the mesh of committee policy, especially as two-thirds in Lincoln and Nottingham and one half in Northumberland were also Education Committee members and/or councillors. They can also in theory express a kind of explicit demand on behalf of their schools, seeking to influence their officers and members on behalf of a particular school or group of schools. How far they were influential is touched on in later descriptive chapters.

Joint Consultative Committees

The Joint Consultative Committee of teachers and members comes clearly in the bracket of potential explicit demand as,—in theory,—the main official channel of teacher opinion. It serves, or should serve, to reflect important teacher opinion as a guide to the authority before and not after decisions are reached. How far such a committee can influence policy, will depend on its constitution and use and in particular on the initiative taken by members and teachers to raise major issues.

In *Lincoln,* a Joint Consultative Committee had existed since the 1930s but had been rarely called or used. After a very brief spell of activity at the time of the 1945 Burnham report the moribund JCC lapsed because under its constitution the Chief Education Officer alone had the right to convene it, and the Teachers' Panel had no right to summon meetings. In 1955, the NUT raised the question of representation on the Consultative Committee which then had nine local education authority members and nine teachers, with a view to revising the representation in relation to the numbers in constituent unions. The Lincoln branch of the National Association of Head Teachers asked for a revised constitution, more activity and for special meetings of head teachers,[23] to be called. After six months of discussion with the local teachers' organizations, the teachers' panel suggested a new constitution of 11 teachers selected to represent different sectors of the service (primary, secondary modern, secondary grammar, further, special education) rather than different teachers' organizations. The Education Committee agreed and the JCC was accordingly reconstituted.

It was consulted on the important 1956 Burnham report.[24] Evidence from the teacher's organizations[25] and from head teachers closely involved at the time[26] confirms that it was pressure from the local branch of the NAHT which led to the 1956 reconstitution of the JCC —the pressure from the National Union of Teachers at the time was for a teacher representative on the Education Committee. The NUT suggests, however, that its fight for the latter was an important factor in persuading the Chief Education Officer to agree to reconstitute the JCC as a sop to Cerberus. It was short-lived. After its single meeting in 1956, the Chief Education Officer did not convene the JCC again before his retirement in 1964, and when meetings of heads were called on secondary education, heads of grammar and modern schools were called together separately.

In 1965, three members of the defunct JCC wrote to the new (fourth) Chief Education Officer asking him to discuss the future and functions of the committee. He recalled the committee and it was agreed that the Chief Education Officer would in future summon a meeting once a term at the request of any three of its members, or whenever in his opinion a matter of importance needed urgent discussion.[27] Even then, as much through lack of teacher initiative as for any other reason, discussions tended to centre on topics like school holidays until the issue of Circular 10/65 on secondary reorganization.

Nottingham's Joint Consultative Committee was well established in 1945, but was divided into two committees, one for primary and one for secondary education. At a joint meeting on 26 April 1945, the teachers' panel asked for teachers to be represented on the Education Committee and the Director in turn suggested the amalgamation of the two committees. This was agreed in May 1945, and the teachers' panel was elected by organizations as follows:[28]

NUT	4
Class Teachers' Association	2
Joint Four Secondary Associations	2
NUWT	2
NAS	2
Head Teachers' Association	2
	14

The request for teacher representation was agreed a year later by the Education Committee on the grounds that

'inclusion of teachers on the Education Committee would be advantageous to the service of education in this city, as it would give the Committee the continuous benefit of the special experience which teachers possess as a result of their daily work in the schools'.[29]

The final constitution of the Education Committee in 1946 was therefore adjusted to 18 members of the City Council, one co-opted member from Nottingham University College (as it then was) and three teachers to represent primary, secondary and further education in the city who would be nominated by the Joint Consultative Committee.

In the early and mid-1940s, there were serious minor quarrels because the original JCC was wholly composed of NUT members. The Director then agreed to admit two men teachers from the NAS, which led the JCC to press for complete representation of all unions, which was achieved by 1947.

The constitution of the JCC was again revised in 1955 following pressure from the local branch of the NUT to consist of the following (previous numbers in brackets):

Education Committee panel	18	(16)
Teachers—	18	(14)
Total		30
NUT	8	(4)
HTA	2	(2)
NAS	2	(2)
NUWT	2	(2)
Class Teachers Association	2	(2)
Joint Four	2	(2)

In 1959 the new Director of Education introduced a supplementary form of consultation, holding frequent area meetings of teachers to discuss problems of mutual interest. The Teachers' Panel of the JCC rarely initiated policy but neither postwar Director would have taken a major step without putting those matters affecting the teachers to the JCC. Occasionally, but infrequently, the Teachers' Panel would meet on its own to discuss new developments.

Northumberland's Teachers' Advisory Committee was created just before the 1944 Education Act mainly to deal with questions arising out of the postwar programme for reconstructing the educational system of the county. It was intended to be, and has remained, a policy committee, and matters affecting salaries and allowance posts have been expressly excluded from its terms of reference. Teacher representatives were nominated by the NUT, the Joint Four Secondary Associations, the NAS, the Association of Teachers in Technical Institutions, joined by two Principals of Colleges of Further Education. The Committee met regularly throughout the survey period, dealing with such varied matters as curricular reform, external examinations, school records and equipment allowances. An early matter discussed was the raising of the school-leaving age in 1947. There were no specific moves to amend the consultative arrangements in any major respect because both the Director and the teachers found the existing arrangements satisfactory and sensibly used.

The extent to which teachers' organizations as such were successful in manipulating their explicit demands to influence policy will emerge as the history of the development of secondary education in each area is explained. It is however pertinent to suggest what kind of role teachers—organized or individually—ought perhaps to play in influencing the use of resources, that is, in planning and in assessing priorities. It should be said that opinions are sharply divided not only between authorities and teachers but between the different groups of teachers. And opinions may differ between national and local groups of the same organizations. A useful starting point however might be a study report produced in 1966 based on international evidence from teachers' organizations over the preceding two to three years, that is the end of our survey period.[30] The concepts produced by the British organizations would seem to have been based on their different past experiences and on their rather different ideologies one from the other. The World Confederation of Organizations of the Teaching Profession prefaces its symposium by suggesting that teachers' organizations ought to further educational planning, the main aims of which were:

'(1) To ensure that the educational system provides for the best economic growth of the country by supplying trained manpower.

(2) To promote social development and political stability.

(3) To safeguard and enhance the national cultural heritage.

(4) To help each individual to develop his or her personal abilities to the full.'[31]

The NUT evidence to this study report suggested that in an ideal situation 'The education service should mirror the current social philosophy of the parents, that is of society'[32] although this could prove dangerous since if parents had been asked in 1870 if they wanted Board schools or in 1876 if they wanted compulsory school attendance, the rates for the former and the loss of income from the latter would almost certainly have produced a majority vote for *negative* action. The influence of the NUT was, they suggested, exerted by direct pressure:

'The profession participates by pressure on the Government and the parties, by submitting evidence to the various committees and, in the case of all continuing committees, by appointing representatives to them'[33]

as well as by publicity and by such specific groups as the Council for Educational Advance and Parent-Teacher organizations.

On the whole the NUT reported broad satisfaction except that as a general principle, it considered that teachers were not consulted often enough over major decisions in education planning. While however the Union considered itself effective at influencing opinion on such issues as oversize classes, it was not yet wholly effective in 'testing targets against available finance', having for example no direct access to the National Economic Development Council. But the Union accepted the socio-economic goal of education.

'Although the union should be mainly concerned with educational progress and objectives, it should be equipped (should the need arise) to justify its demands in the total national economic context . . .'[34]

thus differing slightly in priorities from its fellow unions, the Joint Four who, while they believed that

'educational planning, in the broad sense, is essential to ensure that the manpower and materials available are used to the best advantage, since waste of human material and of scarce resources must be avoided',

nevertheless felt that the quality of the individual came first, and that

'the production of trained manpower, social development, the preservation of national cultures and political stability are subsidiary aims'.[35]

One wonders how an individual can develop to his full however without the production by the society in which he lives of an adequate and appropriate manpower and a healthy social structure.

The Joint Four found, (with reason it will be seen) less room for satisfaction on teacher participation at local, than at national level. Probably the most realistic comment came from the Association of Teachers in Colleges and Departments of Education, that reality in the shape of more children or new legislation tends to overtake educational planning, presumably because resources for expansion do not match policy. If, therefore, teachers' organizations are to be effective in their contribution to educational planning they must have well-informed professional personnel at their disposal.

Not all teachers however are enthusiastic unionists, and one ought also to see a real contribution towards local educational planning from head teachers and senior members of staff in a school, whether or not this is mirrored by formal consultative procedures.

Summary

Within the framework of planning, budgeting and decision-making in the survey areas, the major influence was the personal determination of all six Directors or Chief Education Officers (two in each area) to set their own goals and to tailor their priorities and their budgets accordingly—as well as the administrative practices which translated those goals into reality. Two early Directors out of three relied on a strong though diffuse administration in the period 1945–55, and without a 'quasi-cabinet government'. In all three survey areas there was long continuity of service among administrative staff which led to a fair constancy of standard (whatever that standard may be) and an excessive stability of attitude.

At face value, the influence of committees was likely to be—and was—stronger in Nottingham and Northumberland than in Lincoln, which lacked a 'member pressure group' for secondary education. But in all three areas very strong influences of individual councillors left a permanent and vigorous legacy. Politics (in the sense of defined political coherent priorities reflecting national party policies) were not an important influence before 1965, despite a frequently changing pattern of political control.

Only in Northumberland were women strongly represented on the Education Committee. In all three areas, a considerable majority of members served for less than five years but a substantial number also between five and 15 years. There was a constant overlap which made a strong thread of continuity in all three areas.

Advisory staff were influential in Nottingham (belatedly) and Northumberland (throughout) but not in Lincoln. Similarly consultative arrangements were available in theory in all three areas but were used only once in Lincoln before 1964, mainly in the second decade in Nottingham and throughout the period in Northumberland.

Governing bodies with varying constitutions were available as potential pressure groups in all three areas.

Of all resources money is, and is likely to remain, the main determinant of standards and priorities. The availability of financial revenue (from whatever source, local or central), must be a starting point in any examination of resource allocation. The following chapter therefore attempts to deal with the difficult and complex question of local government finance in the context of the three authorities and their priorities and practice over 20 years. In turn, it will be evident how these affected the basic standard of their secondary education.

Notes

1 MACKENZIE, Gordon N. *National Society for the Study of Education Year Book* 45, 'Developing and administering the Curriculum and Pupil Services', p.22.
2 redesignated thus in 1949.
3 Interview (10.2.69) with a member of the education department.
4 Northumberland, Selection & G.P. Sub-Committee (9.7.43).
5 The magnitude of the task in rural areas was such however that the county was still struggling with the problem when the 1958 national special rural reorganization programme began.
6 Interviews (24.4.69) and (15.4.69).
7 In particular, interview (4.3.69).
8 *Education Act* 1944, First Schedule, Part II, para. 7.
9 Special meeting of Education Committee, Nottingham (5.5.50).
10 Nottingham, Education Committee (22.7.53).
11 *Education* (4.11.1910) quoted in *Education* (4.11.60).
12 *The Education Act* 1944, Part II, First schedule, para. 5.
13 Nottingham, Education Committee (22.5.46).
14 Interview (21.4.69).
15 SIMON, Shena, S. *The Education Act* 1944, Fabian Research Series No. 90. By 1949 the current Fabian pamphlet was admitting that because of lack of capital 'It is proper to state here that completement fulfilment of the 1944 Act in these years is just not possible', *Next Steps in Education*, Fabian Society, June 1949.
16 Interviewed (23.6.69).
17 Interviewed (19.6.69).
18 Interviewed (30.6.69).
19 Interviewed (30.6.69).
20 Interviewed (1.7.69).
21 Nottingham, Secondary Education Sub-Committee (14.5.45).
22 Northumberland, Finance and General Purposes Sub-Committee (1.2.45).
23 Lincoln, Finance and General Purposes Sub-Committee (10.6.55).
24 On which it met however only once on 19.10.56 after which the Education Committee set up a special Burnham Sub-Committee of members only which did all further work on the report.
25 Interviews (5.2.69) (6.2.69) (27.11.69).
26 Interviews (4.2.69) (5.2.69) (6.2.69).

27 Lincoln, Minutes of Joint Consultative Committee (5.2.65) and Finance and
    General Purposes Sub-Committee (15.3.65).
28 Nottingham, JCC (30.5.45) and Secondary Education Sub-Committee
    (11.6.45).
29 Nottingham, Joint Primary and Secondary Sub-Committee (14.5.46).
30 *The role of Teachers' Organizations in Educational Planning,* World Con-
    federation of Organizations of the Teaching Profession, 1966.
31 Ibid. p.31.
32 Ibid. Theme study report p.3.
33 Ibid. p.3.
34 Ibid. p.6.
35 Ibid. p.81.

CHAPTER IV

Finance—
Providing the Resources

'Annual income twenty pounds, annual expenditure nineteen nineteen six, result happiness. Annual income twenty pounds, annual expenditure twenty pounds ought and six, result misery.'

Micawber in *'David Copperfield'*

Many a Treasurer and Finance Committee, caught between the Scylla of ratepayers (behind whom lurk the District Auditor) and the Charybdis of over-enthusiastic chief officers whose annual estimates are, as usual, in excess of the local authority's likely realistic income, must recall Micawber's golden rule. Just as, however, family needs may exceed the social accident of parental income, genuine needs for expansion or improvement of services may well exceed the present level of capital and revenue resources, which the local authority happen to command.

The finance of local government is a fairly complex subject in itself. Not all readers will be familiar with the main structure of the system of financing local government in post-war years, and an outline of the main influential changes which have occurred since 1945 is included for reference in Appendix C.

In 1945, the electorate returned a Labour government with a safe majority of 187. The country was short of labour, timber, steel and money and had to be helped by Marshall aid. Newly elected councillors appointed to reconstruct local government services and the education service in particular, were faced with a decision whether to raise rates to a politically 'dangerous' level to meet the cost of rapidly expanding social and other public services; or to cling to the policy that 'a stable rate is a sign of good government'; or to attempt a typically British compromise.

Some Councils determined their needs and their standards to be met and precepted on the ratepayers accordingly, raising their rates. Others decided on the acceptable maximum level of rate and tailored their policies accordingly to the money then available. The first group stretched the Procrustean bed of rate-yield to meet the giant demands of the expanding education service. The second lopped the size of the education budget (then as now the largest single element in the local budget) to their smaller Procrustean bed of fixed rate-yield.

Two conditioning factors in the local situation are the relative wealth or poverty of the area before government grant is received, and the level of rate in the pound which must therefore be levied to maintain services. An area which is relatively wealthy or which is historically accustomed to high spending will often the more readily adjust its level of expenditure to meet new demands, than areas which have difficulty in raising the necessary funds for basic services or which are traditionally committed to low spending. A politically-conscious authority is perhaps likely to be more sensitive to local pressures against a rising rate if the control of the council is marginal, while a less politically motivated authority may have more freedom to manoeuvre its finances without (or with less) regard to the electorate who, also traditionally, will simultaneously clamour both for lower rates and for improved services.

The financial status of the three authorities is therefore an important factor in influencing the level and type of spending. Local resources and government grants, the balance of tractable to intractable expenditure and the relationship of financial policy to potential educational development, can be critical.

One difficulty arises in that the accounts of the three local authorities were not kept in a uniform way with each other during the survey period. Care must therefore be taken not to compare figures for the three authorities which are not directly comparable. The financial position of the individual authorities may be studied from a close analysis of the tables in Appendix B, and attention is drawn to the footnotes to these tables explaining the different bases for some of the figures. Some figures are however directly comparable and have been used where appropriate. Most of the financial data have been extracted from the published accounts or the estimates of the three authorities. The absence of a philosophy of cost-effectiveness or of regular assessment of standards generally in local authority administration in the survey period, has tended to mean that data have not been kept in a form readily applicable to analytical research.

One of the first attempts to establish clearly the facts on education spending in a national context was published by John Vaizey in 1958[1] and the revised edition incorporating new material by Vaizey and Sheehan 10 years later[2] showed some changes in emphasis in the interval. Although however the 'dramatic improvement in educational statistics' of which the later book speaks makes research an easier task than hitherto, the results still suffer from the difficulty of isolating adequate and uniformly valid financial data and relating them to educational policy. Only in fact in the late 1950s did the concerted work of the IMTA and the County Treasurers' Association achieve a reasonable degree of standardization in the record-keeping of local authority accounts. Nevertheless, there were still some identifiable criteria of resources and of standards which will provide a useful starting point.

Then as now, local authorities were faced with financial techniques the reverse of those of private industries. Private enterprise works on the basis of *minimum expenditure,* and *maximum income* from sales and investment, aiming to cut costs and raise dividends. Local government however is obliged to run its services on the basis of *maximum expenditure* to meet increasing demands for such projects as new schools, old people's homes, children's homes, expanding local health services, often as a direct result of national legislation outside the control of local government; or to meet social needs (for example slum clearance or rising school populations) equally beyond their control. They must however finance this on *minimum income,* that is the lowest rate levy consistent with efficient services (and to avoid political suicide), and the minimum of government subsidies because no government has yet seemed willing to offer more than a carefully estimated minimum grant. Indeed one rough yardstick of a 'good' or 'progressive' authority in the eyes of teachers' unions and other pressure groups is its high level of expenditure compared with the average for all authorities, incurred on such items as teachers' salaries, books or capitation allowances. Authorities have tended increasingly to use the national average expenditure of all authorities as a yardstick for their minimum and maximum standards, since the annual financial analyses of the Institute of Municipal Treasurers and Accountants comparing average expenditure of all county boroughs and all county councils each year have circulated more widely.

Some aspects of the inquiry have of necessity not been limited to the local education authority as such. In particular, financial questions must be seen in the context of the authorities as a whole, especially matters affecting overall priorities between, for example, capital investment in education and housing. The general financial policy of a local authority has of course a direct bearing on its educational planning. The following table illustrates the different financial situations of the three areas:

Table IV (1)

Authority		Total Gross Revenue Expenditure (All Services) £	Total Gross Revenue Expenditure (Education Service) £	Total Gross Revenue Expenditure (Secondary Education Only) £
Lincoln	1946–47	867,900	337,491	108,432
	1964–65	3,139,123	1,779,177	530,276
% increase		361%	527%	489%
Nottingham	1946–47	5,023,056	1,241,574	357,337
	1964–65	18,165,382	7.933,534	2,590,007
% increase		361%	639%	725%
Northumberland	1946–47	3,860,778	1,729,287	363,879
	1964–65	19,595,764	12,382,092	4,575,698
% increase		507%	742%	1,257%

It will be seen how far the proportions vary between authorities, to a different extent at the beginning and at the end of the survey period. It will also be evident how far the different functions of authorities might affect overall budgeting. Nottingham and Northumberland had for example similar budgets for all services in 1965 although Northumberland's total population considerably exceeded that of Nottingham. But the differential for the education service as a whole and for secondary education, more nearly matches the school population differential, than do the local authority budgets as a whole. Nottingham's expenditure on housing, accounts for much of its non-education budget, while that of the county is inflated by high road costs, transport and the administration of justice.

I. The Budget—Where did the Money Come From?

Local authority services are paid for from government grants, from rates levied locally and from miscellaneous income received by the authorities. A distinction must be drawn between the local authority and the local education authority. Lincoln and Nottingham are county boroughs with major responsibility for housing and education but very little major expenditure on roads or transport. Northumberland is a county with heavy expenditure on roads and transport and education but no housing liability. The pattern of their total spending as authorities will therefore vary.[3] Figure 1 on the following page illustrates the all-important rate-level in all three areas.

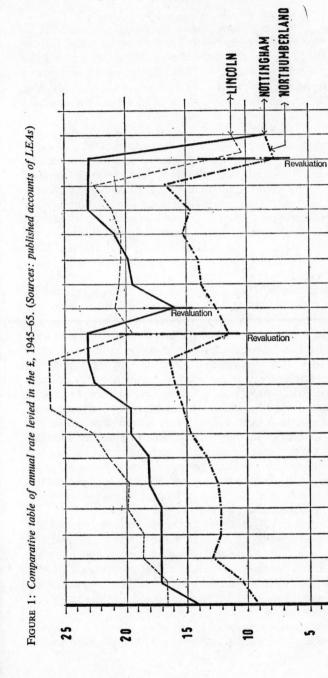

FIGURE 1: Comparative table of annual rate levied in the £, 1945–65. (Sources: published accounts of LEAs)

Income for all services

Figures 2 and 3 which follow, illustrate the different sources of income available to the three authorities in 1946 and in 1964, for the maintenance of all services for which the county boroughs and the county council were responsible. In 1946, *Lincoln* raised marginally more money from rates than it received in government grants, and raised about 22 per cent from miscellaneous income. The rate level was therefore a potential political tool.

Nottingham on the other hand received proportionately less government grant, but received miscellaneous income nearly equal to its rate-yield. Since its rate-income exceeded grants, this became a potential political tool and a conditioning factor. *Northumberland* received more government grant than rate-yield and other income combined, 59·5 per cent in all, and raised a neglible amount (8·7 per cent) by miscellaneous income. (The county had of course no income from rents of council housing.) Figure 1 on page 85 illustrates the actual rate levy in all three areas. This position is very different from many generalizations about sources of local authority income which have been current.

By 1964, the Exchequer Equalization Grant had been replaced by Rate Deficiency Grant and specific grants to the education service had been abolished except for a few special ones for such matters as school milk and meals. The effect of the new Rate Deficiency Grant was to give all three authorities proportionately more government grant than in 1946. In *Lincoln* the change of proportion was hardly significant; in *Northumberland* government grant had always been the major element of income. But in *Nottingham,* the most financially viable of the three authorities in terms of rateable value and rate-yield, the proportion of government grant in fact increased in relation to the two other sources of income. As the least in apparent financial need, it appeared to benefit proportionately more. Its budget was financed almost equally from all three sources of income, while *Northumberland* received massive government grant (63 per cent of total income), raising only 29 per cent from rates and maintaining income from other sources at a modest eight per cent.

By 1964 therefore, *Northumberland* had still the 'protected' position (politically speaking) of high government grant and low rate, *Nottingham,* a higher rate but substantial grant, and *Lincoln* a high actual rate but more money from central government than in 1946 and than from other sources. Lincoln's political consciousness on this factor might well have become less acute, in theory.

Income for the education service

The budget of the Education Committee did not always mirror that

FIGURE 2: *Comparison of total gross local authority expenditure and income, 1946–47. All main grant services. (Sources: published accounts of LEAs)*

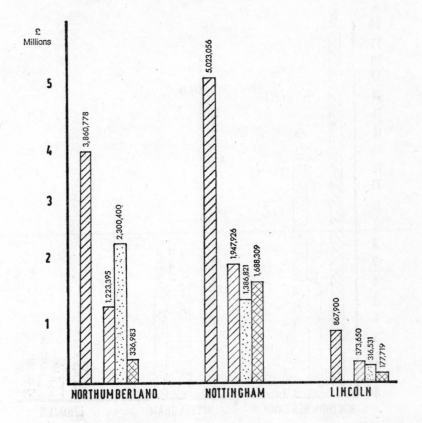

Total gross revenue and expenditure
Income from rates
Income from Government grants
Other income

FIGURE 3: *Comparison of total gross local authority expenditure and income,
1964–65. All main grant services. (Sources: published accounts of
LEAs)*

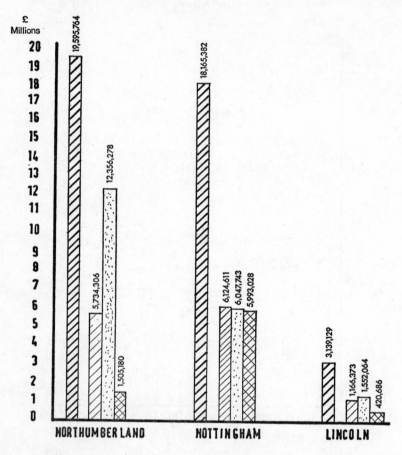

Total gross revenue and expenditure
Income from rates
Income from Government grants
Other income

of the local authority as a whole. Full details of the sources of income for education expenditure appear in Tables III (a) to (c) of Appendix B (pp.B6–B8). Comparisons are only possible for the period up to 1958–59, when percentage grants ceased and government grant was made to the authority as a whole, leaving it to the local Finance Committees to decide how much to allocate as a subsidy to the education service.

Figure 4 on the following page illustrates the position of the three authorities in 1946 and in 1958 (the last year of percentage grants). This and the figures in Tables III (a) to (c) seem to support the theory that percentage grants favoured willing spenders since Northumberland received a consistently higher level of grant than the two county boroughs specifically for education (i.e. exclusive of Exchequer Equalization Grant) and its proportion of income from rates was consistently lower for much of the period. Much of the evidence from Northumberland (see chapters III and VIII) suggests a long tradition of willingness to spend on educational developments.

Rateable value and rate yield

These variations were matched by—indeed partly caused by— variations in the rateable value per head of each authority throughout the survey period. *Northumberland's* rateable value per head was consistently well below that of the other two authorities. This might be expected in a mainly rural county whose urban fringe only bordered the industrial complex on Tyneside the greater part of which paid rates to Newcastle County Borough. In the early years, *Lincoln* and *Nottingham* were not widely different but the latter benefited more substantially from the 1956 and 1963 revaluations (of which more is said in Appendix C). Figure 1 on page 85 shows the level of the rates levied by all three authorities over the 20-year period and it will be evident that Lincoln was obliged to levy a rate well above that of the other two authorities despite its higher rateable value than Nottingham and its relatively high level of government grant. Yet its expenditure per head on education services was lower, as Table V of Appendix B illustrates.

Figure 5 illustrates the different patterns of rateable value per head and Nottingham's especially favourable position. The effect of the 1956 and 1963 revaluations is shown in another, sharper way by the tables in Appendix C (page C.350), which show significant differences in the gains in rateable value per head between the three authorities. Thus *Nottingham* not only had a more favourable rateable value throughout but benefited more substantially from both revaluations, that is its rateable value increased more significantly and its rates fell more sharply. And although *Lincoln*

FIGURE 4: *Annual gross income education service only expressed as % of total revenue and expenditure*

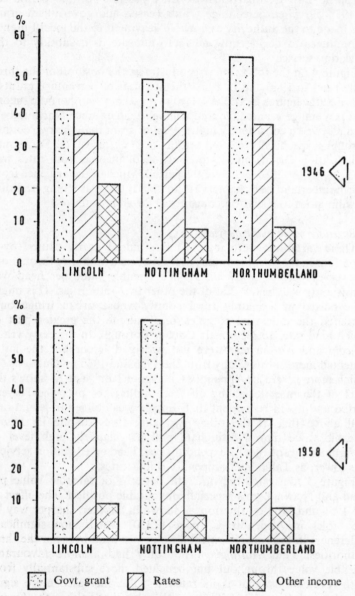

FIGURE 5: *Comparative rateable value per head*

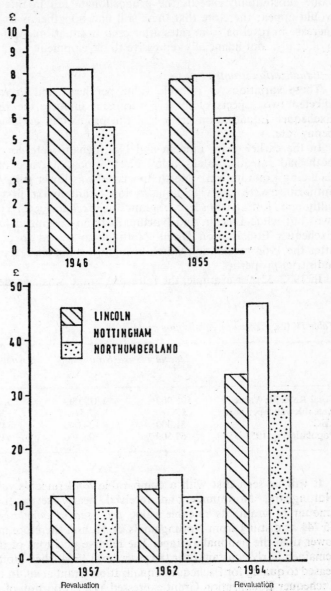

benefited least from revaluation, it still received less government
grant than *Northumberland*. But in all three areas, the rise in rateable
value substantially exceeds the proportionate fall in rate level. It
would appear therefore that there still had nonetheless to be a net
increase in revenue from rates after each revaluation. And this was
'politically' and financially repressive to development.

Equalization grants

These variations in rateable value per head and in rate yield
affected two aspects of local government finance, the receipt of
Exchequer Equalization grant and the product in each area of a
penny rate.

In the earlier years Lincoln and Nottingham were comparable;
both had rateable values below the national average of £6·335
including London, while Northumberland was lower still. All three
authorities were receiving Equalization Grant in the first decade,
(although Nottingham's level of grant was much lower than the other
two) but while Lincoln and Northumberland continued to receive
Exchequer Equalization Grant, Nottingham ceased to be eligible
after the 1963 revaluation which brought it valuable revenue from
industrial properties.

In 1952–53, for example, the following grant[4] was awarded:

Table IV (2): Exchequer equalization grant

	Lincoln £	Nottingham £	Northumberland £
Total Rateable Value	508,000	2,317,000	2,528,000
Rateable value per head	£7·31	£7·51	£5·74½
EEG	31,000	124,000	848,000
Population in 1952–53	69,500	306,600	438,300

It will be seen that with a comparable *total* rateable value with
Nottingham, Northumberland received nearly seven times the
amount of grant, its rateable value *per head of population* being
£5·74½ as distinct from Nottingham's £7·51, and therefore markedly
lower than the national average. The relative positions of the areas
remained fairly constant over the years until 1964 when Nottingham
ceased to qualify for Exchequer Equalization Grant at all. In 1952–53,
Exchequer Equalization Grant expressed as a proportion of relevant
local expenditure showed the same differential:[5]

Lincoln	*Nottingham*	*Northumberland*
%	%	%
4·67	4·73	25·97

Similarly the product of a penny rate varied, and this was of some importance in the light of restrictions placed on local authorities in 1951 by the Ministry of Education on expenditure on minor capital projects at schools. Addendum no. 2 to Circulars 209 and 210 (14.9.1951) which restricted expenditure from revenue on capital projects to 'the product of a penny rate in the authority's area' for the current financial year, severely limited the work which could be undertaken to adapt schools in need of modernization. Even though the penny rate for 1952–53 for the survey areas would have contributed little towards the much needed modernization of old buildings, undoubtedly Lincoln as the smallest authority suffered most, lacking the flexibility that a larger amount will give even if it has to be shared among more establishments:

	1d. rate 1952–53
	£
Lincoln	2,072
Nottingham	9,474
Northumberland	10,613

The revaluations of 1956 and 1963 again affected the level of 1d. rate, thus materially affecting the amount available to the local education authority from revenue to be spent on capital minor work. Thus *Nottingham's* 1d. rate leapt from £10,095 to £17,743 between 1956 and 1957, and from £19,721 to £58,801 between 1963 and 1964. This was to serve a total population of 312,500 (1957) and 315,000 (1964), and a school population of 51,770 (1957) and 51,686 (1964). But *Northumberland's* earlier increase from £10,881 to £16,642 had to serve a total population of 463,900 and school population of 71,752, while the later increase to £57,145 was related to a total population of half a million and a school population of 78,064. Northumberland had therefore a lower penny rate for 50 per cent more school children. The kinds of improvements encouraged by central government using an approved level of expenditure based on the 1d. rate (Chapter V comments on these) were less available to Lincoln and Northumberland where the needs were demonstrably the greater as it transpired. In theory, therefore, 'demand' from an authority to improve conditions in schools using capital from revenue was related to a potential 'resource'—but the Ministry restrictions on use of a 1d. rate, and the poorer position of authorities like

Lincoln and Northumberland, reduced this resource in practice to an insignificant role.

Rate balances

It is worth recording at this stage, that none of the three authorities was able to cushion its rising expenditure by use of substantial balances in hand in revenue account. *Nottingham* however is distinguished from the other two authorities in its use of two Local Government Acts (of 1953 and 1959), enabling and indeed encouraging local authorities to set up additional capital funds with the product of a 3d. rate, to pay for major repairs and renewals and to finance rolling programmes (like the Nottingham five-year plan for re-equipping all housecraft rooms). The Chief Education Officer who took office in *Lincoln* in 1964 was the first officer to suggest building up a 'pool' capital account for renewal programmes; but without success.

Central and local control

Factors like these, that is rates, penny rates and the level of government grant, while they often may seem a technicality to the headteacher or inspector, are among decisive factors influencing city and county councillors to favour or to disapprove new expenditure which may be suggested to meet new needs or new demands. They provide the backcloth against which decisions in full Council are taken. How far can it be argued that increased government grant leads to increased government controls however? How far does this argument outweigh local factors?

A major element in the arguments about the problem of balance of control between central and local government departments, is the proportion of the local government expenditure which is financed by *direct* government grant. It is however questionable whether the correlation of government control with government grant exists other than as a coincidence in time. It is dangerous to show increased grant followed by some increased controls and to argue *post hoc ergo propter hoc*. If this were so, the fall in *direct* subsidy to education in 1959 (see for example Tables III (a) to (c) of Appendix B and Appendix C) would have been accompanied by increased freedom for local education authorities; and it was not.

We have, moreover, seen a marked variation in the level of central grant aid received by both the local authorities as a whole and the local education authorities as such. Chapter V in particular and the succeeding three chapters on the three survey areas will illustrate that they were all nevertheless subjected to precisely the same degree of central controls, that Northumberland which received most grant was the more independent, and that controls increased, rather than decreased, after 1959.

II. Expenditure—Where Did the Money Go?

A number of factors seem relevant to the assessment of an authority's capacity to respond to demand, and to an account of its decisions to do so. First, it is useful to look at growth rates and their relationship to implicit demand. Second, the proportion of tractable to intractable expenditure is relevant to an ability to meet unforeseen or new demand. Third, some improvements in standards have been accepted as at least measurable in financial terms—for example average costs per pupil, or average levels of expenditure on books, stationery and apparatus.

Definition

Almost every discussion published dealing with the costs of education seems based on a different definition of accountable total expenditure. In recent years, the true cost is more accurately computed, for having the cost of service (administration etc.) added in.

References will be made throughout this book to 'gross expenditure' in various contexts and it should perhaps be made clear what this means. Vaizey and Sheehan[6] have allocated certain items of expenditure to central and local government according to their own formula based on grant regulations prevailing at the time and which does not coincide with standard national and local accounting. Their estimates of the source of finance from which expenditure has been met has been separately made for each item, in an attempt to arrive at a realistic, adjusted national figure. Bleddyn Davies[7] on the other hand interprets gross expenditure as

'expenditure incurred in order to secure current standards of provision. We therefore need a concept which measures the total flow of expenditure on resources into the service, *irrespective of when the expenditure was made*. It should also exclude the flow of resources benefiting recipients who are the legal responsibility of other local authorities; but include the value of resources purchased by one authority from others when they are for the benefit of those who are the responsibility of the authority in question.'[8]

Davies' method aims at sophisticated assessment, albeit still an estimated one, which may well prove a good deal more accurate as an estimate of actual resources expended, than simple extraction of expenditure and income figures from revenue and capital accounts.

Davies crosses financial years by his method and adjusts for services provided between different authorities.

Nevertheless, in this work, gross expenditure means the *recorded* total spent on a service, whether the whole education service, or secondary education, or libraries, and so on, and not that figure adjusted to a net figure to show either relevant or loosely related income for the service. There are two reasons. First, it is the gross, unadjusted figure on which the local officers and committees base their decisions to expand or cut a service. If estimates have to be cut, the Finance Committee will expect easily identifiable reductions. Conversely if a chief officer or sub-committee wishes to increase provision for audio-visual aids, for example, or for maintenance and repairs, the case must be made on those detailed estimates in relation to expenditure of previous and future years *on those items*. Second, the important factor when assessing the possible effect of demand on financial resources, is the growth rate in relation to increased need, or to increased cost, or to increased demand. As long as figures over the years are properly comparable, it matters less in the context of demand and supply whether they are adjusted to reflect total cost including hidden costs (except where it is suspected that the latter has developed at a markedly different rate).

Growth rates and average costs

Table IV (4), which follows overleaf, gives the basic growth rate for total expenditure, total education expenditure and total expenditure on secondary education. It will be immediately apparent that *Lincoln's* growth rate on all three is lower than that of the other authorities and that *Northumberland's* is the highest. On the other hand, the county was starting from a much lower relative base—its total expenditure was less than Nottingham's in 1946 for a much larger population, and its education expenditure only marginally higher. Its education growth rates, notably the secondary rate, reflect the reorganization of all-age schools, and greatly increased use of transport for secondary school pupils and of the provision of boarding schools and homes for rural children of secondary age. It will also be seen that only in Lincoln did secondary education expand at less than the general education services. Lincoln's total expenditure on education increased by five times, Nottingham's by six and Northumberland's by seven.

Expressed in another form, table V of Appendix B sets out the growth in expenditure per head of (total) population. Again, Northumberland starting from a lower base increased six-fold as against Lincoln's four times and Nottingham's five-fold rise, yet remained below Nottingham's level for much of the period, mainly because of the problems facing the county on the reorganization of all-age schools which was not fully achieved until the early 1960s. Until then pupils of secondary age in all-age schools were recorded in the primary figures and received resources geared to the primary level and voted to that part of the budget.

Table IV (3): *Gross education revenue expenditure per head of total population*

	LINCOLN £	NOTTINGHAM £	NORTHUMBERLAND £
1947–48	5·9	5·0	4·5
1955–56	9·6	10·4	9·7
1964–65	23·1	25·2	26·0

Table IV (4): *Comparative growth rate of revenue expenditure 1946–64*

	TOTAL GROSS REVENUE EXPENDITURE (ALL SERVICES)* £	TOTAL GROSS REVENUE EXPENDITURE— EDUCATION SERVICES ONLY £	TOTAL GROSS REVENUE DIRECT EXPENDITURE— SECONDARY ONLY £
Lincoln			
1946	867,900	337,491	108,432
1964	3,139,123	1,779,177	530,276
% increase	361%	527%	489%
Nottingham			
1946	5,023,056	1,241,574	357,337
1964	18,165,382	7,933,534	2,590,007
% increase	361%	639%	725%
Northumberland			
1946	3,860,778	1,729,287	363,879
1964	19,595,764	12,832,092	4,575,698
% increase	507%	742%	1,257%

* for the whole county borough or county council.
Note: The figures for 1946 and 1964 are the actual figures for expenditure extracted from the local authority accounts for those years.

Against these growth rates must be set the growth in total and in school population. Table IV (5) which follows, shows some interesting differences between the rises in expenditure illustrated in table IV (4), and the increased population.

Thus, in *Lincoln,* education expenditure as a whole rose more than that for the secondary sector. But secondary school rolls rose at a more significant rate—25 per cent more—than the school population as a whole. Either other sectors of education expenditure rose excessively (and this seems unlikely since the overall growth in education expenditure was still much less than in the other survey areas) or secondary education fell far behind a normal growth rate. Nevertheless with a 69 per cent increase in secondary rolls, at least a proportionate increase in secondary expenditure could be accounted for by implicit demand.

Table IV (5): Comparative growth rate of population—implicit demand

	TOTAL POPULATION	SCHOOL POPULATION	SECONDARY SCHOOL POPULATION
Lincoln			
1946	65,280	8,781	3,096
1964	77,180	12,643	5,230
% increase	18·2%	44·0%	69·0%
Nottingham			
1946	265,090	37,218	13,446
1964	315,050	51,686	20,303
% increase	18·8%	38·6%	50·9%
Northumberland			
1946	412,080	51,778	10,315
1964	494,440	78,064	28,973
% increase	19·9%	50·6%	180·6%

Note: The three main factors were the raising of the school leaving age (1947–48), the rising birthrate (which affected the secondary sector from the mid 1950s) and the increased proportion staying on after 15+ (most significant in the 1960s).

In *Nottingham,* the possible qualitative element of improvement by increased expenditure is more marked. Although the county borough's secondary expenditure expanded at a far faster rate, the rise in both total and in secondary rolls was the least of the three authorities—though still substantial. It did more nearly match the pattern of expenditure however, that is secondary rolls and secondary expenditure both rose more sharply than total rolls or total education expenditure.

The *Northumberland* increases in population again more nearly match its pattern of expenditure. A startlingly high increase in secondary school rolls account for a larger proportion of the equally high increase in secondary expenditure. While, however, secondary expenditure rose at nearly twice the level of total education expenditure, secondary school rolls rose at almost three times the rate of total school rolls. In other words, the rate of expansion of secondary expenditure did not maintain its appropriate relationship to the rate of expansion for all expenditure, which the sharper rise in rolls merited.

This was probably indeed a reflection of the national trend for rising rolls to exceed the rate of rising expenditure. In 1947 the school leaving age was raised to 15 and the 14-plus age group in the country as a whole was predicted to rise from 141,000 in 1947 to 500,000 in 1952,[9] although in practice expenditure was not always forthcoming at the required level to cater for the extra pupils.[10] Nevertheless the extra pupils in 1947–52, and the increased school population following the rise in birthrate caused inevitable increases in maintenance costs, expenditure on furniture, books etc. which can be measured as a proportion of the whole and therefore identified as a basic implicit demand over which local education authorities had no control.

Accepting that minor differences in accounting may well cause these percentage increases to be qualified slightly for purposes of direct comparison, what they do begin to show is the extent to which the three authorities had to expand services mandatorily, because of quite substantial increases in those needing services. They also suggest a growing, if belated, consciousness on the part of two of the three authorities, that planning of expenditure and increase in population are related: which indeed Chapters VI to VIII illustrate.

A footnote is perhaps necessary on the question of assessing standards. However crude, an index of some sort to suggest progress or otherwise, is highly desirable in local government. Costs per pupil have sometimes been used as crude indices of local authority performance. Measurement of educational development is in any case difficult, and opinion is far from agreed on the dimensions in which measurement is either possible or relevant, or on the indices to be used. The extreme idealist may decry any attempt to measure progress of any kind by material indices (such as new buildings or equipment). Even the most liberal of assessors may regard financial aspects as rather tedious administrative restrictions, unlinked with or divorced from the 'real' work of the educator in the classroom.

The IMTA in its 1956 survey of local authority expenditure, suggested, however, that the percentage of secondary school places available in grammar schools, class size and the number of small classes, and pupil-teacher ratios, could all be regarded as valid criteria. To these might be added, with certain qualifications, costs per pupil on for example furniture, books and equipment where it can be established that the majority of schools do not enjoy above-average standards of these. It would be unwise to use the level of capital expenditure unadjusted, since some authorities may have inherited more out-dated buildings than others, and some like Coventry and London, had to build for a decade to replace schools destroyed in the war years. Chapters II and X attempt to relate material resources to the needs of the curriculum, and if the premise that buildings and equipment can predetermine or limit teaching method or curriculum content has some validity, then expenditure on these material resources (and in particular the extent to which this expenditure keeps up with inflation) is a relevant index of a continuing or a declining standard.

The principle of average *costs per pupil* was introduced by the then Ministry of Education in the late 1940s. In 1946–47 the gross cost per secondary school pupil varied from below £22 to above £40 for county councils and from below £19 to above £40 for county boroughs. The *average* cost per secondary school pupil was then £30·39.[11] This not only hides variations between authorities, (Nottingham's gross cost was then for example £25·96) but variations between types of secondary school.

Tractable and intractable expenditure

Another aspect which needs further thought and examination, especially in the context of new educational needs, is the theory that local education authority expenditure can any longer be controlled, cut or redistributed to any marked extent without danger to basic standards. The proportion of the education budget of local authorities which can be regarded as negotiable, or available for other than quite unavoidable expenditure, has steadily decreased over the years. Yet it is from this section of the budget that resources for curriculum reform, new courses and new developments must increasingly come. It is also as a result partly of local policy, partly of centrally agreed wage and salary levels, that the fixed element of the budget is determined. Even in 1956 this had become apparent.

Norman Fisher, writing in the Year Book of Education, suggests that

'A high proportion of costs is intractable: more than 70 per cent is made up of salaries and wages based on nationally or regionally determined scales. In the remaining expenditure are many fixed charges and there is of course an irreducible minimum for such things as the maintenance of buildings or for books, stationery or apparatus.'[12]

The writer's analysis of 20 years of accounts of the spending on education in the three survey areas shows that this margin has narrowed much further over the years in financial terms. An important qualification is, however, that much of this represents the moving of experimental work originally financed from the 'margin', into the basic expenditure. A development of this argument must therefore take account of different interpretations of what is intractable expenditure. Nevertheless, while present criteria apply, once an authority has committed itself to a policy, subsequent cuts must be applied necessarily to the basic levels if they are to be financially significant. This may well then affect the quality and type of education offered.

The three main intractable elements of a local education authority's budget are teachers' salaries, salaries of administrative and non-teaching staff, and loan charges. To these can be added an irreducible minimum expenditure on maintenance of buildings, fuel, light and cleaning, and furniture and equipment. The first group (salaries and loan charges) account for from two-thirds to three-quarters of the budget and the addition of the second group leaves only from three to ten per cent of 'negotiable' expenditure depending on the authority, the Finance Committee and the year.

It is not wholly accurate to regard the entire salary bill as intractable since, in theory at least, one need not employ a full establishment (or one may fail to recruit enough staff). But if one assumes as a matter of policy that a full quota of staff is to be recruited, and that standards, once set, are to be at least maintained, the very substantial majority of such expenditure becomes in fact intractable—short of dismissing staff.

Tables VI (a) to (c) of Appendix B give the proportion of direct expenditure accounted for by some main sections of expenditure in the secondary sector. It must be stressed that each table must be related to the situation within the authority concerned—the footnotes to these tables indicate that the bases of the calculations are not identical and also differ for the period before and after 1959.

Nevertheless, at the time when the annual estimates are being prepared and negotiated, it is in fact crude indices like these which are used. A committee will tend to look at the relative position of expenditure on each aspect of the service and if, for example, expenditure on books or ancillary staff rises at a faster rate than that for maintenance or fuel, it will be identified and questioned. The sophistication of the cost-analytical approach is not likely in the foreseeable future to influence the average Committee member faced with a decision each year to be made on one evening before the rate level is set, on where cuts are to fall or expansion to be approved. Evidence from all three authorities in 1968, confirmed that the detailed work of financial officers is constantly liable to be overruled —in accordance with the basic principles of democratic local government—by decisions by members. Hence, simple indices remain a useful 'political' tool in the non-party sense, and are readily applied in practice.

Loan charges became a steadily larger proportion of intractable expenditure over the years. Nottingham provides a good example of this:

Table IV (6): Nottingham. Education gross revenue expenditure on loan charges (all branches of education)

Year	(A) Total Gross Education Revenue Expenditure £	(B) Loan Charges £	% (B) of (A) %
1946	1,241,574	50,765	4·05
1954	2,961,718	279,341	9·35
1958	4,632,664	596,319	12·9
1964	7,933,534	774,447	9·35

It will be seen that loan charges in *Nottingham* commonly accounted for an average of about 10 per cent of all expenditure; Teachers' salaries accounted for from 77 per cent to about 50 per cent, depending on the basis of calculation, and maintenance increased, for example, in Nottingham to over 10 per cent; educational materials of all kinds accounted for a very small proportion. Administrative costs have not been examined, but these commonly account from five to eight per cent (see Appendix B).

Maintenance of school buildings in Nottingham rose from 2·81 per cent of total secondary expenditure in 1946–47 to 5·22 per cent in 1954–55, doubling to 11·93 per cent in 1959 (when a *fall* in percentage might have been expected following the new accounting procedure under which all secondary expenditure was included in the total figure recorded: See Appendix B, table VI (b)). The Northumberland figure for maintenance of school buildings rose from 3·66 per cent in 1946–47 to 6·4 per cent in 1954–55, remaining constant in real terms, despite an apparent fall to four per cent after 1959–60 when the new accounting procedure operated including all relevant expenditure in the total figure for secondary education. The Lincoln figures remain reasonably constant throughout, and the most interesting factor is the consistently lower percentage of expenditure spent on maintenance of secondary modern schools compared with that spent on secondary grammar schools.

Freedom to operate services, however financed, can only exist if, firstly, revenue can increase faster than the rate of price increases and secondly, the proportion of intractable to tractable expenditure leaves a realistic margin for manoeuvre. Since intractable expenditure, or that fixed by a commitment outside the direct control of the authority, accounts for a substantial and increasing majority of items of expenditure, this limits both the margin for manoeuvre and the extent to which the use of financial grants or approval of annual estimates can operate as a method of control, whether the control is imposed by central government or by the full council over a constituent committee. How in practice is freedom to vary expenditure achieved?

III. Estimates and the Role of the Members and Officers

Annual estimates are prepared on the basis of both short-term and long-term predictions, and over most of the survey period were prepared on the basis of current prices or constant price levels. It is always difficult to estimate accurately future price rises, and no Finance Committee proved willing in practice to anticipate them.

Estimates are prepared each autumn for approval at the turn of the year to take effect from April. They set out the money needed for the payment of services in considerable detail, all of which the Chief Education Officer must be able to justify before the Finance Committee (of the full Council) would be prepared to consider them. How far Eastern bargaining is carried out at Chief Officer level, leaving little action for Committees, is likely to depend on the strength and standing of the Chief Education Officer and the Treasurer. The standard basis on which negotiation will take place is a percentage increase on the previous year, and any abnormal rises will need to be fully justified as essential new policy. Committees on the whole seem psychologically unable to accept a large percentage increase, even on grounds of known price rises, as well as increases planned to meet the cost of desirable educational expansion, and hence a substantial pay award or increased book prices may mean that other schemes may need to be delayed or postponed indefinitely.

The Chief Education Officer will either under- or over-estimate. If the former, he will have to seek Committee approval for extra funds and at worst this might mean a supplementary rate, the bane of the politically conscious. If the latter, his next budget will almost certainly be cut back to the current year's level and another department may have been unnecessarily prevented from carrying out a new scheme. Intelligent guesswork is not always encouraged—committees seemed prepared to allow in estimates for a known impending award if negotiations were completed by the time estimates were printed, but not an expected award still under negotiation. Finance Committees are thought to believe that insistence on accurate estimates based on known data only, leads to financial discipline. It is a fact of life that they are constantly critical of any request for supplementary funds even when wholly justified. There is thus an innate conflict between frequent inflation, which, however, can be spasmodic rather than constant, and the fixing of financial resources at an agreed percentage of increase. When price rises overtake financial resources, as they regularly do, either a supplementary rate becomes necessary or something else must be sacrificed (unless like the former LCC a council is able to hold substantial balances in hand).

Public expenditure, however, has a tendency to grow faster than the national economy and is therefore subject to regular cut-back. An important factor is the base-level of negotiation each year. Thus if a Chief Officer holds back on one aspect of a service, he will not be able to aggregate, say, a five per cent annual rise for five years and ask for a 25 per cent increase, for example, on adult education or library books, even if he can make a case for these. The Finance Committee and the Council will expect growth to be at a more or less even level. Where, then, one aspect of a service is neglected, it is rare that it will catch up and overtake the spiral of rising costs without some dynamic pressure and a deliberate diversion of resources towards that service—probably at the expense of another.

The Financial Climate in the Survey Areas
Lincoln

It is difficult, nearly 30 years later, to assess what motivated the authorities. Comments from older Councillors in Lincoln interviewed in 1969 included 'we were always told by the old guard we were poor' and 'It looked like rank extravagance to increase our spending then'.

A frequent comment was 'They were reluctant spenders even on proven need'. A former Chairman who increased the budget to include an improvement element for the first time in 1966 under the stimulus of the new fourth Chief Education Officer, thought in 1969 that Lincoln was still paying for 'shortsighted rate-pegging' in the 1940s, because he was still negotiating on an artificially low base year. Perhaps the most revealing comment came in 1969 from a former Chairman of the Education Committee. 'We were conditioned against extravagance'. The Chairman in post after 1959 considered Lincoln had suffered from block grant—'The Finance Committee got tougher—we had a rearguard fight for increases every autumn'. Reactionary members of the Finance Committee apparently had commented, 'They managed before the war—they can manage now'. In the period 1960–64, there appeared to be an especial reluctance to commit subsequent committees and a new Chief Education Officer; and spending was artificially 'pegged' thus providing a low base on which to build for the needs of the 1960s,[13] including the comprehensive reorganization which by then many members wanted but the third Chief Education Officer did not.

The Finance Committee in Lincoln was particularly reluctant to approve capital loans, which probably discouraged major programmes of renewal and re-equipment,[14] although a former Chairman of Finance Committee considered that the Education Department had enjoyed a near-autonomy in financial matters after 1948 and could have had whatever the Chief Education Officer had sought.[15] The latter viewpoint is supported by senior administrative and professional staff interviewed, in that they considered the department to have asked for too little in relation to the known needs of the schools. In all, the picture is one of a determined fight by a few keen councillors from the late 1950s, against an excessively stable acceptance of a history of low spending and disinclination for change.

Cuts in already low estimates fell on main curricular items. For the first time in 1962 reductions made by the City Council, led the Chief Education Officer to cut the allocation for teachers' salaries repeated in 1964 to meet a further cut back. Where furniture and equipment were cut, repercussions could have a direct effect on teaching method. In 1961–62, the requests from one grammar school for example included an amount for physics fixed at the level the headmistress and governors expected would be approved, but the head commented:

'This estimate includes only necessary demonstration apparatus. For the classes to take part in practical work, a thing which is extremely desirable, a further sum of £300 would be required. Even then the pupils would be working in groups of three with the apparatus.'

The extra £300 was not granted and the old teaching method prevailed.

Evidence from officers and councillors suggests that the threat of cuts and the knowledge of constant reductions tended to condition the Chief Education Officer, his staff and headteachers to ask for less in the belief that demands for increases would inevitably be cut. If a modest budget is cut, one may be discouraged from seeking larger increases however justified they may be. Nevertheless, in Lincoln the cuts were modest but were on a basically low initial budget.

How far the earlier Chief Education Officer was himself influenced by the Finance and General Purposes committee (of the Education Committee) or by the Finance Committee of the Council is difficult to say. The Chairman who took office in 1956 after the Labour 'landslide' felt that the new and inexperienced councillors were unable to withstand a Chief Education Officer reluctant to innovate, an 'old guard' Labour block who believed in low rates and a concentration of resources on able children, and a Conservative minority opposed to any substantial increase in the Education budget on principle. After 1959, there also developed more pressure from other committee chairmen to axe the Education budget as the departments competed for their share of the new block grant.

In general the picture is nevertheless one of almost complete autonomy of the Chief Education Officer[16]. The long-standing Chairman of the City Finance Committee confirmed the independence and autonomy of the Chief Education Officer in both planning and spending, and doubted whether limitation of financial resources would have held back either the Chief Education Officer or the Education Committee if the former had wished significantly to increase his demands. This view is supported by other members and officers. Other than the regular general annual cuts in estimates, there are very few instances indeed when a specific decision of the Education Committee was adversely affected by the Finance Committee; and no important ones traceable relating to secondary education.

The autonomy of the Chief Education Officer was marked not only in his relationship with committees but vis-à-vis his fellow senior officers. It is not uncommon in county boroughs for the Treasurer to attempt to interpret the Finance Committee's policy and hold back levels of spending in the policy departments. This was not the case in Lincoln. How far the relative freedom won by the Chief Education Officer from financial restrictions other than his self-set ones could be accounted for by the appointment of two successive Treasurers from the school of which the Chief Education Officer was former head, and by the maintenance of a quasi head-master-prefect relationship, must be a matter for speculation. What is remarkable is that the relative freedom of the Education department was not exploited, and, as later chapters will show, standards in schools and levels of revenue and capital expenditure were pegged at an artificially low level until the new regime began in 1964.

Nottingham

The situation in Nottingham was markedly different in many ways; and varied also under the two post-war Directors of Education. The organic relationship between the Education and Treasurer's departments has always been strong. While however in the first decade, the Treasurer's influence on the first post-war Director of Education appears to have been strong, seeking to limit expansion of revenue expenditure to what was financially desirable as distinct from educationally necessary, the later Director working in turn with a new Treasurer negotiated a clearer definition of roles for the two departments which left the Director greater freedom but preserved the close association (on for example, planning of capital programmes).

In Nottingham, a very experienced councillor claimed in 1969 that a rising rate after the war was deliberate Labour policy to meet need. 'If you show people new houses and new schools they don't argue—I've never lost my seat in 39 years'. As in Lincoln, it was suggested by members and officers interviewed that the Finance Committee did not necessarily hold back on major matters, where dynamic pressure was exerted by the Director. The first post-war Director appears to have been essentially an academic, and the capital expenditure in the first decade was more a question of basic need and grammar school expansion. In the mid-1950s however the Director initiated an immediate general drive for modernization and obtained Finance Committee support for two major modernization programmes to be financed from capital loan.

The usual annual cuts in estimates were imposed on the Education Committee by the Finance Committee but with an explicit agreement that supplementary estimates would be approved if the need for the higher level of expenditure really materialised. One must distinguish between cuts imposed as a result of Council policy to hold the rates at a given level, and cuts imposed because of central government directives. Thus the 1949–51 recession imposed by the Government[17] brought cuts totalling £65,175 in the 1950–51 Education Budget of £1,859,196, (but a refusal by the Finance and General Purposes

Sub-Committee of the Education Committee to cut administration as much as the Government wanted) which were on a different plane from the annual interdepartmental negotiations between Director of Education and Treasurer. The latter involved reductions like that of 1956 when the capital from revenue sum for minor improvements to schools was slashed by the Finance Committee from £38,844 to £10,000.[18] Accordingly the following year the Director only submitted a programme of £17,500 which was cut by the Finance Committee to £12,000.[19] Thus level of likely resources reduced the demand. The conditioning process was at work.

In 1957 the Education Committee were informed that the Finance Committee had decided that all Corporation committees should submit a list of all capital projects in order of priority before proceeding with them and the Education Committee submitted this in November 1957. In April 1958, the Sites and Buildings Sub-Committee reported:

'Your Sub-Committee have now received the observations of the Finance Committee on the list of proposed capital projects and have noted the restrictions which the Finance Committee consider should be made in the original programme. Your Sub-Committee consider that these restrictions are reasonable in the light of existing circumstances . . .'[20]

The Director's Budget speech at Education Committee and City Council justified annually any expansion included in the estimates, and like most committees, the Education Committee tended to balk at the smaller items and pass the larger salaries' bills without comment.[21] In most cases if the City Finance Committee in asking for cuts, specified where they should occur, need arose for supplementary estimates later in the year, and in time the Council learned on the whole to let the Director do his own cutting. Estimates are prepared with three phases of increase:

(a) unavoidable (an impending Burnham award or three more schools opening);

(b) committed because of earlier policy (phase II of a pilot experiment; inclusion of more schools in an experimental scheme);

(c) desirable innovation and expansion.

In the nature of things, (a) and (b) are more protected in the estimates than (c) and the section of the Budget which can be sensitive to demand for expansion, is limited therefore on the whole to what is left under (c).

One important instance of serious economies and cuts occurred in 1960, when the Rates Estimates Committee drastically cut the estimates at a late stage; and it was recorded that:

'It has been necessary to make reductions in the provision for teachers, for equipment, stationery and materials etc. . . . Your Sub-Committee have agreed to these cuts with great reluctance because they believe that the expansion of the Education service in all its aspects is essential to the wellbeing of the City and of the nation. The increases in the estimates have arisen principally from better pay for teachers, from the expansion of secondary and technical education and from the building of urgently needed new schools. The reductions now reported have impaired the fabric of the service.'[22]

The confidence of the Council and the Education Committee in its sub-committees, is summed up in a story, probably not apocryphal in the light of other evidence, of the Chairman of the Sites and Buildings Sub-Committee who presented a report to the Education Committee, for belated 'confirmation' of a decision by the Sub-Committee increasing the capital programme after negotiations with the Ministry. A senior member asked 'What, Mr Chairman, will happen if we were to say no?', to which the laconic Chairman replied 'The likelihood of such an occurrence is not one which has ever crossed my mind; nor will it'.[23] On the whole, in *Nottingham*, however, the picture is one of steady expansion with a budget rising faster than rises in prices, and increased pupil numbers, would account for. The City Council and the Education Committee showed a general concern for standards which was only intermittently consciously subordinated to other influences.

Northumberland

In Northumberland the education service also seemed to enjoy near-autonomy and the county status of the authority shielded it from the more acute of pressures from members.[24] It was slightly complicated by the presence of the Divisional Executive at Wallsend, whose budget is compiled separately and dealt with by Wallsend Education Committee, which had right of direct access to the Education Committee. The Chairman of the Wallsend Committee considered (on interview in 1969) that he 'got what he wanted'. One leading councillor remembering rising post-war rates thought in 1969 'they took no heed until loan charges were crippling' while a councillor from a rural area remembered 'they all fought for the county to clothe the skeleton of a service—Tories and Labour alike', with little heed for rate fixing till the late 1950s.

Evidence from Northumberland officers is unanimous that the very powerful personality of the former Chairman of the Education Committee allied to the work of their equally strong Directors, meant that rarely if ever, did either Committee or Council reject schemes even if they involved increased expenditure. The usual Finance Committee reduction of Education Committee annual estimates operated, but the cuts were modest and the Director was left freedom to prune his own Budget. Not until the mid-1960s were the cuts serious, but in 1965, after scrutiny by a special sub-committee of the Finance Committee, the County Council reduced the estimates by £822,415 gross for the total county budget, and in recording the sub-committee's appreciation of the co-operation of the chairmen of committees and of Chief Officers 'they are especially conscious of the contribution made by the Education Committee'[25]. (Even then the increase on the previous year's estimates was 8·62 per cent).

Evidence from officers on the reason for the continued success of both Directors in obtaining approval for increased expenditure for experimental work as well as for basic improvement, attributes success to two causes. The first was the quality and calibre of the Chairman of the Education Committee (an ex-miner, later a parson) who held office for most of the period—'a man of stature in his own special way' and 'he had a genuine almost passionate interest in education for which he fought', were typical comments[26] while another described him as 'a canny fighter who only cared for his schools and the kids in them'. He succeeded in creating a climate of opinion in which if the Director argued for a service on grounds of educational deprivation, need or quality, it was almost automatically granted. 'We will have decent education in decent schools'.

The second major factor was Northumberland's pride in being 'progressive'[27] and the pre-conditioning against 'extravagance' which was apparent in both county boroughs was markedly absent in the county. There were some constituency fights—one famous example was of a rural councillor who fought for a bridge across a stream (cost £1,000) in order that children from an outlying village could reach a newly built secondary school without a 17-mile detour. His success was at the expense of £900 for replacing gaslighting in old schools in Wallsend.[28] The example is an interesting, perhaps historic, contradiction of the theory that all expenditure was approved in relation to demand, since there was a substantial element for educational innovation in the same budget which cut the replacement lighting.

There is however no history in the county of significant cuts in estimates after first committee approval, except in 1950–52 and 1960–62 as a result of national directives (see Chapter V), and these were only slight.

All councillors interviewed considered that the rural and urban balance was fairly maintained in the allocation of resources. Three leading councillors attributed the success in obtaining a high capital programme, in large measure, to a 'communion' between the second post-war Director and the Chairman of the Sites and Building Sub-Committee to whom the Education Committee had delegated considerable power. The general picture in the county was one of considerable autonomy in the Education Department, and of a Committee with faith in both Directors to the extent of raising the 'implicit ceiling' of expenditure on demand and on justification.

Conclusion

The importance of the factor of local 'conditioning' begins to emerge from the foregoing account. Some of the relationships between natural resources and growth rates are predictable, others need further explanation.

We have looked at the suggestion of 'planning for inequality'. The three authorities started from very unequal bases. Their rateable values and rate yields were permanently unequal and revaluation gave to Nottingham which needed least and widened the gap between the best and worst. Exchequer Equalization grant did not equalize. Among other things, Lincoln had the highest rates but the lowest expenditure per head; worsened by revaluation. Nottingham's proportion of overall income from government grant increased over the years although its financial need was least (Figures 2 and 3). Lincoln's increase in government aid was offset by a massive reduction in miscellaneous income. The pattern is not consistent however. Figure 4 isolates education service income. Northumberland benefited most, which seems right—it was a high spender under a percentage grant system and had the highest need; but Nottingham again benefited more than Lincoln despite the latter's poorer rateable value, higher rates and greater need.

The base year (1945) on which they built was unequal in that the inherited base for negotiation was in inverse ratio to need, (see table IV (4) above and table V of Appendix B). Northumberland had the lowest expenditure per head but the greatest need. This was reversed over the years—despite the county's inherited need it ended in 1965 with the highest expenditure per head—an attempt to meet its major demand for more secondary education. Lincoln's acute needs were not met financially—on a low base year of 1945, its expenditure per head was consistently lowest throughout the decade of 'the bulge'—1955 to 1965.

And the yield from a penny rate was unequal (see above) thus diminishing the possibility to improve schools from the 'capital from revenue' budget.

Implicit demand from rising school rolls was unequally met, not necessarily in direct relation to need. (Chapters VI to VIII comment in more detail on this). In Lincoln, secondary education expenditure grew more slowly than other sectors (table IV (1)). The secondary school rolls grew faster and proportionately more than secondary expenditure (Tables IV (3) and (5)). Even at the most basic of levels, the demand was not matched. Nottingham is arguable—secondary revenue growth rates did at least exceed the rate of rise in school rolls. In Nottingham, the correlations more nearly matched. Northumberland's expenditure rose so dramatically more as to ensure that the implications of rising rolls and the opening of more new schools were financially met at basic levels. But on closer examination, the secondary rolls rose at three times the rate of total rolls, secondary expenditure at only twice the rate of all education expenditure. Was there still a shortfall?

The burden of intractable to tractable expenditure also fell unevenly. Taking the three main intractable elements of teachers' salaries, loan charges and fuel and maintenance, the acute need arising from Northumberland's rural reorganization, meant more massive increases in these three intractable elements in the county because of the necessary capital programme—in theory reducing its tractable element more than in the other areas. All three had diminishing margins for an improvement element in the budget by 1965.

Finally, the brief account of the financial climate establishes widely divergent attitudes towards each authority's responsibility to provide financially to meet defined needs. Chapter III commented on some objectives of the administration. These were reflected in financial practices. Readers may draw their own conclusions as the jigsaw begins to fit together.

The authorities worked in very different local situations, and therefore in theory the argument of a direct correlation between central government grant and control over local authorities, should have led to a difference in the central controls exercised over the three authorities. The following chapter shows however that controls were exercized with no regard for the individual and different positions of local authorities; but in an overall national context.

Notes

1 VAIZEY, J. (1958). *The Costs of Education*. London: Allen and Unwin.
2 VAIZEY, J. and SHEEHAN, J. (1968). *Resources for Education*. London: Allen and Unwin.
3 Sometimes quite unaccountably. 'Lincoln's high expenditure does not fit easily into any classification—it is confined mainly to sewage, refuse and administration' . . . *Local Expenditure and Exchequer Grants*. IMTA 1956, p.87.

4 Extracted from tables 1A and 1B of *Local Expenditure and Exchequer Grants*, IMTA, 1956.

5 Ibid.

6 VAIZEY, J. and SHEEHAN, J. (1968). *Resources for Education*. Unwin University Books, Chapter III. London: Allen and Unwin.

7 DAVIES, B. (1968). *Social Needs and Resources in Local Services*. London: Michael Joseph.

8 op. cit. Writer's underlining.

9 Circular 145 (6.6.47) of Ministry of Education.

10 For example, although 1182 practical rooms were provided altogether in the country as a whole, in many areas specialist rooms, gymnasia and halls had to be used as classrooms, there were too few libraries and 'perhaps the most serious deficiency of all was the lack of books'. *Education in* 1948, Ministry of Education. London: HMSO, pp.10–12.

11 Ministry of Education, *List* 50. *Costing Statistics, London:* 1946–47, *and* 1947–48.

12 FISHER, N. (1956). 'Fiscal Management in an English LEA', in *The Year Book of Education*, 1956, page 357.

13 Interviews, June 1969.

14 Interview with former Chief Education Officer (29.5.69).

15 Interview (21.4.69).

16 Even though the Chief Education Officer had few delegated powers, and all items over £100 had to be individually approved by Committee, the latter rarely if ever refused the Chief Education Officer's requests.

17 which caused the famous or infamous Circulars 209 and 210 (28.10.49) to be issued by the Ministry of Education restricting building programmes and asking for cuts in administrative costs, aid to pupils and other revenue expenditure.

18 Nottingham, Sites and Buildings Sub-Committee (12.4.56).

19 The full £38,844 for 1956 and £17,500 for 1957 had of course been first approved by the Education Committee.

20 Nottingham, Education Committee (23.4.58).

21 The fact that salary increases are intractable and smaller improvements are not, does not alter the interesting psychological fact that a committee will raise supplementary estimates for national pay awards without resistance but would balk at a 1d. rate rise for improvements.

22 Nottingham, Finance and General Purposes Sub-Committee (16.3.60) and Education Committee (24.2.60).

23 When one compares Nottingham's capital expenditure with that of Northumberland (Tables IV (b) and (c) of Appendix B) it is evident that in the first decade, Nottingham had a higher programme in relation to school population.

24 County Councils meet quarterly, not monthly and delegate more to both officers and sub-committees.

25 Northumberland, County Council (4.11.65).

26 Interviews (4.3.69).

27 A comment from members, officers and teacher representatives alike.

28 Interviews (30.6.69) with both protagonists (separately).

CHAPTER V
Central and Local Controls

'Quod enim mavult homo verum esse, id potius credit.'
(*For what a man had rather be true, he more readily believes*)

Francis Bacon (*1561–1626*)

This chapter suggests that central government directives and policies prevented both implicit and explicit demand from being met even at the (differential) levels accepted as desirable by the three local education authorities. It is also suggested that government has indulged in a form of 'double-think', constantly recommending simultaneous expansion and recession with Protean changeability in the same exhortatory breath. The list of achievements narrated in annual government reports on the education service reflect but scantily the massive backlog of needs and demands in each survey area—and doubtless elsewhere—which the national planning in stop-go phases preserved until the end of the survey period and which we are still attempting to meet.

The balance of control between central and local government over the administration of educational services has formed the centre of two major controversies since the early days of the establishment of the Board of Education. One is the democratic desirability of greater local autonomy, in direct contrast to the tendency of some continental countries to organize some of their social services on a centralized basis. The second controversy is whether the balance of control is directly linked with the proportion of the financial contributions of central and local government respectively to the cost of running the local education services.

These matters of principle have been of concern not only to local education authorities individually over the years, but to the associations representing local authorities corporately, that is, the Association of Municipal Corporations (representing county boroughs), the County Councils Association, and the powerful Association of Education Committees. Of the three organizations it is the latter which appears to have exerted the most effective pressure on both central and local authorities. For 70 years since 1902, the AEC has in fact been something of a successful anomaly. It has given the Education Committees of local authorities, direct representation alongside county boroughs and county councils. Both

Chief Education Officers and chairmen of committees are appointed to the AEC and both have voting rights. This combined informed opinion with which the AEC has sought to influence both central and local government policy, including its own sporadically recalcitrant members from time to time, has probably been the stronger and more influential, for its unity between members and officers.

On 19th January 1945, a special meeting of the AEC was convened to consider first, its own reconstitution and second, the effect of the recent report of the Burnham Committee on the salary structure of teachers. Hitherto only a comparatively small number of county education authorities had been members of the Association, but following the recent negotiations, the AEC had considered it likely that in the new climate of post-war redevelopment and in the light of the new Education Act, most if not all local education authorities would join. Its secretary, William Alexander, saw a need for a strong and united Association for education which might hope to influence the Ministry of Education and other bodies by a coherent policy based on local opinions coordinated nationally.[1] That the AEC saw itself both as a respected and credible pressure group and as a monitor of identifiable basic standards of provision is undoubtedly true. It was also a potential watchdog to safeguard local autonomy, and this role might have been even more influential. Was it?

Increased Delegation to Local Authorities?

In the late 1940s the Government set up a special committee to investigate methods of improving both relationships between central and local government departments and the efficiency of certain aspects of local government. The Committee's report finally appeared in print in December 1951.[2] The Ministry of Education sent an advance advisory circular to local education authorities supporting the committee's main recommendations

'which will result in a considerable increase in the delegation of responsibility to local education authorities, in accord with the policy of the government'.[3]

Whether this policy was in fact carried out will be for the reader to judge in due course, but the principle of increased delegation had at least been clearly stated and endorsed by central government. Fifteen years later, this principle was restated in another more substantial government-sponsored report, the Redcliffe-Maud Report.[4] The case may perhaps be best summed up in one of the main policy statements of the report:

'Our terms of reference also require us to bear in mind the need to sustain a viable system of local democracy: that is a system under which government by the people is a reality. This we take to be of importance at least equal to the importance of securing efficiency in the provision of services. . . . Local government is the only representative political institution in the country outside Parliament. . . . Central government tends, by its nature, to be bureaucratic. It is only by the combination of local representative institutions with the central institutions of Parliament, Ministers and Departments, that a genuine national democracy can be sustained'.[5]

The Commission was writing in a climate of growing concern from local authorities about the steady and unobtrusive assumption by central government departments of increased control over local authority administration. In particular financial controls had been eroded, severely limiting the freedom of local authorities to determine the rate at which they wished to develop their services; which accords ill indeed with the theory advanced in the late 1950s that the purpose of replacing percentage grants by block grants was to increase local financial freedom. The Royal Commission, while accepting that a significant degree of central control of the rate of expansion of services was unavoidable, strongly recommended the delegation of more discretionary powers to local authorities.[6] The problem had been recognized at a time of the most marked of the post-war increases of control over capital expenditure in the early 1960s. One of the most experienced and gifted civil servants of our time, Dame Evelyn Sharp, wrote in 1962:

'Genuine efforts have been made by central government in recent years to check the trend; and to get rid of unnecessary controls. But we cannot escape the fact that central and local government are now locked in a tighter partnership than ever before and they must learn to accommodate themselves to this. But I don't think this means we have to resign ourselves to a diminution of local government. The increasing power of central government means, surely, that it is more than ever important to foster an effective and independently minded system of local government; to provide a counterpoise'.[7]

One must however recognize that as far as the education service is concerned, the Minister of Education in 1945 had a double duty, first that of securing

'the effective execution by local authorities under his control and direction of the national policy for providing a varied and comprehensive educational service in every area'[8] and second, that of ensuring with his colleagues in the Cabinet, that the national economy was both restructured and controlled according to the needs of post-war England, as they saw them at that time.[9]

The educational 'control and direction' was subsequently subdivided into six key points of control by the Local Government Manpower Committee in 1951, that is:

(i) securing an adequate quantity and variety of educational facilities;

(ii) ensuring efficient management of educational establishments in terms of staff, equipment and maintenance;

(iii) protecting the rights of individuals, including parents;[10]

(iv) ensuring the proper qualifications of teachers and other professional staff;

(v) ensuring an adequate and appropriate standard of fees, awards and allowances;

(vi) ensuring reasonable minimum standards of educational premises.

One essential corollary of the first requirement outlined above, was an adequate supply of teachers in each local authority's area, and by 1948 by mutual agreement with the local authority associations, a quota system to control the recruitment and supply of women teachers had been imposed on local education authorities by the Minister 'to avoid a breakdown in the education service in several of the industrial towns'.[11] The quota system was later extended to cover all full-time teachers. This central control was at least with the agreement of the local authorities.

The state of the national economy at that time and subsequently, also made it necessary for the Minister of Education to exercise direct and detailed control both over the level of capital expenditure represented by the annual education building programme, and over the general level of revenue expenditure. From time to time specific aspects came under scrutiny, in particular administrative costs; and discretionary services (notably adult education and youth service) proved especially vulnerable sectors when financial cuts were sought.

A further and essential control imposed in the period 1945–1952 in the light of the condition of industry in England in 1945, and of the country's new needs, was however central control by the Minister of Education and the Minister of Works of the raw materials for post-war new building, that is labour, timber and steel. Many cities such as London, Coventry and Plymouth had suffered from bomb damage so badly that extensive areas of housing and factories, hospitals and offices as well as up to a quarter of their schools were in immediate need of replacement or of substantial repair. Simultaneously the new Labour Government with a safe majority of 187 in the House in 1945, was setting a new order of priorities before the nation, in the forefront of which was a massive housing programme to replace inner city slum areas and to provide for a rising population. Ironically, as rationing of food and clothing eased, rationing of raw materials for the construction industry and for local authorities grew more strict.

In the same way in which the building needs of housing and education clashed with other services in the battle for raw materials, priorities between education and other social services were assessed centrally in relation to capital and revenue expenditure. The estimated expenditure on the new National Health Service for example rose nearly threefold in the period 1948–1953:

National Health Service Expenditure

	ORIGINAL ESTIMATE £	SUPPLEMENTARY ESTIMATE £
1948–49	150 million	37 million
1949–50	260 million	99 million
1952–53	402 million	58 million[12]

(The Guillebaud committee set up in 1953 to inquire into the Health service largely justified the increase in terms of real expansion of the service).

It was expected, then, that the Cabinet should expect stern control over education expenditure which accounts for so large a proportion of public spending.

Four key controls, then, had developed, over capital and revenue expenditure, over resources and over administration. In one sense, the latter was fundamental to the remainder, since the number and calibre of senior professional staff might be expected to influence the competence of the local education authority in the expansion of services. How were the survey areas affected if at all by early attempts at controlling expansion of administrative services?

Control of Administration, 1945–1955

In 1945, the Ministry of Education was reorganized to take account of its rapidly expanding work. A single Schools Branch replaced the two branches which had dealt separately hitherto with Elementary and Higher (including secondary) Education. A Buildings and Priority Branch was established also, working through Regional Priority officers (based geographically in the regions) through whom the allocation of raw materials and manpower for the building programme was controlled.[13] The central administrative, professional and clerical staff of the Ministry had been increased from 157 in 1944 to 250 in January 1948 to enable the Ministry to handle its increased work,[14] reasonably enough it seemed.

Simultaneously, however, with the sharp increase in work facing local education authorities, and in contrast to the increased establishment at the Ministry of Education a directive was issued by the Ministry of Health (then responsible for local government) asking in fact for a cut in local authority staffs in order to reduce administrative costs.[15] *Nottingham* refused to consider reducing its education staff and on the contrary endorsed the Director of Education's view that extra staff would be needed to carry out the statutory duties of the 1944 Education Act and the increased work caused by a rising school population.[16] There is no evidence that either *Lincoln* or *Northumberland* agreed to cut staff as early as 1947. All three authorities were conscious of the demands that preparation of the required Development plans, the resultant substantial building programmes, the raising of the school leaving age, and the expansion of teacher training would make on their staff.

Here we have an early example of central government dichotomy, on the one hand the Minister of Education directing a policy of expansion of educational services and on the other, the Minister of Health (and Local Government) seeking a reduction in staffing establishments. Shortly afterwards indeed the Ministry of Education turned its attention to administrative costs. In 1949 the grave state of the national economy led the government to call for a review of all government expenditure. The circular issued comments with a faint tone of surprise, not to say mild reproach, that

'Expenditure of local education authorities under this head (administration) has been rising rapidly in recent years and is now, at some £12 and a half million, nearly double what it was in 1945–46 . . . local education authorities should review their procedure and establishments so that at least interim reductions are made to take effect in 1950–51'.[17]

It is difficult at this distance in time to see where the 'room for considerable entrenchment' lay of which the circular speaks. *Nottingham* refused a second time to consider any serious reduction in administrative costs, limiting its contribution to leaving two advisory posts vacant and one deferred, and a clerical vacancy unfilled.[18] *Lincoln* could not offer any realistic cut[19] and *Northumberland* offered no economies on staff at all.

Two years later however, the Ministry of Education returned to the attack, and in a circular which asked for a general cut in revenue expenditure of five per cent commented wistfully that

'Notwithstanding the review which they were asked to undertake two years ago, the expenditure of authorities or administration has continued to rise and is now running at the level of about £13 million as compared with less than half that figure six years ago'[20]

and asked local education authorities for further cuts. Lest authorities should turn a Nelsonic eye, a reminder came some months later that

'Authorities are also asked to state the amount of the economies which they estimate to make in administration and Inspection (other than Medical Inspection) in the financial year 1952–53 as a result of the review of administrative costs under para. 3 of circular 242'.[21]

Lincoln finally conceded, and left vacant the newly created post of Assistant Education Officer which was to become vacant in February 1952 on the resignation of the current holder, 'partly with the need for economy in mind, as outlined in circular 242'.[22] This however proved a rash step for the additional measures needed to cover the work resulted in a net saving of only £575, while the work had to be transferred to existing staff who were redesignated as organizers. The administrative responsibility for detailed work on secondary education and for the building programme had to revert to the Chief Education Officer. The resulted understaffing at senior professional level was to last until 1964. *Nottingham* offered no reduction on administrative costs[23] and *Northumberland* only an insignificant cut in the rate of expansion of clerical assistance at schools, and no major administrative saving.[24]

It was no doubt the ineffectiveness of this attempt to control local administrative costs centrally, that led the Minister to announce that

'she has in mind so to vary the application of the education grant formula that greater responsibility for controlling expenditure in the field of administration would rest with authorities'.[25]

The passive resistance of the local authorities had had its effect, and little more was attempted in this respect, despite the potential control which the percentage grant system made possible until 1958. It is important to note however that the increased devolution to local authorities recommended by the Local Government Manpower Committee 12 months earlier, still seemed alien to the Ministers of Health and Education in 1951.

Control of Capital and Revenue Expenditure—1945–55

The Ministry of Education's determination to control the general level of capital and revenue expenditure was more constant, although with sporadic effect in practical terms.

The theory behind the control of expenditure is presumably that it helps to stabilize the national economy by checking the rate of expansion, and that since the private sector is beyond immediate control the public sector must be used in an attempt to retard the spiral of inflation. This theory seems to be widely accepted by local authority administrators on surprisingly slender evidence. Does government control of local authority expenditure have any widespread economic effect? Can the Government in fact control expenditure at all? And how far do directives from the Ministry of Education for expansion of services coincide with contradictory instructions for economy?

On the one hand for example, local education authorities were urged to provide for 'The New Secondary Education' as outlined in Ministry of Education Pamphlet No. 9 in 1947 in which it was suggested that

'The Modern school will be given parity of conditions with other types of secondary school; parity of esteem it must secure by its own efforts'.[26]

The new policy also presupposed expansion of secondary technical education and therefore of technical accommodation in secondary schools, and even more important, the early reorganization of the many remaining all-age (5–15) schools into primary and secondary schools.[27] To reorganize these, however, would mean not only substantial new capital building but increased revenue on staff, equipment, specialist furniture and books as courses developed and widened in scope.

But by 1949 the Ministry of Education had introduced two 'watchdogs'. The first was the principle of costing statistics—the published annual figures of average costs per pupil of primary and secondary education to be used as yardsticks[28] and the second was a regular (annual or biennial) directive on the overall level of revenue expenditure which the central government found acceptable.

In 1949 the Ministry of Education issued circulars 209 and 210 asking for a general cut back in capital and revenue expenditure by local education authorities because of the serious national economic crisis. Circular 210 opens with an apparently reassuring placebo that

'Local education authorities . . . will also have noted the announcements that the Government do not contemplate any major change in policy which would result in a reduction in the scope of the services for which the Ministry of Education is responsible'.[29]

It then goes on to instruct authorities to restrict capital expenditure from revenue in 1949–50 and 1950–51 to the amount included by them in the 1948–49 estimates for this head—itself a year of severe restraint because of the cost-cutting effect of earlier circulars culminating in circular 191 issued in December 1948. Minor improvements and repairs to schools are financed out of capital funds from capital or revenue account, and the restriction (which lasted for many years conflicted directly with a directive from the Ministry repeated in its 1948 annual report that despite controls on major capital expenditure,

'In the meantime, much can be done to make conditions in some of these old buildings more pleasant; not least by greater attention to cleaning and decorations. Minor improvements to offices[30] and playgrounds will often make a great difference to the conditions under which the schools will have to work. The greater discretion in the matter of minor building works of this kind given to local authorities in circular 191 . . . will it is hoped speed up such improvements.'[31]

The greater discretion was in fact illusory. It was true that local education authorities no longer had to seek individual approvals for minor capital works at schools; but they still had to raise the money. A restriction on expenditure of either the product of a penny rate or on capital from revenue generally made the freedom to choose what to do, decidedly illusory.

Moreover, painting and decorating was one of the few 'tractable' or discretionary elements of the revenue budget which could be cut significantly without drastic measures like leaving classes without a teacher—or without a classroom. It tended therefore to be cut regularly by both Education and Finance Committees either to reduce the level of rate increases or in response to government control of expenditure, mainly in the absence of any other element of the budget large enough to be significant which was not also intractable.

Circular 210 also demanded cuts in transport costs, and in provision for recreation and social provision (including Youth service), disallowed any further grants for school uniforms and instructed local education authorities to increase charges for school dinners and for evening classes.

Lincoln's general cuts were infinitesimal although new kitchens at two secondary schools had to be postponed yet again.[32] *Nottingham* cut back by a total of £64,465 which, if set against its actual 1949–54 gross revenue education expenditure of £1,738,196 represents a cut of about 3·6 per cent. Of this £6,090 was for secondary education, a modest cut on £532,056 but it is significant to the argument in the foregoing paragraphs that £10,000 was from painting and decorating and £12,000 from capital from revenue for minor school improvements.[33] There is no record of the actual cuts in *Northumberland* but as the county's Director of Education was invited to serve on the new national committee set up to consider economies in education costs it can be assumed that the estimates approved on his recommendation in January 1950 took serious account of the circular.[34]

Economies on such a small scale however, even multiplied by the total number of authorities, can have done little to redress the national economy. Doubtless political honour had, however, been satisfied.

A more important result of circular 209 which was to have lasting results, was the setting up of a national committee of officers of both central and local government and of HMIs to look into the reduction of costs in school building.

'The Committee is viewing its task from three angles: economy in scale of provision, economy in planning and economy in construction . . . for projects to be started in 1950 the objective must be to achieve a 12½ per cent reduction in cost on the average costs in 1949'.[35]

A year later however the Ministry assured local education authorities that

'The Minister . . . is anxious however that authorities should regard the Ministry not only as operating statutory controls but as providing an advisory service which may be used with advantage during the formative stages of projects'.[36]

The effect of this new development was in practice drastically to restrict the amount per pupil and the amount per square foot of building which local education authorities could spend on major school building. In the earlier post-war years it had the beneficial

effect of making education architects consider more ingeniously and
more thoughtfully how best to design schools at lower cost. In later
years it resulted—and still results—in abortive and lengthy negotiations over individual projects which need for one reason or another
to cost more than the average, almost always either resulting in some
concession from central government departments that the local
education authority was right in its original definition of need or in
the cancellation of the project thus adding further to the backlog of
unmet needs.

Meanwhile by 1950 the national economic situation had worsened
for a variety of reasons, and in 1951 the political control of the
country changed. The General Election in 1950 had greatly weakened
Labour's position in the House,[37] and on 25th October 1951 a
Conservative Government was returned:

Conservative	321
Labour	295
Liberal	6
Irish Nationalist	3
	625

Florence Horsbrugh became Minister of Education in place of
David Tomlinson. The Korean war was well under way and for this
and other reasons defence expenditure leapt. There appeared to be
pressure from all political groups for expansion of social and military
services—although their priorities were vastly different—and it may
well be that either political party would probably have been faced
with severe retrenchment in public expenditure in any event. This
must be a matter for speculation. What is sure is that in December
1951 the first of the new series of steps for retrenchment was taken.
In Circular 242 of the Ministry of Education, local education
authorities were instructed again to cut overall revenue expenditure
by five per cent.

This time *Lincoln* cut by £7,120, or 1·9 per cent of the gross
education revenue budget for 1952–53.[38] Again, predictably a major
part (£3,820) was for painting, improvements and maintenance of
buildings. *Nottingham* also cut by 1·9 per cent overall, or £40,415
but the Sites and Buildings Sub-Committee refused to offer reductions and pointed out that with new schools opening their estimates
would need to increase. (Both the Education Committee and Council
accepted this). The City Council asserted its growing independence
of central government by a firm statement that

'This Council, recognizing that a five per cent cut in education services as enjoined on local authorities by the Ministry of Education would inflict irretrievable harm on the citizens of the future, instructs the Education Committee to submit any suggested cuts for examination by the full Council before forwarding them to the Minister'.[39]

The Council supported the Education Committee's action in deliberately limiting reductions to a maximum of 1·9 per cent. *Northumberland* Education Committee offered a reduction of £48,285 of which £25,500 was for evening classes alone, which expressed in relation to the actual 1952–53 expenditure of £3,196,615 was again about one per cent.[40] Accordingly, the Ministry of Education protested to the authority that its cut was not realistic in relation to Circular 242. The Education Committee approved on 28.5.1952 a draft reply declining to offer further cuts, and decided to refer the whole question of the economies to the North Eastern Council of Education Committees.[41] Pressure was also exerted from second-tier authorities and other local organizations, although to little avail. The effect of the 1952–53 economies and especially the retarding of the school building programme brought direct protests to the Minister of Education for example from such organizations as Prudhoe and District Trades Council, the Miners Lodge at Wallsend and the Wallsend Plumbing Trade Union.[42]

The following chapters outlining developments in the three survey areas, comment on their building programmes. In the face of increasing and acute need for new secondary places, for new technical schools and for reorganization of all-age schools, the Ministry issued Circular 245 of 1952 cancelling the whole of the 1952–53 building programme and substituting a drastically reduced revised programme for each authority to cover the period 1951–53.

The general effect was radically to cut back all capital investment for three years. Earlier policy decisions of the Ministry were therefore negated—including two important educational developments, provision for the growing Vth and VIth forms, and for the reorganization of all-age schools. The first was recommended as early as 1949 when the Minister drew the attention of local education authorities to the striking increase in pupils staying on beyond the statutory leaving age:

'It is emphasized that the task of catering for the needs of the older children involves secondary schools of all types. The Minister wishes to satisfy himself that suitable steps will be taken to provide adequate accommodation for children of this age.'[43]

Unfortunately this pious hope was not matched by any increased allocation of capital resources by the central government in the event.

The irony of this struck the *Nottingham* Education Committee in June of the same year when the same Ministry (a different branch) refused to allow the new Bilborough school to be built with Vth form accommodation. It was to be planned as an ultimate four-form entry school offering a five-year course (that is a 20-class school); but only the first instalment of 16 classes (I—IV years) was allowed to be built in the 1949–50 programme.[44] One wonders what would have happened if the majority of the 120 IV-formers had opted to stay on for the new technical five-year course which Nottingham had started to develop in its new schools. Educational 'rationing' was decidedly still with us.

The second issue had already become the centre of a battle between central and local government departments by 1949. The reorganization of all-age schools had been recommended as early as 1926 by the Hadow Committee but the rural counties in particular had been quite unable to obtain adequate building grants or building approvals. In *Northumberland* in 1935–36, only 17 senior schools existed, three all-standard schools had senior departments and 194 all-standard schools contained senior pupils.[45] As late as 1958 in addition to 20,013 pupils in secondary schools, there were still 6,691 seniors in Northumberland primary all-age schools[46] whose accommodation and staffing was largely related to primary school needs. Yet the authority's readiness to build was negated by the cancellation of much of its agreed programme. Already in the late 1940s, the Director of Education could foresee a need for massive building programmes to eliminate all-age schools, and already it was apparent that in the central allocation of capital resources, the increased demand from local education authorities could not begin to be met.

The County Councils Association therefore pressed the Ministry of Education on behalf of county education committees, and an important meeting was held at the Ministry on 25th May 1949 between the CCA and Ministry representatives. The CCA was seriously concerned at the continued complete refusal of the Ministry to include any building projects to help rural all-age reorganization. The Ministry agreed that reorganization was essential, that reports from HMIs showed that it was very difficult to obtain any benefit from the extra year of schooling except in reorganized secondary modern schools but the 'brute facts' were that more places needed to be built to cope with the rising birthrate and to serve new housing estates. 'This made it absolutely clear that there was no prospect at the moment of allowing any reorganization proposals as such.'[47] Pressure from CCA representatives for even a gesture towards rural areas of projects of a few thousand pounds each—'to build instalments of a few classrooms' met with the 'blunt truth that the Ministry programme was not enough to allow even the smallest additions'. The pressure was ineffective. In fact, the Treasury had pinned the Ministry to a given level of capital resources and no educational argument or pressure seemed capable of altering this.

By 1951, the AEC had entered the lists, and its representatives had discussed with the Ministry the total level of building programmes, the impossibility of keeping within approved cost limits for school buildings, and the continuing difficulty: the supply of steel.[48] The cost limits were not, however, increased by the Ministry until 1953[49] and then only by a modest amount. The new cost limit in itself was still however *lower* than the original 1949–50 cost limit. How far the rise in cost limit was due to pressure and how far to an acknowledgement by the Ministry that Education Committees could not attract realistic tenders, is hard to say. The AEC pressure, however, was ineffective in that no improvement took place for two years during which school building had to go ahead based on out-of-date price limits.

A pattern of control over capital and revenue resources began to establish itself on which local pressures only had sporadic and relatively minor effect, that is annual approval of acceptable levels of expenditure and regular reviews of the overall financial position. This pattern continued almost throughout the whole survey period. The key controls on capital expenditure were (and still are) the centrally controlled maximum cost per school place, and the need to obtain the approval of the Ministry of Education for each major capital project in advance of the programme year.

In the early 1950s, the Ministry introduced a further control (which again remains despite the ostensible desire for greater local autonomy), an annual limit to each local education authority's allocation for minor capital work[50] for the improvement of school buildings. Circular 209, addendum 2, referred to above, severely limited the level of minor works expenditure but Circular 245 issued on 4th February 1952 accepted that

'Many authorities will now have to carry out additional minor projects in order to make good the loss of places in new schools resulting from the cut of the main programme'[51]

for which supplementary allocations could be sought. *Nottingham* was successful for example in more than doubling its 1953–54 allocation from £23,774 to £48,744[52] after pressure from both Director of Education and the Committee.

Not in fact until 1955 did the Ministry feel able to include any improvement element in major building programmes, which had hitherto been limited to the strictest application of 'roof over heads'. In December 1954, Circular 283 (3.12.54) superseded the earlier Circular 245, and for the first time conceded the need to start reorganization of all-age schools especially in rural areas so that new places in properly equipped secondary schools would be available when the pupils born at the time of the high post-war birthrate reached secondary age in the late 1950s. As from the 1955–56 programme therefore it was announced that special priority would be given to rural reorganization; and the cost limit on minor capital works was raised to £10,000 (maximum per project).

One important qualification, however, which was to have far reaching effects on the development of new educational courses and on education for the average child in particular, was the Ministry's insistence (mainly and at times wholly applied to secondary modern schools) that during the period of severe restraint from 1952 to 1960, the Building Regulations would not be strictly applied in assessing the future use of new buildings. For example a four-form entry school with a five-year course should have had 20 classrooms suitable as form bases, together with from 6—10 specialist rooms. Circular 283 however describes how a school built for four-form entry (i.e. 600 pupils on a five-year course) could accommodate five or six form entry on a four-year course by using four specialist rooms as form bases (thus obviously restricting their use for specialist purposes) and by assuming that no Vth year pupils would stay on. The expedient is described as 'some inconvenience'.[53] It accords very ill with the Ministry's insistence in earlier circulars on the need to provide for Vth-formers, on the growth of external examinations (GCE having replaced School Certificate in 1951) and on the apparent shift of emphasis on standards in 1951 that

'whereas the 1945 Regulations came to be regarded as prescribing maximum as well as minimum standards, the revised Regulations, particularly those dealing with teaching accommodation, should be regarded as providing minimum standards only'.[54]

In other words, with one breath local education authorities were exhorted to improve teaching accommodation to meet new educational needs, and in another they were precluded by the Ministry from providing for five-year courses and even pressed to overcrowding the new schools by the equivalent of 20 per cent. It could be argued by the Ministry that we could not afford to build classrooms for non-existent Vth-formers. It could also be argued however that five-year courses could not be developed at all if aspirant

Vth-formers had neither classrooms nor specialist accommodation; and that technical education would become an unattainable myth if laboratories and housecraft rooms had to be used for non specialist class teaching.

In the same period, the Ministry continued specific controls over revenue expenditure of which perhaps the best example arose over *Nottingham's* transport policy for secondary pupils. The normal minimum distance beyond which local education authorities had liability to provide special free school transport for secondary school pupils was three miles[55] in accordance with the 1944 and 1953 Education Acts. Nottingham chose to be more generous because of the traffic dangers in the city, and provided free transport after $2\frac{1}{2}$ miles up to February 1953 when the Education Committee proposed to reduce the limit to two, thus acting in direct contravention of Circular 242 (quoted above) which asked local education authorities to economize on transport costs. The City Council agreed to the Education Committee's proposal. In 1953 the Ministry accordingly told the authority it must send in a separate statement of expenditure on transport for secondary pupils living less than three miles from their schools, and that grant would be disallowed on this expenditure.[56] The Education Committee sent its Chairman and Vice-chairman to London to exert pressure on the Minister partly because of traffic dangers and partly because the City's inability to build secondary schools fast enough (because of Ministry restrictions) meant more pupils had to travel further to school to fill what vacant places there were. The Education Committee asked that approval be given to a $2\frac{1}{2}$ mile limit. By December the Education Committee had lost its case, and the Ministry accordingly withheld £2,700 grant for the current year—unless the local education authority agreed to reinstate the statutory three-mile limit.[57] When the full City Council learned they would in fact lose grant, the Council rescinded its earlier decision and agreed it would conform with the Ministry standard.[58]

Thus in addition to controlling general levels of expenditure, the Ministry exerted detailed control even when a local education authority considered that unusual local circumstances justify a special local policy.

Before moving on to the second decade, it is necessary to pause here to look briefly at the third important control during the first decade which fortunately did not continue indefinitely—control of material building resources. While these restrictions were severe, they were fair, and the Ministry was in this instance to be congratulated in handling the situation with a combination of skill and realism. Nevertheless, the combination of the materials crisis with capital controls, proved almost fatal to authorities like Northumberland.

Control of timber, steel and labour

Pressure from local education authorities for larger building programmes has already been mentioned. The national crisis over timber, steel and labour meant, however, that acute lack of resources constantly depressed the level of demand as authorities tended year by year to ask for much less than they really needed in the knowledge that more would not be forthcoming until the materials crisis was resolved.

For by 1947 it was evident that the varied demands of the country's home needs (housing, hospitals, schools, children's homes after the 1948 Children's Act which was in draft in 1947) were competing both domestically [and with the acknowledged need to [redress the economy by increasing exports. Local authorities were warned that

'The national deficit of building labour is likely to be matched— and in the next year or two, exceeded—by the shortage of certain principle building materials, notably steel and timber, and will inevitably entail drastic curtailment of new works programmes generally'.[59]

while Dalton writes of the period when he was Chancellor of the Exchequer (1947),

'The capital investment programme was to be cut by £200 million . . . agreement was reached at next morning's Cabinet, on a cut less drastic than at first proposed *based in effect on the quantity of timber available*'.[60]

The programme immediately facing the Ministry seems modest by present day standards—demand from local education authorities for £5$\frac{1}{4}$ million for the raising of the school age from 14 to 15 years, £4$\frac{3}{4}$ million for schools for new housing estates and a further £3$\frac{1}{4}$ million for the extra secondary places. But by December 1947 authorities had been instructed to defer all but essential building (buildings for nursery pupils, adult education and youth service stood automatically deferred) and to restrict proposals for new schools either to those needed to serve new housing estates, new primary schools to provide for the sharply rising birthrate, or to projects to help expansion of technical education.[61]

The Chancellor of the Exchequer issued a report early in 1948 on capital investment, warning in particular that

'The volume of new investment undertaken must be brought into proper relation with the reduced supplies of materials, industrial capacity and manpower that we can afford to make available for this purpose. These limited and valuable resources must be concentrated as far as possible on those types of investment which will most quickly strengthen our capacity to export.'[62]

The report restricted the scope of education priorities to the three mentioned above, adding a caveat which was to have an unfortunate repressive effect on standards in old schools for many years after the worst of the economic crisis had been weathered:

'No building proposal for children of compulsory school age will be sanctioned unless the Ministry (of Education) is satisfied that the fullest use is being made of all available existing accommodation and that no improvisation is practicable.'[63]

Improvisation was interpreted by the Ministry as using school halls, libraries, science laboratories as general teaching spaces thus clearly limiting their specialist use: hiring church halls; and enforcing a general level of 10 to 15 per cent overcrowding in all schools before any additional new places would be approved. The overcrowding rule still applies in 1974 and is increased to 15 per cent—no new places are normally currently agreed until all existing secondary post-war schools are overcrowded by 15 per cent.

Restrictions on labour and materials were accordingly in operation by 1948;[64] timber was only available on licence; iron and steel were rationed on licence on a quarterly basis. Enterprizing authorities like *Nottingham* and *Northumberland* began to look at ingenious ways of using aluminium as a substitute in new primary schools. It was fortunate that the three survey areas did not have the added problem of war damage which faced London, Plymouth and Coventry.

Nottingham provides a good example of the restrictive effect of the lack of national resources on its demand for secondary school expansion. In the period 1946–49 it pressed for three additional new secondary schools (apart from five primary schools) and 37 new hutted class and practical rooms for the raising of the school leaving age; but by 1949 it had only succeeded in negotiating 240 places at Wigman Road Secondary School, was faced with housing secondary pupils in accommodation built for primary pupils and had no projects in the Ministry's reserve list. This must however be seen against a background of a worsening national situation, as the Ministry's Regional Priority Officer reported:

'The priority given to projects on the Prime Minister's list to agriculture and to factories to assist the export drive has had an unfavourable effect on all school projects, both as regards materials and labour. In particular a cement famine over much of the North Midlands, grave shortages in engineering equipment and electrical switchgear . . . have gravely dislocated the HORSA programme.'[65]

The Committee records for the period 1949 to 1952 make frequent reference to reports of crises resulting from the steel situation of which a typical one was the 1949 award of only 206 tons of steel for primary school projects and none for secondary places. But Nottingham needed 300 tons for its new secondary school alone, and only after a strong fight did the authority obtain a licence in September 1949 for an instalment of 180 tons of steel for its Wigman Road Secondary School.[66]

By 1951 steel was no longer licensed but was scarce; but in 1952 national priority had swung to armaments and defence, and licensing was reintroduced. Nottingham applied for 937 tons of steel for its approved school building programme for 1951–53 and by January 1952 had only received authority for 74 tons. The Authority pointed out to the Minister that unless more was authorized promptly the schools would be delayed and children would be out of school.[67] The revised 1952–53 programme was again at risk—

'No assurance is given that the steel allocated will match up to the revised 1952–53 programme set out above, and your Sub-Committee fear that should the steel not prove adequate, it may be necessary to redesign some of the schools to use less steel or to substitute alternative schools requiring less steel for those now in the programme.'[68]

Only in 1953 was it possible to remove the control on steel, and the Ministry of Housing and Local Government ceased the control on 6th May 1953,[69] but the situation was still serious enough to affect the 1953–54 programme, which was to remain at the level of the (already drastically cut) 1952–53 programme largely because of the limited supplies of steel.[70]

The effect of these national restrictions was to leave the Ministry and the local authorities at the end of 1954, with a drastically reduced capital programme. The Ministry had established firm central controls over both the level and detailed aspects of revenue expenditure. The next decade shows some, not all of the same problems.

Control of Capital and Revenue Expenditure 1955 to 1965

The general election of May 1955 had returned the Conservatives to Westminster with an increased and viable majority of 60. Almost immediately, however, the Government decided that the country's economy needed yet sterner measures, and in November 1955 the Chancellor of the Exchequer addressed a message to all local authorities further to curb capital expenditure and to exercise restraint—by now a familiar message.[71] Local education authorities had recently been exhorted by the Minister of Education to re-organize their all-age schools and to develop secondary education, and the call for economy accordingly seemed likely to fall on deaf ears. Lest authorities should grow over enthusiastic to follow the advice of the Ministry of Education, the Chancellor therefore announced in the Commons on 17th February 1956 'measures to deal with the present economic situation' which the Minister of Education translated into a now familiar pattern of 'reshaping the building programme'; which meant postponing most of it.[72] While control over minor capital works (under £10,000 a project) was not yet reintroduced, the Minister 'relies on authorities however to defer for the time being any jobs which are not urgent'.[73] It is difficult to see what work could genuinely be regarded as non-urgent after 10 years of the most stringent control on all school building, deferment of improvements and regular cut-back in maintenance and repairs.

Nottingham had just, for example,

'received with great satisfaction the Ministry of Education Circular 283 . . . which announced the abolition of the limit placed on Minor capital works. Immediate steps were taken to formulate a programme for modernising old schools which are so far below the standards set by present regulations of the Ministry.'[74]

The satisfaction was shortlived—faced with a strong directive from the Ministry, the Education Committee had to fight its own Council's response to the Chancellor's message, a proposal to post-pone the Committee's programme for relighting old schools (replacing gas with electricity), and for basic improvements.

Nottingham noted with regret that the Ministry of Housing and Local Government had asked local education authorities to curb capital expenditure for 1955–56 to the level of 1954–55, itself a drastic reduction of the authority's claim.[75] The 'expansion' of secondary education appeared likely to be stillborn. *Northumberland,* with some strength of mind, merely received the Chancellor's request with no comment and declined to curb minor works,[76] but *Lincoln,* deferred half of its very modest minor works programme for both 1956–57 and 1957–58, its standard of 'urgency' being markedly different from the other two local education authorities whose general approach to school building tended to be more vigorous (and both of whom by contrast had a fully staffed Sites and Buildings administrative section).

By 1955, secondary technical education had developed strongly, and external examinations were becoming a legitimate educational goal for other than grammar school pupils[77]. Conceptions of new and wider needs of both secondary grammar and secondary modern schools were being studied by the Ministry's Development group who had recently completed the new Wokingham, Berkshire, school, subject of Building Bulletin 8 issued in December 1955 as a guide to local education authorities. The Development group were also planning the new secondary selective school at Arnold, Nottinghamshire, subject of Building Bulletin 17, based on smaller teaching groups, wider subject choice and larger VIth-forms than hitherto.

It was the more discouraging therefore to those local education authorities not selected by the Development group for pilot experiments, when they wished to try innovation in new design to meet new curricular needs, to be faced with Circular 301 of 26.4.56 which admitted on the one hand that building costs had risen by 53 per cent since 1949, but which refused to raise the cost limits for school building on the grounds that it would add £4 million to the 1956–57 building programme alone, 'the amount by which the value of that programme would have to be increased to offset the rise in prices since April 1955'. The Secretary of the AEC summarized the feelings of the local education authorities about the House of Commons Debate, in his editorial:

'The Minister then claims credit for circulars 301 and 304 on the grounds that they have the effect of holding down the amounts that can be spent per new school place, on the equipment in new schools and on the building of those schools. So far as the cost per place is concerned the Minister has already virtually admitted that this may well lead to schools being built below existing regulation standards. Surely it would be more to the point to alter the standards if the nation is unable to afford even the minimum standards now laid down by the regulations. . . . The figure for secondary schools would appear to constitute a severe cut . . . the evidence seems fairly strong that rural reorganization, in which local education authorities were encouraged to go ahead as quickly as possible, is being deferred . . .'.[78]

The National Association of Divisional Executives for Education was equally concerned:

'Circulars 301, 303 and 304 have caused consternation among some authorities and even the AEC has been excited. There are likely to be grave consequences in many areas . . .'.[79]

The NADEE evidence suggested that the deferral of the building programme (cut to £55 million from £89 million) meant that

'The effect on the new secondary modern schools is likely to be considerable, and the children who will shortly be entering them, having endured the privations of the "bulge" years in the primary schools, are to be offered scant recompense in the secondary field'.[80]

With the repercussions of the new restrictive circulars 301 and 304 barely dying with the old year in 1956, local education authorities were already apprehensive in 1957. But meanwhile a more fundamental battle had begun to be fought, on the probable replacement of the percentage grant for education by a block grant to the local authority who would then decide at its own discretion how much of this it chose to use to subsidise the education service. The *Nottingham* Education Committee was typical in opposing the new grant scheme.[81] Its relevance here is the now specious argument generally put forward by representatives of central government that it heralded an era of greater freedom for local education authorities.

Even as the debate wore on however, local education authorities were directed by the Ministry of Education to cut back still further—this time on expenditure of capital from revenue, the sole remaining uncontrolled source from which to finance improvements to schools. Circular 334, issued on 27.1.1958, severely restricted not only capital from revenue, but the rate of replacement of old furniture and equipment, following a similar circular from the Ministry of Housing and Local Government to the local authority—'Any expenditure which can be deferred, should be deferred.'

It will be recalled that, formerly, up to a 3d. rate could be spent from revenue to improve schools—in *Nottingham's* case in 1958, a yield of £47,000; but the new restriction cut this to £25,000.[82] *Northumberland's* meagre allowance of £31,896, meant a cut in its estimates and deferment of urgent work.[83] All three authorities had now had their major programme slashed, 'non urgent' minor works deferred and now a limit imposed on minor capital work from revenue. The appearance in that autumn of the Government's new policy document 'Secondary Education for all: A New Drive'[84] and its accompanying circular 342 of 3.12.1958 must have had a hollow ring in the ears of the frustrated local education authorities. The circular spoke of 'the reality of secondary education for all', and for the first time since the serious programme cuts in 1951, announced the intention to reinstate the Building Regulations for school premises which had been consistently suspended since their creation in 1951 and amendment in 1954. We could at last afford, it seemed, in the forthcoming 1960–62 programme, to apply the standards first created in 1951 and recently revised in 1959. The minor works limit (for each project) was raised to £20,000, but at first no increased allocations were forthcoming. Steady pressure from the local education authorities nationally and through their associations, resulted in an increased national allocation for minor works in 1959, while simultaneously detailed guidance on 'The Remodelling of Old Schools'[85] announced a new drive to improve old schools. Authorities began to hope that at last the completion of the rural all-age reorganization was in sight; and they could begin to catch up on their backlog of other secondary school improvements. Hopes were even expressed that a new freedom to local education authorities on matters affecting school building, would follow introduction of the block grant.

This latter however had never been seriously considered by the Ministry of Education and indeed it is difficult to see how the Minister could delegate powers to local authorities and still retain necessary control over capital investment for education on behalf of his Cabinet colleagues. (The Government was still unchanged—the 1959 election had returned a Conservative government with an increased majority of 100.)

So far from increased freedom, control of cost became still more acute. The Minister refused again to increase school cost limits in 1959 despite rising prices, on the grounds that

'There is ample evidence that at the present time schools which satisfy the requirements of the Building Regulations and which are of good quality of construction and finish can still be built within the current limits of nett cost per place',[86]

and agreed only with extreme reluctance after the strongest pressure from the local authority associations, to increase cost limits for secondary schools by 10 per cent in 1960[87] and again from £290 to £310 in 1961[88]. It is perhaps fair to add that while local authorities were sure that cost limits were raised as a result of their pressure, the official Ministry reason was given that

'tendering for education building projects, which had been very keen throughout 1958 and most of 1959, became markedly less so during 1960 *with the growth of investment in the private sector*'.[89]

This would seem difficult to reconcile with the general cut back in capital investment in the public sector on grounds of the interest of the national economy. Over the period as a whole, cost limits rose at a much slower rate—and belatedly—than the equivalent rise in building costs, causing declining standards in later years in the amount of teaching area provided:

Table V (1): *Changes in school cost limits authorized by the Ministry of Education*

CIRCULAR with effect from:	SECONDARY SCHOOLS		
	with kitchen £	with scullery £	% increase %
Circular 209 (1950 programme)	290		
Circular 215 (1951 programme)	240		— 17·2
Circular 264 (10.3.53)	250	246	+ 4·2
Circular 274 (Add. 1) (7.4.55)	264	260	+ 5·6
Circular 6/60 (1.4.60)	290	286	+ 9·8
Circular 6/60 (Add. 1) (1.3.61)	310	305	+ 6·9
A.M. 13/63 (22.11.63)	329	323	+ 6·1
(1.4.64)	338	330	+ 2·7
A.M. 13/66 (1.7.66)	367	358	+ 8·6

And by 1961 when cost limits finally rose after a long interval, one problem had been solved only to be overtaken by another, a now familiar pattern reasserting itself. A national economic crisis equal to that of the period 1949–52, led to the issue of circular 13/61 drastically cutting and restructuring the 1961–1963 agreed building programme, much of which was in the end deferred *sine die* and irretrievably lost. The Minister was obliged to tell local education authorities that

'In the course of Wednesday's debate in the House of Commons, the Chancellor of the Exchequer gave details of the measures the Government intend to take to restrain the growth of public expenditure and to improve the efficiency of the country's economy . . . there will be reductions in authorizations for minor works . . .'[90]

and that priority for scientific and technical education would take precedence. New local major building programme allocations 'on a very restricted basis' would supersede the hitherto agreed 1961–63 programme.

The scale of the setback can be measured by the final award of a national programme of £55 million instead of the £127 million which local authorities had sought, of which about £90 million could have been built without difficulty with existing technical resources. Twenty-seven authorities had no programme at all, and Durham, whose problem of rural reorganization was acute, only £1·7 million out of a submission of £6—8 million. *Lincoln* had asked for £908,000 and had no programme. *Nottingham* was awarded £183,000 out of a submission of £505,000 and *Northumberland* £612,000 only out of £2,199,000.[91] Even allowing for a certain possible over-bidding on the part of the authorities, the programmes could bear no relation whatever to the scale of need.[92] Or indeed to the now massive backlog of deferred building—casualties of previous crises.

The Association of Education Committees debated with some bitterness the inadequate programmes at its annual conference in 1963, rejecting with acerbity the Minister's suggestion that local authorities had asked for more than they needed. The pressure from local authorities resulted in a final modest additional £5 million for the country as a whole.[93]

The satisfaction expressed in the Ministry of Education report for 1962, of progress despite and not because of national conditions, must be seen against this picture of economic turmoil and erratic frustrations. The total cost of the programme for rural reorganization over the five years from 1958 to 1962 was £300 million—

'a milestone passed in converting the title of the White Paper from intention to reality . . . there has been some rise in costs over the period, but cost control in educational building has helped in getting value for money spent'.[94]

The achievement had however been at the expense of and not in addition to, the many other developments sought by local education authorities—arguably a correct priority if the choice had to be made, but to set it in context, a priority set *primus inter pares*.

It is important to recognize that the Minister of Education could, however, only win for the local authorities such resources as he or she succeeded in negotiating in the annual Cabinet debates on priorities for expansion (or retrenchment). It is perhaps not without significance that the post of Minister (now Secretary of State) for Education is to this day regarded as a post of middle rank and not of senior statesmanship—a stepping stone to higher posts of government. The average length of tenure in the later years became two years or even less, a sad reflection on the extent to which the needs of the services are subservient to the concept of relative status of Ministers in the House. Or as the 1962 report went on to say,

'continued progress, like politics, is an art of the possible . . . continued advance on education must, therefore, turn on the identification and acceptance of priorities, both as between education and other social services, and within the education service itself'.[95]

But hardly had the balance begun to be redressed in 1963 and 1964 when an echo of the 1949 building troubles cast a shadow on the renewed enthusiasm of local education authorities—

'the volume of demand for building is likely to rise by over 50 per cent in the next ten years, and the building force to expand only slightly',[96]

and efforts were renewed to perfect methods of industrialized building. Nothing daunted, authorities nationally put forward a bid for an expanded building programme which in many areas, took account of new consortium building techniques. They were however faced in 1965 with an all too familiar declaration of retrenchment. The clarion call of circular 10/65 (urging local authorities to re-organize their secondary education on comprehensive lines) the natural corollary of which was swift development of capital invest-ment, was immediately followed by circular 12/65 issued on 24th August 1965 reporting new measures which the Chancellor of the Exchequer[97] had announced in the House of Commons on 27th July to correct the balance of payments.[98] These deferred all educational building *except schools* (in deference to circular 10/65) for six months, and asked for further restraint in local education authority spending. Authorities could be forgiven for reflecting that 'plus ça change, plus c'est la même chose'.

As it happened, all three authorities surveyed had already turned their attention to the reorganization of secondary education, antici-pating circular 10/65 by over a year; and all three authorities stoutly ignored the Chancellor's appeal, in pressing their committees to leave untouched their proposed rate of expansion of the secondary education service.

Probably of the four key controls referred to so far, the meticulous control of capital expenditure exercised by the Ministry of Education made the most immediate and the most lasting impact on the policies of the local education authorities.

The National Picture

The tables which are given on the following pages show the actual capital expenditure of all local education authorities in England and Wales for the period 1945–65, separating major and minor building programmes. The figures are supplied by the Building Intelligence Team of the Department of Education and Science. They are particularly interesting in the light of the assurances of central government departments that the introduction of block grants in 1959 should lead to greater freedom for local education authorities. In fact, however, capital expenditure fell drastically in 1957 compared with the 1956 level, and when the rising costs of school building are taken into account the reinstatement in 1960–63 of the 1956 level of expenditure was more apparent than real, while further drastic cuts were made by the Department of Education and Science in 1963–65.

Table V (2): England and Wales—major building programmes (all services). Authorizations 1945–65 (at prices current in the year of award)

YEAR	PRIMARY AND SECONDARY £000	Index	TOTAL, INCLUDING FURTHER AND SPECIAL EDUCATION AND TEACHER TRAINING £000	Index
1945/47	28,038	100	28,038	100
1947/49	9,453	32	13,972	49
1949/50	55,045	196	65,879	234
1950/51	46,440	165	55,143	197
1951/52	14,169	50	19,195	68
1952/53	45,642	163	51,762	185
1953/54	45,937	164	52,183	186
1954/55	48,286	173	56,392	202
1955/56	72,590	259	91,241	325
1956/57	73,571	264	91,193	324
1957/58	24,474	85	44,590	159
1958/59	50,121	179	69,521	298
1959/60	41,294	146	64,449	230
1960/61	78,427	278	91,065	325
1961/62	81,659	289	100,070	358
1962/63	71,013	253	95,211	340
1963/64	55,535	198	78,795	282
1964/65	53,259	189	77,803	278
Total	894,953		1,146,502	

Between 1958 and 1963 there were in addition four special additional teacher training expansion programmes totalling £50,718 not voted to any one year.

Source: Department of Education and Science Building Intelligence Team

Table V (3): England and Wales—schools minor building programmes—1945-65 *(money spent) (at prices current in the year of award)*

YEAR		TOTAL VALUE OF		
		Work started £000	Index	Work completed £000
1946/47		9,825	100	6,459
1947/48		6,735	68	5,846
1948/49		6,993	72	7,367
1949/50		8,894	90	9,322
1950/51†		6,793	69	6,477
1951/52		7,141	73	4,941
1952/53		7,296	74	6,354
1953/54		7,315	74	7,804
1954/55		8,123	82	8,506
1955/56		13,374	136	12,406
1956/57		14,703	150	14,031
1957/58		15,726	160	16,704
1958/59		11,394	116	12,723
1959/60		13,983	142	14,939
1960/61	(15,430)*	21,040	215	18,746
1961/62†		12,713	130	15,165
	(14,405)*			
1962/63		19,367	197	14,188
1963/64	(10,086)*	21,055	215	20,913
1964/65	(11,672)*	23,396	238	23,058

Notes: * The figures in brackets from 1960/65 represent the actual revised authorized *allocations* awarded by the Secretary of State.

† The figures for 1950–51 and 1961–62 represent a deliberate cut-back by the Chancellor of the Exchequer of the time.

Source: Department of Education and Science Building Intelligence Team

It will be recalled that Circular 245 of 1952 cancelled the original 1951–53 schools' building programme and substituted one which was much reduced. The Ministry had already conceded the need urgently to provide 'roofs over heads' for the rapidly increasing primary school population, and the need which would arise from 1956 onwards for extra secondary school places for the same reason. Faced with the kind of regular 'economic crisis' to which the earlier sections of this chapter refer, successive Ministers of Education held back the level of capital expenditure to that agreed with their Cabinet colleagues and in particular with the Treasury. After a cut in early 1951 by nearly three-quarters of the previous level of expenditure, the programme returned to the 1950 level for three more years before increasing to provide for the then backlog of overdue projects—for a mere two years. Moreover of the £73,571,000 awarded for 1956–57, 30 per cent was carried over from 1955–56, and accordingly the programme was really no higher than that for 1954 in real terms.[99]

The Minister of Education announced in 1957 that

'Yesterday the Chancellor of the Exchequer outlined in the House of Commons the measures which the government proposes to take to *stabilize capital investment in the public sector in 1953–59 and 1959–60 at this year's level*'.[100] (writer's emphasis)

But the 1957–58 level had been fixed at a mere £24,474,000, only a third of the 1956–57 programme which in turn was only two-thirds of the previous year's. And for two years thereafter the government held investment to a fixed low level, until pressure from the local authority associations increased the allocation from 1960 onwards.[101]

In looking at the table of major building approvals for the period 1957–65, one might well recall with some surprise, the enthusiastic tone of the Government White Paper 'Secondary Education for all—a New Drive' issued with Circular 342 on 3rd December 1958, urging local education authorities to make 'a reality of secondary education for all'. At no point would it appear in looking at the trend over the years that Ministerial calculations have taken account of the constant backlog of work which accumulated after each of the major cuts, notably those of 1951, 1957 and 1963. In the period under survey, those local education authorities which had a rising school population, especially those like Northumberland having to provide for inner city overspill, were not able even to meet basic need, still less to programme projects to improve or replace old schools.

It will be seen that the Ministry did in 1960 attempt to help authorities by providing an extra £10 million for minor improvements. But this too was slashed in the 1961–63 cuts back to the 1955–57 level, and the restoration to £21 million in 1963 did not more than attempt to catch up with rising building costs.

The programmes must indeed be seen in relation to the regular and substantial rises in building costs over the period under survey which tended to erode any (temporary) rise in apparent value of the annual programmes. In 1956 the Ministry estimated that building costs had risen by 53 per cent between 1949 and 1955.[102] But the programme had increased in annual value by only 25 per cent. Similarly secondary school building costs limits in 1960 were increased by the Ministry by 9·8 per cent to take account of recent

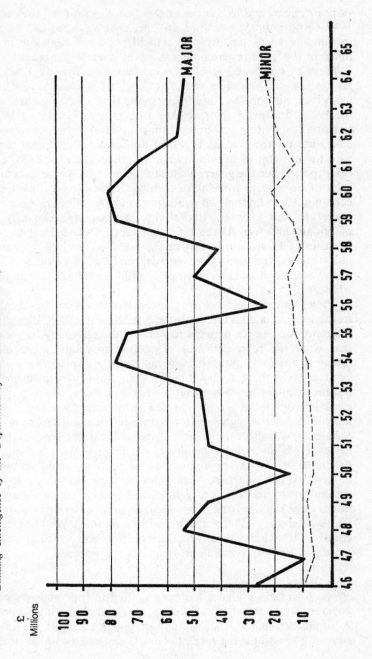

FIGURE 6: *Major and minor school building programmes—primary and secondary schools, 1946-1965. England and Wales. (Source: Building Intelligence of the Department of Education and Science)*

wage increases, and by a further 6·9 per cent in 1961. Of the restored 1960–63 programme therefore, 16·7 per cent was absorbed by a rise in building costs, and despite a further 8·8 per cent rise in cost limits in 1963, the programme was _cut_ by over 20 per cent.

There is, on this evidence, a *prima facie* case for suggesting that national capital resources were not allocated in relation to demand from local authorities, since for example they asked for three times the 1963–65 award.[103] Nor do they seem to be allocated in relation to rising costs, rising numbers in school or new policies for secondary education on the part of the local authorities; but in accordance with the amount of capital investment which the education service can expect, when the government of the time reviews the 'acceptable' level of investment in relation to other demands on the country's economy. One example of pressure from the AEC has been given earlier in this chapter. Its activity in 1963 was similarly only marginally effective. At the 1963 conference, the AEC called on the Minister of Education to restore the previous level of programmes and deplored the inadequate awards. Sir Edward Boyle could only promise them a possible further £5 million for the country as a whole.[104]

While, however, successive Ministers have used the argument that restrictions on capital investment are 'in the interests of the national economy' one ought perhaps to qualify this reasoning by recalling that what the representatives of central government are in fact saying to the local authorities, is not that the capital resources are not there. On the contrary it is the local authorities' own financial resources, albeit borrowed over a period of years, which pay for a capital programme. It is that the government of the day has temporarily set a higher priority on another service, or on other policies which affect the capital element of the country's economy, for example increased expenditure on defence, new housing, new hospitals or clinics, or remissions of tax, or increased welfare benefits, which must be met from savings elsewhere. In these circumstances, the most energetic efforts by local education authorities to meet local demand, from whatever source (teachers, governing bodies, parents) will be always subject to this overriding central control, the vicissitudes of which are clearly shown in the two tables of national school building programmes just quoted.

Conclusions

The foregoing evidence has been limited to four main aspects of governmental control only, but, it is suggested, the four key controls. A similar examination of matters of policy on other priorities in education[105] and the concurrent control of resources would probably reveal the same dilemma, that it is not possible to expand all aspects of a service either concurrently or even in accordance with a pre-determined long term plan, given limited resources.

It would seem that the recommendations for increased delegation to local authorities quoted at the beginning of this chapter, have not been carried out, so far as control over capital expenditure is concerned on which most educational expansion depends. On the other hand, there is some evidence that control over general revenue expenditure by central government is less effective, in that local authorities refused to cooperate to the desired extent and in the last analysis the local political situation is probably more decisive (in controlling rate-increases) than directives from central government. Moreover, strong local authority resistance in the early years resulted in local victory on the control of administrative costs which rose in accordance with local education authority needs and not in relation to levels determined centrally. In a situation of national shortage of material resources however the control—or rationing—by central government was highly effective in the period 1947–1953.

The continued apparent need for central control of public capital investment despite total lack of control of private capital investment, really makes any longterm effect of local authority response to implicit and explicit demand, only minimally possible. Individual authorities may marginally improve their position in the national 'league table' in the queue for major building programmes by skilled negotiations. Organizations like the AEC may succeed—and have succeeded—in increasing the education service's slice of the national cake, as it were. This did not however, hasten rural reorganization by any significant period. It did not free local authorities to spend as much as they would have liked on minor improvements to schools which figured in the Ministry's 1962 Building Survey as among those seriously deficient in standards of accommodation. It did not even leave them free to spend their revenue on minor capital works, since in due course this, too, became regularly subject to cuts or controls. And such 'growth' element in major building programmes as did survive Treasury cuts was steadily eroded by rising building costs, thus adding another element of 'intractable' expenditure to offset an apparent growth rate in response to demand. (Chapter X refers to the impact on accommodation standards of the failure not only of the national cost limits but the formulae of the Building Code to match the need for more school places or new and nationally accepted curricular needs.)

Furthermore, the replacement of percentage grant by block grant did not bring greater freedom in these particular aspects—the key controls. The only probable improvement was that the Nottingham transport issue, for example, had it arisen after 1959, would have been left to the discretion of the local education authority since the factor which influenced the Council in its final decision on the transport of secondary pupils was the withdrawal of percentage grant by the Ministry.

There is, interestingly, no conclusive evidence that either political party in power was more or less strict on control of capital investment. The pattern of slight expansion followed by rather drastic retrenchment, followed by only partial reinstatement of earlier levels of expenditure (in real terms) was a constant one whichever party was in control at Westminster. The survey period starts with a Labour Government in 1945 and ends with one in 1965, with a long period of Conservative rule after 1951. But the fundamental dilemma remained the same throughout the 20-year period.

Finally, the six points of control outlined by the Local Government Manpower Committee in 1951 and referred to at the beginning of this chapter, were (perhaps fortunately for the authorities) only partly tackled by the Ministry. In theory the Minister was responsible for ensuring an adequate 'quantity and variety' of services; in practice it was the authorities which attempted to set the pace of expansion. The 'efficient management of establishments' was—properly—left to the discretion of local education authorities. The maintenance of minimum standards was attempted in two main ways—the agreed system for a quota of teachers for each authority, and the (notional) imposition of Standards for School Premises. On the latter point however, the stringency of control on capital programmes from 1951 to 1960 meant that these standards were suspended for that period; and the Building Code specifications had to be regarded as maximum as well as minimum standards because of the rigidity of the cost per place limits which limped behind massive increases in building costs, putting a strait jacket on imaginative design for all but the most ingenious.

The three local authorities fared very differently, as might be expected, and the following chapters will attempt to show for each, how some local factors influenced the development of and the demand for, secondary education, given the financial problems outlined in chapter IV and the central controls outlined in this chapter.

Notes

1 Nottingham, Secondary Education Sub-committee, report of Director of Education. Minute 1944–46 Vol. 1 p.41.
   The AEC proved right and all local education authorities did become members, including Nottingham.
2 *Report of the Local Government Manpower Committee.* December 1951. HMSO.
3 Ministry of Education, Circular 208 (1.2.1950).
4 *Royal Commission on Local Government in England* 1966–1969. HMSO
5 Ibid. Vol. I para. 28.
6 Ibid. para 34 and Chapter XIII.
7 SHARP, Dame Evelyn, *Public Administration* 1962, Vol. 40 pp.378–9, article on 'The future of local government'.
8 *Education Act, 1944,* Section 1 (1). The word 'comprehensive' did not of course have in 1944 the connotation which it now has in relation to secondary education.
9 For example, Marshall Aid was not suspended until 1951, increasing from £144 million in 1948 to £239 million in 1950.
   DALTON, Hugh, *High Tide and After,* memoirs 1945–60. Frederick Muller Ltd. 1962. page 304.
10 embodied for example in Sections 68 and 76 of the Education Act, 1944.
11 *Education in* 1948, Ministry of Education, HMSO, 1949.
   Even so, Nottingham failed for years to recruit its full quota of women teachers. A later chapter comments more fully on teacher resources.
12 DALTON, Hugh. *High Tide and After,* 1945–1960. Frederick Muller Ltd. 1962 p.364.
13 Later to become Architects and Buildings Branch in 1949.
14 *Education in* 1948, Ministry of Education, June 1948. HMSO.
15 Ministry of Health, Circular 96/47.
16 Nottingham, special Education Committee (7.7.47).
17 Ministry of Education, Circular 210 (28.10.49) para. 4.
18 Nottingham, Finance Committee (16.12.49) and Education Committee (28.12.49).
19 Lincoln, Finance and GP Sub Committee (28.11.49).
20 Ministry of Education, Circular 242 (7.12.51).
21 Ministry of Education, Admin. Memo 421 (8.4.52).
22 Lincoln, Finance and GP Sub Committee (20.12.51).
23 Nottingham, Education Committee (23.1.52).
24 Northumberland, Finance and GP Sub Committee (17.12.51).
25 Ministry of Education, Circular 242 (7.12.51) para. 3.
26 Ministry of Education *The New Secondary Education* 1947 p.30. But the Building Bulletins issued as a guide to planning and design over the following 20 years, specified very different standards for different types of school, much more generous schedules of accommodation being prescribed for grammar schools.
27 Ministry of Education circular 142 (9.6.47).
28 Ministry of Education Admin. Memorandum 323 (22.4.49).
29 Ministry of Education, circular 210, para. 1.
30 lavatories.
31 Ministry of Education *Education in* 1948.
32 Lincoln, Finance and GP Sub Committee (28.11.49).
33 Nottingham, Finance Sub Committee (16.12.49) and Education Committee (28.12.49).

34   Northumberland, Education Committee (4.1.50).
35   Ministry of Education Circular 209 (28.10.49). For 1951 a reduction of more than 12½ per cent was predicted.
36   Ministry of Education Administrative Memorandum 371 (20.9.50).
37   Labour 315, Conservative and Liberal National 298, Liberals 9, Irish National 1 and Speaker 1.
38   Lincoln, Finance and GP Sub Committee (28.1.52) and 1952 annual report, p.7.
39   Nottingham, special Education Committee (25.2.52).
40   Northumberland, Education Committee (2.1.52).
41   A regional constituent of the AEC.
42   Northumberland, Education Committee (26.3.52).
43   Nottingham, Secondary Education Sub Committee (10.1.49).
44   Nottingham, Sites and Building Sub-Committee (22.6.49).
45   *Education in Northumberland* 1953–58, page 21.
46   Ibid. p.22.
47   Northumberland, Education Committee (28.9.49) and Appendix E, Schedule XIII pp.316–317.
48   Northumberland, Buildings Sub Committee (13.7.51).
49   Ministry of Education Circular 264 (10.3.53). The full cost per place rose from £240 to £250 (secondary) and £140 to £146 (primary).
50   At that stage, projects costing less than £6,500 each, which in 1952 for example could enable 2 new classrooms to be added to a new school.
51   This piecemeal adding to new schools (or to remodelled schools) is not only uneconomic, but leads to bad design of schools in curricular terms.
52   Nottingham, Sites and Building Sub Committee (4, 12 and 16 February 1953).
53   Ministry of Education Circular 283, Appendix, paras. 3–7.
54   Ministry of Education Circular 240 (5.10.51).
55   between a pupil's home and school.
56   Nottingham, special Education Committee (26.8.53).
57   Nottingham, Secondary Education Sub Committee (8.12.53).
58   Nottingham, Secondary Education Sub Committee (8.2.54) and Education Committee (24.2.54).
59   Ministry of Education Circular 143 (2.6.47).
60   DALTON, Hugh. *Hide Tide and After* 1945–60. Frederick Muller Ltd. 1962, p.268.
61   Ministry of Education Circular 155 (1.12.47).
62   *Capital Investment in* 1948, Treasury Cmd 7 268, HMSO, Page 4.
63   Ibid. p.14, para. 34.
64   Ministry of Education Circular 180 (16.8.48).
65   Nottingham, Sites and Building Sub Committee (14.1.48). HORSA Hutted Operation for Raising of School Age.
66   Nottingham, Sites and Buildings Sub Committees (12.1.49) and (15.9.49).
67   Nottingham, Sites and Buildings Sub Committee (10.1.52).
68   Nottingham, Sites and Buildings Sub Committee (14.2.52). The schools built with less steel were likely to have higher maintenance costs later.
69   Nottingham, Education Committee (24.6.53).
70   Ministry of Education Administrative Memorandum 413, Addendum 3 (18.8.52).
71   Northumberland, Education Committee (15.12.55).
72   Ministry of Education, Circular 298 (23.2.56).
73   Ibid.

74 Nottingham, Annual report 1955, p.4.
75 Nottingham, special Education Committee (7.12.55).
76 Northumberland, Education Committee (15.12.55).
77 See for example Circular 289 (9.7.55) and BANKS, Olive, *Parity and Prestige in English Secondary Education,* Routledge & Kegan Paul 1955, pp.216–219.
78 *Education* (3.8.56), p.145. William Alexander's Editorial.
79 NADEE pamphlet 4, July 1956.
80 Ibid. para. 7.
81 Nottingham, special Education Committee (12.9.57). See in particular the AEC pamphlet *The Threat to Education,* 1957 for the LEA's case against block grants.
82 Nottingham, Secondary Education Sub Committee (10.2.58).
83 Northumberland, Finance and GP Sub Committee (7.3.58).
84 Cmd 604, December 1958, a Government White Paper.
85 Ministry of Education Circular 10/59 (3.9.59).
86 Ministry of Education Circular 4/59 (26.5.59). Subsequent maintenance costs of this generation of schools have however proved the authorities right and the Minister wrong. Inability for example to build pitched roofs because of low cost limits has meant spending sums of up to £20,000 within ten years of a school's opening, on repairs to flat roofs.
87 Ministry of Education Circular 6/60 (13.4.60).
88 Ministry of Education Circular 8/61 (31.5.61).
89 *Education in* 1960, Ministry of Education, HMSO (writer's emphasis).
90 Ministry of Education Circular 13/61 (28.7.61).
91 *Education* (11.5.62) pp.942 and 967–968. The figures cover both primary and secondary schools.
92 Need which was itself starkly described in the Department of Education and Science's own *School Building Survey* 1962, published in 1965.
93 *Education,* (12.7.63) pp.114–5.
94 *Education in* 1962, Ministry of Education, HMSO, p.2.
95 *Education in* 1962, Ministry of Education, HMSO, pp.7–8.
96 Ministry of Education circular 1/64 (28.2.64) commenting on the new White Paper *A National Building Agency,* Cmd 2228.
97 It is perhaps important to record that he was, by now, a Labour Chancellor, Labour having taken control from the Conservatives in 1965.
98 See also circular 2/65 of the Ministry of Housing and Local Government.
99 *Education* (6.7.56). Answer to questions in the House of Commons 28.6.56. See also Circular 306 of 1956.
100 Ministry of Education, Circular 331 (30.10.57).
101 AEC Minutes for 1959 and 1960.
102 Ministry of Education, Circular 301 (26.4.56).
103 *Education* (15.11.63) and AEC minutes, Autumn 1963.
104 *Education* (12.7.63).
105 for example within the survey period the persuasion in the reports published in 1960 on grants to students (the Anderson Report) the Youth Service (the Albemarle Report) and the 15–18 age group (the Crowther report) or in the White Paper *Better Opportunities in Technical Education,* Cd 1254 issued in 1961.

CHAPTER VI

Secondary Education in Lincoln, 1945-65

'Lincoln . . . instead of advancing in the progress of ameliora-tion, there seemed every appearance of its soon sinking into complete insignificance. . . . But it is . . . highly gratifying to the inhabitants of Lincoln to observe the spirit of improvement daily gaining ground. . . . We may fancy we see this opulent city emerging from this apathy, which has too long enchained it and approaching by rapid strides to that state of grandeur and magnificence which it formerly possessed.'

E. Baron 1810[1]

One can only speculate how significant an influence on Lincoln's slower than average rate of change in the 20th century, may have been the lingering tradition of those symptons of inaction and apathy described by Mr Baron in 1810. The account which follows, and the brief general profile in Appendix A (I), suggest that in fact in Lincoln, the dominant principle in the allocation of resources was that of 'conditioned demand'. That is, there appeared to exist an artificially low 'ceiling' set both on the resources available and on the level of demand, by officers and by head teachers in particular. This led to the application of the subsidiary principle, that lack or limit of resources, in turn depressed demand.

It is perhaps important to restate here that what follows relates strictly to the secondary school sector only. The level and quality of provision made by local authorities for different sectors of their services, may quite understandably vary; and it would be wrong for example, necessarily to apply the evidence on the secondary sector in Lincoln, to its other services. Nevertheless, the secondary sector is of such importance as to be a not untypical illustration of the main principles by which the Lincoln authority operated.

It is also important to remind readers that the survey ends at the year 1965. Since then, all county secondary modern schools have been closed, and a scheme for comprehensive schools developed which will result in September 1974 in a three-tier scheme in which three out of five high schools (12—18) are purpose-built and the two remaining in adapted accommodation built in 1937 and 1956 respectively. The 10-year period 1964–74 has seen growth in the city relatively exceeding that for the previous two decades together, including curriculum development, a strengthened role for advisers and development of in-service education for teachers.

The base on which this later development has had to be built was, however, artificially depressed—financially (see chapter IV) and psychologically (see chapters II and III). It has been suggested that basic principles governing supply and demand underly many aspects of the development of secondary education, and that such factors as the strength of the administration, the control of capital resources by central government and the presence or absence of pressure groups can help to determine the level and allocation of resources. Was this so in Lincoln? Does an identifiable pattern emerge from the developments which took place in the city? Earlier chapters have set the curricular, administrative and financial scenes and Appendix A gives a brief profile of the city. It will also be recalled from the preceding chapter that the controls by the Ministry of Education over capital building programmes were stringent throughout most of the survey period, and that pressure even from the local authority associations had only a marginal effect on the national allocations for new school buildings. In Lincoln, the position was further complicated by the very strong views held by the third Chief Education Officer on the way in which secondary education in the city should develop, which in turn determined his priorities in negotiations both with his own committee and with the Ministry of Education.

The Inherited Position

The dominant pre-occupation of the early educators after the first World War was increased provision of 'scholarship' places, and a new girls' county grammar school was therefore created in temporary accommodation in 1922 and rebuilt in 1937. The technical school for boys was enlarged and reorganized to provide extra secondary grammar places for boys in two stages, firstly in 1922 and then in 1936. Thus by 1945, grammar places were available for 25 per cent of the relevant age group; but there was little new accommodation for the non-grammar sector. This pre-occupation with the able children has lasted throughout most of the post-war period, and can be summed up by the following quotation from a grammar school headmaster in 1965.

'The citizens like to feel that there is some return for their money, in addition to past history. On the educational front this return is provided by the possession of four good grammar schools.'

Secondary education in Lincoln in 1946 was provided partly by four single-sex grammar schools taking about 25 per cent of the 11-plus age group each year. Five secondary modern schools then recently formed from senior departments of former elementary schools, had also a total of 1520 pupils on roll in 1946. (Records of the secondary school population show at times in the survey period, almost equal numbers of actual pupils on roll at the two types of school, but children of secondary age in all-age schools were shown as in primary schools, and secondary modern schools keep pupils for four years only (11—15) and not seven (11—18)—hence the apparent discrepancy.) The Roman Catholic church maintained one all-age (5—14) school and the Church of England an all-age (5—14) school and a secondary modern school in very old premises, scheduled to close in due course. The Education Committee shared the avowed aim of the then Chief Education Officer to give priority to maintaining a level of recruitment to grammar schools of 25 per cent of the age group, to match the rapidly rising school population.

The Development Plan

An important factor which affected the early plans for the development of secondary education, was the change of Chief Education Officer in 1948. The Chief Education Officer in post in 1945, was formerly the headmaster of a primary school in the city, with a sympathy for the less able and the non-academic. The preliminary proposals for the city's Education Development Plan included firm proposals to provide technical education for secondary modern pupils.

The Chief Education Officer had declared in the Annual Report for 1946, in fact, that

'for the pupils in the secondary modern schools it is proposed to develop still further the practical side of the curriculum so that they may continue to make and strengthen their contribution to the needs of industry and commerce and the future skilled craftsmen employed thereon'.[2]

Officers employed in the department at the time confirm that it was then the intention to offer the new secondary modern schools technical facilities to make this possible.[3] There were also significant numbers of pupils of school age (from 13 to 18 years) following junior courses at the Technical College and the College of Art—as many as 151 boys and 29 girls in 1948 and 60 and 57 respectively in 1949.

The Chief Education Officer was, however, due to retire in 1948. His place was taken by the headmaster of the city's largest (boys') grammar school, holding views diametrically opposed to those of his predecessor. The new Chief Education Officer designate, it is suggested by colleagues who worked with him in that period, had a strong influence on the Education Committee and on the Development Plan even in the period before he took up post.[4] The then Chairman of the Education Committee moreover shared his view that resources should not in fact be directed to less able children because 'the country's future depended on the clever child'.[5]

In the event, Lincoln's Development Plan for primary and secondary education was finally approved by the Minister on 17 March 1949 and was based on a bipartite system of secondary education, providing grammar and modern schools, but no technical schools. The Minister expressed concern however at the lack of provision for secondary technical education in the Development Plan (especially in the face of plans for new secondary technical schools, bilateral schools and multilateral schools elsewhere). An earlier resolution of the Education Committee had suggested that this would partly be provided in the secondary modern schools.

'where the curriculum already included a certain amount of practical work which could readily be extended'.[6]

The new Chief Education Officer, however, in direct contrast to his predecessor persuaded the Committee in 1948 that this work should go to the grammar schools:

'The Minister agreed to this (bipartite) arrangement only after much discussion and after an assurance had been given that the courses in the grammar schools will afford the variety of curriculum envisaged for both normal grammar schools and secondary technical schools.'[7]

It is to be seen whether this happened in practice.

Certain aims may be set by the authority, by the officers and by the teachers; and made possible by a subsequent and purposeful allocation of the necessary buildings, staff, equipment and money. One may then expect that the administration would respond to pressures, subject only to limitations imposed by central government (outlined in the previous chapter), or by lack of financial resources from constraints such as those outlined in Chapter IV. The following section suggests some of the aims which might be expected to have affected the allocation of local resources. The succeeding section attempts to narrate how far practice followed theory, while the final section draws conclusions on the success or otherwise of pressures.

Aims, Policy and Conditions in schools

The predominant aim of the new Chief Education Officer was to preserve a level of recruitment to the grammar schools of 25 per cent of the age group, to maintain which in times of a rising birth rate, meant increased places and more money for the grammar schools. It appeared that a concurrent aim was to provide technical education in the grammar schools (see above). The Chief Education Officer also deliberately aimed to restrict courses in secondary modern schools to those of a very general nature and strongly to oppose any introduction of special 'bias' or extended courses for less able pupils. In an interview in 1969,[8] he reaffirmed, despite the many developments in secondary education over the 20 years which had passed, that in his view it was wasteful to equip secondary modern schools with specialist rooms since the less able child needed only basic literacy and a general education. The place for specialist teaching was the grammar school or the Technical College. He had, he admitted, strongly opposed the creation of head of department posts in secondary modern schools on the grounds that there was, or should be, no high calibre 'academic' work to justify them. Secondary modern schools were 'not expected to produce technicians or skilled workers; if they teach their pupils good manners they will do well'. He considered 15-year-old pupils in secondary modern schools too immature to tackle external examinations, and hence had strongly opposed the introduction of these in the non-grammar schools.

His views appeared to be shared by most leading Education Committee members in Lincoln until the late 1950s. It will be recalled that the two dominant personalities leading the Labour group on the Committee until 1956 were solely concerned with preserving 'the scholarship' ladder to advanced education, and regularly attacked proposals put forward by co-opted members of the Education Committee to improve the secondary modern schools, as frivolous spending and a waste of ratepayers' money.[9] It appeared that the Chairman of the Finance Committee throughout most of the period held the same views. He admitted on interview in 1969, that his priority was for the able boy (not girl). He saw no relationship whatever between extended courses for secondary modern pupils, and their entry to further education or to employment offering skilled training (despite the minimum entry requirements for both of these). He had accordingly opposed the spending of money on secondary modern schools, other than for the basic essentials needed for a general education.

The aims of the new Labour group who took office in 1956, however, were diametrically opposed to those of their predecessors (see chapter III) and it was the new Chairman of the Education

Committee and not the Chief Education Officer, who initiated the scheme for transferring secondary modern pupils at 15 plus to the grammar schools, in lieu of extended courses at their own schools. The new proposals met with opposition from the Chief Education Officer, but were supported by the secondary modern head teachers who were anxious for increased opportunities for their able pupils.[10] It should be noted that the proposals were only supported for the *pupils'* sakes; the secondary modern heads remaining firmly of the view that the non-grammar schools should be offering five-year courses to 'O' level, transferring able pupils at 16+ and not 15+. The new Chairman's efforts in the late 1950's to reorganize secondary education on non-selective lines, also failed in the face of the Chief Education Officer's refusal to agree. Both matters were consequently deferred until the appointment of a new Chief Education Officer in 1964.[11]

The head teachers were equally divided in their aims. The heads of the four grammar schools took their lead from an early (1946) resolution of the local Joint Four Secondary Associations that it was useless to expect increases of salary for grammar school teachers 'unless and until the public could be convinced that grammar and modern schools were not equal . . . the big stumbling block to any change of grammar school salaries is the principle of parity of esteem. . . . These ideas must be attacked'.[12] And while the gulf between the two groups of heads did narrow over the years, the grammar school teachers did not in fact support the principle of widening the curriculum in the secondary modern schools. They did support the Chief Education Officer's insistence that any additional provision for older pupils must be made at the four grammar schools, and not at secondary modern schools.

The heads of the secondary modern schools fought hard in the early years for their own schools but on their own admission gradually gave up the battle for new buildings, equipment, staff and new curricula in the face of constant lack of resources or of encouragement. It proved possible to interview most of the secondary modern head teachers holding office for the greater part of the survey period and four gave evidence simultaneously as representatives of teachers' organizations.[13] Extended courses for the less academic pupils were not generally common until the mid 1950s, and Lincoln was not alone in offering a limited curriculum in the early post-war years. The secondary modern head teachers, however, soon began to press the Chief Education Officer for extra accommodation and staff to establish new courses, even though they still lacked adequate resources for their basic work. For example, the Chief Education Officer recommended to his Committee in 1947 that the city did not need any of the special huts on offer from the Ministry of Works at a special rate for the raising of the school-leaving age (from 14 to 15), which would have provided much needed practical rooms for housecraft and handicraft. Instead, the Committee hired church halls, and used school halls, libraries and science rooms for general teaching.[14] Evidence from staff in the Education Office at the time suggests that this was a straight economy measure—the Committee and the Chief Education Officer could see no case for capital expenditure on practical rooms, despite the statement quoted above on the expansion of practical education.

The heads of the two boys' schools promptly protested to their governors, opposed transfers of their able boys at 13 plus to the Technical College and asked for improved facilities for technical education[15] but with no success. Three of the schools had no library facilities whatever; one boys' school had no metalwork room; a girls' school had a shorthand teacher but neither typewriters nor a commerce room in which to work. However limited the conception of a commerce course might then have been, one can sympathize with staff who try to offer relevant courses to older pupils, despite lack of suitable resources. Pressure on accommodation was such, however, that another school was using huts dating from the 1920s at half a mile distant, a church hall, 'and occasionally even the corridors in the main school'.[16] By 1951, all specialist rooms were being used for general class teaching, science was being taught for half of the syllabus in ordinary classrooms and every school hall but one had a class.[17] This situation was to remain in some schools, throughout most of the survey period. By 1962, one typical boys' secondary modern school still had no library, no gymnasium, no second science room, 'inappropriate furniture in the geography and art rooms . . . in the woodwork room much of the machinery is out of date . . . the biggest single deficiency being well chosen books . . . apart from one period of nature study in form 1C, the C forms have no science . . . biology is taught in a classroom'.[18]

At the request of the head teachers in 1950, a pre-nursing course was started at the Technical College for girls of 15 plus, after the repeated failure of the heads to convince the Chief Education Officer that it should be at the girls' schools. At this point over half of the girl leavers tended to enter routine office jobs, about a third of boys entered engineering firms, one third the building trade and 10 per cent of boys (but very few girls) entered further education. It is not without significance that the school which sent more boys than any other into skilled employment or apprenticeships and to further education (from 37–40 per cent into engineering firms and 28 per cent to the technical college in 1952) was the only school to have the complete range of facilities for woodwork, metalwork, technical drawing and science, even if both inadequately equipped and over-crowded; and a headmaster holding a BSc (Engineering) degree.

It will be seen that there was already a case for (a) more secondary school places to relieve overcrowding and to allow for Vth-form expansion, and (b) capital expenditure to improve conditions in the schools. By 1953 pressure from the head teachers led the Chief Education Officer reluctantly to propose a three-year GCE course at the College for 15-year-old girl leavers from secondary modern schools, who wished to become teachers, the Chief Education Officer still opposing the introduction of any external examinations into non-grammar schools. A year later, following renewed pressure from the girls' schools for a pre-nursing course, the Committee approved a scheme for transfer of secondary modern school girls at 15-plus to the girls' grammar schools specifically for this.[19]

As yet the Church of England school was not reorganized (5—15). In 1954 the Minister approved the creation of a secondary modern (11—15) CE secondary school, by adaptations to the old school premises. The greatly increased primary school population was soon to transfer to secondary schools and by 1956 the secondary modern schools were already faced with 200 pupils for whom no places were available, even taking account of the overcrowding of specialist rooms.[20] The steady increase in applicants for further education courses at the Technical College led the heads to press again for either extended courses in their own schools (preferably) or for a second school leavers' course at the college.[21] Predictably, more boys than girls from secondary modern schools went on to further education (53 boys and 27 girls in 1957). In 1958, of two schools of comparable size, the boys' school sent 19/59 in summer and 23/61 at December to vocational courses at 15-plus, while the sister school sent a total of 8 and 10 respectively. The Committee, in the face of strong resistance from the College, whose staff felt they were doing the school's work, authorized a commercial course to complement the boys' technical course. The college entry from the girls' schools doubled. It is a tribute to the schools staffs that so many pupils met the entry requirements, for there were still no spare rooms to teach specialist subjects even reasonably. One school could offer housecraft once a fortnight to half of the school and not at all to the rest,[22] while at the brother school, only two out of five year groups could be taught any handicraft at all because of lack of specialist rooms. (It will be recalled the City had built none in the special programme in 1947–49 for raising the school-leaving age.)

It is interesting to reflect that by this time, the Crowther report (1959) had recommended the raising of the school leaving age to 16, the expansion of extended courses for less academic children in the second quartile of ability, and a target of 50 per cent of boys and girls receiving full-time education to 18 years instead of the 12 per cent (to 17) and six per cent (to 19) then current.

The secondary modern head teachers in Lincoln had for some time now, from discouragement, ceased to press for any new facilities on new courses in their schools, with rare exceptions. The only new school built in the period had been deliberately designed for a four-year course with no external examinations. Any 'late developers' were moved to grammar schools at 13 plus or at 15 plus. Two heads interviewed attributed this to the Chief Education Officer's unshakable ideas about 'fixed intelligence' on which he based the Lincoln selection techniques and which underlay his opposition to examination work for the 'bottom 75 per cent', so to speak.[23] Accordingly the heads did not resist very strongly when their renewed pressure for more opportunities for their abler pupils was met by the establishment of a second (15—17) course at a grammar school. By 1962 this transfer scheme had been operating for 10 years, and 137 pupils had been transferred in the 10-year period—a relatively small number out of an annual age group of about 1300 for 10 years (about one per cent). Of these 27 either failed or did not sit the GCE but the remainder succeeded in obtaining certificates:

Table VI (1): GCE 'O' level

	NUMBER SUBJECTS PASSED							
	1	2	3	4	5	6	7	8
Number of pupils	17	27	18	12	14	15	6	1

One wonders how far this supports a 'cost-effective' argument—the return is not a high one for the additional staffing required. Would not relatively straightforward extra staffing in the secondary modern schools have offered both these pupils and their borderline peers the possibility of an average of three to five passes in common core subjects in their own schools? At a time when the average grammar school pupil passed in from five to nine subjects, the majority of transferred pupils obtained fewer than five passes and over a third, fewer than three.

The CSE had meanwhile also failed to commend itself to the Chief Education Officer, who rebuffed an offer from the Joint Four to help on any advisory boards set up locally—'The policy of the Education

Committee is not to provide for external examinations in secondary modern schools'.[24]

In 1964, however, a new Chief Education Officer was appointed. His first remit from the Education Committee was to prepare a report on the reorganization of secondary education on comprehensive lines (a year before the issue of circular 10/65).

The new (fourth) Chief Education Officer's priorities were quickly established both in his department and in the schools. Within 12 months he had revised the structure of capitation allowances to replace the differential rate between grammar and modern schools by a 'rate for age' allowance, and concurrently had arranged for CSE courses to be offered in secondary modern schools in 1967, the earliest date by which planning could be completed. He negotiated substantially increased major and minor building programmes and persuaded the Education Committee to create two new posts and to appoint an experienced Deputy Chief Education Officer and a new Assistant Education Officer for secondary education, to take over detailed planning for further and for secondary education respectively. The Joint Consultative Committee of Teachers was recalled and reconstituted, and a programme of in-service training for teachers established for the first time with the help of newly appointed advisory staff. Unlike his predecessor, the new Chief Education Officer held the view that services would expand and developments materialize as and when he appointed experienced staff especially designated to look after specific sectors of the service. He accordingly appointed enough supportive administrative staff to create two sections within the office to handle respectively the administration of schools and of Sites and Buildings. Within 18 months the minor works programme had jumped from £8,000 to £51,000; the increased major building programme allocations were diverted to providing new secondary modern schools or places which would later be used as part of a plan for comprehensive education. Revenue expenditure for the next three years, after swift negotiations with the Finance Committee, increased for the first time at a significantly higher rate than the cost of living.[25]

Two additional needs which will have been identified from the foregoing account, were (a) to provide more school places to relieve overcrowding, and (b) to use capital resources to improve conditions in the older schools. But there is little evidence that the third Chief Education Officer or the Education Committee accepted these as valid aims with any degree of priority. One form of *implicit demand* however which faced all authorities in this survey period was that of rising numbers. How was Lincoln affected? Was this demand met?

Implicit Demand—Rising School Rolls

Since the schools were already overcrowded in 1946, the raising of the school leaving age and the rising birth rate would not have alone accounted for the total need for new places between 1946 and 1965. Adding the three factors together and bearing in mind that much of the rising revenue expenditure was intractable, it would be reasonable to suggest that expenditure should have risen at no less than the rate at which the school population rose. This would be necessary to maintain a minimum constant standard, before any account were taken of other factors like price rises or improved standards. The base standard in 1945 was of course artificially low because of the rationing and restrictions of the war years.

In Lincoln's case, this meant a minimum overall percentage increase of about 44 per cent and of 70 per cent for the secondary sector:

Table VI (2)

	TOTAL SCHOOL POPULATION	SECONDARY ONLY
1946	8,781	3,096
1964	12,643	5,230
% increase	44%	70·5%

The secondary school rolls thus had risen at a much faster rate than the school population as a whole. But revenue expenditure on the secondary sector in Lincoln rose at a *slower* rate than total education revenue expenditure:

Table VI (3)

	TOTAL EDUCATION GROSS REVENUE EXPENDITURE £	TOTAL SECONDARY GROSS REVENUE EXPENDITURE £
1946	337,491	109,432
1964	1,779,177	530,276
	527%*	489%

* This includes expenditure on further education, special education etc. as well as primary and secondary. But neither of the former developed very fast until after 1964.

It is therefore arguable that unless the total increase in expenditure concealed a major element of improvement (which is unlikely in the light of the evidence about the secondary sector) the secondary schools received less than the increase needed to maintain the same general standard as in the service as a whole. Nevertheless, expenditure did rise for other reasons than mere extrapolation of the effect of rising rolls since the growth rate on costs very substantially exceeded the growth rate of numbers of pupils. Expressed in another way, Table VI (4) which follows shows the relative growth of secondary rolls and secondary expenditure using 1946 as the base year. Clearly part of the increased expenditure (about a third in crude terms) could be accounted for because of implicit demand from rising numbers. This of course conceals differences for pupils under and over 15 and in grammar and non-grammar schools.

Table VI (4)

Year	Total Gross Direct Secondary Revenue Expenditure £	Index	Secondary School Population	Index
1946	108,432	100	3096	100
1948	124,428	115	3289	106
1951	153,631	142	3387	109
1953	162,759	150	3366	108
1956	240,731	222	4411	143
1959	349,035	323	5316	172
1962	448,648	415	5228	168
1964	530,276	491	5230	168

Tables VI (2) to (5) suggest that there were other factors causing increased expenditure. Among these, improved standards and price rises would, in an average authority, be dominant factors. Before looking further at revenue expenditure however, the capital programme over the survey period is described since this would be a major resource for providing the extra school places—over 2000—needed between 1946 and 1964. Its effect on subsequent revenue expenditure can normally be seen partly from increased loan charges and partly from higher costs of maintenance, equipment and services to newer buildings.

Capital Resources—Implicit and Explicit Demand
The previous chapter referred in some detail to national policy and national controls, and in particular to the general growth in national

capital expenditure with, however, sporadic severe cuts, notably in the early 1950s and the early 1960s.

Lincoln, like most other local education authorities, was obliged to give priority to new primary schools in the first five years after the approval of its Development Plan because of the rising birth rate which affected primary schools from 1950 onwards. A project for new secondary modern places in the south of the city was, however, put forward for the 1949 programme, before being withdrawn by the Chief Education Officer after pressure from the Ministry to do so in 1950. The city's need in the first 15 years was undoubtedly mostly for more places for secondary modern children (since 25 per cent of the secondary school children had grammar school places already). Lincoln had a grammar school provision of well above the national average, much to its credit. Even by 1952, the national average was only 20·5 per cent of 12-year-olds in grammar schools (*Education,* 22.5.53) while List 69 of the Department of Education and Science for 1964–65 gave an average of 18·6 per cent of boys and 20·1 per cent of girls in grammar schools in the Counties and 16·4 per cent and 17·3 per cent respectively in County Boroughs, with a further six per cent (all abilities) in comprehensive schools. By 1950 there were 300 extra pupils of secondary age, by 1955 over 1,000 extra pupils and by 1964, over 2,100 more than in 1946. It should have been possible for the Chief Education Officer to project these figures 15 years ahead, as soon as the 1946–1950 birthrates were registered. Even then, preserving the 25 per cent recruitment to grammar schools would leave a substantial deficiency of places, bearing in mind that all secondary modern schools were already seriously deficient in specialist accommodation in 1946; and that the Education Committee had decided, on the Chief Education Officer's advice, that no extra practical rooms were necessary for the raising of the school leaving age in 1948, and hence had provided none. Migration in and out of the city was not statistically significant. There were, therefore, no spare secondary places in 1949 at all to house the increased number of pupils.[26]

The actual capital programmes approved by the Ministry for the secondary sector in the survey period are given in Appendix E for all three authorities. There was no building programme for secondary schools from 1945 to 1954. Of the total in *Lincoln* of £¾ million for the period 1945–1965, only a small proportion actually provided new places. The early programmes from 1954–1957 provided secondary *replacements* for the old St. Hugh's senior department, and the old Sincil Girls' School and for the dividing of a small and marginally viable old coeducational secondary modern school into two even smaller single-sex modern schools.[27] Not until 1960–62 were even 270 new modern places provided, by extending two existing schools. A relatively small capital sum was spent on increasing the four grammar schools from two- to three-form entry each in order to maintain the 25 per cent level of recruitment but this did not bring the two girls' schools fully up to the standard of the boys' schools, and they still remained deficient in scientific and technical facilities when surveyed in 1968–69.

Figure 7 which follows shows the actual total education capital expenditure; and the secondary school programme, from 1954 to 1965. (No secondary schools were built or extended between 1937 and 1954.) By 1964 there were 1515 more secondary modern pupils under 16 years of age than in 1946. But only a net gain of 270 new places had been provided. The remaining pupils were housed by redeployment of unimproved old buildings or by overcrowding. Of the increased grammar school rolls, most were adequately, though not generously, accommodated. Yet the Ministry had drawn attention to the need to provide extra places in 1955, and the national programmes from 1955–1962 provided nearly three times as many secondary places as primary, in sharp contrast to the early 1950s.[28] In Lincoln, however, all 450 places provided in 1959–1960 were for grammar schools, to maintain the 25 per cent intake, and not until two years after the 1960–62 programme did any new *additional* secondary modern places come into use. By this time the largest age groups resulting from the very high post-war birthrate had in any event worked their way out of the schools, without the benefit of either extra non-selective places, or an extended course except for a handful of pupils who were able to take an academic course by transferring at 15 plus to one of the grammar schools.

It would seem at face value as if the implicit demand from additional numbers was not fully met for the 75 per cent of children who were allocated to non-grammar schools. Resources therefore did not match either the demand created by the extra numbers, or the constant demand from the heads of the non-grammar schools for more and for better accommodation.

It is the more interesting in the light of this, that the Education Committee, advised by the Chief Education Officer, did not in fact ask the Ministry for any major building projects at all either in 1957–58 or in 1958–59, and effectively none in 1959–60, since the minor extensions at South Park High School were for children from the Lindsey county which had no grammar school for girls in the nearby county district. The Minister accordingly awarded no programme at all in 1962–63 although the Committee had revived sufficiently to ask for the replacement of the City Boys' grammar school; and two new secondary modern schools, for girls in the north

FIGURE 7: *Comparison of total capital education expenditure and secondary major building projects—Lincoln*

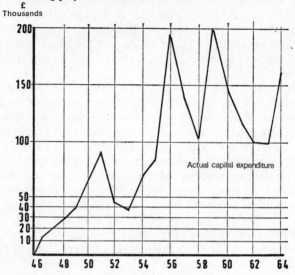

Major building programme allocations secondary schools only

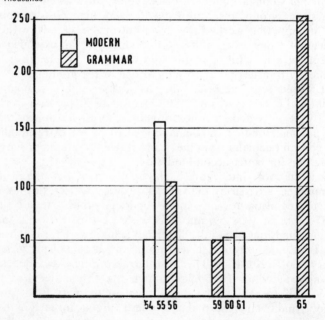

of the City and for boys in the south. Significantly, however, the Deputation which finally saw the Ministry to appeal against the refusal to award any school building programme, was instructed that the first priority must be for the replacement of the City boys' grammar school, which was undoubtedly hampered by totally inadequate 19th century premises and lack of good specialist rooms; as, however, were the six county secondary modern schools.

The subsequent award of the new City grammar school replacement in 1963 for the 1965–66 programme, after the intervention of the Lincoln MP, and the Ministry's concurrent refusal to award the two new secondary modern schools is particularly interesting in that there was at that time in theory, no money for 'improvement' projects, the national programme being limited to places needed without which children would otherwise be out of school. The latter situation in fact then threatened in Lincoln, where the lack of the extra secondary modern places meant that overcrowding was acute. In 1959, two schools had 431 boys and 475 girls in accommodation for 300 each; in 1961, 642 girls in accommodation for 480; 439 girls in places for 300; 409 boys in places for 300. One can only speculate on the pressures which resulted in the Minister's final decision, particularly in the light of events that followed. For by 1965, Lincoln had a new Chief Education Officer and Parliament a new (Labour) government, and building programmes nationally had increased significantly. The new Lincoln Chief Education Officer promptly and successfully negotiated a three-year programme which included the missing extra secondary modern places in both the south and north of the City, and provided the means ultimately to reorganize the schools on non-selective lines by, among other things, providing extra places at the new City grammar school to convert it from a three-form entry grammar to an eight-form entry comprehensive school.

In many authorities, deficiencies in the school major building programme[29] were made good by extra minor works allocations for which the authorities fought. The Ministry's central allocation for these[30] is usually shared out between the local authorities on the basis of £X per 100,000 head of total population and it is left to local authorities to negotiate additions if they can justify them. A county borough of Lincoln's size could probably have expected a basic allocation of £5,000 in the very early years, an annual average of £20,000—£30,000 in the late 1950s and from £60,000—£80,000 by 1965. From time to time between 1951 and 1961, the Ministry declared in principle and in theory that it did not need to approve expenditure on minor works; but in practice the 'freedom' was regularly revoked by instructions to curb capital expenditure and temporary reimpositions of control.

Lincoln spent very little per head of school population throughout the whole period on either minor works, or other minor capital expenditure from revenue, by marked contrast with Nottingham and Northumberland. Annual expenditure for these in the period 1946–1953 rarely exceeded £2,500. (It is not possible to separate expenditure on primary and secondary schools for minor improvements and the figures that follow cover both.) By 1953 the Ministry was asking local education authorities how much they wished to spend (in order to grant loan sanction) and for four years the authority asked for nothing but decided belatedly to spend about £5,000 a year towards the end of each programme year, and in each case underspending the Ministry's allocation by about £2,000. By 1957, the authority had told the Ministry it required no allocation at all (despite termly requests through almost all governing bodies for urgently needed building improvements to both grammar and modern schools). Consequently from 1957–1960 the Ministry made no award at all. In 1960, the committee, surprisingly, asked for an allocation of £12,920 but the Ministry predictably scaled it down (as it is wont to do for authorities that regularly underspend) to an allowance of £5,000. The authority's request for £23,450 for the period 1961–1963 similarly fell on deaf ears and £8,000 only was awarded. No allocations at all followed for 1963; but on appeal the authority was awarded £6,972 of which Lincoln only in fact spent £4,284. The authority sought no allocation for 1964, was awarded £6,500 and only spent £2,572. At this time some other county boroughs of comparable size were spending sums of the order of £30,000—£50,000.

However, in 1964, the new (fourth) Chief Education Officer took over negotiations and in 1965 an allocation of £51,000 (which the authority spent) was followed by allocations of up to £80,000 for succeeding years, which were also fully spent.

By the time the Committee had begun to make realistic bids for minor capital allocations in 1961, it would appear that the Ministry had become conditioned to Lincoln's low level of spending at less than £5,000 a year, and accordingly awarded programmes at that level until the 'credibility' of the authority was re-established in 1964. When one recalls also that each time the local authorities were asked by the Ministry to cut or defer capital expenditure, Lincoln proved more than willing to do so, (e.g. after Circular 209 of (1.11.50) and Circular 298 (23.2.56)) one may speculate whether the Committee and the third Chief Education Officer genuinely saw no needs currently in the schools; or were reluctant to see any increase in rateborne expenditure and therefore held back capital expenditure on which heavy loan charges would be payable. A third theory put forward by both members and officers interviewed wondered whether perhaps either the Education Committee or the Chief Education Officer had fully understood the purpose or the potential use of minor works allocations? Two former Chairmen in fact confirmed that they had had no idea that sums of, for example, £20,000 could have been spent, outside of major programmes, to remodel schools; nor that requests for increased allocations could have been made. This is supported by officers closely concerned with Committee work. It would seem that the absence of an Assistant Education Officer or an administrative officer specifically responsible for and experienced in development and building programmes meant that all work, negotiations and decisions rested at Chief Education Officer level; and that he could see no case to be fought.

Revenue Expenditure and Material Resources

One may perhaps expect that deficiencies in major building programmes which can be partly attributable to factors outside the Education Committee's control (such as central control of capital expenditure) might be offset by increased expenditure where the local education authority has freedom to spend with little central government control; that is revenue expenditure. The level of capitation allowances, expenditure on furniture and equipment, or special allowances for educational experiments and new teaching methods, can increase at whatever rate the local Chief Education Officer the Education Committee and the Council choose. Lincoln's expenditure appeared to be unaffected from outside the Education Department.

Appendix B, tables IV (a) and V give full details of the general rate of growth expenditure on secondary education, Table VI (a) details of the proportion of the budget taken by different elements of expenditure and Tables VII (a) and VIII to X the different rates at which expenditure increased for different aspects of the service. To relate these to the apparent policy of the Education Committee it is necessary to look at a number of aspects of secondary expenditure.

Intractable Expenditure

Some elements of intractable expenditure were lower in Lincoln than elsewhere mainly because of its general conditioning towards low spending. Administrative costs were lower than average, falling in fact from three per cent of the budget in 1946 to 2·3 per cent in 1964. Loan charges (for the complete education capital programme) were below even the county borough average, itself low compared proportionately with, for example, Nottingham:

Table VI (5)

Year	LINCOLN General rate fund loan charges as % of total council revenue expenditure %	Education loan charges as % of total education gross revenue expenditure %
1947	5·1	3·1
1954	4·2	4·3
1959	6·35	5·8
1963	7·7	5·7

Table VI (a) of Appendix B gives a more detailed breakdown of expenditure. Most of the teachers' salaries were intractable and the standard of maintenance and furniture and equipment were kept to the irreducible minimum.[31] From 80—85 per cent of the secondary budget was accounted for by teachers' salaries, maintenance, furniture and educational materials. If an appropriate proportion of the three per cent of administrative costs, five per cent loan charges and such items as transport, fuel light and cleaning etc. are added, it is evident that the real margin for innovation and improvement is very small indeed.

The Grammar/Modern Differential

Detailed reference has been made in chapter II to the sharp differential operating in favour of the grammar school pupils and against the modern schools. This was especially relevant when assessing the effect of price rises on what was in real terms a diminishing budget. For in some years some secondary grammar and secondary modern costs in Lincoln in fact fell both in proportion and in actual terms. For example, Table X in Appendix B, shows that teachers' salaries in modern schools rose by 19·1 per cent from 1950 to 1951, but the cost per pupil rose only very marginally. Therefore some other costs must have been *cut* to pay for the rise in teachers' salaries.

Explicit Demand

Two outside sources of pressure were potential sources of influence. The AEC and Publishers Association on the one hand were concerned to persuade local authorities to increase school allowances because of rising prices for books and apparatus; and some teachers' associations had strong views on standards in schools, both material and financial. Table VII (a) of Appendix B gives full details of rising expenditure on educational furniture and apparatus. But the increases barely kept pace with rising numbers, and in some years expenditure was actually *cut* (1956, for example). The implicit demand of rising prices and the explicit pressure from the AEC and Publishers' Association had no traceable effect in Lincoln.

For within this period there were substantial price rises which meant that allowances ought to have risen by similar percentages if they were even to retain their former purchasing power. And it must be recalled that the late 1940s were poor years on which to base negotiations for necessary increases, because of the inheritance of the war years and the rationing, especially of paper and books. The Chief Education Officer reminded the Ministry on 1 April 1949 for example that 'we are very short of furniture. There has been practically none obtained for nearly ten years and with the increased birthrate we must have more'.

Typical examples of some price rises follow. If these are related to the actual expenditure on books and stationery over the years as set out in Table VII (a) in Appendix B it will be seen that expenditure actually *fell* in real terms in some years, as rising numbers in school were matched by rising prices. In 1950, paper costs rose by 15 per cent, and all paper goods from E. J. Arnold rose in price by $7\frac{1}{2}$ per cent from 1 July 1950.[32] In 1951, the Publishers Association was so concerned as to write to all authorities. The cost of paper had doubled in 18 months and was then six times the level of pre-war prices. To provide the same quantity of books in 1952–53 as in 1951–52 would mean increasing book allowances by one-third. The Lincoln authority asked the Chief Education Officer to look at the situation and hold a meeting of head teachers 'to discuss whether it is possible to effect economies in this direction'.[33]

At the same time, paper costs went up by a further 25 per cent from 2 April 1951, although they were later cut by 10 per cent on 1 November 1952.[34] They continued to rise, other recorded increases being five per cent in 1955, and 15 per cent in the cost of new books in 1956. There are no parallel records available of price rises in costs of equipment; but since the cost of steel and refined metals rose sharply in the early 1950s, one may assume that equipment for science and handicraft in particular became regularly more expensive.

From the mid 1950s onwards, costs rose steadily. But expenditure on educational materials increased no faster than the proportionate rise in rolls, and moreover expenditure on books, stationery and apparatus had dropped by nearly half, as a proportion of the total budget—see table VI (a) of Appendix B. It had therefore *decreased* in real terms:

Table VI (6)

YEAR	SECONDARY SCHOOL ROLLS	% INCREASES	FURNITURE AND EQUIPMENT £	% INCREASE	BOOKS STATIONERY APPARATUS £	% INCREASE
1949	3328	—	2,815	—	11,126	—
1959	5316	+59·7	4,315	+53·3	17,636	+58·5
1962	5228	— 1·6	7,968	+84·7	17,463	— 1·0

(extracted from table VII (a) in Appendix B)

There is indeed another source of evidence which supports this—that of the teachers' organizations. The following section suggests that their influence was less than one might have expected but that pressure both for more resources and for a different allocation, met with little practical success until after 1964.

Explicit demand from teachers

The active associations in Lincoln within the survey period were the National Union of Teachers, the Joint Four Secondary Associations and the Association of Head Teachers. They worked on the whole entirely independently of each other, and this in some measure probably weakened their position.

It proved possible to interview representatives of all three associations, including two former secretaries of the AHT (from secondary modern schools), a former secretary of the Joint Four, and the long-serving secretary of the NUT who was also the teacher representative on the Education Committee. The following is based on records of the Education Committee, interviews with Council members and officers, interviews with members of the teachers' associations and evidence based on the records of the teachers' associations available to those interviewed.

The *National Union of Teachers* can perhaps claim the most significant contribution. The third Chief Education Officer's policy had been only to consult the NUT on legal matters, and to seek occasional observations from the head teachers as a group (but not as a union) on matters of policy. It was, moreover, practice from 1948 to 1964 to call meetings of heads of the selective and non-selective schools, separately. While the local Association of Head Teachers concentrated its pressure on the need to reconstitute the Joint Consultative Committee, the NUT consistently fought for representation of teachers on the Education Committee. There is general agreement that NUT pressure before 1959 (when the first teacher representative took his place on the Education Committee) was wholly ineffective, the two questions at issue being pressure for an increase in capitation allowances and for the establishment of head of department posts in the non-grammar schools after 1956 (which the authority had discretion to award; but was not so obliged).

In 1959, Lincoln was second to lowest among county boroughs in the national average costs per pupil, and in particular for capitation allowances, and for furniture and equipment. The teacher representative appointed to the Education Committee was appointed specifically as a representative of the NUT, a position apparently accepted by the other unions, and his first remit from the union was to press the Committee for a substantial increase in school capitation allowances and for an improvement in the allocation, which at that time gave secondary modern schools less than half, for each pupil, of the grammar school rate. The Committee and later the Chief Education Officer countered the argument that Lincoln's spending was low, by suggesting that some expenditure was met from capital account. The audited accounts of the Corporation however show no evidence of this at all, and there would seem a firm case that Lincoln's allowances were in fact well below average. The Association of Head Teachers joined the NUT in 1962 in reminding the Chief Education Officer that the published figures of the IMTA for 1961 showed that Lincoln was still second to bottom among County boroughs, and asked that the Joint Consultative Committee be recalled to consider this. The Chief Education Officer refused to agree.

After a considerable battle, the Chief Education Officer finally agreed in 1963, his last year of service, to produce a new scheme of capitation allowances based on the 'reasonable' allowances recommended by the Association of Education Committees. His successor in 1964 was quick to review the whole scheme, and promptly recommended a considerably improved scale to the Education Committee which also removed the inequality between selective and non-grammar schools to the extent that it was based on a common 'rate for age'.

The other important issue raised by the NUT was the unwillingness of the authority to use discretionary powers under the 1956 Burnham report to establish head of department posts in secondary modern schools. It was of course predictable that as long as the Chief Education Officer and the Education Committee opposed any form of extended course or V-form development in the non-selective schools, they should fail to see a need for these posts there.[35]

The Joint Consultative Committee was reconvened specifically to discuss the 1956 Burnham report, and the teachers' representatives from the secondary modern schools argued strongly for new head of department allowances at secondary modern schools,[36] but the Chief Education Officer advised the Committee not to agree, 'especially since opinions among teacher representatives were clearly divided' (the Joint Four opposed the idea). The Committee even refused to use its discretion to award graded posts in Group III schools. The Burnham Salaries Committee of the Education Committee on 22 January 1957 confirmed that the authority would not agree to the new head of department posts and moreover refused to use the discretionary power to increase existing special allowances for women teachers to the men's level, insisting on adjusting allowances over a seven-year period.

After intermittent pressure, the contest was renewed when the 1961 Burnham report was published. It was again left to the teachers, in this case the secretary of the NAS and the local AHT to renew pressure for head of department posts in secondary modern schools. The teachers pointed out dryly that as a neighbouring authority had already done this, Lincoln was losing a steady stream of teachers to new schools over the county boundary. The Committee deferred the matter several times, until the NUT pressed in June 1961 at a full meeting of the Education Committee that Lincoln was the only authority (out of five) in Lincolnshire not to award the new allowances. In July the NAS sent a further lengthy written case to the Finance and General Purposes Committee, which, however, again deferred the whole matter.

Early in 1962, national guidance from the AEC, together with ceaseless pressure from the local head teachers and unions, persuaded the Education Committee to make the minimum award in 1962. The new Chief Education Officer however in 1964 submitted a revised scheme nine months after his appointment which radically improved the position in all secondary modern schools.

Meanwhile, a regular series of appeals from head teachers and governors either for additional posts or for upgrading of existing posts in *grammar schools*, had met with consistent success.

The local Joint Four secondary associations took a rather different attitude on the role that they should play. (See chapter III for the policy of the national unions.) It is true that in 1945 the Joint Four pressed unsuccessfully for a grammar school representative on the Education Committee in the light of the new Act; but thereafter they disassociated themselves from later NUT pressure for teacher representation. Evidence from officers of the Joint Four[37] confirms the consistent opposition from these associations to any extension of special courses in the non-grammar schools, and to any joint discussions with the NUT on the application of the 1956 and 1961

Burnham reports. Evidence from assistant teachers suggests that some would have supported a general campaign for better capitation allowances, but were dissuaded by the secretary of the Joint Four on the grounds that 'the local education authority could be trusted'. In fact, the Joint Four held no formal meetings at all between 1949 and 1956 when the reconstitution of the Joint Consultative Committee was discussed, and none between 1956 and 1961 when again the major issue was the new Burnham report.

In 1963, the new secretary raised the matter of the 'unconstitutional actions of the Lincoln JCC on Education'. It was agreed 'that further action should be postponed till next year when the new Chief Education Officer would be in office'.[38] In 1964, a new spirit took root, and it was agreed that joint meetings with other unions should take place (for the first time) about the proposed reorganization of schools to encourage 'an exchange of viewpoints among teachers with experience in different types of school'.

Evidence from senior officers of all three unions, (the NUT, AHT and Joint Four) confirmed that after years of pressure, head teachers and union secretaries tended to give up an unequal battle, and to tailor their demands to what they thought either the Chief Education Officer or the Committee would concede, and not what they thought really desirable. 'It was a vicious circle of discouragement leading to inaction leading to falling standards leading in turn to depressed discouragement.'[39] 'We were so short of basic equipment, we were almost starved of books. . . . We were used to the inevitability of the habit of a lifetime.'[40]

Asked to account for their lack of success, most of those interviewed quoted the faith of the Committee in the Chief Education Officer, and the strength of his clearly defined view of secondary education albeit opposed to that of many teachers; the lack of mobility of staff, who had no outside yardstick by which to measure standards; and the absence of outside middle-class pressure groups.

Outside pressures

The birth of specific voluntary (i.e. non-professional) groups whose purpose is to exert pressure on local and national education departments is relatively recent. In 1960, the Advisory Centre for Education (ACE) was established as an offshoot of the Consumers' Association with similar functions, and *Where*, an educational magazine not dissimilar to *Which?* was established for parents and for the general public. The avowed aims of ACE were to press for 'equality of educational opportunity at all levels' and for improved standards in education. In 1961, the first Association for the Advancement of State Education was formed in Cambridge, originally initiated by a group of parents involved in a difficult dispute over a local school, but quickly taking on wider functions. By 1967 there were over 100 such associations throughout the country, all affiliated to a central body, the Confederation for the Advancement of State Education. These organizations tend to be centred in urban areas and to be organized by middle-class parents. By 1967, CASE estimated a membership of between 5000 and 8000 members[41] and had formed a national policy in favour of comprehensive education. The Comprehensive Schools Committee became active in 1965, and its opposite, the National Educational Association (committed to preserving grammar schools) although dating from 20 years back, revived, claiming to number 300 individual members by 1967[42] with between 10,000 and 20,000 affiliated through parents' committees and old pupils' associations.

An attempt was made in the early 1960s to establish a branch of the Confederation for the Advancement of State Education in Lincoln. The initiative came from a member of the Education Committee who was also a governor of a secondary school. The lack of support (fewer than 20 people with a serious interest) meant that the group did not reach the stage of a formal constitution (by sharp contrast with branches in some areas of South Eastern England such as Richmond-on-Thames and Wimbledon whose membership numbers hundreds). Of the 20, most were already involved in some other group such as political parties or teachers' organizations.

The potential founder attributed the lack of interest to three factors. First, the lack of a real middle-class with a tradition of involvement in education. (The small and shortlived Fabian group, now defunct, worked very much as an 'in' intellectual group and had no dynamic or functional relationship with other groups, social or industrial, in the City.) Second, a local 'complacency' that Lincoln standards were good, born (it is suggested) of geographical isolation and lack of interchange with other areas. Third, a long tradition of pride in the grammar schools (which were without question as good as most) and concurrent lack of interest in other secondary schools, going back to pre-war days. It was also suggested, and evidence from others would support this, that the only successful organized groups in Lincoln were the political parties, not because issues were in fact necessarily political but because the parties had a ready organization, standing committees and the involvement of lively local people as it were, ready made, without the need to think out new aims and methods of organization.

Industry
Similarly, there appears to have been little or no influence on

educational services from the established industries of the city. Yet industry has, or should have, a large stake in the development of educational services, partly because of the need for the content of secondary school curricula adequately to equip school leavers either to become immediately competent in employment, or to profit from training for skilled work. Partly also because, about two-thirds of secondary modern school leavers will insist on staying within ten or 20 miles of home, and even the more able school leavers prefer to stay in their home region. The local pattern of industry and in particular, changes of emphasis in industrial techniques, training opportunities and minimum requirements for recruitment may therefore have a marked effect on local secondary education.

Lincoln had only one representative from industry on its Education Committee, a director from the largest engineering firm in the city. Officers and members of the Committee interviewed in 1969, described him as predominantly preoccupied with the able boy, (Lincoln appeared to regard girl school leavers as inexorably destined for shops and offices) and concerned with the graduate entry to engineering, rather than the 40—70 per cent of boy leavers (depending on the school) who entered the industry as apprentices or at semi-skilled level. His main contribution appears to have been to attempt to restrict apprenticeships to grammar school leavers[43] and to support employers in demanding that preference be given to 16-year-old leavers with successful results in the examinations of the East Midlands Examination Board.[44] But both the industrial representative and the Chief Education Officer refused to allow the secondary modern schools to present boys for these examinations when repeated requests for this reached the Education Committee.

Reference has been made to the very limited industrial representation on the Education Committee. School governing bodies were similarly unassailed by industrial interest. Two-thirds were local councillors, the remainder nominated from names approved by the Education Committee. Moreover, the influence of governors seems strictly limited in practice.

Explicit demand from governors

In theory, governing bodies were responsible for the annual estimates of their schools, for staffing, for approval of special items of expenditure, and for the general management of the school. In practice all these matters are handled by head teachers and by officers of the authority. Resolutions of governing bodies are however considered by the Education Committee (or by an appropriate sub-committee) and important requests from head teachers will usually be accompanied by a supporting resolution of the governors. The foregoing sections account for substantial rises in expenditure from factors often beyond the control of the authority. The effect which governors can have on estimates must therefore be mainly limited to pressing for special increases in staff or allowances over and above the necessary ones needed because of salary increases or rising numbers. Did they press for improvement, and was it effective?

Three main comments were made by almost all officers, head teachers and Committee members interviewed. First, that governors were not aware of conditions in schools, because they rarely if ever visited. Second, that when they did support a head teacher, their views were not seriously considered and their pressure was ineffective. Third, that governing bodies in Lincoln, whether of grammar or of modern schools, were not used by the Chief Education Officer or by the Committee for discussion of any matters of major policy affecting secondary schools.[45]

Reports of the governors of the grammar schools seem preoccupied with records of school leavers going on to higher education and with requests for regular upgrading of senior members of staff (very rarely for the establishment of new posts). Each of the four grammar schools had its own governing body. The single governing body for the six county secondary modern schools expressed itself firmly on a number of topics over the years of which the three most constant were the serious need for extra accommodation especially for specialist subjects, opportunities for more able pupils to follow courses leading to GCE, prenursing and preapprenticeship qualifications, and additional opportunities for further education. The governors' resolutions appear to have had no effect whatsoever except in so far as the Education Committee accepted the need for further opportunities for girls from secondary modern schools to study for the minimum qualifications for a nursing career. The Committee however insisted on providing them at the Technical College and the girls' county grammar school. Occasionally governors would protest at lack of suitable staff—a girls' school had no scientist in 1953, a boys' school no metalwork master for eight years—but it is interesting that there is no record of the major battle over the establishment of head of department posts, in the minutes of the secondary modern school governors.

The effect of the governors' annual discussion of school estimates appears to have been negligible. About 70 per cent of the direct expenditure with which they were (notionally) concerned was in any event voted to teachers' salaries, and there is no evidence of pressure for more or for different types of teachers, except in the case of grammar schools where occasional upgradings of teaching staff were requested. There was before 1964 no clearly defined scheme for capitation allowances and much local evidence suggests that this was deliberate policy on the part of the third Chief Education Officer. It is therefore difficult to quantify true demand with curricular supply since the heads worked to a depressed unknown level. There is no evidence in Committee minutes of pressure from governors on capitation allowances, which is the more surprising in the light of evidence from the teachers' unions on a long-standing battle between teachers on the one hand and the Chief Education Officer and Education Committee on the other.

During the structured interviews of all head teachers, officers and committee members, a number of questions were put, on the role of governors. Were they effective? If the answers were to be yes, what did effective mean in the context of Lincoln City? Were any decisions altered because of pressure from governors? Did governors succeed in improving staffing of schools, equipment allowances or annual estimates? Where governors had passed a resolution, would the Chief Education Officer or Committee have taken the required step without any request from governors? Did governors initiate any major policy?

The answers may be briefly summarized, with considerable unanimity of evidence. Governors were considered to be generally ineffective and time-consuming. They had no effect on estimates, staffing or equipment allowances. No Committee or Sub-Committee appeared to alter a decision or concede a governor's request if it clashed with Committee policy. If it did not so clash, the head teachers' request would have been granted anyway without the support of the governors. No record exists of governors disagreeing with a head. No matters of major policy even reached the governors before 1965.

The two Chief Education Officers were agreed on the general ineffectiveness of governors as makers of decisions or influences on resource allocation. Senior officers considered that a strong head with weak governors could do more than a weak head with a lively governing body since the key relationship, it was suggested, was that between the head and the administrators.

Members of the Education Committee interviewed were also candid that resolutions of governing bodies would not be likely to alter Committee policy. One former Chairman considered they were a useful moral and social support for a school and three former members considered governors did not know either the conditions in schools or the needs of the schools partly because they never visited schools and partly, it was claimed, because heads were diffident to complain to governors, when they were sure in advance that it was useless to do so.

The teacher member of the Education Committee (representing the NUT) agreed that governors had had no decisive role in Lincoln, but felt that their social and supportive work for a school in its locality was more marked when schools had their own governing bodies. As long as the six modern schools had one governing body he claimed the governors' reports made no impact. When in the 1960s, each pair of local schools was given its own governors, their comments made more impact on the Committee. He nevertheless could not remember any occasion when a decision had been altered or additional resources allocated, because of any intervention of governors.

Head teachers and heads of departments

All but two head teachers considered that they had not fought as hard for improved resources as they might, and that the cumulative effect of constant refusal of requests for extended courses, for extra specialist rooms, for higher capitation allowances and for new books, led them to cease 'to waste energy fighting the inevitable' to quote one headmaster. Two considered they had fought unceasingly—the only two to be recruited from outside the City. One, a headmistress, increased her school's estimates by 20 per cent in her first year, doubled her school allowance for three subjects, and started a GCE course and the teaching of French in the secondary modern school in defiance of the Chief Education Officer. She attributed her success to her experience elsewhere in the country, and the yardstick it gave her for arguments based on an outside standard.

Within the schools—grammar and modern alike—every head admitted to allocating school allowances according to the degree of demand from each department. A strong head of department could fairly easily obtain a proportionately higher allocation than he or she might normally expect, when discriminating pressure was exerted on the head. The latter usually justified this on the grounds that it is sound to invest more money in good enthusiastic staff. Different heads accounted thus, for example, for the markedly better technical facilities in one boys' school, the significantly better art rooms in a girls' school, the possession of good geography rooms and equipment in a third, and so on, in schools that were otherwise fairly poorly equipped. All but two of the Lincoln schools were organized internally on mainly 'authoritarian' as distinct from 'democratic' lines, in that lines of communication and demand within the schools went direct from head to head of department or class teacher.

All heads—grammar and modern alike—volunteered without prompting that the constant refusal of the Chief Education Officer and the Committee to provide new accommodation and other than the minimum of capitation allowances and equipment, depressed the general level of demand. Comments ranged from 'Even our books were thirty years old—we gave up asking for equipment like projectors' to 'The new regime in 1964 was like a breath of fresh air through a clogged system'. In the period 1964 to 1967, all schools were encouraged to develop CSE, to purchase film projectors and tape recorders, to prepare proposals for pupil-centred science courses. The level of demand nearly doubled, with substantial success in the award of extra resources.

What appeared totally absent, was an objective assessment of the use of resources in relation to priorities in curricular development. Nor is there any trace until after 1964, either in schools or in committee records, of a conscious measurement of standards attained over a period of years; even by the crude index of, for example, examination results against national averages, or of standards of literacy at 13+ or of the destination of school leavers. The key question, in planning terms, of the Chief Education Officer's or Committee's conception of an ideal or viable size of school for optimum use of limited resources, appears nowhere as a matter for an educational debate, in the committee or departmental records. Yet these are matters closely to be considered at times of financial stringency and of educational reforms.

The supply of teaching staff has been deliberately omitted from the three chapters on the local areas, being dealt with in full in Chapter IX.

Conclusion

The pattern in Lincoln over the 20-year period is consistent. First, as a poor authority with a low level of spending in the base year of 1945, it seems a clear example of lack of resources depressing demand. This was evident both in the schools and in the education department. There is only slender evidence until 1964 of dynamic demand releasing or reallocating resources. After 1964, demand (from a new Chief Education Officer, encouraging demand in turn from head teachers) very substantially altered the pattern of resource allocation as well as the level of resources awarded by the Department of Education and Science (capital) and by the local authority (revenue). Group tactics, whether in committees, in and between schools, or from outside pressure groups, played little part. And neither explicit nor implicit demands were fully met in the survey period.

Lincoln's flow chart would be a very simple one for the period 1945–1964 uninfluenced by outside demand. That is:

Education Committee

↓

Chief Education Officer

↓

School

↓

Head of Department

For there was no decisive influence at sub-Committee level, nor from assistant education officers nor inspectors. Demand from teachers' unions, the teachers' consultative committee and the governors could be traced; but was not effective. Demand from industry, pressure groups and parents was untraceable. The reports of national consultative committees seem to have made no impact[46] and the AEC recommendations on equipment allowances were only very belatedly followed.

Chapter III outlines the Committee structure of the Lincoln Authority. It is probable that had there been, as elsewhere, a Sites and Buildings Sub-Committee and a Secondary Education Sub-Committee the development of secondary education would not have remained as static as it did; nor would the authority have underused its capital programme for so long. For as will be seen in the two other survey areas, a group of lay members identified with a special sphere of activity can stimulate discussion, call for regular reports and act as a pressure point (of elected members) both in Council and at national level.

The individual influence of Council members on the other hand did seem decisive. Evidence from all officers interviewed, from Council members and from four teachers' organizations combines to confirm the picture of personal influence which emerges from the events outlined in chapters III, IV and VI and the role of leading Committee members.

Controls from central government were not as strong a factor as in the other two survey areas since the authority tended to under-bid for capital resources.

On the other hand the fact that the city was poor (as explained in Chapter IV) appeared to have a generally depressing effect. A decisive influence was the concern of the City Council's Finance Committee to hold the rate level as low as possible (see Chapter IV and Appendix C) despite inevitably rising expenditure as basic costs rose. The whole service appeared conditioned towards economy and minimum cost—in itself not necessarily unwise, provided however that it is an attitude measured stringently against an identifiable and defensible minimum standard, which is related to assessed (and changing) needs.

But in the event, standards, some of which were mentioned in earlier chapters, were met by neither an appropriate level nor method of allocation of resources. To take certain, admittedly crude, indices of standards, for example the level of grammar school places, Lincoln will be regarded as successful in that from 1945–65 it provided advanced academic education for 25 per cent of the 11 + age group, well above the national average, with a further one per cent or so transferring to grammar schools at 15 +. On the other hand it must have been one of very few authorities to provide no facilities at all for the remaining 75 per cent to follow an extended course in technical education; or to take external examinations (until after 1964); or to provide only a basic common-core curriculum.

While the allocation of the building programme enabled the authority to provide additional advanced academic (grammar) places as the need gradually increased, new secondary modern places followed, did not precede, need in terms of rising school rolls. The growing national demand for increased Vth form places was met only by the one per cent entry to grammar schools at 15 +. The hypothesis that implicit demand from rising numbers, curricular developments, and national influences in educational policy had an effect on resources in Lincoln, is only partly valid. Extra capital and revenue expenditure were certainly disbursed to cater for the additional pupils, but largely at the expense of, not in addition to, the additional allocations that should normally have been made for curricular development, improvement of material standards from the poor base-line of the 1940s, and increased provision for older pupils. And the general level of capital expenditure was low by national standards. Finally, the non-grammar schools did not achieve the promised 'parity of esteem', by whatever criteria one may assess this.

Explicit demand was no more successful in altering policy. The preceding sections show that outside pressure groups (like AASE) did not exist; that industrial influence was tenuous; that pressure from teachers (both individually and collectively) was largely ineffective with only partial influence even on the capitation issue; and that governors while a useful moral and social support had no influence on the development of the pattern of secondary education or on the direct allocation of resources.

Overriding all, however, was the decisive influence of each Chief Education Officer in post. Despite the conditioned approach of the

1945 Labour Council ('a grammar school place for every child'), the earlier (second) Chief Education Officer (before 1948) with a teaching background of elementary schools, had injected into the draft Development Plan, proposals sympathetic to the needs of the less able. These were reversed by the third Chief Education Officer in 1948 who successfully also resisted the influence of the newer Labour Council of the late 1950s for the reorganization of secondary education on non-selective lines and for the development of the non-selective schools, until his successor took office in 1964. The absence of any significant supportive staff below Chief Education Officer level before 1964 other than for primary and special education, effectively removed any remaining chance of counter-influence or longterm planning by other educationalists within the department who might have identified with a particular branch of the service—in this case secondary education.

The schools survey is dealt with in chapter X and school leaver destinations in chapter XI. The next chapter looks in turn at events in Nottingham, only 40 miles distant but very different from Lincoln.

Notes

1   *The History of Lincoln,* printed by A. Stark, for E. Baron, Bookseller at Lincoln, 20 April 1810. pp.259–261.
2   Lincoln, Annual Report 1946, p.5.
3   Interviews, February and June 1969.
4   and 5 Interviews, (10.2.69) and (3.6.69).
6   Lincoln, Finance and General Purposes Committee (28.4.47).
7   Lincoln, Annual report 1949, p.5.
8   Interviewed (25.5.69).
9   Interviews in 1969 with two former Chairmen of the Education Committee, three former councillors, and two coopted members. Evidence is unanimous on this point also from officers interviewed in 1969.
10 Confirmed in interviews in 1969 with two Chairmen of the Education Committee, and with officers handling committee work.
11 There is unanimity on this in evidence from both officers and members of the Committee, and from the new Chief Education Officer appointed in 1964 to whom his predecessor confirmed his opposition to both proposals.
12 Evidence from a representative of the Joint Four in 1969.
13 Interviews held on (10.10.68) (11.10.68) (4.2.69) (5.2.69) (5.6.69) and (9.6.69).
14 Lincoln, Annual reports 1947, p.4 and 1948, p.4.
15 Governors (22.4.47) and (23.4.47).
16 Governors (25.11.49).
17 Governors (26.2.51). It will be evident that the quality as well as the quantity of secondary education must have been at risk despite valiant attempts by teaching staff to compensate for the restrictive conditions.
18 A report in 1962. Four other schools were in a similar condition.
19 Lincoln, Education Committee (12.5.53) and (14.12.54).
20 Governors (12.7.56).
21 Governors (16.1.58) and (9.7.58).

22 Governors (8.7.59).
23 Interviews (5.6.69) and (9.6.69).
24 Lincoln, Finance and General Purposes Committee (16.7.62).
25 Evidence concerning this general progress was given by both members of the Education Committee and by senior officers of the department.
26 See chapter V for the national building programme demands.
27 which released accommodation for Sincil Boys' School which had been overcrowded by 30 per cent or more until the girls' school was replaced and its accommodation reallocated.
28 In 1951–52 22,000 out of 69,000 new places in England and Wales were secondary; in 1955–56 187,000 out of 262,000. *Education in England and Wales,* Ministry of Education. HMSO 1955.
29 a project becomes 'major' over a given cost fixed by the Ministry, £10,000 in the early years, £20,000 in the late 1950s, £30,000 in the late 1960s and now (1974) £45,000. As usual, the award of an allocation is in fact permission to spend an LEAs own money.
30 see the table at the end of Chapter V for details of national allocations from 1946–1964.
31 Officers, head teachers and committee members were agreed on this on interview in 1968; and the writer's survey of schools confirmed this assessment.
32 Lincoln, Finance and General Purposes Committee (28.6.50).
33 Lincoln, Finance and General Purposes Committee (30.10.51). This continuing policy no doubt accounted for the girls school whose library in 1968 held large stocks of books dated 'Pupil Centre 1927'.
34 Lincoln, Finance and General Purposes Committee (23.4.51) and (30.9.52).
35 at that time the criteria for head of department allowances were more rigidly related to 'academic' responsibility than in later Burnham reports— see chapter IX.
36 Minutes of JCC (19.10.56).
37 interviewed in June 1969 and on 17 November 1969.
38 Records of the Lincoln Joint Four Associations.
39 Interview (6.2.69).
40 Interview (6.2.69).
41 The Times, (24.1.67).
42 Ibid.
43 Interview with a senior officer of the Education Department (10.2.69) and with two Education Committee members (5.6.59) and (3.6.59).
44 Ditto.
45 see also Table D (vii) in Appendix D, illustrating that most head teachers considered governors ineffective.
46 Certainly neither the Crowther nor Newsom reports had any measurable effect before 1964.

CHAPTER VII

The Development of Secondary Education in Nottingham

'We have built a house that is not for time's throwing.'

Rupert Brooke

Readers will recall that Nottingham is about four times the size of Lincoln, that unlike Lincoln it had a School Board in the 19th century and that its administrative structure in 1945 was already quite well developed. It was an industrially wealthy city with no need for substantial Exchequer Equalization or Rate Deficiency grants for most of the survey period. As a willing spender, the City received, however, a high level of grant under the percentage grant system.

The Post-war Inheritance

In 1945 the city inherited a legacy of secondary modern and senior schools which were the result of the energetic policy of the pre-war Director of Education who started the reorganization of all-age schools in fact before the Hadow report of 1926. By 1939 all county schools in Nottingham were already reorganized, and the authority had used the building grants of the 1930s lavishly to build new secondary modern schools. In 1945 the city had, however, too few grammar school places, offering only 12 per cent of the 11+ age group a selective place, including places taken at the two direct grant and independent High Schools. The authority established at the outset of its planning of post-war reconstruction, that two main aims were the establishment of more grammar school places[1] and the expansion of secondary technical education in some form.

'One of the most important tasks confronting the Committee is to decide on the number and type of the more specialized schools.'[2]

It is difficult to set the grammar school position against a coherent national pattern at that time. The Ministry of Education's circular 73 of 1945–46 suggested that under normal conditions 25—30 per cent of the age group should be in grammar or technical schools and 70—75 per cent in modern schools. The Spens Committee in 1938 had suggested that 15 per cent of the age group would benefit from selective education. On the other hand, the Ministry of Education in

The Nation's Schools in 1944 had suggested that no further expansion of grammar school courses would be justified for the country as a whole and that some authorities might even reduce their provision. Since the grammar school percentage throughout the country varied then from about eight per cent to nearly 30 per cent of the age group the generalization appears of doubtful use.

It is interesting to note that, unlike the position today—especially in the South-East—when parents of most social backgrounds appear to be vociferous in expressing views and demands, Nottingham parents in 1945 appeared to play no part in pressing for their children's rights to immediate equality of educational opportunity in the wake of the new Act of 1944. So far from the parents fighting for an increase in the 12 per cent of selective places in the city, many did not take up those places which were offered. In 1944 for example only 91·6 per cent of boys and only 80·9 per cent of girls who were offered grammar school places, accepted them. A year later, 92 per cent of boys and 84·5 per cent of girls offered selective places accepted them. From then until 1956, when the bilateral system was introduced, about 10·0 per cent of both boys and girls offered grammar school places refused them, while the level of available provision increased only slowly from 12 to about 15 per cent in competition with a steadily rising school population. It would not appear on the evidence that parental demand significantly exceeded supply.[3]

Aims and Policy

As well as the expansion of grammar and technical education, the authority declared as a major aim in 1945 that for the former elementary, now secondary, schools:

'It is a matter of supreme importance that these new secondary schools should be given as soon as possible the same standards of staffing, buildings, equipment and general amenities as those enjoyed by the old established secondary schools and that they should be afforded every opportunity to develop courses of study suited to the ability and aptitude of their pupils.'[4]

The corollary to this of course was massive diversion of resources for levelling up old non-grammar schools.

The Development Plan

The influence of the two post-war Directors, of other sources of pressure or demand, and the actual pattern of capital and revenue expenditure and distribution of resources, should be seen against the main developments in secondary education over the 20-year period. In 1945 there were three grammar schools housing about

2200 pupils, with a further 11,730 pupils on the roll of 31 other secondary schools, including the three technical schools for art, building and for the textile trades opened in 1941, 1942 and 1944 respectively. Together the latter accounted for about a three-form entry each year.

As a deliberate act of faith (unlike the Lincoln authority) Nottingham grouped its secondary schools in governing bodies covering from five to eight schools and in such a way that each group included a grammar or technical school as well as several modern schools. The Education Committee had already agreed that all post-primary schools must have the same standards of buildings, playing fields, equipment and staffing under the same code of regulations[5], but the Government White Paper on Post-war Reconstruction had also warned that the rate of educational development would depend on 'the financial resources available having regard to our existing commitments, to the claims which we may have to meet and to such orders of priority as may have to be laid down'[6] which led the Director to comment dryly that 'there is an ominous and all too familiar ring about these phrases which gives cause for some anxiety'.[7]

The Ministry pressed the authority to submit its development plan by 1946, when the Director advised his Committee that the Nottingham non-selective schools could be developed to offer special courses including engineering, commerce and other technical studies, and that there was considerable demand from industries in the city for these. The plan as submitted provided for reorganization of non-selective schools as bilateral schools, the replacement of old inner town schools by new schools in the outer districts related to proposed new housing estates, and for rapid expansion of grammar school provision.

Viable Schools

It will be seen from the tables in Appendix D that in all three authorities, the Development plans had been based on small schools, in the case of modern schools mostly three-form (450 pupils) or four-form entry (600 pupils). Lincoln's plan was largely a rationaliza-ation of the inherited position. In Nottingham, the Director and the Committee decided that in their view, schools of about 600 were viable and accordingly their plan was deliberately so designed.

'It has been pointed out to the Ministry that the great majority of the new secondary schools in the City are large schools accom-modating about 500 pupils, that they will become larger with the raising of the compulsory school age and that there is therefore the opportunity of organizing in each one of them more than one course of a technical or practical type . . .'[8]

Most of the schools in the plan were designed for from 420 to 680 pupils, and if this seems small by modern standards, it must be remembered that even by 1947, the considerable majority of schools in England and Wales had in fact less than 401 pupils on roll.[9]

This makes even more interesting the issue of circular 144 of the Ministry of Education (16.6.47) stating as a principle, among other matters, that any school which was to become bilateral must be at least nine-form entry (1350 pupils); since clearly the corollary of this in relation to the many development plans which were then suggesting bilateral or multilateral school organization, would be a massive building programme to enlarge many of the 2765 secondary modern schools with less than 401 pupils, or to build additional new nine-form entry schools. However, the Ministry was already aware in 1947 that a policy of roofs over heads of the new 15-year-old pupils, was as much as could be expected for several years and that massive building programmes could not be guaranteed—as Chapter V has illustrated.

Nottingham, however, remained adamant that it rejected any tripartite organization

'as tending, almost inevitably, to placing the modern school in a position of inferiority in public esteem'[10]

and even more firmly rejected the concept of large schools as undesirable and, from the aspect of site acquisition, impracticable.[11] The Director, backed by his Committee, also flatly and somewhat pertinently refused even to attempt to define a timetable for the implementation of the plan on the grounds that:

'I am to point out that the Ministry have as yet given no indication of the year when local education authorities will be allowed to proceed with building schemes.'[12]

The authority was quickly developing a considerable independence of spirit which served it well in the forthcoming vicissitudes of negotiations on crucial building programmes. The Development Plan was finally approved based on proposals for bilateral schools of 600–700 pupils only.

The authority had conformed to Ministry guidance and had consulted the Church authorities on draft proposals in the context of the Development Plan put forward by the Diocesan authorities. Nottingham, as historians will recall, was one of the towns which in the early days of the 19th century phase of the industrial revolution, hit the nadir of utter poverty, figuring pejoratively in a number of reports by national commissions on social conditions. Partly for this reason, early development of schools and of an education system by the Church had failed to gain any ground in the City, which had therefore a weak history and tradition of church education and few church schools.

The main pressure from the Diocese of Southwell was for the replacement of the St Mary's CE modern school by a new CE grammar school, and although the authority resisted the inclusion of a CE secondary school in the City's Development plan, the Diocese succeeded in establishing the new Bluecoat CE school in the 1966/67 building programme after some years of inaction because of Ministerial refusal to award a relevant building prgramme. The Development plan had included from the outset the equivalent of seven-form entry RC modern and three-form entry RC grammar/ technical places, and after complex vicissitudes and negotiations between the Diocesan Commission, Nottingham and the Ministry, a two-form entry RC secondary modern school succeeded in finding a place in the 1956/57 programme, in successful competition with the CE grammar school project which did not. Projects to enlarge and reorganize both grammar and modern RC schools were approved in 1960/61 and, mining subsidence problems finally resolved, the two-form entry Bishop Dunn RC modern school at Aspley was approved for the 1963/64 programme.

The revised Development Plan was in fact finally approved by the Minister on 24th May 1951 and subsequent negotiations for building programme projects varied little from it until the early 1960s. The Director and the Education Committee were agreed that not all able and gifted children were academically inclined, nor would they necessarily profit from the traditional academic curriculum. There was grave concern that although it was not yet available, a total provision of extended education for from 20 to 25 per cent of the age group was desirable.[13] Early building programmes, while balanced, gave priority to immediate expansion of grammar school provision (three new grammar schools were included in building programmes from 1951–1955) but the rising school population and the need to devote most of the building programme to new schools to serve outlying housing estates made it apparent to the Committee by 1957, that

'a very substantial increase in the number of grammar school places could not be achieved within the next few years in view of the restrictions on the building programme.'[14]

This, in the early years of the newly appointed Director, combined
with his new educational ideas on increased flexibility of school
organization and curriculum, led the Committee to make an
immediate decision that a third of its schools should reorganize as
bilateral schools in advance of completion of building programme
proposals arising from the Development Plan, and that additional
staff, new senior posts and other resources would be diverted or
added to enable the reorganized schools to offer comparable
education with that in the grammar and technical schools. As from
1957, four schools were reorganized as grammar/modern schools,
offering a total of six-form entry academic places (180 per year) 13-
form entry non-academic places (390 per year), while seven more
schools were reorganized as technical/modern schools offering nine-
form entry technical places (270 per year) and 23-form entry modern
places (690 per year). By 1958, enough staff and extra resources had
been diverted or added, to level up the selective provision to cover
over 30 per cent of the age group.

Table VII (1): Grammar school places (at 11 +)

YEAR	AGE GROUP		PLACES	PLACES AS % OF AGE GROUP
1945	4000		394	9.85
1948	3850		426	11·10
1951	3700		451	12·2
1954	4426		447	10·1
1955	4950		834*	16·8
1956	4600		698	15·2
1957	4700		794	16·9
(Introduction of bilateral scheme)				
1958	4790	grammar	731	15·2
		bilateral†	776	16·2
			1507	31·4

* opening of new High Pavement (SB) grammar school, establishment of Forest
  Fields (SM) grammar school, and opening of Clifton Hall (SG) grammar
  school.
† grammar streams only.

By 1959, the growing success of the bilateral schools led the
Secondary Education Sub-Committee to decide (1.7.59) that the
technical schools should close and the pupils transfer to bilateral
schools. The Textile School closed in 1961 and the Building School

in 1965. By 1965, about 100 pupils a year were transferring to the VIth forms of grammar schools at 16+ from the bilateral schools. For throughout the 20 years of planning, the authority had opposed any development of additional sixth forms to those at grammar schools and all developments in non-grammar schools were therefore planned for the age ranges 11–16 only.

Only one major example of political influence has been traced in Nottingham, and this relates to the establishment of the city's only comprehensive school. It might be cited as an example of 'political demand'. It might conversely be regarded as a typical example of the logistics of coherent educational planning taking precedence over individual or group pressures. The history of the establishment of the school is told in more detail in the thesis of which this book is an abridged version. It is perhaps adequate to record here that after negotiations between City and County on the transfer of the Clifton estate projects south of the Trent to the City, Nottingham's building programme was inflated by the addition of schools to cater for the new estates. After a review of secondary need, grammar places and the future of Mundella (mixed) school, it was agreed to build a large comprehensive school for boys at Clifton and it was built in the usual instalments between 1955 and 1960, as part of a political 'lobby' for reorganization—but as a pilot experiment.

Both the Conservatives and the teachers as represented by the Joint Consultative Committee, pressed for a promise on educational grounds that no further comprehensive schools would be built for at least seven years, after which time Fairham would be reviewed. The more moderate Labour group were not opposed to the bilateral scheme which had been approved in 1956, and hence were reluctant to press for a comprehensive scheme. The promise was honoured, and in 1968 Fairham was still Nottingham's only comprehensive school. The general view of the officers and members interviewed in 1969 was that the initial political fight was swiftly overtaken by complex factors of educational planning, such as the balance of boys' to girls' places and of selective to non-selective places. These were in turn dictated by previous decisions made by the Committee on the development of new schools.

This, then, was the general pattern of the development of secondary education in Nottingham. Some powerful forces in the City influenced the allocation of resources which made this possible. Predominant factors were the distinctive personalities of the two post-war Directors of Education and their conception of the role of their colleagues in the service. We have seen in Lincoln how the influence of the Chief Education Officer was paramount, and it has been suggested that the lack of strong supportive professional staff in

Lincoln was one factor which led to underuse of capital resources. The position in Nottingham was very different.

The Leadership

To understand the influence at work in Nottingham one must picture the leaders of the service as their colleagues and their committees saw them, for that in turn influenced Council and Ministry as well as the teaching profession. It will be recalled that the first post-war Director had been in post since 1938, his predecessor having been described by a contemporary as 'a fighter, a wise despot, lively, determined and a fast worker'. He was quoted as having said

'There will always be those to fight for scholarship children; I want a modern school for every elementary schoolchild in Nottingham.'

He had come near to achieving this when he retired on the eve of world war II. His concern for the less privileged was not limited to less able children—more of the grammar school places then available were for boys and he was responsible for building the Manning girls' grammar school to provide equal opportunity for all able children, and not just boys, at the level thought appropriate in the 1930s. But the City had still, as we have seen, too few grammar school places.

His successor in 1938 was described in a series of interviews in 1969, by both former colleagues and by teachers and council members as essentially an academic, though a competent administrator. He tended to be rather remote—both committee members and colleagues recalled having always to make appointments to see him—and he was not inclined to delegate. There was consequently little team work. He was by nature, more interested in academic grammar school education, preferred single-sex education and many heads felt that his remoteness and background led him perhaps to underestimate the problems of teaching the lower 80 per cent of ability—the majority of children. On the other hand there is complete unanimity that he believed with integrity, in real parity of esteem—a contemporary head teacher commented:

'he would have no truck with the concept of tripartite education which had a modern school at the bottom.'

Many suggested that his lack of impetus for the modernization of older schools and for the practical task of closing the gap of resources between grammar and non-grammar schools, arose more from lack of practical experience of the real conditions and needs of the poorer non-selective schools, than from lack of motivation. Equally, many paid high tribute to his foresight and skill in negotiating in advance, in the earlier post-war years land purchases for school sites, and substantial building programmes, which put Nottingham well ahead of many comparable authorities. His natural inclination towards the education of the able children together with the City's acute problem in meeting their needs with so low a provision as 12 per cent of grammar school places, made it inevitable that he should be remembered for his fight to redress the balance of the situation he inherited.

His administrative competence showed immediately in his insistence on substantial increases in the establishment of senior administrative staff in the period 1944–1947 and in particular the appointment of a professional assistant specifically to handle the developments arising out of the new Education Act of 1944. The continuity of staff at middle management level over the crucial period 1948–1960 undoubtedly reinforced the authority's strong position in arguing for increased resources from both the Ministry of Education and from the City Council[15].

The second post-war Director was appointed in 1956 (from the post of Assistant Director within the authority). His extensive experience as the professional officer in charge of sites and buildings development had given him an almost unprecedented detailed knowledge of conditions in the schools, of the moods and techniques of the Ministry of Education with regard to capital programmes and of the possibilities for future development. The picture painted by his colleagues from schools, from the administration and from the Education Committee is completely convincing in its consistency, and is supported by personal interviews by the writer held in 1969. He was described as having a deep interest in the underprivileged; and as a creative educationalist. Common adjectives used were dynamic, impulsive, courageous in decision making, determined, competent. An enthusiast, one colleague described him as preferring to be the 'fons et origo', reluctant to delegate, but keen to carry his staff in a general drive towards modernization and development. He aimed, it was said by a senior colleague (in 1969 on interview) for 'all round curving improvement rather than jagged peaks of prestige development'.

The immediate tasks he set himself on appointment were to bring to life the dormant bilateral scheme, still only approved in principle; to sponsor swift and extensive development of libraries in secondary schools; and to continue the longterm programme of modernization of specialist rooms (especially housecraft and handicraft) by special capital loans—if he could carry his Finance Committee. And he did.

As a corollary of the bilateral developments, he restructured the scheme of school allowances for material resources (books, stock etc.) so as to minimize and in due course eliminate the differential then operating between grammar and non-grammar schools, which it will be recalled remained in operation in Lincoln until abolished by the fourth Chief Education Officer in 1964/65. He particularly aimed at helping the development of external examinations and bias courses in the non-selective schools.

Implicit Demand From Rising Numbers

Two aims created implicit demand, a policy of expansion of grammar and technical education, and a positive desire for parity of esteem between schools. The next most immediately measurable factor of implicit demand is that of rising numbers.

It will be recalled that in Lincoln, revenue expenditure rose at just over twice the rate of increase of the school population. In Nottingham however a much smaller proportionate element can be accounted for in this way. The following table illustrates the different growth rates of total direct secondary school expenditure and secondary school population using 1946 as the base year. The cost figures after 1959 are slightly inflated by the addition of elements not counted before then (see the footnotes to tables VI (b) and VII (b) in Appendix B)—but the main point of the table is not invalidated by this addition, since this table relates to total expenditure and not to separate elements within it. On the basis of the average annual increase of previous years, not exceeding 100 points between 1958 and 1959 are caused by the new method of accounting but after 1959 growth is again pure. The figures are unadjusted.

Table VII (2)

YEAR	TOTAL GROSS DIRECT SECONDARY REVENUE EXPENDITURE £	INDEX	SECONDARY SCHOOL POPULATION	INDEX
1946	357,337	100	13,446	100
1948	468,542	131	17,312	129
1951	681,497	191	17,537	131
1953	720,007	201	18,022	134
1956	1,021,054	286	18,294	136
1959	1,924,574	535	20,711	154
1962	2,355,570	651	20,510	153
1964	2,590,007	725	20,303	151

Thus the implicit demand of rising school numbers would have accounted in crude terms for a rise of only about 50 per cent in basic expenditure to maintain about the same standard as in 1946. In fact, however, the expenditure rose by over seven times. There were clearly in Nottingham other reasons and other pressures.

On the other hand, the growth in the secondary school population clearly had implications for future capital building programmes. Before looking at the allocation of financial revenue resources, it is necessary to look at the outline development of the capital building programme which both provided new places for the majority of secondary school pupils, and determined by implication much of the revenue expenditure in the second decade.

Capital Expenditure and the Building Programme

The capital programme provided in all for 2,560 grammar places and 13,140 new secondary modern bilateral or comprehensive places by new building or by major adaptations to old buildings in the period 1949–1965, but it is not possible readily to estimate how many places were taken out of use by closure of old schools as new ones were built, and thus to measure a net addition. What is impressive, is that about two-thirds of Nottingham's secondary school pupils are now receiving education in post-war buildings despite the severe national restrictions on capital expenditure.

Nottingham's total capital expenditure over the period 1946–65, appears in full in Table VI (b) in Appendix B, while the secondary school building programme appears in Appendix E. The capital building programme had of course been subject to very detailed control by the Ministry of Education and in particular the 1950–53 and 1960–63 periods were subject to severe cuts. The account already given of the Ministry's role in directing priorities (roofs over heads in the first decade; reorganization of all-age schools and improvement of scientific and technical facilities in the second) suggests that the theory announced by successive governments, of increased freedom for local education authorities was largely illusory, and that authorities have on the whole had substantially to alter or curtail their policies because of government economies. Nottingham was no exception, but with considerable independence of spirit succeeded in finding some alternative ways of achieving the same ends in the later years.

In the early years the Director advised the Committee that the most urgent need was for additional secondary school places to house children transferred to the many new housing estates then being built on the outskirts. The Ministry priority for 'roofs over heads' and for housing estate schools matched the authority's own priority which was to provide new and more suitably designed secondary schools in outer districts and to remodel the vacated older secondary schools in the city centre for improved primary school places. The city's further needs in 1952 already justified a £1,500,000 programme for providing eight new secondary modern schools. While the Ministry did not disagree on the need however, it was unable to approve any projects to relieve overcrowding or for improvement or to complete the reorganization of all-age voluntary schools. By 1952, the authority had been awarded a programme of £784,725 for 1948–50 providing 1,760 new secondary modern places, and a further £670,840 for 1951–52 aimed at providing 2,590 places. But the revision of the 1951–53 programmes, deleted so much of this, carrying some forward to 1953, that the net gain on 1951 was in fact only 550 grammar and 1,460 modern places *or less than half of the defined and previously agreed need.* Building labour was scarce as the national defence programme increased, but the authority refused to curtail its advance planning of new schools or its intention to build. The urgent need for new places which the Ministry could not authorize, meant that most class sizes in secondary schools exceeded 40 pupils and every teaching space was used as a class base.[16] The standard of education in this period, despite outstanding work by the teachers, cannot but have been deficient of much that the new Act had hoped to introduce, including new and widened curricula, and extended opportunities.

Unlike Lincoln, which rarely spent even such minor works allocations as it was awarded, Nottingham therefore persistently attacked the Ministry for not providing an adequate major building programme and demanded additional minor works allocations to remedy in part the deficiencies with which it had to live—either by building small extensions to existing schools or by remodelling old schools which had to face a longer life. In the rather disastrous 1951–53 period for example—in the face of a truncated major programme— the Director, backed by the Sites and Buildings Sub-Committee, increased the city's original minor works allocation from £19,685 to £41,658 and subsequently to £68,815. The following year he doubled the allocation from £23,744 to £48,744—with the result that the first offer from the Ministry in 1954/55 was £44,942 instead of the £20,000 offered in 1952. Again in 1958–59, soon after the introduction of the bilateral scheme, the original £30,000 allocation was increased to £50,000 and the authority, with confident disregard for central control, in fact apparently authorized and spent £72,239 in minor projects. There is no evidence of repercussions from the Ministry and it may well have been with their tacit agreement because of under-spending in another region. The 1961–63 cuts reduced the original two-year allocation of £200,000 to £63,000 but the authority (predictably) succeeded in negotiating an increase of its revised allocation of £73,000 to £87,000.

While there is strong evidence in Committee minutes that this constantly increased demand and ceaseless negotiation, combined with the authority's undoubted reputation for matching its promised schedule in building, did increase the resources available, it must be added that this still did not match the authority's view of its own assessed needs. The authority had prepared schemes for remodelling schools, none of which on examination seem excessively lavish or in advance of real need, and could readily have put in hand work costing £252,000 in 1960 for example instead of the £100,000 authorized by the Ministry, since Nottingham was by then well staffed for building work and prepared to use private architects if need be. In particular, Nottingham suffered from the recession of the mid 1950s and the dichotomy of the two main government departments, Education and the Treasury in 1956 which announced with one voice (Education) that restrictions on minor capital works were abolished and with another (the Chancellor of the Exchequer) that all 'non-urgent' minor capital works should be deferred.

'The Education Committee noted with particular regret the restrictions on capital expenditure announced by the Treasury in December 1955. It was precisely a year earlier that the Ministry of Education had announced the abolition of restrictions on minor capital works, and the Education Committee had prepared a substantial scheme of improvements to old schools.'[17]

The Nottingham Finance Committee of the City Council, not feeling able to assert quite the degree of independence which the Education Committee demonstrated, deferred the education re-lighting programme (presumably as long as children could actually see, the enforcement of the new lighting standards set by the Ministry of Education's technical officers was classed as 'non-urgent').

Also partly as a result of the government's continued requests to curtail capital expenditure, the Finance Committee of the Council decided for the first time seriously to review all capital projects proposed or in preparation, and to restrict forward planning to an agreed level for the whole Council.

'Your Sub-Committee have now received the observations of the Finance Committee on the list of proposed capital projects and have noted the restrictions which the Finance Committee consider should be made in the original programme. Your Sub-Committee consider that these restrictions are reasonable in the light of existing circumstances.'[18]

The authority nevertheless put forward 12 secondary school projects for the 1960–62 programme, and from five to seven for all successive years, a programme made largely necessary by the Ministry's earlier refusal to allow the authority either to build for a full Vth year, or to build a whole school in one instalment. Thus, schools programmed in the 1950–55 period were costed for a four-year course despite the authority's Development Plan which stated that all schools should be designed for a full five-year course ready for the raising of the school leaving age. All county schools in the period 1958 to 1965 had to be built in instalments as were the early William Sharp Modern and High Pavement grammar schools, a wasteful process and one leading to serious organizational difficulties both in the interim and in the long term. It also led to overcrowding until further instalments were approved, since in all the cases examined here, the authority's original predictions of future school rolls submitted with the draft building programmes, proved highly accurate, justifying the full projects at the outset.

Figure 6 in Chapter V gives in graph form, the pattern of the national building programme for primary and secondary schools. Figure 8 on the following page here, gives the relationship of *Nottingham's* secondary building programmes to its overall capital expenditure. It will be seen that Nottingham had an above-average secondary programme until 1955 after which it broadly followed the national overall pattern of cuts and growth. On the whole priority had to be given to primary schools in the early years (hence the high actual capital expenditure from 1949–1952); but the secondary programme suffered unduly badly in the 1956–1959 lean years. The national priority for example in 1960–65 was in fact for secondary schools over primary; yet Nottingham's post-1960 secondary programme falls below the national trend. No doubt this was because the rural counties were still reorganizing all-age schools with the aid of the special building programme following circular 283, and Nottingham had already done this, organizationally in the 1930s and materially with new schools in the first post-war decade. (The peak of actual capital expenditure in the city at a time when the secondary programme dropped in the late 1950s represents expenditure from the 1954–56 programme carried forward and the city's new further education programme.) Much of Nottingham's crucial building took place in the first decade or so, which meant that the development of new policies in secondary education in the later years, (both inspired by the second post-war Director and encouraged by the 1958 White Paper[19] of the central government) could be made almost immediately effective because so many schools were post-war. Even if earlier restrictions had not enabled the City to build initially for a five-year

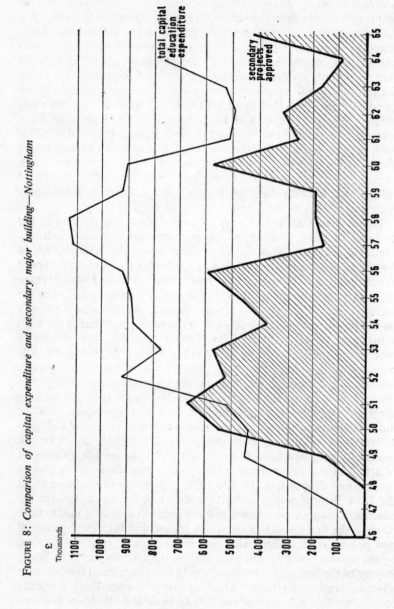

FIGURE 8: *Comparison of capital expenditure and secondary major building—Nottingham*

course, judicious use of minor works had enabled it unobtrusively to bring many new schools up to a five-year standard in time. The later building programmes not only fell in monetary value but even further in real terms because of rises in building costs.

This pattern of capital expenditure will clearly have had a significant effect on subsequent revenue expenditure, and particularly the intractable element of the budget (for example loan charges, maintenance and to some extent, teachers' salaries and educational materials). In addition, the introduction of the bilateral scheme meant immediately higher costs in salaries and in school allowances— since children following an extended course were given a better staffing ratio and a higher capitation allowance. To double the percentage of grammar places meant to increase revenue costs significantly.

Revenue Expenditure

Remembering that Nottingham had no apparent innate problems financially and that both Directors and the Committee were deeply concerned to raise standards, one might expect that revenue expenditure was an aspect largely free from central controls which the authority would use to meet the demands of the schools and indeed, other more explicit demands (for example the establishment of the Textile school which started in rented premises with all costs met from revenue). Were they in fact, free to do so?

The following section looks at the relative growth rates of expenditure, the intractable element, and one aspect of inherited attitudes towards priorities for the allocation of resources.

Growth Rates

In Lincoln, it will be recalled that secondary expenditure rose at a slower rate overall than total education expenditure. Tables IV (b), VI (b), and VII (b) of Appendix B give fuller details. Table IV (5) in Chapter IV gives the comparative position for the three authorities. The *Nottingham* growth rates are given again below, together with the population growth:

Table VII (3)

(a) growth rates—population

YEAR	SCHOOL POPULATION	SECONDARY SCHOOL POPULATION
1946	37,218	13,446
1964	51,686	20,303
% increase	38·6%	50·9%

(b) growth rates—expenditure

Year	Total Gross Revenue Education Expenditure £	Total Gross Revenue Direct Expenditure— Secondary Only £
1946	1,241,574	357,337
1964	7,933,534	2,590,007
% increase	639%	725%

Thus the growth rate for secondary expenditure more than kept pace with the general growth rate and considerably exceeded the impact of demand from rising numbers. Some of the other factors which affected the substantial increases in secondary expenditure differed from those of Lincoln, and a number arise from the substantial capital building programme in the first decade. Much of this is intractable.

As chapter IV illustrated, from four to 12 per cent of the annual total education budget was already committed for loan charges before any question of adjusting or improving educational standards could be considered. Figures for the secondary sector for later years show loan charges as an identifiable item, and the loan charges for the *secondary* capital programme accounted for over £300,000 in an average year. In most years this would have represented over 13 per cent of the secondary budget. There were moreover other intractable elements which in addition, reduced the residual budget which was available for the Director and for the Committee with which to respond to new and changing demands.

Table VII (4): *Gross revenue secondary expenditure*

Year	Furniture, Equipment, Books, Stationery and Apparatus £	Index	Maintenance £	Index	Fuel Light and Cleaning £	Index
1946	22,258	100	7,174	100	22,681	100
1949	52,061	234	38,916	556	37,848	167
1952	62,812	283	27,142	386	57,765	255
1954	62,645	275	41,571	592	72,892	322
1956	75,763	342	42,116	610	100,559	442
1958	90,152	405	58,338	832	132,346	585

FIGURE 9: *Nottingham—Comparative table of gross revenue education expenditure,*
1946–58

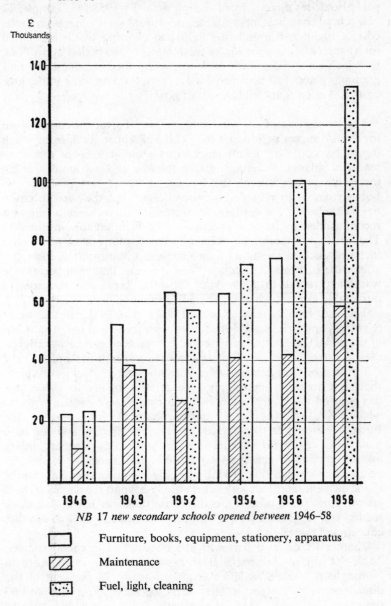

NB 17 *new secondary schools opened between* 1946–58

☐ Furniture, books, equipment, stationery, apparatus

▨ Maintenance

▦ Fuel, light, cleaning

Other elements in the budget rose partly as a result of the capital programme—it is not possible to isolate its effect completely since part also arises directly from rising prices. By 1958 for example, 17 new schools had been opened, and this meant steady increases in the cost of maintenance and fuel light and cleaning which accounted for an increasing proportion of the budget. In the period up to 1958, by which time about 8,000 new secondary modern and 1,650 new grammar places had been provided, expenditure on some intractable costs had risen four-, eight- or six-fold.

The proportion of the total budget taken by these items is given for the full survey period in Table VI (b) of Appendix B, from which it will be seen that maintenance costs grew at a faster rate than teachers' salaries or educational materials, and accounted for an increasing proportion of the budget. A small part of furniture, books etc. can be regarded as discretionary but the need to equip new schools and the desirability of meeting the minimum standard recommended by the AEC makes most of it intractable in practice. The fact that the secondary section of the accounts in 1959 and after included such elements as loan charges, administrative costs etc. affects the percentage of course—but it means that each percentage was likely to fall in 1959. They all did—except maintenance, an intractable element which increased substantially.

The very high increase in actual costs of non-educational items (eightfold and nearly sixfold) coupled with the rise in the proportion of the budget which they represented for this sector, steadily reduced even further the margin for experimental expenditure open to the Director. For the principle is firmly established in local government that next year's estimates must be related mainly to percentage increases on the current year, except for negotiable special items on which a limit is always set. It was customary in Nottingham for the Finance Committee to agree an overall growth rate, and for both 'committed' extra expenditure (e.g. for price rises, teachers' salary awards, staffing of new schools) as well as desirable innovation, to be contained within that growth rate. Clearly in these circumstances if one element increases very substantially beyond the agreed overall growth rate, some other expenditure must be cut back. One main section still regarded by the Committee as liable to cuts was in fact educational materials.

Chapter IX deals in part with the question of teachers' salaries. Table VI (b) in Appendix B shows that in the early years in Nottingham teachers' salaries absorbed nearly 70 per cent of the direct secondary budget; in later years, between 50 per cent and 60 per cent. The rise in financial terms was from £278,246 in 1946 to

£1,475,425 in 1964. The latter figure is probably more accurate since the total of which it is a proportion includes *all* expenditure on secondary education, indirect and direct alike. It is a substantial proportion. Expressed in monetary terms its growth rate however, while highly significant, is less than that of some other intractable elements. (This however was largely because of slow growth in the first decade because the city could not recruit its full quota of women teachers. In 1953 the authority was 30 below quota of women teachers and by 1956 even though recruitment had improved, 10 housecraft and five metalwork rooms were closed because there were no qualified staff.) The sharper rises tend to coincide with either the implementation of a new Burnham report, or the opening of a batch of new schools (e.g. 1956, 1958, 1961).

So far, some examples of 'implicit' demand have been covered. The school population rose by 51 per cent; but the total expenditure by sevenfold. Intractable items not affected by educational policy accounted for substantial rises, not only in amount but in proportion. But furniture, equipment, books and apparatus rose by less than all these (only four-fold) and yet this is one major possible influence on educational planning—the introduction of new equipment, environment and materials is integrally related to the introduction of new techniques and of new educational goals.

Inherited Assumptions and Attitudes

Within this aspect of the allocation of revenue expenditure, lies hidden a kind of subculture of inherited educational prejudices which becomes translated into a differential allocation of money and equipment (less on grounds of actual assessed educational need, than of unexamined automatic assumptions). For example, in Nottingham as in Lincoln in this particular respect, the grammar school child had a higher per capita allowance than other children. After 1956, the new Director reorganized the scheme to enable children following a five-year course in a bilateral school to qualify for the grammar school rate of allowance on the obvious grounds that their course costs were the same as those of children in grammar schools. But this still left the less able children in bilateral schools a long way behind.

The scheme operating in 1965 however also gave a substantially higher rate for *new* schools than for *existing* schools:

	grammar	*other secondary*	*VIth form*
existing	£5. 5. 6.	£3. 5. 0.	£8. 7. 6.
new	£9. 12. 0.	£6. 19. 6.	£9. 12. 0.

This appears to suggest either a philosophy of 'to him who hath shall be given' or an assumption of excessive permanence of existing materials (i.e. that books and apparatus in existing schools last indefinitely) or that all new schools start without a single text book or tape recorder. Despite evidence that books lasted an average of 10 years in pre-war years and even in the 1940s, the average life of books in the later years after about 1958 was no more than five. Some of the schools built in the period 1946–53 may well have started with no 'inherited' resources. Those built after 1956 were however mainly built to enable older unsuitable (and smaller) schools to close, and in one case, a 10-form entry bilateral school inherited 6,000 quite adequate library books and a complete range of text books from its contributory schools—yet it qualified, as 'new', for over twice the book allowance of its 'downtown' neighbour. An assumption is prevalent (indeed a desirable one) that one cannot equip a new school with old furniture and materials. But least of all should one equip an *old* school thus. Children in older schools have the more need to have their obsolete geography books, their vintage iron-frame desks, their Reynard-the-Fox readers, replaced by modern books and equipment, to compensate for their other environmental disadvantages.

Nottingham, however, from early post-war years, recognized this need—at least in one respect. Authorities have been known to suggest that their apparent 'average' costs per pupil as assessed by the IMTA are underestimated because some expenditure is met from capital loans, not revenue. Lincoln's argument thus, was specious—there were in fact no significant capital loans. Nottingham's claim is partly justified. In 1948, the authority decided to start a vigorous programme of replacement of obsolete furniture—loan sanction for £28,588 was approved for this. It will be recalled that the first post-war Director declared his belief in 'parity of esteem' and high standards. He persuaded the authority to follow the 1948 replacement programme with three more—the general renewal of secondary school furniture in 1954 (£25,000), the remodelling of housecraft rooms from 1955 (£12,500) and a key development—the establishment and expansion of libraries in all non-grammar secondary schools, from March 1956 (£28,060).

Libraries

Both post-war Directors attached great importance to the place of the library in the school and in the curriculum, and this is one striking example of the extreme importance of the educational philosophy and administrative competence of the Director in post. As early as 1949 the School Libraries Advisory Committee pressed for increased library allowances.[20]

By 1953, the Education Committee could record that
'There was a time when the school library was exclusively the
treasured possession of the grammar schools. The Committee has
however pursued the policy of making such provision in all of its
schools.'[21]

And it was as a result of a detailed review of all schools that the 1955
major loan was sought in order to establish new libraries in 31
existing secondary schools.

While therefore, inherited assumptions about the relative cost of
the needs of grammar and non-academic children did underly the
capitation scheme, both Directors showed a genuine and a highly
practical concern for some of the other needs of the non-grammar
schools.

The evidence so far suggests that the influence of the Directors'
own philosophies of educational priority, and the intractable
demands of factors outside the control of the authority, were
dominant.

Informed Comment

How important in fact are resources in helping to set and achieve
standards in schools? Both local authority inspectors and HM
inspectorate[22] considered them of influential importance—pupils and
teachers alike tended to live up to the expectations of their environment or of its limits. A drab classroom, too few test tubes, old text
books and poor equipment, the wrong art materials, a gym too small
for free movement; and both pupils and teachers would work to a
depressed standard. Interestingly, four of the schools surveyed in
Nottingham had taken in teaching staff from older schools closed
down as new ones were built (or amalgamated); and in each case
both head and staff accounted for low initial demand for money,
equipment and books, by years of conditioning in a declining school.
It appeared that when a school is known to have a limited life, there
is a reluctance on the authority's part to spend money on it, and
staff themselves give up at a very early stage, seeking any improvement—'You wait for the glass-lined Elysian fields down the road
and put up with dogeared books and no tape recorder',—which is
extraordinary since all equipment is in fact transferable even when
the old school does move to new buildings. But six examples of this
were found in Nottingham.

For a variety of reasons, the parity which both Directors wished
to achieve between grammar and modern schools did not materialize.
Firstly, the limited capital programme prevented earlier schools
from being built with either enough classrooms or enough specialist

accommodation (through no fault of the authority's) and prevented the replacement at all of many old schools still existing in 1965.

'The most serious problem however remains lack of approval of capital expenditure as a result of which such buildings as those of Highbury, Clarement, Trent Bridge and Dale Secondary Schools seem likely to remain in use for a number of years to come . . . this hold up is preventing the Committee from implementing their policy of having all children in schools with full GCE courses at "O" level. It can be said that much has been done, and that the City's record will stand comparison with any in the country. Nevertheless there remains the problem of the 20 per cent in "modern" schools.'[23]

Secondly the increasing proportion and size of the intractable element of the budget narrowed the Director's margin to remedy basic deficiencies of accommodation. A larger margin would have enabled the authority to create a more favourable educational environment from proportionately increased revenue expenditure on furniture and equipment, for example—though many improvements were undoubtedly made. Thirdly, inherited attitudes by Directors and Committees on the considered needs of 'able' and less able or non-academic children, perpetuated a very significant differential element in awarding annual capitation and equipment allowances. These inherited attitudes were by no means mirrored in all schools.

On the other hand, dynamic demand did release resources in that the authority successfully negotiated increases in its major and minor building programmes in the first 15 years of the 20-year period which improved conditions for two-thirds of the children of secondary school age. Similarly both Directors achieved a much larger general growth rate than was evident in Lincoln.

Examinations

Nottingham attempted to check its own standards in external examinations, admittedly one index only of performance in education. A fuller account appears in the writer's PhD thesis. Summarized, the relative performance of the bilateral group in 1962 seemed more impressive. In September 1957 the first 630 pupils were admitted to the selective streams of bilateral schools, *after* 15 per cent (or about 700) had first been selected for grammar schools. In other words, there was not free choice as in an area offering both comprehensive and grammar schools. These were the less able 10 per cent of the top quartile. The following table is of interest, showing the first batch of GCE results in 1962, compared with five years previously.[24]

Table VII (5): Passes at 'O' level

		5 *or more*	4	3	2	1
1956	grammar	198	53	49	62	81
	other	18	15	15	18	36
	total	216	68	64	80	117
1962	grammar	325	102	77	80	54
	other	114	78	88	111	148
	total	439	180	165	191	202

The Ministry of Education statistics for that time showed that nationally 24 per cent of grammar school pupils failed to obtain more than two passes at 'O' level—Nottingham appeared to be slightly worse than the national average. The Director used these results to suggest that

'the discouragement of the less successful pupil in the grammar school contrasts with the encouragement received in the bilateral and other schools by their more able pupils'.

But in practice in 1962, 44·5 per cent of grammar school pupils obtained five or more passes at 'O' level and 14·7 per cent of the bilateral entry. Bearing in mind an entry at 11+ of 15 per cent of the age group to grammar, and 16 per cent to bilateral schools, one wonders how far the bilateral 'O' level achievements would have been greatly improved had they had grammar school staffing, accommodation and financial resources from the outset.

It would take further research to account for the detailed results (which are not untypical and are probably mirrored elsewhere). Wastage at VIth-form level is predictably less than at Vth form. If however, one acceptable defined goal of advanced academic or extended secondary education is to pass external examinations in order to qualify for entry to further or higher education, skilled employment or other professional training it must be a matter of concern whether a failure rate at 16+ of from 25 per cent to 35 per cent is caused by entering candidates not really sufficiently able; or because lack of adequate staff and equipment have hindered development of more relevant teaching methods; or from other factors within the school or home. On the other hand, faced with the impossibility of obtaining a capital programme large enough to double its grammar provision in the mid-1950s, Nottingham had clearly attempted to use its resources as effectively as it could to offer this extended opportunity to so many more pupils than would otherwise have benefited. The bilateral results are from the early years of the scheme and would seem wholly to justify the Director's insistence on attempting to staff and equip these schools on the same scale as grammar schools for the able pupils although this proved impossible in the early years. The disparity of cost for the less able in non-grammar schools is another matter.

Explicit Demand

Chapter I outlines in some detail the likely sources of explicit demand. Most but not all, were present in Nottingham. Most were not significantly influential.

Industrial influence

In Nottingham, industrial influence tended to be more evident and more effective than in the other two survey areas. There was a long history of this—Appendix A gives an outline description from which it will be seen that locally inherited traditions had an impact of 50 or 100 years experience behind them. Among the main industries of textiles, lace, hosiery, bleaching and dyeing, light engineering, cycle manufacture, cigarettes and tobacco and mining, lace was one of the oldest (though declining in 1945). It was nearly a century ago that a Commission commented that

'The manufacturers of Nottingham speak with no uncertain voice of the important influence of the local school of art on the lace manufacture of that town.'[25]

Over the 20-year survey period, lace, mining and textiles have tended to decline while engineering, electronics and the manufacture of ready made clothing have increased substantially.

Textiles and hosiery were strong enough in the early 1940s, however, to rouse explicit and strong pressure from the textile industry for the establishment of a junior secondary technical school for the hosiery trade[26] later amended to cover all textiles on the lines of the existing technical schools of art and of building. It is interesting to note that the pressure aimed at the Education Committee came jointly from the hosiery section of the Chamber of Commerce and from the Hosiery Workers Society. The principle of shared resources was established at the outset—the trade would provide special machines and equipment if the local education authority would provide premises and staff.[27] The school opened in 1944 with 19 boys and 17 girls and, after pressure from the lace trade, with a more widely based curriculum than originally envisaged. Recruitment was partly at 11+ and partly at 13+. The school catered especially, although not exclusively, for potential recruits to the combined trades until it closed in 1960 after the successful establishment of bilateral (grammar/technical, grammar/modern and technical/modern) schools in the late 1950s. In common with Nottingham's general policy of close involvement with industry, an advisory committee similar to those existing for the other technical schools, and with trade representation was established. The courses in the technical schools were strongly vocational. By 1952 of 89 leavers from the Building School, 48 boys went into craft apprenticeships in building, 21 into office work with builders, surveyors and architects and 14 into engineering. Sixty of the 96 leavers from the Textile School went direct into the textile trades.

Industrial links between the education service and local firms were strengthened by the establishment of a standing Education Consultative Committee of the Nottingham Chamber of Commerce to provide a link between industry and commerce and the educational institutions in the city, and

'to advise on school sixth form curricula and to recommend which subjects should be studied at school and which reserved for part-time advanced training'.[28]

Consultation remained lively, a conference being held in 1954 between representatives of the Education Committee, the Chamber of Commerce and all types of secondary schools

'to provide a full and frank exchange of views between the representatives on the qualities and abilities expected of boys and girls entering industry and also to afford head teachers an opportunity of explaining their aims and objectives'[29]

Links with industry remained a little haphazard but another concerted effort was made in 1958 when the Director approached all Trades Associations and the Trades Council to discuss relationships between secondary modern schools and industry and to improve links. Discussions covered visits by teachers to factories, courses for local employers on the education service, visits to schools by them and the establishment and credibility of internal leaving certificates. A conference of industrialists and representatives of the education service followed in January 1959.

Notwithstanding these very positive efforts on behalf of the authority regularly to involve industry in educational planning, comments from officers and members interviewed in 1968 produced conflicting views on the real effectiveness of the involvement of employers and of industry in general. One experienced officer considered that cross-representation between industry and the Education Committee was a form of lip-service, while another senior colleague attributed strong social responsibility to the older family firms, who led the way on day release and the education of young workers. The network of strong advisory committees in the further education sector indirectly gave rise to the meetings between heads and industry which in the view of several officers and members helped to strengthen the case for the development of technical courses in the bilateral schools. There is, however, little practical evidence of industrial influence on major policy or on the direct allocation of resources, and some evidence (from headteachers) of real uncertainty of the respective roles of the education service and industries in providing for the education and training of the 15- to 18-year-old. One head of a mixed bilateral school has successfully developed a work experience scheme including the donation of substantial electronic equipment to the school by a local firm, but in his view the contact took a disproportionate time to negotiate. Several heads saw a need for a central educational industrial co-ordinator to help integrated planning and sharing of resources between industry and schools.

Committees and the administration

Chapter III outlined Nottingham's Committee structure and suggested that evidence was unanimous on the powerful role in Nottingham of the Sites and Buildings Sub-Committee. With two Directors also determined in their own way to secure maximum resources for the city and to further their own educational philosophies, the authority succeeded in extracting a substantial building programme even in the lean years. The presence also of a highly skilled administrative head of section whose sole task has been for the 20 years from 1952 to deal with the education programme, was however the key factor which translated the Directors' will to develop services fast, into the real ability to do so. Of the two factors, the administrative strength of the department is probably the stronger. Officers are agreed that Committees and Council alike backed the Directors by providing capital resources at the necessary level—in this sense the implicit demand from rising numbers (1945–58) and from changing needs (1958–65) was backed by explicit demand in the form of a substantial and carefully prepared draft building programme presented to Committee each year (unlike Lincoln which made no bid for several years) always in excess of the likely award from the Ministry although always related to realistic need. There was a unanimous concern on the part of the Education Committee to raise standards, and party politics did not distort this. But like most committees 'they will authorise £2 million at a nod but will argue on £200'.[30]

The role of the Secondary Education Sub-Committee seemed less decisive but there is evidence of requests for regular reports to this sub-committee both on the general development of the new secondary schemes; and on standards. There were for example, annual reports on the level of grammar or selective places, on capitation schemes and staffing and on examination results. Such a degree of positive member interest would have made it more difficult for Nottingham to have followed the Lincoln pattern (had it so wished) of developing different sectors of secondary education at different rates and standards.

The fine political balance made the city councillors rather 'rate-conscious' however and although Nottingham used its powers to spend capital from revenue quite generously to improve conditions in schools, this was an element that successive Treasurers tended to cut.[31] The first Treasurer would appear to have held back the first Director from initiating a number of minor educational developments requiring a growth rate in revenue expenditure exceeding that thought appropriate by the Treasurer. The second decade was quite different—a picture of interdepartmental planning, project co-ordination and greater freedom for the Education Committee within an overall 'ceiling'—the result of closer cooperation between the new Director and a new Treasurer.

Table III (2) of Chapter III gives membership of the Education Committee by length of service. In Nottingham although 53 per cent of all members in the survey period served for less than five years, as many as 18·5 per cent served for 10 years. And the influential leaders were almost without exception, the longest serving, including the eight per cent who served for over 15 years. Continuity was reasonable in that at any one time, nearly half had served for over five years on the Education Committee.

Influence of teachers

The teacher organizations in Nottingham do not appear to have played a direct role in policy making in the sense of initiating major ideas. On the other hand, the genuine concern of both Directors to involve teachers in the running of the service created a very different climate of teacher involvement from that of Lincoln. Nottingham had both teacher representatives on the Education Committee and a Joint Consultative Committee which functioned efficiently, throughout the survey period.

In examining this aspect, it proved possible to interview present and past secretaries of the NUT, the current secretary of the Joint Four and some headteachers who had been involved in union affairs, in addition to senior professional staff and committee members in the education service. Opinion varied, understandably, between officers and teachers on the extent to which the latter initiated pressure or ideas for new policy. Evidence from the Director and senior colleagues and members of the Education Committee suggests that while teacher opinion was sought and carefully considered by the Committee or by the Director before major (or indeed some minor) changes initiated by the Director were put into effect, the teachers saw their role more as one of producing 'feed-back', than of creating new policy for the consideration of the authority. Typical comments from the administration include 'teachers lack the habit of initiating' or 'they advise *how* best to do what we have suggested, rather than *what* we should do next'. One leading and experienced councillor spoke of 'a climate of disincentive for pressure' because the Committee tended to want to do 'the right thing' following for example the issue of Burnham reports or revision of nationally recommended standards for allowances for educational materials (by the AEC). One NUT representative thought actual pressure (as distinct from consultation) in the second decade was rare because the Director tended to consult teachers at a very early stage in forming new proposals. The first Director used formal consultation. The second, while continuing to use the JCC, preferred to call regular meetings of heads, and to encourage leading members of organizations or of the profession generally to 'look in on me and sow seeds of ideas when they feel like it'.

A distinctive feature in Nottingham by comparison with Lincoln, was the swiftness with which shortly after the war, the teachers' associations buried their differences and recognized that strength lay in unity.[32] The staffs of selective and non-selective schools alike, were unanimous in pressing for parity of standards across all schools, and later in expressing concern on the low level of grammar school places. All groups of staff supported development of GCE courses in non-grammar schools in the early 1950s and in due course, the establishment of the bilateral scheme.[33] Any inter-union difficulties which might have arisen were resolved in the Teachers' Panel which met before each meeting of the JCC. As in Lincoln, the NUT appears to have dominated both teacher politics and teacher participation. For example, the former secretary of the local NUT was the teacher representative on the Education Committee from

1946–1958, and was a former National President of the NUT[34]. Having been a headmaster of both grammar and non-selective schools, he was a highly accredited spokesman for both. As head-master of a secondary modern school he established a GCE course in the early 1950s with the tacit approval of the Director,[35] and this was regularized by the new Director in 1956, whose immediate task was to reform the allowance structure of both teaching staff and of equipment. 'There was no need for our unions to use pressure tactics—resources were offered to us to encourage GCE'. Pupils were still transferred at 16+ from non-grammar to grammar schools—one grammar school had a VIth form in 1965 of whom a third were from neighbouring bilateral schools.

All teacher representatives regarded nominees to the Education Committee as delegates of the Joint Consultative Committee who were expected to report back to the JCC. On the whole, the records of the JCC support the view of the officers that issues of major importance were not raised—agendas were predominantly composed of school holidays and administrative matters. Evidence from NUT members interviewed suggests that the JCC did, on behalf of all organizations, express concern about low provision of extended courses in the 1950s, but teachers did not feel that they needed to press, recognizing that the administration was already using its capital resources to best advantage.[36] Teachers interviewed also suggested that they pressed for an adjustment of the revenue allocation when in the late 1950s it was necessary deliberately to divert resources to secondary schools as the increased numbers moved from primary to secondary schools. This pressure was ineffective largely because the needs of the reorganized secondary schools were so great that the Director and his Committee could see no alternative to giving preferential treatment to the secondary sector even at the expense of other sectors. It is only fair to record that while 'the bulge' was in the primary sector, the reverse position was evident—primary costs rose at a faster rate than secondary at that time.[37]

Several heads and teacher representatives could remember the 1950–52 cuts, and suggested that they had a long term depressive effect on the level of ordering school equipment and materials for some years afterwards with the result that the base line for negotia-tion on equipment allowances by the teachers' unions in 1958 was artificially low. It was at this stage that the JCC began to look at the national statistics of the IMTA which however then showed that Nottingham ranked as 'good average' on secondary but below average on primary expenditure. Some representatives appeared to be conditioned by the general atmosphere of 'rate consciousness' and suggested that this discouraged the teachers from asking for expansion. This is only partly true. Where new schools were established demand for new curricular resources was high, but the pattern of depressed demand was very evident in the old or re-organized schools.

As in Lincoln, the Joint Four did not appear to recognize for themselves the role attributed to them by the parent associations at the world conference referred to in Chapter III. The secretary of the Nottingham Joint Four was interviewed in 1969, together with the former secretary of another East Anglian branch. The four associations took part in JCC activities, but neither secretary could remember an issue of policy on which the local Joint Four as an organization had initiated or discussed taking any specific action. The Nottingham representatives confirmed the Lincoln evidence that very few directives or requests for views were received from head-quarters.[38] During the interview, the work of other unions in pressing for teacher representation on local authorities or for higher capitation allowances was discussed, but neither representative (nor, they thought, their colleagues) would have considered it a valid task for their professional associations to become involved other than as 'watchdogs' on the JCC. Whereas, for example, the NUT headquarters specifically advised its local branches in the late 1950s to use the IMTA statistics to press local authorities to improve standards,[39] the Joint Four local groups had received no such directive.

The general conclusion on teacher involvement in Nottingham is that all post-war administrations have valued teacher consultation and have used it,[40] but that on the kind of issues which affect distribution or level of resources, the need for pressure did not arise because both Directors were already concerned to raise standards and did so within the limits of those national and local controls which teachers accepted were valid. The NUT appeared to play the leading part in influencing policy during consultations, working mainly however within an agreed co-operative framework of a viable Teachers' Consultative Committee.

Governors

Evidence from the Director and from four senior colleagues, produced an interesting gloss on the general agreement in Nottingham that while governors were a useful moral and social support to a school they were not effective in either altering decision-making or diverting or increasing resources. It appeared that councillors themselves frowned on 'lobbying' for a particular school. Both members and officers accounted for this partly by the grouping of the schools—a governor had a loyalty to all six schools in the group—and partly because most were councillors anyway and would have to carry out the policy of their own Education Committee in that Committee later. The two administrative staff most closely concerned with school management both considered[41] that the relationship between head teacher and the Assistant Education Officer or section head was the crucial factor in determining the school's likelihood of extra resources or a different allocation. With or without pressure, the established educational priorities still existed and only major decisions of the Education Committee were likely to alter existing concepts of educational priority.

Records of governors' meetings show no preoccupation with any major matters—minutes more often relate to such matters as display boarding or draining boards. In 1969 all but two chairmen of governors were councillors, however, and four heads considered that the only instances in which they could recall an issue being strongly supported by governors, was at a time when their chairman also held an influential position in the hierarchy of Education Committee and Sub-Committees. On subsequent questioning, all four considered they would have ended with the same decision had the matter rested between themselves and the Director. A leading member of the Education Committee[42] considered that governors tended to support a head teacher's recommendation blindly from respect for professional judgement and had neither the knowledge nor the desire to alter priorities within school budgets submitted for governors' 'approval' each autumn. His committee colleagues interviewed in 1969 supported this.

The only major example of specific explicit pressure from governors arose over *Mundella Grammar School*, the fuller story of which is told in the writer's thesis. In the original development plan, this mixed grammar school was due to reorganize as a single-sex boys' school on the opening of a new girls' grammar school in the south of the city. By 1949, the Mundella PTA and old Scholars' Association were pressing the Education Committee to agree that the school should remain coeducational but the Education Committee resolved to reaffirm their earlier decision on the grounds that single-sex schools were preferable.[43] A long fight by governors, the associations and one or two councillors followed from 1950 to the mid 1960s. In fact the school did remain mixed but it would be dangerous to argue *post hoc ergo propter hoc* in this case since the head and staff of the school, and the administration, while appreciating the involvement of the governors, PTA and Old Scholars' Association considered that the final decision was dictated by the new need to plan for the south of the city as a whole in 1955 and not because of pressure. Both Committee members and officers took the line that rightly or wrongly they were there to judge what was educationally best, free of vested interest (whether coeducational or single-sex organization is 'educationally best' is in the end, a matter of a collective value judgement).

Of the nine schools visited, seven thought governors had no influence and two thought at first that they were a useful pressure point but on subsequent analysis of the examples given, agreed that the result of the request or pressure from head teachers direct to the Director was likely to have been the same, with or without the intermediary of governors.[44]

Conclusion

The evidence in Chapter IV on finance and the foregoing account of relative growth of both capital and revenue expenditure, seem to suggest that neither the authority nor the Directors of Education appeared psychologically inhibited by limited local financial resources. The growth rates of expenditure more than outstripped implicit demand from rising numbers.

The capital programme in Nottingham is a clear example of both principles outlined in Chapter I, that is lack of resources depressing demand, but dynamic demand releasing resources. The authority was successful in increasing its minor works allocations in several years, and negotiated a very substantial programme of secondary school building in the first decade as a result of its strength in administration and on the Sites and Buildings Sub-Committee. On the other hand, the full demand from the authority was not met in that the draft building programmes, realistic assessments of need, put up by the City always considerably exceeded the programme awarded. Chapter V and an earlier section of this chapter suggests that even given 'demand' for development of extended courses and improved conditions on the part of the Director and the Committee, the central control of capital building programme prevented the local education authority's full policy from being carried out. The Authority's intention to build five-year schools to offer extended courses in the first decade, was also frustrated by the unaccountable insistence of the Ministry in cutting projects in major programmes to accommodate either a four-year course only, or only half of the Vth year. Stringent controls on both major and minor works allocations and the growing backlog over many years of authorities' claims on these, made it unlikely that money would later be available, moreover, to remedy these initial deficiencies of the new capital projects—for to do so in the face of needs of older schools, even though the newer school may lack its complete accommodation, would be to follow a permanent policy of 'to him who hath shall be given'.

Implicit demand arising from the authority's policy of developing the bilateral scheme was again only partly met. Revenue expenditure did rise substantially. Improvements were made to the equipment and staffing allowances; but mainly for the able or older children only, for most of the period. The new schools were as well designed as the Ministry controls would allow but older schools did not receive the same standard of furniture and equipment and general environment as new schools. The goodwill and intention of both Directors to ensure parity of esteem between types of school and to develop constantly improving standards was hampered also by the rising proportion of the budget accounted for by *intractable* expenditure.

Inherited factors

A major determinant in establishing priority for the allocation of resources in the first decade was the deficiency in grammar school places, a factor beyond the control of both the Committee and the Director in 1945. Conversely the City's inheritance of a viable structure of reasonably sized modern schools (with only three all age schools) in 1945 materially influenced the pattern of the early post-war building programme and the development of technical education in non-grammar schools. Unlike Lincoln, however, the authority did successfully provide for technical education, both in technical and in bilateral schools. The standard of technical facilities in those schools offering extended courses was as adequate as the Ministry cost limits would allow in new schools; but left something to be desired in some older schools, for whom the authority had been unable to negotiate remodelling schemes from a limited minor works programme. The need significantly to expand opportunities for able pupils to follow extended courses, influenced the allocation of revenue resources since the extra grammar and (selective) bilateral places carried a proportionately higher standard of staffing, capitation etc. with its resulting additional annual revenue cost.

Explicit Pressure

Some *industrial* influence was noticeable particularly in the early years in relation to the three technical schools. Most schools and all officers considered that in general in Nottingham industry had had a general conditioning effect creating a favourable climate towards the development of technical education; but that no other practical effect on resources had been measurable, and that technical education as such had tended to move from the secondary to the further education sector in the later period. *Governors* were unanimously regarded as ineffective both as a source of pressure to influence decision-making; and as a factor of potential demand affecting the level and distribution of resources. *Teacher participation* was only partly effective in influencing major policy and was not apparently a significant factor in determining or in altering priorities of allocation of resources, although consultation with teachers was constant throughout the survey period. There was no traceable influence from outside bodies such as AASE or parents' associations within the period 1945–65. There appears to have been no major influence from *advisory staff* other than the control of a relatively small annual 'pool' of money for curriculum development.

The personality and philosophies of the two Directors appear the two major determinants, particularly in that both shared considerable administrative competence with strong educational ideologies (even though the latter differed). And they both took care to staff their departments for effective growth.

Notes

1 'The existing provision of schools of this type in Nottingham is quite inadequate'. Education Committee (17.3.43).
2 Secondary Education Sub-Committee (11.6.45).
3 With a level of provision so low, the places refused were in fact filled by the next 10 per cent on the waiting list. For further comment on possible parental influence see BANKS, Olive. *Parity and Prestige in English Secondary Education*, Routledge & Kegan Paul 1955. pp.197–209.
4 Nottingham, Annual Report 1945. p.2, reinforcing a similar statement of the Education Committee on 17.3.43.
5 Education Committee (17.3.43).
6 Education Committee (29.7.43).
7 Education Committee (29.7.43).
   The pattern of control outlined in Chapter V suggests that the Director's anxiety proved not unfounded.
8 Secondary Education Sub-Committee (8.1.46).
9 Ministry of Education, *Education in* 1947, p.120 Table 12. Interestingly even in the LCC as late as 1954 only half of its secondary schools were larger than 401 pupils (166) while the remaining 163 schools had less than 400 on roll, 90 having less than 300.
10 Secondary Education Sub-Committee (8.7.47).
11 Ibid.
12 Letter to Ministry September 1946.
13 Secondary Education Sub-Committee (15.6.54). Nottingham was not alone in its difficulty. By 1954 there were still 27 per cent of all local education authorities who had grammar school places for less than 15 per cent of the age group.
14 Secondary Education Sub-Committee (11.3.57).
15 The strength, experience and influence of Nottingham's senior administrative staff was referred to by most Committee members interviewed, and by HMIS.
16 Sites and Building Sub-Committee (8.10.53). The use of specialist rooms as class bases severely restricted the teaching of specialist subjects.
17 Nottingham, Annual Report 1956. p.4.

18 Sites and Building Sub-Committee (10.4.58).
19 Ministry of Education. *Secondary Education for all—A New Drive* CMD 604 December 1958. HMSO.
20 Successfully; because the Director agreed with the Committee. Nottingham, Annual Report 1949, p.66.
21 Nottingham, Annual Report 1953, p.27.
22 Interviewed in April 1969 and November 1969.
23 Annual report 1965, p.20.
24 School Government Sub-Committee (3.10.62).
25 *Royal Commission on Technical Instruction,* the Samuelson Report, second report, Vol. I, 1884. Part IV, pp.513–14.
26 The hosiery trade alone employed about 25,000 in 1943–45. Hosiery in this context included knitwear, woollens and lingerie as well as hose.
27 Nottingham, Higher Education Sub-Committee (12.4.43).
28 Secondary Education Sub-Committee (10.9.45).
   Fortunately its terms of reference were not interpreted so literally.
29 Secondary Education Sub-Committee (12.4.54).
30 Senior officer interviewed in 1969.
31 There is unanimity among officers that the Treasurer, not the Finance Committee, had a more decisive influence in determining budgetary expansion or regression in the survey period.
32 See Chapter III for composition of the JCC.
33 It is interesting to note, however, that Nottinghamshire County Council, like Lincoln, had banned GCE in non-grammar schools at that time, though it later altered its policy.
34 Interviewed in 1969.
35 Tacit in that the Director did not oppose it as a policy but with the financial recession of the early 1950s, would promise neither additional staff nor extra allowances.
36 Interviews 1969.
37 Evidence from administrative officers and files.
38 In marked contrast with the NUT.
39 Evidence from the NUT in all three authorities.
40 Director, 1969 'I could not and would not have gone ahead with the bilateral scheme without the fullest backing from the teachers in 1957'.
41 In separate interviews in 1969.
42 With 43 years experience of local government, most of them serving on Education Committees.
43 Secondary Education Sub-Committee (12.9.49).
   31 out of 36 secondary schools in 1949 were single sex.
44 See for example table D (viii) of Appendix D.

CHAPTER VIII

The Development of Secondary Education in Northumberland (1945—1965)

*'No child shall be at a disadvantage educationally by virtue
of being born and educated in the county.'*

Education in Northumberland 1953–58

Northumberland was between six and seven times the size of Lincoln,
nearly twice the size of Nottingham and markedly poorer than either.
Its inheritance of a low level of provision of secondary education in
1945 and an equally low budget, left a backlog of need not fully met
even in 1945 despite the county's valiant efforts.

The Inherited Position in 1945

After the war, the pattern of secondary education was mainly
bipartite with one or two nascent technical schools. Grammar places
were available for only 10 per cent of the age group, and over half
of all children of secondary school age were in all-age schools with
poor facilities, financed at the primary (elementary) and not
secondary rate of allowances and staffed accordingly. The three
immediate demands facing the Education Committee were the need
to complete the Hadow reorganization; the need to increase the
number and proportion of selective places; and the rapidly rising
birthrate which, combined with Newcastle overspill, created an
urgent demand for a massive secondary building programme. The
county itself saw a fourth need, to improve or rebuild many existing
schools. (Of the 11 existing senior schools in 1942 for example, five
had no library, none had adequate science and all were overcrowded,
mostly with class sizes over 40.) At the request of the Board of
Education, a junior technical school had been established at Wallsend
in old buildings to stimulate the intake of recruits to skilled work in
the building trades[1] but there was little other 'technical education'
then available.

By 1943, pressure was building up in favour of educational
reconstruction, especially from the 'disfavoured' rural areas. 'Public
opinion is most strongly roused . . . reform most urgently demanded'[2],
because there were too few selective places in many districts;
children had to travel long distances; premises were poor; and over

half of children over 11 were in all-age schools. Individual pressures came from Newburn, Prudhoe, Alnwick and Berwick[3] for new secondary schools in their areas. One immediate placebo was applied by way of a 13+ transfer scheme to grammar schools to help the operation of which the Teachers' Advisory Committee resolved that 'the grammar and technical schools and the A forms of modern schools should have a common curriculum'[4] although the latter did not really happen in practice.

The Development Plan and the County's Policies

The main task of preparing a new Development Plan fell to the then Deputy Director (later appointed Director in 1953). The final plan was presented in what must have been record time in 1946, based on tripartite organization of grammar, technical and modern schools; and embodied a number of basic principles. The need for larger schools (for educational reasons) was to be balanced against increased travelling time, transport costs and boarding of children, and the need to retain village schools for community reasons. Uniform planning was not considered necessary or desirable.[5] The authority specified an order of priority for future building programmes, the provision of new technical schools, new rural modern schools, new urban modern schools, primary remodelling or remodelling of existing grammar schools, believing that

'the most urgent problem, educationally speaking, is to provide for the full choice of schools at 11+, and therefore it is considered that it is really vital to provide Technical schools and to complete reorganization of primary and secondary schools.'[6]

In calculating secondary requirements, the authority assumed a need for future secondary places as follows.

Table VIII (1)

	GRAMMAR	TECHNICAL	MODERN	TOTAL
New places	1,090	3,570	16,368	21,028
Remodelling places	2,860	930	9,125	12,915
Total	3,950	4,500	25,493	33,943

The Director had persuaded the Committee in 1947 to amend the Development plan in order to establish the campus principle for five areas and to develop a modified campus plan for four more. The Director defended the continued provision of small schools, but suggested that shared campus facilities would overcome some disdavantages.[7] The authority did not establish any major policy on the desirability of single-sex or coeducational schools—each area was to be considered on its merits. Both the Roman Catholic and Church of England church authorities co-operated well with the county (and vice versa) and although church education is not strong in Northumberland, the inclusion of church schools in, for example, the Ponteland and Alnwick and Longbenton districts was the result of effective negotiations by the Dioceses.

The Leadership

Even more strongly than in other areas, the personal qualities, idiosyncrasies and philosophies of the two post-war Directors and the long-serving chairman of the Education Committee, pervaded the whole process of the development of secondary education in the county.

Two characteristics were constant. A tradition of close and lively consultation with teachers—formally and informally—and a ceaseless striving for reform, innovation and the widening of educational opportunity were ingrained in the attitudes of both Directors. The evidence which emerges from the train of actual events, is very largely confirmed by verbal evidence from contemporaries of both.

The first post-war Director was generally described as 'energetic, thoughtful and educationally sound'. He built up a strong inspectorate and a climate of teacher-involvement in the 1930s and despite inadequate funds, started the Hadow reorganization. The schools built in the 1930s were provided with specialist rooms reasonable by the then standards (if somewhat inadequate when reviewed unaltered in 1968). He saw the education service as 'a partnership'; and the achievements of the early post-war years are tangible evidence of an administrative skill not common in 1945. Despite the shortage of revenue and capital resources in the period 1945 to 1953, firm aims were set of desirable standards to be attained which materially helped the development of better educational services in the county. But a former contemporary colleague interviewed in 1968, described him as unconcerned at the low grammar percentage— he believed (as his contemporaries at Nottingham and Lincoln) in 'investment in the able'. The problem of the technical schools was deferred effectively until his successor's appointment in 1953, from the post of Deputy Director, who considered as late as 1968 that he owed much to his training under the early regime.[8] This however would do less than justice to his own individual contribution. 'He was constantly vigilant for rising standards.'[9] Senior professional staff described him as energetic, skilful at handling his Committee, 'a man of unquestioned integrity',[10] but an educationalist rather than an administrator—and a Director should be both. In common with four out of five of the other post-war Directors he was reluctant to delegate, and ran a diffusely organized Department. It is interesting to speculate that some of the more distinguished achievements in two of the three areas happened under a largely 'directive' organization.

The second post-war Director encouraged his inspectors to play a major part in the formation of policy; in the design of schools; and in curriculum development. They were for example responsible for initiating drives to improve libraries, to increase the supply and use of visual aids, and for the modernization of facilities and techniques in the craft subjects. This accounted for some anomalies. Average general expenditure on books, stationery and apparatus in the county was for example below the national average at a time when the cost of visual aids and extra curricular activities in the county had rocketed to three times the national average. Yet the county was among the first to introduce teachers' centres, the extended day, Nuffield Science and French, project technology and the use of short-term residential centres (both general centres to widen pupils' educational horizons and the specialist field study centres at Catton and Howtell). The county's policy on boarding education pre-dated national trends by about 10 years.

The Director's priorities, with hindsight, are interesting. There is unanimous evidence from senior colleagues, financial officers and members that neither he nor the Committee made a practice of regularly taking stock of the financial implications of a fast rate of innovation from a minority of pupils. The assessment of the incidence of premature leavers from grammar schools and of GCE results which were used in the 1959 revision of the Development Plan, was not matched by conscious assessment of priorities between sectors of secondary education; and there was little monitoring of overall basic standards. Educational planning was by conviction rather than by coherence.

'There was a tradition of experiment'[11] and 'we had experimentation by instalments'[12] were not untypical comments. A financial adviser suggested that 'the county could never resist an experiment—prestige projects were paid for at the expense of basic standards'[13]. The only section of the estimates rarely cut was the budget for curriculum development and for new schemes—a highly desirable tradition and in one sense the life-blood of a developing service. Teachers in less privileged schools deficient in basic resources were, however, predictably more doubtful about the price paid for innovation where this failed to be generally applied.

The passionate concern of both Directors to maintain steady development and to achieve real equality of opportunity for Northern children was matched at Committee level, led by the Chairman. A driving force for 20 years, the Chairman, once convinced by the Director that money for a certain development or improvement was necessary for the good of Northumbrian children, carried his own party, the opposition, the full County Council and where necessary, the Ministry in the tide of his determination. 'A man of stature', with 'a deep and abiding concern for children' coupled with 'a driving force that blew like the wind across Seahouses'[14] and with a real respect for teachers and their views, he combined with the Director to make a force for development regarded with unease by some of the financially conscious County Council members. But as a team, the Director and Chairman were rarely opposed with any seriousness by the authority who appeared to recognize the needs represented to them as valid and urgent.

Grammar and Technical School Provision

A fundamental influence, modified only in the late 1959s was the county's strongly held view that only a maximum of 15 per cent of children could benefit from an academic (grammar) education. This sprang partly from the personal conviction of the then Director and partly from the research work of the authority's Examinations and Research Officer whose results pioneered the Northumberland Selection Tests in the early 1940s. In practice grammar school places were provided as follows (including those admitted to direct grant and independent schools):

Table VIII (2)

Year	% OF 11 + AGE GROUP QUALIFYING FOR GRAMMAR SCHOOL PLACES %
1946	10·1
1948	13·2
1952	13·9
1956	13·4
1959	14·8

(But the county had proposed to build 15 technical schools offering courses ranging through agriculture, mining and engineering, commerce to building, art and homecrafts.)[15] The authority had developed a system of late transfers to grammar schools at 12+ and at 13+ which gave an extended academic education to a further two per cent of pupils, for whom 'special forms are started in several county grammar schools'.[16]

During the 1950s, however, under a new Director, the principles underlying the early Development Plan were reviewed. Nationally considerable doubt had been cast on the rigidity of tripartite classification (which stemmed predominantly from the influence of the Spens report) and a fundamental review initiated by the second post-war Director led to a complete revision of the Development Plan, finally published in 1959. The revised plan adopted a bipartite system of grammar/technical and technical/modern schools, on the grounds that

'it is extremely difficult to define a Technical type of pupil as such, but it is possible to differentiate with reasonable accuracy between children endowed with a facility for acquiring knowledge by the abstract means of the written or spoken word, and those for whom practice in the crafts is an essential means for the acquisition of knowledge and the expression of ability.'[17]

As a direct result of Ministry cuts in capital programmes, the county in fact succeeded in programming only two technical schools, Haydon Bridge and Wallsend, the former opening in 1962 and the latter in 1960. The combined grammar/technical selection rate improved in the last five years of the period:

Table VIII (3)

YEAR	% OF 11 + AGE GROUP QUALIFYING FOR ENTRY TO GRAMMAR AND TECHNICAL SCHOOLS %
1960	17·7
1961	21·7
1962	25·0
1963	23·1
1964	25·8

The rising birthrate indeed was to create a major problem in that the need to maintain the *existing* level of selective places and to reorganize existing all-age schools conflicted with the need to provide more new places for additional pupils. By 1955 for example, the 11 + age group had increased by 30 per cent on the 1952 level,[18] and by 1958 (the peak year of 'the bulge') the age group was 70 per cent higher than in 1952,[19] dropping to 55 per cent over the 1952 figure in 1959, an implicit demand which even the Ministry might have recognized.

Non-grammar Schools and Extended Courses

Table VIII (1) above shows a need for over 16,000 new secondary modern places and the section which follows this, on capital investment, illustrates the county's difficulty in building schools fast enough to meet the needs of less able pupils largely but not wholly because of excessive governmental controls and a 'stop-go' policy of national capital investment. Northumberland accepted from the outset the need to establish some form of extended education for non-grammar pupils, particularly in the early years.[20] By 1954 the authority was concerned at the lack of involvement of secondary modern schools in external examinations.[21] The presence of able children in modern schools (in the absence of enough grammar and technical schools), the need for parity of esteem and the desirability of an incentive for the pupils led the Director to consult the Teachers' Advisory Committee and subsequently to recommend that both GCE and the examinations of the Northern Counties Technical Examinations Council be permitted in non-grammar schools with a preference for the latter.[22] In 1954, only four out of 45 modern schools entered pupils for external examinations, but by 1957, all but six modern schools and most of the larger all-age schools entered some candidates, 815 of whom were under 16. The pass rates for the NCTEC pre-technical and pre-National certificate courses were 77 per cent and 90 per cent respectively. In 1957, seven modern schools offered GCE courses in some subjects. By 1961, some rationalization of bias courses was suggested after consultation with head teachers, and the committee accepted the need to meet the cost of travel (over three miles) and of lodging where necessary to give pupils access to a wider range of courses.

Interviews with senior professional staff and with teachers' representatives in 1968 confirms that the real drive for extended courses in non-grammar schools arose because of concern at the low percentage of the county's children staying on after 15 + compared with the national average. The development of a range of courses in the non-grammar sector was widely discussed at meetings of heads of (all types of) secondary schools and with the senior professional staff before the Director submitted a policy document to his Committee.

Boarding Education

It was regarded by both Directors as essential for the county to develop residential provision to enable pupils from rural areas to benefit either from selective education not available near their home or from a wider range of educational opportunity than could be offered in small rural schools (some with catchment areas of from 100–200 miles). Hostels were built at Allendale (to serve an outlying rural modern school), Haydon Bridge (to serve the agricultural technical school), Alnwick (grammar school) and Hexham (to serve both sexes attending the grammar school), at an overall cost of £250,000. In 1956, the authority bought Bellingham and Marton school camps from the National Camps Corporation to offer pupils over 13 years an opportunity of a period of boarding education in a rural setting. The initial costs were £25,000 and £23,000 respectively. Subsequent improvements amounted to over £60,000 for both camp schools together. The county used generously its power to send pupils to recognized boarding schools (notably Barnard Castle and Whitley, King Edward). The authority took the opportunity to lease Ford Castle (former home of the Joyces) when it became available, and developed it as a short term residential centre. By 1962, the Education Committee declared a formal policy that

'In the light of their knowledge of the great educational and social benefits derived from an experience of boarding education by county children . . . the Education Committee have already laid down as a principle that provision shall be made to enable all children at some time during their secondary school course, to have the opportunity of at least one week's education under residential conditions'

in addition to the long-term provision. The Director was authorized to look at the possiblility of using redundant rural schools (at Beal and Kielder for example) for development as residential centres, to supplement the two residential Field Study Centres at Howtell and Catton. Northumberland's well-developed boarding provision seemed in advance of its time, and accounted in part for some of the justifiably high spending on secondary education (a later section on revenue expenditure gives details).

Capital Expenditure and the Secondary Building Programme

The actual capital building programme for the secondary sector is given in full for the period 1946–64 in Appendix E, which should be read in conjunction with this chapter. Figure 10 on the following page illustrates it diagrammatically and can be sharply contrasted

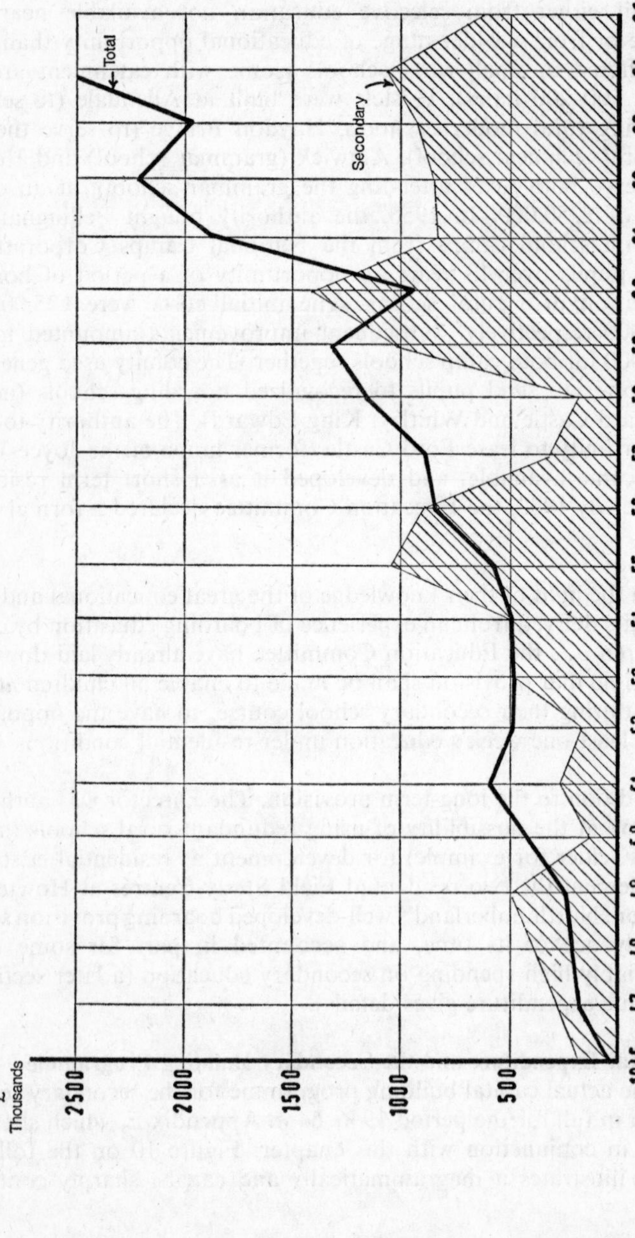

FIGURE 10: Total education capital expenditure and secondary building programmes—Northumberland

with Figures 7 and 8. The later programmes are inflated because of the need for extra schools to accommodate pupils on Newcastle overspill housing estates and in the two new towns. Newcastle's slum clearance programme produced a 90 per cent increase in the secondary population in South-east Northumberland between 1957 and 1963, in addition to the earlier overspill programme which created the need for schools at Longbenton and Newburn in the early 1950s. And clearly the needs and policies touched on so far had very substantial implications for capital building programmes. It will be recalled (from Chapter IV) that the county was basically poor, relying heavily on government grant to maintain its services. But as Appendix E illustrates, the county's building programme was substantial although its final total costs were proportionately higher than Nottingham's because of a late start.

The County Council's independence from central government was established from the outset *despite its dependence on government grant*. The Development Plan established that building programmes must match the

'material outlook of nearly every village and town in the county . . . to preserve the traditional architecture of this lovely county.'[23]

The first battle was fought over the HORSA huts issued by the Ministry of Works for the raising of the leaving age in 1947. The county refused to order them, and designed its own prototype, enlisting the aid of the County Councils Association and the AEC to fight the Ministry. It instructed its Planning Committee to refuse planning consent for HORSA huts. The County's specially designed mobile classrooms were eventually approved by the Ministry and erected, the total programme exceeding £55,000.[24]

The phasing of the Northumberland programmes in the first decade defies ready explanation thirty years later. Some projects were approved by the Ministry and then promptly cancelled a year later as part of the regular cuts (for example the technical schools at Ashington, Blyth and Wallsend), others were deferred by agreement with the local education authority because of site difficulties of subsidence (Wooler, Prudhoe) or ownership (the aristocracy owned many of the suitable readily accessible sites . . .). Nevertheless, the county regularly submitted programmes for approval greatly in excess of the level awarded, programmes for which there was an irrefutable case on grounds of rising numbers, all-age reorganization and development of technical education; and less than one half of which were awarded. Table VIII (4) on the following page gives the most marked examples.

It has indeed often been argued that authorities indulge in 'Eastern bargaining' and that they could not have built the full programmes submitted even had the Ministry awarded them. And there is some evidence from both members and officers that some projects were

Table VIII (4): *Secondary Building Programmes—Selected Years*

Year		Estimated Value of Authority's Submission (Secondary) £	Value of Secondary Programmes Approved by the Ministry £
1951–52		750,181	257,280 later cut to 128,640
1956–57		1,569,662	913,378
1957–58		1,224,362	312,779
1958–59	main Newcastle overspill	1,890,013 / 405,141 / 2,295,154	157,405
1959–60	main Newcastle overspill	1,300,480 / 204,036 / 1,504,516	1,037,696
1960–61		1,687,141*	1,421,866
1961–62		1,747,550*	817,376
1962–63		2,229,968*	850,983
1963–64		2,267,198*	903,873
1964–65	main Newcastle overspill	1,150,055 / 2,211,645 / 3,361,700	1,082,170

* Newcastle overspill not readily identifiable, but included in the total.

lost from the very early building programmes because of inadequate staffing. Architects blamed this on low salaries of technical officers offered by local Government in the North East compared with industry and with other regions. The position stabilized, however, in the mid-1950s and from 1956 onwards evidence is unanimous that technical resources were in fact available for a larger programme than that awarded. When the programmes were awarded at a higher level, the additional schools were built. Moreover, if the building programme in Appendix E is related to Table VIII (3), to the rapid growth in the school population and to the fact that as late as 1958 there were 6,691 seniors in all-age schools, it will be evident that Northumberland's draft programmes related realistically to acute *actual* unmet need. An analysis of the detailed draft programmes shows that the county made convincing cases for new modern schools and additional selective places throughout the 1950s, but while the first real phase of rural reorganization was awarded in 1955–57, the drastic cut in the 1957–59 programme halted this, causing a backlog from which the county could not recover. This was exacerbated by the subsequent need to house children from Newcastle-overspill housing estates for which no proportionate increase in the county's building programme was awarded. Not until the early 1960s did the county itself consider it feasible to include any improvement projects even in its draft programme. Even however the effective and *explicit demand* from the local education authority, only succeeded in marginally increasing its programme. The County Council invoked the aid of the CCA in 1949 to press for extra capital allocations for new rural schools; although unsuccessfully. A regular pattern of visits to the Ministry began in 1951 when the Chairman of the Education Committee and the Director went to London to press for North Sunderland modern school's inclusion in a programme and for a substantial programme in 1952. The derisory revised 1952–53 programme (£128,640 out of £1½ million) caused a further full Deputation which produced a marginally higher programme in the following year, but a third of which was for Newcastle overspill. The Authority recorded with some bitterness its concern:

'All this in spite of Development Plan proposals, which seems to suggest the shelving of the plans for a while.'[25]

Despite regular deputations from 1953 to 1958 the programmes were only marginally increased on negotiation, although in 1954 Circular 283 actually pressed authorities to submit proposals for rural reorganization of all-age schools suggesting that an *addition* would be made to the national programme for this. But Table V (2) (on page 140 of Chapter V) shows that when the building cost increases between 1949 and 1955 are taken into account, together with the sharp rise in the age group, the annual £77 million approved nationally for 1955 and 1956 represented no more than a re-instatement of the 1949 level of programme. The dramatic fall in 1957 to £24 million and the timelag of three years until even the 1955 level was reinstated, puts gravely into question the seriousness of the Ministry's policy statements on secondary development of 1954 and 1958.[26] In 1958 the Ministry recorded that 'further projects for all-age reorganization cannot be accepted at present' because the national priority was still for 'roofs over heads' due to housing developments or high numbers, and the small margin for develop-ment had to go towards improving scientific and technical facilities in grammar schools (undoubtedly another genuine need). Priority for rural schools was shortlived.

But not only were new places not available for 'roofs over heads' but existing schools were deficient. 'Laboratory facilities are totally inadequate.' 'The premises of this grammar school would not grace the 19th century.' 'This girls' grammar school is in quite appalling premises.' 'This boys' grammar school is in a highly inconvenient building over 100 years old surrounded by a conglomeration of dilapidated huts.' 'We cannot offer these secondary modern pupils the practical education they need.' The county—members and officers alike—were driven by a desire to offer the fullest educational opportunity to their pupils.[27] The capital resources were not forth-coming from the national budget until the early 1960s. Circular 6/60 must have had a hollow ring in the county's ears:

'The school building programme for 1960-61 marks the beginning of five years of increased effort to improve the quality of primary and secondary education. Large building programmes are also in hand for technical education . . .'[28]

Tables V (1) and V (2) provide as they stand, evidence of the dichotomy of central government's declared and its actual policy.

Implicit Demand From Rising School Rolls

The relative growths in school population and in expenditure in the three areas are given in Tables IV (4) and IV (6) in Chapter IV. The sharper increases in revenue expenditure in the county compared with the county boroughs is largely attributable to the factor of all-age rural reorganization which affected both its capital programme and the subsequent increases in revenue expenditure as more pupils moved from the primary sector (in old buildings and with low allowances) to the secondary sector (in new buildings with improved allowances). The 1946 base of both secondary school population and secondary expenditure per head was also abnormally low.

The extent to which rising numbers caused increased expenditure, although more in actual terms, was less *proportionately* than in the county boroughs, as Table VIII (5) illustrates when compared with similar tables in chapters VI and VII:

Table VIII (5)

YEAR	DIRECT GROSS SECONDARY REVENUE EXPENDITURE £	INDEX	SECONDARY SCHOOL ROLLS	INDEX
1946	363,879	100	10,315	100
1949	533,025	147	13,785	142
1953	783,472	216	15,214	157
1956	1,271,000	350	18,088	185
1959	2,451,291	674	23,374	240
1961	3,127,188	860	27,366	253
1964	4,575,698	1250	28,973	259

Secondary expenditure in Northumberland increased in fact at nearly twice the rate of the total education budget, and increased over 12 fold from 1946—1964 while the secondary school rolls increased less than threefold. Substantial though the implicit demand of rising rolls may be, it was perhaps not the only major factor.

Intractable Expenditure

As in Nottingham the most readily identifiable intractable elements of revenue expenditure were teachers' salaries, loan charges and maintenance. Appendix B gives full details of the financial pattern of some aspects of the county budget. The increase in *teachers' salaries* was proportionately greater in the county than in the county boroughs partly because of the original low base in 1946 (a majority of children being in all-age or 'senior' schools) and the low grammar provision. Chapter IX clearly illustrates the very substantial differential of salaries and allowance structures between selective and non-grammar schools. The increase from 10 per cent to 25 per cent provision of grammar and technical places would carry a major implication for the salary bill; and so it did. It was however less marked than it might have been because the quota system was negotiated on a base year of 1938 when Northumberland was understaffed.

Table VIII (6)

Year	(A) Total Direct Secondary Expenditure £	(B) Teachers' Salaries (Secondary) £	% (B) of (A)
1946	363,879	270,606	74·4
1951	661,719	451,780	68·3
1957	1,441,643*	881,366	61·2
1959	2,451,291†	1,142,364	46·6
1962	3,702,306	1,695,435	45·8
1964	4,575,698	1,938,078	42·4

* the first year of the phased introduction of equal pay.
† see footnote to Table VIII (c) in Appendix B for a change in the basis of calculation from 1958.

Even allowing for the difference in the method of calculating the total secondary expenditure after 1958, the impact of reorganization can clearly be seen in an expenditure of £2 million for teachers' salaries alone. (It is not possible to add back the cost of loan charges, transport etc. to the total figure before 1958 because these figures were not broken down into sectors of the service.)

Loan charges, as might be expected, accounted for a significant element of the budget. The loan charges for the total education service increased from 3·2 per cent of total gross revenue expenditure in 1946 to 9·9 per cent in 1964, a trebling in proportion. Table VIII (7) shows the loan charges for secondary education in some later years at the peak of the effect of the building programme:

Table VIII (7)

Year	(A) Total Direct Secondary Expenditure £	(B) Loan Charges £	% (B) of (A) %
1958	2,054,239	234,390	11·4
1960	2,784,148	350,833	16·3
1962	3,702,306	538,545	14·5
1964	4,575,698	843,746	18·4

Northumberland was therefore obliged to pay a heavy price for the lateness of the peak of its secondary building programme, because of the heavier actual cost of loan charges and the rising proportion which it took of the direct secondary budget.

Another mainly intractable element which was proportionately higher in later years in the county boroughs, was *maintenance* not only of buildings but of grounds. Sites of rural schools tended to be larger—16 to 20 acres—and their maintenance depended on gang mowers and staff travelling 60 miles or more each month to each school from the nearest depot.

Table VIII (8)

Year	Maintenance £	% of Direct Secondary Expenditure %
1946	13,330	3·6
1956	56,361	4·4
1959	107,325	4·4
1964	175,666	3·9

The three elements quoted above, when expressed as expenditure per head of secondary school population, show a higher level of spending than the percentage of the budget shown here would indicate at first sight. One probable reason for this is the addition to the total secondary budget of other elements either not present or less substantial in that of the two county boroughs. Administrative costs were higher in the county because of a larger inspectorate. The latter in turn, accounted for a substantial and increasing budget of in-service training of teachers after 1960 which was often directly related to the curriculum development so keenly encouraged by the Director. And boarding and transport costs were higher.

Tractable or Discretionary Expenditure

Brief mention was made in an earlier section of the implication of the Development Plan for boarding education and for the transport bill. In this also the county's needs—and expenditure—were greater:

Table VIII (9)

Year	Expenditure on Boarding* £	Expenditure on Transport (Secondary) £
1947	115	not known
1955	13,633	not known
1958	89,753	55,634
1964	130,225	142,161†

* Boarding hostels, camp schools etc. but excluding Ford Castle and the curriculum-based centres.

† out of an overall total of £283,552 for transport.

By 1964, the county's combined costs of boarding hostels and schools and transport (largely of rural children to new secondary modern schools) accounted for six per cent of the total secondary budget. Despite the difficulties which the authority experienced in providing full equality of opportunity, it appears to have taken a number of measures to attempt to compensate both for potential geographical disadvantage and for belated building programme approvals, by transporting children to services where these could not be taken to children.

Curricular Resources

Table VII (c) of Appendix B gives the rise in expenditure on curricular resources, and its proportion of the total budget. After 1959, loan charges, transport etc. are added back to the total, and the fact that even so, expenditure on furniture, equipment, books stationery and apparatus still accounted for 5·6 per cent to 7·0 per cent of the total secondary budget, meant a rise in real terms—unlike the position in the county boroughs.

Table VIII (10) which follows relates increased costs to the growth rate of secondary rolls, and should be read in conjunction with Table VII (c). Before 1959, the rate of increase of expenditure when related to rising numbers seems to have done no more than to meet normal price rises. By 1964, it included a substantial increase for curriculum development and innovation.

Table VIII (10)

YEAR	FURNITURE APPARATUS EQUIPMENT £	INDEX	BOOKS STATIONERY MATERIALS £	INDEX	SECONDARY ROLLS	INDEX
1949	20,487	100	27,347	100	13,785	100
1950	13,099	49	26,913	99	14,238	104
1955	27,192	133	46,406	170	16,185	118
1959	64,846	318	106,712	388	23,374	170
1961	67,712	333	108,637	396	27,366	200
1964	109,610	535	148,713	543	28,973	211

Northumberland, in common with the other local education authorities operated a scheme of school allowances weighted in favour of first, grammar school pupils and later, older pupils, throughout most of the survey period. The system was revised in due course to remove the differential between types of school, only retaining a higher allowance for pupils over 15+. Evidence from the inspectorate, the teachers' organizations and the schools supports the suggestion that this review arose out of a growing concern from heads of all-age and rural schools expressed at the regular meetings of heads called by the Director. A working party of teachers and officers produced the revised scheme which, amended to allow for price rises, was operative in 1968.[29] It was combined work on the part of the teachers (both the organizations and the heads) and the inspectorate which produced the county's programme to make sure that all schools had a minimum of visual aids (projectors, cine projectors, etc.) and that the funds did not go only to the vociferous. It was, too, the inspectorate who developed the mobile film unit to serve small schools scattered in rural areas.

The *library service* was another example of 'demand' from within the service. The county inherited a 'shocking position' in 1945 with no branch or mobile public libraries[30] and both Directors worked ceaselessly to improve both the general library provision and its service to schools. The new schools were given grants of £1,000 per annum for the first few years after opening but older schools often had no libraries at all and a programme of providing Terrapin classrooms from minor works money was encouraged by the Director, to release rooms in older buildings for conversion to libraries[31] which then qualified for initial grants. Schools without purpose-designed libraries were given generous loans from the public library service. By the early 1960s a mobile library for schools of 3,000 books was in operation and it is relevant to note that in the early years *priority was given to non-grammar schools*. The scheme was only extended to grammar schools in 1963.[32] It supplemented a fleet of mobile public libraries.

Inherited Assumptions

The same inherited attitudes on the needs of the less able and the able, of boys and girls were as prevalent in Northumberland as elsewhere and there is little new to add except on the question of viable size of school. A correlation between inadequate resources in small and rural schools, discriminatory timetabling between boys and girls, and a high level of entry of girls into unskilled employment in the county became evident. Professional opinion in the county was adamant that 300 was an ideal size for a school and 450 was tending to be large. This attitude was defended on the grounds that any larger school would fail to provide pastoral care. Consequently in several districts, from two to four small schools were (newly) built at three-form entry or less within easy travelling distance—in two cases, actually on the same site. Yet Walbottle, Whitley Bay and Ashington grammar schools were all enlarged in phases from 2/3 to 5 form entry, making schools of over 1,000 pupils at a time when modern schools were still being designed for 400 pupils with an intake across 80 per cent of the ability range. Either grammar school pupils did not need pastoral care (which is arguable) or the 'cost-effective' argument was held to be valid only when providing breadth of opportunity for able pupils. In practice, although rationalization of courses and special subjects was sought between neighbouring schools, 13+ transfers and cross-timetabling were so rare as to place the theory of shared resources in doubt. In view of the evidence in Chapter XI on the destination of the county's school leavers, and notably the girls, it is arguable that the pastoral care of teenage pupils might have been less crucial to many than the acquisition of an adequate scientific education, modern languages and craft skills which they would need in adult life. Most rural and small schools could offer only a severely limited curriculum even though this was often brilliantly taught on the evidence of the 1968–69 survey. A well adjusted 15-year-old may become a maladjusted adult if inadequately equipped to find skilled work outside his own region when need arose—as it increasingly will. It is suggested that the county's assumption that any school above 450 was 'large' and that pastoral care was impossible above that size, was inherited and unexamined n relation to the needs of the time.[33]

Standards

The county regularly reviewed the progress of pupils in its grammar schools, following the tradition of assessment of academic achievement set by Miss Lambert as Examinations Officer in the early 1940s. The county seemed in its reports well satisfied that its losses at 15+ were below the national average; but so was its grammar provision. If the selection tests pioneered by the county had much validity and so few as 10 per cent to 12 per cent went to grammar school, then there ought to have been minimal loss at 15+. The high early rate of leaving gives credence to the regressive Northern attitudes towards advanced education touched on by the University of Newcastle's survey on school leavers mentioned in Chapter XI.

Table VIII (11)

Year	Premature Leavers at 15 + from Grammar Schools %
1952	12·9
1956	12·8
1959	7·0
1961	6·3
1964	4·5

The national average in 1953 was 20 per cent and in 1964 10·5 per cent.

In a study of secondary selection in Northumberland, Victor Hancock suggests that this might be partly

'that the preparation in the modern school before transfer for the work which will be encountered in the grammar school afterwards is inadequate'[34]

although there is no evidence cited that more pupils transferring at 13+ left prematurely than those entering at 11+. Hancock also establishes that Northumberland's VIth forms were well below the national average. The GCE results which he cites for 1959 are not wholly impressive for such a limited selection rate

Table VIII (12): 1959 GCE 'O' level

	GRAMMAR/TECHNICAL		OTHER	
	Number	*%*	*Number*	*%*
Candidates	784	13·1	91	1·6
Candidates taking 5 subjects	772	12·87	49	0·8
Passed 5 subjects	506	8·43	18	0·3
'good'*	347	5·78	1	0·02

Note: The percentage is of the age group of 6,194 admitted to all county
secondary schools in 1954 at 11 +.

*English Language, Maths, Science, Foreign language plus 2 others.

It is generally accepted that entry to further education, universities
or skilled employment is directly related to performance at least at
'O' level. That only eight per cent of the age group passed five
subjects and only five per cent in the kind of subjects needed for
further advanced education and training raises serious questions
about the accommodation, staffing and material resources available
to that generation of children as well as about the type of teaching.
It is difficult to suggest that these results are solely the result of
inadequate motivation and it can hardly be held that the top 12 per
cent of the age group were less able than elsewhere. The question
also arises, what level of achievement the 88 per cent in non-grammar
schools reached in terms of qualifying for adult life.[35] Of the 3·6 per
cent of modern pupils entered for 'O' level in 1961, 19·2 per cent
passed in five subjects and 32 per cent in four subjects. The evidence
in Chapter XI is hardly surprising in the light of these findings. On
the other hand, the county made a serious attempt to substitute an
internal leaving certificate but

'it soon became clear that neither parents nor employers relished
the arrangements . . . if the universities themselves were not willing
to leave general education on trust to the schools, it could hardly be
expected that the professions and employers would.'[36]

The county's adoption of the NCTEC's school certificate was more
popular and in 1961 2,506 pupils took it with a 69·1 per cent success
rate in an average of five subjects.[37]
Standards of accommodation and equipment are partly dealt with
in Chapter X and in Appendix D. The authority was little different
from the other survey areas in that the older schools which the
authority had failed to programme for rebuilding were woefully

deficient in specialist facilities, and the new buildings suffered from the Ministry's insistence on 'instalment' building, low cost limits and imposition of a maximum teaching area. The county un- doubtedly achieved the best available in limiting circumstances; always excepting its syndrome of 'small schools'.

Explicit Demand

In Northumberland, there was little evidence of explicit demand with one or two notable exceptions.

AASE

In 1963 a Tyneside branch of AASE was established which expanded from a Parent-Teachers' Association at a Tyne valley school. The current secretary was interviewed in 1968 and records checked at County Hall. Tribute was paid by AASE to the co-operation of the Education Department in providing information and in discussing major issues of concern (such as the cutting of annual estimates). On the other hand there seems no evidence of real success as a pressure group. Most of the issues raised were related to local districts (the need for a new school at Ponteland). AASE expressed early concern at the uneven provision of different aspects of education over the county and did succeed in using managers and governors to air issues concerning poor facilities. How far success was due to AASE and how far to the normal concern of the Director and inspectorate for raising standards, is hard to say. AASE raised also at an early stage the difference between the level of recruitment to grammar schools (percentage of places at 11+) between town and country districts, and the fact that, coincidentally, it correlated highly with the difference in the accommodation available. The debate was still under way when circular 10/65 on comprehensive reorganization was issued. AASE appeared to begin to make an impact on this by 1965, but was not hopeful of major reorganization to redress the balance despite strong pressure. The former Chairman of the Education Committee discounted AASE as a pressure group but saw their contribution as creating a 'climate of interest in education'.[38]

Teachers' organizations

Representatives of several teachers' organizations were interviewed including one past President of the NUT who served as teacher representative on the Northumberland Education Committee from 1948. The Teachers' Advisory Committee dealt with a wide variety of issues from the design of schools, equipment allowances and use of visual aids to the controversial issue of technical education in schools during the 1956–59 revision of the Development Plan. The Advisory

Committee set its face against selection for technical education at 11+ thus dealing the final death blow to the concept of the widespread provision of secondary technical schools. It was the NUT rather than the Joint Four who pressed for some form of technical education in both grammar and modern schools. The teachers used the IMTA statistics on capitation allowances effectively to improve the average level of spending in the county. The scheme of allowances for heads of departments following the 1956 Burnham report was drawn up by a joint working party called together by the Director, including the NUT, Joint Four and the inspectorate. Discussion between teachers and the Director tended to be informal (though useful) and latterly the teachers have pressed for a Joint Consultative Committee with more power than the Advisory Committee. The teachers interviewed spoke warmly of the tradition of co-operation and confidence which operated in the survey period. 'Demand' was not necessary—development tended to happen by consensus with a strong lead from the Director.

Governors

There was widespread scepticism about the ineffectiveness of governors except as potential 'school community committees'. On balance they seemed more 'involved' and articulate in the rural areas where all schools tended to serve the community in the widest sense. The views of heads are included in Appendix D. One councillor suggested that 'few of them after all have themselves had proper secondary education, especially in mining areas' which she implied led to a lack of understanding of the real educational issues.[39] One councillor for a deprived area defended his parochial interest, discarding the need for a synoptic view. 'That's the other chap's job, not mine. Too bad if he isn't canny—that's life.'[40]

Wallsend Excepted District

The position of Wallsend was examined with some care at each stage of the research. Schools in the District were visited and the Divisional Education Officer and Chairman of Wallsend Education Committee interviewed. The District's standing was discussed with officers and members at County Hall. There is no evidence that the presence of an Excepted District made any difference whatever to capital, revenue or staffing resources. In theory the Wallsend Committee had the right to go direct to the County Council or even the Ministry. In practice, it was simply one of 54 county areas. Those interviewed were asked two questions. Either the Excepted District made no difference—was it then a waste of money? Or it did make a difference—in which case was it not then unfair on say Berwick,

Allendale or Longbenton. Majority opinion considered the Excepted District 'an expensive and wasteful process of apparent democracy which if it worked, would take more than its share of resources'.[41]

Industry

There is no firm evidence of the influence of industry with the exception of agriculture. Apart from the agricultural technical school, most of the rural schools taught a form of science based on natural rather than physical sciences. There was no traceable influence whatever of the engineering and shipbuilding bias of Tyneside. On the contrary, more Tyneside schools had half-empty craft workshops than other schools, some were deficient in technical facilities and one technical school exported a majority of leavers to routine clerical work and to teaching. There was markedly less involvement than in Nottingham.

Conclusion

The 'climate of spending' to achieve 'decent education in decent schools' referred to in Chapters III and IV can be clearly seen in the foregoing account of developments in the county. Despite an inheritance of problems in the early post-war years, the authority is an impressive example of dynamic demand releasing resources. It suffered more acutely from Ministry controls (although it received the highest government grant, the controls were related to national and not local conditions).

Explicit demand from teachers, governors and outside groups appeared to play a lesser part because of the apparent readiness of the county itself to sponsor improvement and development. The apparent inequality of its rateable resources did not hinder the Director or the County from expanding the secondary budget at a remarkable rate although the financial position became a more real restraint in the 1960s.

Nevertheless, the results achieved did not lead to full equality of opportunity. On the one hand, a wide and rich range of new educational experiences was developed for some—not all—pupils. But the level of grammar provision was below average for most of the period and is still uneven from district to district. Most of the pupils for threequarters of the period had to be educated in either old or unreorganized schools. And (as Chapter X will illustrate) many schools were deficient in accommodation and other resources even in 1968. Many pupils left school underachieving by national standards both in external examinations and on entering adult employment.

How far the allocation of resources accounts for these results is a matter of individual judgement. It may well be that to achieve a more consciously even distribution of educational opportunity, more meticulous assessment and monitoring of the relationship of educational development to the distribution of resources will be essential. Certainly the principle of 'compensation' which produced the boarding and transport schemes should be extended to more active compensation of resources to small and to rural schools which suffered from the lack of viability touched on in Chapters II and X. A county so ready to accept new ideas as Northumberland has been, may well already be planning this.

Two words most commonly used in speaking of Northumberland county, by members, officers, teachers and others, are *independence* and *unity*. With such a conception widespread during the survey period, the chain of pressures illustrated in Diagram A in Chapter I might well prove secondary to consensus under a benevolently directive Director.

Notes

1   School Building Sub-Committee (8.5.42). The Nottingham Building School dates from the same period and was created for the same reason.
2   Higher Education Sub-Committee (5.5.42).
3   primary school managers, miners' unions, district councils town council, Higher Education Sub-Committee (7.9.43).
4   Secondary Education Sub-Committee (8.5.45).
5   Development plan page 2.
6   Development plan page 4.
7   Finance and General Purposes Sub-Committee (22.10.47). In practice it only materialized in two districts.
8   'In many respects I reaped where he had sown'. Interviews 30 June and 1 July 1969.
9   Interview with former Chairman (23.6.69) speaking of the second Director.
10 Interviews 4, 5 and 16 June 1969.
11 Teacher representative (4.3.69).
12 Former chairman (23.6.69).
13 Interview (5.3.69). For example, a proposal to buy a redundant castle took precedence over the metrication programme.
14 Interviews with members and officers, March and June 1969.
15 Finance and General Purposes Sub-Committee (13.1.48). Of the 15 proposed schools, 4 were to be for boys, 4 for girls and 7 were to be mixed.
16 Education Committee (27.6.57).
17 *Education in Northumberland, 1959—1962*, pp.25–26.
18 Education Committee (30.3.55) Appendix B, Schedule III.
19 Education Committee (23.6.58) Appendix A, Schedule II.
20 The Secondary Education Sub-Committee in 1952 asked for a report on initiating commercial courses in modern schools for example.
21 The county had instituted an internal County leaving certificate following the 1947 report of the Secondary Schools Examination Council.
22 Table IX of Appendix D gives the actual distribution of courses in all non-grammar schools as at 1965. Some modern schools could only offer CSE even in 1968.

23 Development Plan, p.3.

24 A repetition of an earlier battle in 1925 when the County again insisted successfully on its own design instead of the 1919 governmental prototype.

25 Buildings Sub-Committee (12.2.52).

26 or more kindly perhaps highlights the incapacity of Ministers of Education to convince Treasury colleagues of the seriousness of the country's *economic* need for a more highly developed education system; if reasons of justice and equality were unacceptable.

27 This is evident in records as well as from interviews.

28 Ministry of Education, Circular 6/60 (13.4.60). The 1962 national programme was no higher than in 1955 and was less in *real* terms. The 1963–65 national programme was no higher than in 1949 and was less in *real* terms.

29 Interview with NUT (4.3.69).

30 Interviews with members (18.6.69) and (23.6.69).

31 Notwithstanding, some of the schools deficient in facilities in 1968 and included in Appendix D, were in Northumberland.

32 Education Committee (12.12.63) Appendix E, Schedule IX.

33 Interviews with inspectorate and heads, March and June 1969. One officer commented 'To build one six-form entry instead of two three-form entries would have been unthinkable'.

34 HANCOCK, Victor, 'Secondary Selection in Northumberland'. Unpublished MEd dissertation, University of Durham.

35 Hancock, somewhat incredibly, uses his results to argue that therefore only 7 per cent of pupils should receive a grammar school education, which begs the question of achievement by pupils in other regions.

36 MELLOWES, Charles, *The General Certificate of Education,* Department of Education, King's College, Newcastle on Tyne.

37 op. cit.

38 An overzealous pressure group can breed a defensive hostility.

39 Interview 24.6.69.

40 Interview 30.6.69.

41 Interviews June and September 1969.

CHAPTER IX

Teaching Staff

'Let the method of teaching lessen the labour of learning so that nothing be a stumbling block to the pupil, and deter from perseverance in study.'

Comenius (17th Century)

There are few who would not agree that more influential than any other single 'resource' in schools are the teachers themselves, whose ability or otherwise, whose skill in teaching methods and whose quality of personal education will set the framework for learning (for good or ill) which will remain with children all their lives. The capacity for ordered thought, for educational discovery, for the application of principles, and the acquisition of essential knowledge and culture, will come to a pupil perhaps most effectively through a successful teacher. It may be for this reason that, faced with priorities of choice when allocating a limited budget, most chief officers and committees will retrench in any other sector than in the establishment of full-time teaching staff (and its consequent expenditure on salaries). Improvement of pupil/teacher ratios or of specialist teaching, command high priorities. The element of an authority's budget earmarked for teachers' salaries is therefore an important factor in influencing growth or retrenchment in other aspects of educational planning since major increases in the salary bill either because of pay awards or because of increased numbers of teaching staff, may (and often did) cause the growth rate in other elements of expenditure to slow down or even cease temporarily. The maximum total political 'ceiling' on the increases allowed for the education budget, related to the maximum acceptable rate increase, means that pay awards and increased staffing, hold back other 'tractable' growth in the education budget.

Salaries of teaching staff have been described as 'mainly intractable' expenditure because the level of salaries and allowances is determined nationally by the Burnham Committee of employers and teachers, and because the mere fact of rising school rolls makes it necessary to employ proportionately more teachers, assuming that even if growth in the sense of improved ratios is not possible, at least current standards are to be maintained. But there is a further refinement of the simple equation that extra pupils require extra teaching staff. This introduces a *tractable* element if one questions the inherited assumptions on which the policy is based; but adds a further *intractable* cause of rising expenditure if the Education Committee and Chief Education Officer accept without question, inherited principles of staffing for older pupils—which they did in all three authorities surveyed. This refinement is the especially favourable staffing ratios for older pupils regardless of the method and content of their teaching. A questionable assumption is made by the Department of Education and Science when determining an authority's quota of teachers, and by the authority when approving staffing establishments for secondary schools, that children may be taught adequately in groups of 30 up to the age of 14 but should be taught in progressively smaller groups (regardless of pupils' ability and the teaching methods generally used) from the age of 14 to 18 years. Thus, additions in school population will have a very different impact on the teaching staff salary bill depending on where in the age range they occur. The basic minimum on the generally accepted minimum standard of 1:30 in lower forms of secondary schools may be regarded as legitimately 'intractable', but any increase above that becomes subject to a value judgement on the different needs of the pupils. There are many who will suggest that remedial pupils, for example, should be regarded throughout their school career as 'weighted' for small teaching groups in the same measure as VIth form groups, obviating the need for head teachers to 'borrow' staffing from other main curricular classes or groups which therefore must be increased to 35 or more to 'subsidize' a remedial group of 20.

The position on future recruitment and supply is further complicated by relatively lavish and esoteric methods of staffing for the 26 per cent or so of 15- to 18-year-olds now in full-time secondary education. We ought not to assume, perhaps, that an increase in Vth and VIth form numbers necessarily implies that the present favourable staffing trends for this age group will be simply extended. But the assumption is still widespread. On the contrary, it may well mean achieving a more economic use of scarce specialist staff—given that the vexed question of allowing choice of subject options can be solved. A secondary school teacher is not only a teacher of young people but of history or mathematics, and some 'overstaffing' on the basic ratio has undoubtedly been necessary in smaller schools to ensure that not only are John or Mary taught, but that they are taught Latin or advanced physics. A second value judgement applied in this context, is the importance or degree of difficulty of the teaching and learning which takes place. Traditionally academic work is more highly paid than teaching dull children to learn; and teaching older children, more highly paid than teaching Upper Fourth formers. One is the more surprised that such an odd reversal of true values should not only be accepted, but condoned by practising teachers on the Burnham Committees. There can be few who would not find a C-stream group of 14-year-olds more difficult to teach and more demanding educationally, than older, more motivated examination candidates. The teaching of 'advanced level' languages for example, while intellectually demanding, is less complex and less strenous than the creation of suitable techniques, programmes and class activities to transmit a sense of language communication and a skill in the practical application of modern languages, to less articulate IVth and Vth year children in the middle two quartiles of ability. That this is a second value judgement does not make it necessarily less valid than the traditional acceptance of academic work as the main appropriate criterion of special financial recognition.

However, the principle of a higher rate of pay for graduates and for teachers of advanced work, has in fact persisted throughout the post-war years and accounts for substantial rises in the teaching staff salary bill after each Burnham award as the differential between the non-graduate and the 'good honours graduate' and between the teacher on basic scale and the allowance holder has widened.

Teacher Supply

A brief idea of the scale of the increased staffing in the schools may be helpful together with an illustration of the pattern of growth. The two main factors which become evident are the high proportion of women to men teachers, and the very substantial actual increase in the overall teaching force, over the survey period. The general pattern, however, seemed to be one of relatively slow growth in the first decade and very substantial growth in the latter part of the second decade.

Growth in Teaching Force

This was the major effect of *implicit demand* from rising rolls and rising standards. Massive resources were diverted to teacher training to provide the extra teachers.

The following table[1] illustrates the growth rate for the decade 1953—1963 in the provision of teacher training places.

Table IX (1)

YEAR	STUDENTS IN TRAINING (COLLEGES AND DEPARTMENTS OF EDUCATION)		
	M	W	Total
1953–54	6,825	19,858	26,683
1959–60	10,571	24,013	34,584
1963–64	18,510	39,168	57,678

The early 1950s were largely a period of consolidation, before the major expansion of the period 1958–65 and subsequent further expansion following the Robbins report. The percentage increases for the three-year periods from 1953 to 1956 and 1956 to 1959 were 6·4 per cent and 21·4 per cent respectively, while the increase for the four-year period from 1959 to 1963 was 67·5 per cent.

This clearly had repercussions on national capital expenditure on teacher training. Table I of Appendix E gives the complete national building programmes for all sectors, from which it will be seen that the teacher training capital programme ran at about £1 million per annum from 1947—1956 except in 1955 when an exceptional programme of £2,081,000 was approved. A reduced programme in 1957 was followed by a special programme of major expansion over the period 1958—1963 totalling £50,718,000, supplementing the normal programme of about £1 million per annum.

Standards

It is impossible to measure the degree of improvement this long-term trend meant in educational terms. In crude statistical terms, the teacher/pupil ratio is illustrated thus:

Table IX (2): *Overall Teacher:Pupil Ratio**

	1956	1959	1965
County Council average	25·9	25·3	25·5
Northumberland	26·6	25·9	25·9
County Borough average	26·9	26·4	26·4
Lincoln	26·5	26·2	26·2
Nottingham	26·8	26·0	26·5

* It is not possible readily to separate primary and secondary school ratios.[2]

In other words there was little overall improvement in the second decade but the teaching force had at least kept pace with the rising school rolls. In 1963, the Minister of Education in his annual report, estimated that to eliminate oversize classes, (i.e. secondary classes over 30 and primary classes over 40) a further 149,000 teachers were needed by 1971 in addition to those in posts in 1962,[3] and it could be argued that therefore not all sectors of the service had benefited equally by the massive increase in the teaching force. On the other hand, from 1952 to 1962, school rolls had increased by 12 per cent overall; the teaching force by 21 per cent.[4]

One improvement which might be interpreted qualitatively, as well as quantitatively was the increase in the proportion of graduate teachers as well as the actual numbers of teachers. The following example from Nottingham shortly after the establishment of the bilateral schools is not untypical:

Table IX (3)

	SEPT. 1956	SEPT. 1958
(a) *Total teachers in secondary schools*		
men	477	585
women	392	458
total	869	1,043
(b) *Percentage of graduates newly entering secondary schools*	30%	47%

While a graduate is not necessarily a better teacher, the academic training of a graduate may well be regarded as more appropriate to the academic curriculum followed by more able children. But the impact of the increase of graduate recruitment on the salary budget, like that of the award of equal pay, was considerable.

Central controls over supply and recruitment remained but unlike other governmental restraints, these commanded strong support from the local authorities, in the overall interests of the education service.

Despite the higher proportion of women to men teachers, so many authorities were short of women teachers in the early post-war years that by national agreement with the local authority associations, a quota system for women teachers was introduced under the control of the Ministry of Education. The purpose was to assess how many teachers an authority needed in direct relation to the size and nature of its school population and to limit the number to the essential average, thus restricting those authorities fortunate enough to attract as many applicants as they needed (or more) in order to release a pool of teachers for those authorities who consistently could not attract enough teachers to maintain basic standards. For example,

Nottingham was awarded a quota of 934 women teachers for 1951–52 but in the event could only recruit 906.[5] Like many other authorities similarly placed, *Nottingham* established special opportunities for pupils—mostly girls—educated at secondary modern schools specifically to enable them to make up the appropriate GCE qualifications for entry to teacher training.[6] This was as much a response to national *demand* for teachers, as a conscious widening of educational opportunity for the pupils.

By 1956 the National Advisory Council on the Training and Supply of Teachers recommended the abolition of the quota system for women teachers and the introduction of one controlling distribution of all teachers. The Minister agreed the former but not the latter, and asked the more fortunate authorities to exercise voluntary restraint.[7] The rising secondary rolls meant an urgent demand for more secondary trained teachers and Circular 313 (18.9.1956) therefore restricted the admission of children under five to school, on the grounds that if more infant teachers were needed for under fives they were not available to fill gaps in primary schools to release teachers of juniors to transfer to secondary schools. Circular 318 (5.12.1956) referred to consultation with the associations of local authorities and of teachers, producing 'a strong sense of partnership and goodwill' and an acknowledgement that some authorities would accept a worsening of standard in order to benefit colleagues elsewhere. The 'voluntary' quota would continue, but sanctions would have to be introduced if this failed. It did; and the quota system was restored 12 months later. Circular 14/59 (18.12.59) endorsed the quota system, but gave slightly improved staffing standards for the 15+ age group and redesignated temporary teachers as 'off-quota' to allow some flexibility to authorities willing to recruit above standard.

By the end of the survey period, part-time teachers were also becoming a permanent and important element of the total teaching force—having increased from 5,000 in 1954 to over 30,000 in 1964.[8]

The factors which emerge so far are therefore direct growth in teaching establishments, improved standards and control of quotas— all of which would directly affect the largest slice of the local education budget. The final factor was the introduction of equal pay —as a majority of teachers were women, this long overdue social reform absorbed much of the 'growth' element of local education authority financial resources. For before the second world war, 66 per cent of the teaching force were women (all unmarried); by October 1951, two-thirds of the teaching force were women (of 225,000 teachers nationally, 84,750 were men and 140,250 were women); and in 1963, 60 per cent of the 280,000 full-time teachers, were women, of whom two fifths were married.[9] These figures cover both primary and secondary schools, although more of the women would be in primary than in secondary schools.[10]

Burnham Salary Awards

Pure growth in numbers created major budgetary demands. So necessarily did the shift in emphasis of the main Burnham agreements. A fuller account appears in the writer's thesis (of which this is an abridged version). The constant injection into the basic salary structure, of more sophisticated methods of awarding additional special allowances to the basic scale—thus widening the differential between teachers on the basic salary and those holding above-scale posts, and (because of the very nature of the criteria for allowances) between teachers in primary and in secondary schools was a major factor. In the secondary sector, the differential between salaries of teachers in grammar or bilateral and in modern schools widened for similar reasons. Thus, the different policies of the three local authorities surveyed, will have resulted in differences in the impact of the Burnham awards on their secondary school expenditure.

Inherited assumptions about the curricular needs of pupils, the value of the contribution made by different kinds of teacher and the financial rewards which teachers of different backgrounds merit, are directly identifiable in both national and local sources. This is important, in that *explicit* demand from some sectors of the teaching profession appears to have been successful, but the *implicit* demand of the needs of less able pupils and of teachers of less able pupils, does not appear to have been met.

Thus the basic cost per teacher with no additions to salary above the basic scale, more than doubled from 1945 to 1963 both at the minima and maxima of the scales and in the case of women at the maximum, almost trebled. This part of the Burnham agreements was wholly mandatory and allowed no discretion and was therefore wholly intractable. To some extent, a total rise in the salary budget may have been mitigated by the fact that the larger teaching force was, according to the Department of Education and Science, also getting younger—in 1963 23 per cent of all men teachers, but 36 per cent of all women teachers were under 30 years of age (and therefore at lower points on the salary scale). Allowance posts above the basic scale, however, have always involved an element of discretion in the way in which local authorities have applied them and it is here that the educational philosophy and priorities (and the inherited traditions) of local authorities and of Chief Education Officers begins to become marked.

The graph on the following page (Figure 11) shows the pattern of teachers' salaries from 1945 to 1965, including the earlier dif-

FIGURE 11: *Teachers' salaries—assistant teachers' basic scales with no additions, 1945–64 (excluding incremental adjustment for equal pay after 1956)*

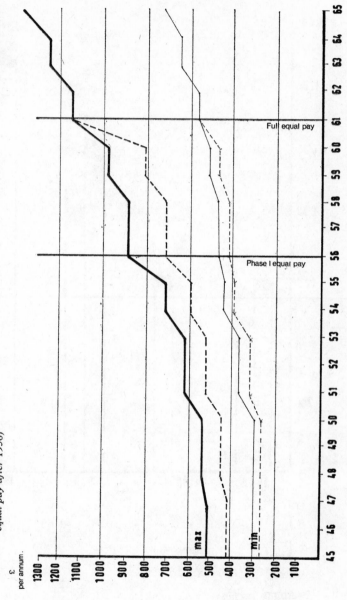

£ per annum.

Full equal pay

Phase I equal pay

max

min

FIGURE 12: *Teachers' salaries, 1945–61. Additions to basic scale*

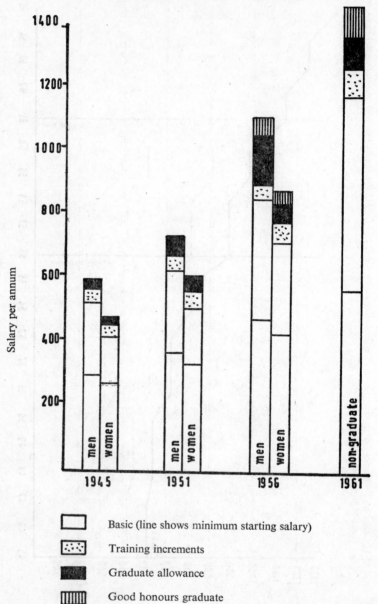

Basic (line shows minimum starting salary)

Training increments

Graduate allowance

Good honours graduate

ferential rates for men and women. The diagram which follows, (Figure 12) illustrates the relationship between the basic scale and additional increments for years of training and for graduate qualifications.

Discriminal Awards

The discriminal principles illustrated in Chapter II were applied equally to pay awards. Discrimination by ability of pupils taught was consistent. Discrimination by sex of teacher and of school lasted until the early 1960s.

The 1945 award instructed that 15 per cent of full-time qualified teachers would be regarded as eligible for above-scale posts. All three authorities gave major preference to able pupils, to which Lincoln added discrimination by sex of school. For example, *Lincoln* applied the 1945 Burnham report by allocating 26 special allowances between the four grammar schools and six between six secondary modern schools.[11] At this date, the boys' schools tended to have a more favourable structure than the girls' schools even taking size of school into account, while in 1951, a boys' and a girls' grammar school of comparable size in Lincoln had allowance structures so widely divergent as to give the boys' school nearly twice the allocation as the girls' school. The former had a total entitlement of £1,400, the latter of £790, a differential significantly higher than the 20 per cent basic differential between salaries of men and women teachers in 1951. The remaining schools reflected a lesser but still marked inequality:

Table IX (4)

SCHOOL	1945 NUMBER AND TOTAL VALUE OF ALLOWANCE POSTS	1950 NUMBER AND VALUE OF ALLOWANCE POSTS
Two FE grammar boys	6 (£500)	6 (£650)
Two FE grammar girls	5 (£320)	5 (£440)

Nottingham applied the strict Burnham rule of 15 per cent of all full-time qualified teachers, and awarded 144 allowance posts selectively on the basis of 16 posts to each of three grammar schools and one senior allowance to each of 32 other secondary schools with over 200 on roll. (i.e. 48 posts between three grammar schools and 32 between 32 other secondary schools).[12] *Northumberland* also noted the 15 per cent rule, but, discreetly evading a request from the Northumberland Joint Four Associations that allowances should be

awarded to 50 per cent of full-time qualified teachers,[13] succumbed
to the inherited influences mentioned above and decided to award
allowances to between 30 per cent and 40 per cent of grammar
school staff, 25—30 per cent of staff in technical schools, and to
modern schools 'according to the roll' which tended to mean one
post per modern school (or 16·83 per cent of the secondary modern
staffs).[14]

Since the percentage of grammar school places in *Nottingham* and
Northumberland was then at about the 12 per cent level, with an
added three per cent in technical schools in Northumberland, this
meant that in *Nottingham* over half of all allowance posts were held
by teachers of the top 12 per cent of the school population and under
half by teachers of the remaining 88 per cent. In *Northumberland*
nearly twice as many staff teaching the brighter 15 per cent held
allowances as the total staff teaching the remaining 85 per cent. In
both authorities most of the top quartile of ability in the non-
grammar schools would have received education in a selective school
had they been in another authority's area.

This particular aspect of 'choice' in the allocation of resources
above the basic scale would not appear to have been influenced either
by teacher demand or by the educational needs of all, as distinct
from the most able, pupils.

The 1956 Burnham report was however a major report of reconstruction and innovation, and it was perhaps fitting and significant
that its chairman was Lord McNair.[15] Its main provisions were the
introduction of equal pay and the rationalization of the allowance
structure particularly for heads of departments. The report added
more than 15 per cent immediately to the salary bill but the Minister
in his reply to Lord McNair commented that

'the Government believe that the taxpayers and ratepayers will
approve this increase in cost in spite of the financial difficulties of
the present time, so vital is it to expand and improve on schools
and colleges. Sound policy calls for strict economy in other directions
in order to put more emphasis on the teachers as the main-stay of
the education service.'[16]

The report recommended the full award of equal pay from 1st
April 1961 (in 1945, the minimum salaries for men and women
respectively had been £300 and £270, and the maxima, £525 and
£420). Meanwhile equal pay increments would be paid to women,
based on the proportion of difference between her salary and a
man's salary 'with equivalent qualifications, training, and service
employed in a similar capacity'. It will be recalled that nearly two-

thirds of the total teaching force were women, although since they were largely in primary schools, fewer women than men would be receiving the top salaries with full special allowances. The impact of this on the local authorities' budgets was significant. For example the effect of full and immediate equal pay in Lincoln would have been an additional £28,000 on a total education revenue budget of £677,937, or 4·15 per cent of all expenditure on the education service in 1955.[17] Taking as an example the minimum and maximum basic salaries as at 1956 and 1961 for men and women (i.e. before and after equal pay):

Table IX (5): Teachers' Basic Salary

	Minimum £			Maximum £	
	M	W		M	W
1956	475	430		900	720
1961	570	570		1170	1170
% increase	20·0	32·6		31·0	62·5

The financial impact of equal pay can be seen even more sharply by the following table, illustrating the effect of the award on head of department allowances:

Table IX (6): Head of Department Allowances

Grade		1956 £	1961 £	% Increase
A	M	125 ⎫	165	⎧ 32%
	W	100 ⎭		⎩ 65%
B	M	200 ⎫	260	⎧ 30%
	W	160 ⎭		⎩ 62·5%
C	M	275 ⎫	355	⎧ 29%
	W	220 ⎭		⎩ 61·5%
D	M	350 ⎫	450	⎧ 28·6%
	W	280 ⎭		⎩ 60·5%
E		—	545	—

* The percentage increases represent the difference between the basic women's rate as laid down in the 1956 Burnham report and the 1961 rate, and exclude phased incremental allowances towards equal pay.

It will be recalled that the percentage increases between 1956 and 1961 at the maximum of the basic scale, for men and women respectively, were 31·0 per cent and 52·5 per cent.

The committee also recommended that posts of heads of department should be established, and that they should be mandatory in schools offering advanced work but discretionary in other secondary schools—another inherited attitude on 'allocation of merit'.

'In secondary schools in which advanced work is undertaken . . . the local education authority *shall* . . . establish posts of Head of Department of such number as the authority may determine . . . In other secondary schools the local education authority *may* establish posts of Head of Department of such numbers as the authority may determine.'[18]

This report first introduced the principle of a guide to appropriate allowances for different sizes of schools—thus a school from groups 0—VIII would normally only qualify for posts at Grade A, a school from VIII to XII at grades A and B, and so on until very large schools at group XVII would qualify for a full range of posts from A to D.[19] The inherited assumption that allowances should go to teachers of older children led to the formula for calculating the Burnham group of a school, that children count as 'points' on a scale on which the Burnham group (I to XXVII) is based, thus affecting the level of teachers' salaries:

Age of children	Points
Under 13	1
13—14	2
15	4
16	6
17+	10

It will become apparent that some secondary modern schools without a Vth form, or any bilateral or other secondary school without a VIth form, would inevitably have a lower Burnham grouping than grammar schools of lesser size. A three-form entry grammar school (450 pupils from 11—16 and 100 VIth) would have a unit total of 1660, while a four-form entry non-selective school (with 600 pupils aged 11—16) would have a unit total of only 1200. If the authority chose not to apply the discretionary clause to non-selective schools, the grammar school would have a wide range of allowance posts and the modern school none. If the clause were applied, the modern school would still qualify for less. *Lincoln,* it will be recalled, consistently refused to create heads of department posts in its non-selective schools. The Director in *Nottingham* recommended they be awarded immediately to bilateral (11—16) schools, but delayed the introduction to modern schools until 1958 when posts were created in all secondary schools, mostly allocated to maths, sciences, and handicraft.[20] *Northumberland* appears to have shared Lincoln's view in 1956:

'Secondary modern schools would appear to be adequately provided for by the graded posts and deputy headships. It is not a compulsory requirement that advanced work should be undertaken, but in general it would not appear to be intended that departments will be created where such work is not undertaken.'[21]

In the event the posts were limited to grammar (and later technical) schools until 1960 when, anticipating the 1961 report, Northumberland remarked that a number of authorities had made use of the optional clause, and accepted a recommendation of the Director that provision be made in the 1960–61 estimates for a number of Grade A posts in modern schools above Burnham Group VII, while a more generous scheme of allowances was also approved for the grammar schools.[22]

No new major principles were introduced in 1959. The overall increase was less marked than in 1956, and of *Nottingham's* secondary school salary bill in 1959, at least £34,785 was directly attributable to the new Burnham report for the half year September 1959 to March 1960 (out of the year's full salary bill for secondary schools of £966,694; that is 3·5 per cent).[23] *Northumberland's* extra cost for the secondary sector was £48,632 (out of a secondary staffing bill of £1,142,364 or 4·2 per cent).[24] It should be stressed that with the exception of the 1956 report, most of the reports before 1961 gave the major benefit to teachers on the basic scale which therefore would affect the primary more acutely than the secondary sector of expenditure.

By 1961, it was evident that many authorities had already anticipated the trend and had created significant numbers of allowance posts in non-selective schools, which was in fact a corollary of the development of extended courses and bias courses to which reference is made in earlier chapters. The 1961 Burnham report made it mandatory to establish allowance posts in all secondary schools of whatever type of group VIII and above, and left a discretionary power to award posts in smaller schools. The committee also increased the span of allowances by creating a new Grade E.

By the end of the survey period, all three authorities were broadly in line with the national average of above-scale posts in secondary schools. *Lincoln* had consistently deferred the secondary modern issue until the NUT and NAS pressed for full implementation of the 1961 Report, when the Education Committee conceded the minimum number. The position altered radically with the coming of the new Chief Education Officer in 1964 and within a year of the new appointment, the staffing structure in the non-selective schools had been significantly improved. *Nottingham's* scheme seemed reasonable, though not generous to the few remaining secondary modern schools, while *Northumberland* approved a more generous than average scheme following the 1965 Burnham report using discretionary as well as mandatory powers and creating many new senior posts in non-grammar schools.

The Impact on Selective and Non-academic Schools

It would appear, then, that inherited assumptions and attitudes rather than the demands of all groups of teachers have influenced the way in which resources in the form of salary have been awarded. Certainly it could be argued that demand from grammar school or graduate teachers was met but that demand from those teaching less able or younger children was not. To the extent that salary structures influence recruitment, there would seem to be little relationship between the increased implicit demand of the expansion of the secondary modern sector, and increased *proportionate* expenditure on the salaries of teachers in that sector. And while the 1961 report eliminated inequality of pay as between men and women, it did not (nor have subsequent awards) eliminate inequality as between teachers of and schools for the able and the non-academic.

The unit total of a school is based on the number of children on roll and on their ages. The 1948 report counted each child under 15 as one point, 15-year-olds as four, while pupils of 16+ and 17+ were each worth seven and 10 points respectively. The effect on teachers' salaries of the development of Vth and VIth forms was therefore likely to be considerable; and the gap between selective and non-selective schools began to widen:

Table IX (7)

age	2 FORM ENTRY GRAMMAR SCHOOL (1948)		4 FORM ENTRY MODERN SCHOOL (1948)	
	pupils on roll	points	pupils on roll	points
11—14	240	240	480	480
15	60	240	20	80
16	40	280	—	—
17	30	300	—	—
	370	1060	500	560
	Burnham group XI		Burnham group V	

The head teacher of the grammar school was therefore paid £460 (women £405) but the head of the modern school £220 (women £195) in addition to basic salary, because these allowances were related to the Burnham grouping of the school.

A comparison of four actual schools chosen from one of the survey areas is given in tables 8 and 9. In 1956, of two schools of completely comparable size (but different distribution of age) the grammar school had a unit total of twice that of the modern school, entitling the head and deputy head of the former to nearly twice the special additional allowance of those appointed to the latter. Moreover, the grammar school entitlement of above-scale graded posts (15 points) was two-and-a-half times that of the modern school. The head and governors of the grammar school could recommend the equivalent of 15 staff for an above-scale allowance (a typical pattern however would be three posts of scales I and II and two of scale III adding up to 15 points) while the head and governors of the modern school could only recommend the equivalent of six (of which a typical pattern would be two posts at scale II and two at scale I).

Table IX (8): Comparison of selective and non-academic schools' entitlements under the 1956 Burnham report
The two sample schools are actual schools from one of the survey areas; a three-form entry boys' grammar school and a four-form entry boys' modern school, but with the same total rolls.

Age	Number on Roll		Points	Total Points and Burnham Group	
	grammar	*modern*	@	*grammar*	*modern*
11—12	155	252	1	155	252
13—14	154	236	2	308	472
15	82	25	4	328	100
16	62	—	6	372	—
17 +	47	—	10	470	—
Total	500	513		1,633	824
				Group XVI	Group IX
Entitlement by Burnham groups				*grammar*	*modern*
Head Teachers' allowance				£815	£490
Deputy Head's allowance				£320	£180
Entitlement to graded posts above basic scale				15	6
Grading of Heads of Departments*				A to C	A and B

* assuming the local authority used its discretion to award them in non-grammar schools.

By 1965, as table IX (9) on the following page shows, the difference between the respective salaries of heads and deputy heads had narrowed, but the score for graded posts, while not so divergent as in 1956, was still double in a grammar school that for a modern school of similar size and therefore more staff would qualify for allowances. And the highest allowance a teacher in the modern school could reach was £420 (C) while his or her grammar school counterpart would be graded at £540, not necessarily for more work or more responsible work. One grammar school with a science VI of 23 had a head of physics, and a head of chemistry at grade C each and a head of science overall of grade D—aggregate £1,380 while the single head of science in a modern school of the same size was pegged at grade B (£300).

Table IX (9): Comparison of selective and non-academic schools' entitlements under the 1965 Burnham report

The two sample schools are actual schools from one of the survey areas; a three-form entry girls' grammar school and a four-form entry girls' modern school, but with the same total rolls.

AGE	NUMBER ON ROLL		POINTS	TOTAL POINTS AND BURNHAM GROUP	
	grammar	*modern*	@	*grammar*	*modern*
11—12	142	210	1	142	210
13—14	193	304	2	386	608
15	75	49	4	300	196
16	87	—	6	522	—
17 +	47	—	10	470	—
Totals	544	563		1,820	1,014
				Group 9*	Group 7†

* formerly groups XVII—XIX
† formerly groups XI—XIII

Entitlement by Burnham group	*grammar*	*modern*
Head Teachers' total salary	£2,750–£3,050	£2,325–£2,625
Deputy heads' allowance	£635	£455
Entitlement to graded posts above basic scale	21	10
Grading of Heads of Departments	A—D	A—C

Clearly this situation, referred to at the outset of this chapter, could be interpreted as a consciously unequal assessment of the value of teachers by those controlling the level and structure of teachers' salaries. Either it is that we value more highly the quality of work of teachers teaching more able and older children. Are they better teachers in fact? Or is the market perhaps scarcer or more vulnerable to outside competition? Or indeed it may well be that the task of teaching able or older pupils is considered more onerous and more difficult in itself. A counter-theory might well be suggested, that to teach pupils who are mainly in larger classes, who tend to be less motivated, and whose span of ability ranges over three quartiles of ability and not one, is both more difficult and more challenging; and does equally validly meet the needs of the pupils which is reputedly the aim of the teaching process. If, therefore, one suggests that the allocation of resources (including salaries) should in fact be directly related to need and to demand, the evidence of the history of teachers' salaries seems to suggest that the gradual codification over the years of the principles introduced in successive Burnham reports, widens rather than narrows the gap between need and demand on the one hand, and appropriate salary resources on the other.

Successive Burnham reports (after 1956) have also laid down standards of the level, as distinct from number, of head of department posts a school should have, in relation not to its actual size (that is, say, 500 pupils) but its distribution of pupils by age and ability. It has been left partly to local education authorities to decide how many posts at which level to award each school. The ways in which this can vary is illustrated by the following examples (also taken from actual schools in one of the survey areas).

Table IX (10): *Comparison of 4 grammar schools in 1957 after the 1956 Burnham report*

| School | Burnham Group | Head of Dept. Posts | | | Total | Total Value £ |
		A	B	C		
boys' grammar	XVI	2	5	3	10	2,075
boys' grammar	XII	2	5	3	10	2,075
girls' grammar	XII	5	2	3	10	1,685
girls' grammar	X	2	6	–	8	1,160

The first two schools which differ in size and in distribution of older pupils, have the same allowance structure and value of posts. The girls' school of exactly comparable size with one boys' school has fewer senior posts and a smaller total value, while the second girls' school varies again both in size and structure.

Two important factors emerge from this. The first has been referred to—the different resources received by selective and non-selective schools respectively. The second is the impact on the local authority budget. An earlier section of this chapter touches on the effect on the teachers' salary budget, of the increased numbers of teachers recruited to meet extra need; and on the effect of equal pay, both of which were mainly intractable elements. While, however, the level of allowance posts is intractable, the number and distribution are not. An authority could therefore in the survey period control one element of its salary budget by its generosity or otherwise, and by its assessment of educational priorities—in the award of graded posts above basic scale and of head of allowance structures. The cost is, of course, enhanced by the fact that most teachers experienced enough to have been awarded a responsibility allowance will be nearer the maximum than the minimum of the basic scale. Heads of departments in grammar schools also tend to have good honours degrees which inflate salaries further.

To summarize, the scale of the effect on the budgets of the rise in teachers' salaries in secondary schools in the survey areas for the two major awards of 1956 and 1961 not only was influenced by the discriminal principles operating at the time, but was out of proportion to the scale of increase in school rolls. Table IX (11) which follows sharply illustrates this; and if related to the tables in Chapter IV on overall growth of the secondary budgets (and to Appendix B), shows also that intractable salary increases were paid for by cut back in development elements of the education budget.

One element of the rise in 1957 will have been the award to women teachers of the third seventh of the difference between women and men's pay scales. Between four and six per cent could be due to rising school rolls (making the employment of extra teachers necessary). There would still seem to be an identifiable element for 'improvement' as distinct from basic staffing, but this could only have been modest after the two factors above are accounted for. In 1962 however, more of the increase may be due to improvedstaffing standards or to more substantial use of discretionary powers, together with the mandatory new allowances for non-grammar schools above group VIII. For the school rolls had fallen or remained static, and full equal pay had already been achieved by 1961.[25]

Table IX (11): *Comparative table of increases in teachers' salaries and of total secondary school rolls*

		LINCOLN £	NOTTINGHAM £	NORTHUMBERLAND £
Teachers' salaries (secondary)	1956	168,422	665,183	760,212
	1957	198,614	792,700	881,366
	% increase	16·9	19·2	16·0
Total secondary roll	1956	4,411	18,294	18,088
	1957	4,671	19,028	19,299
	% increase	4·5	4·0	6·7
Teachers' salaries (secondary)	1961	284,515	1,116,873	1,425,883
	1962	319,455	1,248,094	1,695,435
	% increase	12·3	11·8	18·9
Total secondary roll	1961	5,374	21,311	27,366
	1962	5,228	20,510	27,894
	% decrease or increase	—2·7	—0·37	+0·19

Explicit Demand From the Teachers' Organizations

The brief accounts given in Chapter III and in the description of secondary developments in each of the survey areas refer to lively activity by the NUT and to a tacit acceptance by the Joint Four of a relatively passive role in decision making, out of the context of the Burnham Committee. It was possible to interview two past presidents of the NUT both of whom had served on the Burnham Committee, one continuously since 1948 and the second from 1954 to 1956 and from 1961 onwards. Both considered that the major contribution of the teachers' unions in general and the NUT in particular was the achievement of equal pay in 1956, which was rejected by the Authorities' panel (as well as by government spokesmen) until the negotiations leading up to the 1956 report. A concise and pertinent summary of the role of the NUT and other unions in the period 1944 to 1956 is contained in Asher Tropp's detailed work on the development of the teaching profession[26] which there is no need therefore to repeat here. Teachers interviewed by the writer, both representing organizations and in individual schools, confirm Asher Tropp's account of the pressure tactics used on the several questions of equal pay, differentials between the basic scale and head teacher allowances, and head of department posts. Where the evidence in the survey areas differs in emphasis is on the question of graduate allowances, which cannot be disassociated from the problem of recruiting subject specialists in scarcity subjects. Tropp suggests that the award of special allowances for maths, sciences or other subjects as well as for good honours degrees, was regarded by most as degrading.

'To many besides the teachers (*including here the majority of graduate and grammar school teachers*) the recent changes appear degrading to the profession.'[27]

In the survey areas, opinion, however, seemed evenly divided, the one agreeing with Asher Tropp's interpretation (and the writer's view) that salary should be paid in relation to value of work and assessed need, and that advanced examination work is neither more 'valuable' nor more 'responsible' than work with less able children. This view was held by a majority of teachers interviewed in non-grammar schools, but a minority of heads and senior staff in grammar schools—this minority almost without exception being teachers involved in the government of teachers' organizations or in regional or national committees concerned with educational matters.

The contrary view, that graduate allowances and head of department and other above-scale allowances should be predominantly the prerogative of staffs of grammar schools (or teachers of able and older children) was held mainly, but not exclusively, by grammar school staffs, predictably enough, since they tend to be the product of a grammar school and to have been students with ex-grammar school pupils, and therefore to know less of the educational processes of teaching the less able (often in unstreamed situations).

Theories vary on why with so strong a representation on the Burnham Committee in the early years the NUT lost the battle on special allowances, ceding its case for improvements to the basic scale, although it did win the concession that allowances would be paid for all advanced work and not merely for shortage subjects. The most commonly held view (by teachers) is that when its majority was safe (in 1945 and 1948) the Union had not clarified its policy and by the time the acute shortages of the 1950s stimulated the Authorities'

Panel to seek 'carrots' with which to attract unwilling horses to the grammar school pond, as it were, teachers opinion was more divided in the light of the new organizational problems of multilateral, bilateral and comprehensive schools. Where the profession was divided, the employer's side was not likely to concede.

This issue is not only a question of priorities in the allocation of resources. The children themselves (the *raison d'etre* of the teaching profession) are sensitive to the values set by adults. If they see that the senior posts in a school go to graduates, and that more senior posts are held by graduates in maths, science and languages than in geography, music, art or physical education, they will tend to value these subjects in that order. They will tend to achieve to the level expected of them—and they know when more resources (from teachers to tape recorders) are given to either their more able peers or those following a traditionally academic course. And pupils do know. The most revealing diagnosis of a school often comes from the third- and fourth-year pupils—not from the established teacher.

Staffing and Viability of Schools

Earlier sections of this chapter have referred to the distribution of men and women teachers, the quota system, and to the selective/non-selective school syndrome. A fourth factor is relevant, the control of the supply of the right kind of teachers. This is one criterion of the viable size of a school, which should be decided in direct relation to policies on the supply and allocation of all resources. For example small school A offers both pottery and chemistry to GCE 'O' level. Both the chemist and the potter leave and are replaced by a painter (with subsidiary weaving) and a biologist (with subsidiary chemistry). The languages department thrived under a French specialist with subsidiary German and Italian, so French was the first language, German the second and Italian a VIth form option. The best new candidate from a (limited) field however is a German graduate with subsidiary Russian. Both these languages are increasingly commerically and vocationally useful. Does the school stand out for a chemist or francophile, or appoint the best teacher on offer and shift the emphasis of the curriculum? This can only be done if there are enough specialist teachers in each department to adjust the timetables of other staff offering chemistry, pottery or French to secure the completion of the courses of pupils halfway to 'O' or 'A' level. In practice this becomes possible in a four- or five-form entry grammar school or a six- to eight-form entry comprehensive school. (An 'academic' example has been chosen as the easiest to illustrate. It is as valid for the middle band of ability halfway through a two-year CSE course of integrated studies.) But the third year in the smaller school must now be 'offered' different options related to the 'market place' offers of the staff and not to the needs of the individual pupils. Similarly the recruitment to a secondary modern school of a good general scientist may inhibit introduction of specialist sciences—or vice versa. More research is needed into the whole concept of viability as related to the freedom of pupils' options on the one hand and the balance of curriculum on the other.

Finally, the whole pattern of staffing resources for schools may well change in the next decade with the increasing number of schools designed or remodelled on 'open-plan' lines, and with the gradual introduction to varying degrees of the team-teaching approach. This is extensively discussed in Warwick's recent book[28] (in which problems of school organization, use of teachers and school design are related). Any widespread application of the approach suggested by Warwick will involve a critical reappraisal of the whole rationale of the allocation of resources (both staff and salary allowances), and of the historical values on which this has been based in the past.

Conclusions

The recruitment and distribution of teachers, a major aspect of resource allocation, would appear therefore to have been partly affected by both explicit and implicit demand, and by the kind of inherited attitudes referred to in Chapter II.

Firstly, the actual number of teachers, both nationally and in the survey areas, has increased substantially over the 20-year period with a resultant and intractable increase in actual expenditure. Preceding chapters and tables VI (a) to (c) in Appendix B, show that teachers' salaries have maintained or increased their proportion of the total secondary budget despite other growing claims (such as loan charges or maintenance of school buildings). The increase arises mainly from implicit demand of rising school rolls (both overall and at V and VI form levels) based on a tacit assumption that authorities should at least maintain and preferably improve, current national staffing standards. *Secondly,* a markedly explicit demand from the teachers, secured the introduction of equal pay in 1956 which had a substantial, and again, intractable effect on local authority budgets. *Thirdly,* the inherited attitudes which continued largely unchanged, perpetuated the principle that more staff were needed to teach children of 15 and over, and that many of these staff should be paid at nearly twice the rate of a teacher on the basic scale. Most of the application of this principle in successive Burnham reports was intractable since the training and graduate additions and the salary level of special allowances, were all mandatory. Part was tractable in that local authorities were given discretion in 1956 on the allocation of head of department allowances to non-grammar schools; and on the number, in both 1956 and 1961 for all schools. Pressure from the teachers to alter the policy of the authorities on discretionary elements was unsuccessful in Lincoln until after 1964; and was largely considered to be unnecessary in Nottingham and Northumberland because the authorities consulted the teachers closely throughout the restructuring of both the secondary school systems and the schools' allowance structures, in the second decade of the survey period.

Fourthly, inherited attitudes on most aspects of teacher supply and distribution both between and within schools appear to be a stronger determinant than a value judgement of pupils' needs in different bands of ability, different age ranges and in different types of school. Those responsible for the allocation of resources within the structure of the government of education, appear to have given much thought over the 20 years towards 'education according to ability' in allocating favourable staffing resources to able children; but not to the less able (whether the result is desirable or not is a matter of opinion). Some thought has been given to education 'according to age' in that the 15–18 age group has overwhelmingly favourable staffing resources. Less thought seems to have been given to education 'according to aptitude'. In staffing as in design of schools, such subjects as music, drama, art, housecraft and handicraft and physical education come low in the hierarchy of relative status.

Finally, as in other aspects of the national allocation of resources, central control has grown, not diminished over the survey period, partly for good and partly for ill. It was wholly necessary for central government to take a synoptic view of the national development of teacher training and to promote the expansion of training colleges on the one hand and a fair distribution of teachers between local authorities on the other. There is no traceable dissentient voice that the Ministry of Education's control of the national quota of women teachers and later of all teachers, and of overall staffing standards, was fair, necessary and constructive.

A different view may well be taken, however, on the issue of teachers' salaries. In the earlier years the recorded evidence[29] suggests that the balance of control lay between the local authority associations and the teachers' organizations with the decisive control on the whole with the former. By 1955, other factors began to influence negotiations, including the scarcity value of science graduates but the Minister of Education nevertheless approved the recommendation of the Independent Committee. But by 1959 the Minister made warning noises, and by the early 1960s a major dispute between the teachers, the local authorities and central government led to the suspension of the traditionally independent Committee and the introduction of a decisive role on the part of the Secretary of State for Education and Science with whom the major control in practice still rests even though the Burnham Committee has now been properly reconstituted. All recommendations of the Committee have been subject to approval by the Board or Ministry of Education, but only since the early 1960s has the detailed control and the major formation of policy moved so markedly from local to central government. This issue among others, has raised the vexed question of whether payment of teachers' salaries should be transferred from the local authority budget to the National Exchequer,[30] although this has been successfully resisted so far.

There will need to be major changes in the next decade, as indeed there have been some in the period since 1965. In particular the proposed continued expansion of higher education (22 per cent of the 18+ age group by 1981 instead of seven per cent in 1961 and 15 per cent in 1971)[31] and the possible introduction of a Diploma in Higher Education make it necessary to reconsider both our educational values and the competition or otherwise from other industries for the diplomates and graduates available for recruitment to the teaching profession. At a time of graduate unemployment, it no longer follows that the recruitment policies and the salary structures of the past are still relevant. And with 'educational rationing' increasing, the deployment of the salary element of the education budget, as related to quality of education in schools and to needs of pupils, becomes of increasingly pertinent interest.

Notes

1   Ministry of Education, *Training the Teachers*, Reports on Education No. 7. January 1964.
2   Ministry of Education, Circulars 318, 345 and 1/65.
3   Ministry of Education, *Education in* 1963, Cmnd 2316, HMSO, page 76, para. 12.
4   Department of Education and Science, *Staffing the Schools,* Reports on Education no. 6. December 1963 p.1.
5   Nottingham, Annual report 1952 p.12.
6   *Education,* (13.2.53).
7   Ministry of Education, Admin. Memo. 524 (9.2.56).
8   Department of Education and Science, *Part-Time Teaching in Schools,* Reports on Education no. 21 (21.5.65).
9   Ministry of Education, Circular 222, (29.6.50)—a forward estimate from those in posts in 1950, and Department of Education and Science, *Staffing the Schools,* Reports on Education No. 6. December 1963.
10 Department of Education and Science, *Staffing the Schools,* December 1963, p.1.
11 Lincoln, Finance and General Purposes Committee (29.11.45).
12 Nottingham, Joint Primary and Secondary Sub Committees (29.1.46).

13 Northumberland, Finance and GP Committee (10.1.46).
14 Ibid.
15 As Sir Arnold McNair he chaired the committee appointed by the President
    of the Board of Education to consider the *Supply, Recruitment and Training
    of Teachers and Youth Leaders* in 1942–44. The McNair report had a
    seminal influence on the post-war salary and grading structure of the
    teaching profession.
16 David Eccles to Lord McNair (28.6.56).
17 Lincoln, Education Committee-in-Committee (8.5.55).
18 1956 Burnham report. Writer's italics.
19 By 1961 allowances ranged from £165 for Grade A to £545 for the newly
    created E.
20 Nottingham, Secondary Education Sub-Committee (2.7.58).
21 Northumberland, Finance and General Purposes Committee (26.9.56).
22 Northumberland, Finance and General Purposes Committee (18.9.60).
23 Nottingham, Secondary Education Sub-Committee (2.9.59).
24 Northumberland, Finance and General Purposes Sub-Committee (3.9.59).
25 It is impossible to compute the effect of turnover of staff, that is loss of
    experienced staff and recruitment of younger staff on a lower salary. On
    the whole authorities find in budgeting that it is rarely significant.
26 TROPP, Asher. *The School Teachers,* Heinemann 1957. pp.250–270.
27 Opus cit. p.259. writer's underlining.
28 WARWICK, David. *Team Teaching,* University of London Press, 1971.
29 Burnham reports, local authority records, NUT records and published
    accounts (TROPP, Asher, *The School Teachers*).
30 see for example GOULD, Sir Ronald, *Year Book of Education,* 1956, 'Factors
    Affecting Teachers' Salaries in England and Wales', Chapter 14, p.455.
31 *Education: a Framework for Expansion,* Government White Paper, HMSO,
    1972.

CHAPTER X

The Schools Survey and Curricular Resources

'Inopem me copia fecit.'
('plenty makes me poor')
Ovid, *Metamorphoses*
(iii) 466.

The relationship of material resources to the curricular needs of schools and pupils was one aspect considered in the context of the sample survey of schools undertaken by the writer in 1968–69. A fuller account of the survey appears in Appendix D and in its accompanying tables. This chapter seeks to relate some of the findings to the hypotheses underlying this research.

Chapters VI to VIII commented in some detail on the progress made in each survey area from 1945 to 1965 and on some important influential factors. How far can it be suggested that the general pattern or rationale which has been traced, is mirrored in the schools? What was the general standard of resources achieved by the local authorities in their schools, either because of or in spite of the factors of demand and supply operating in each area?

Design of Schools

Fundamental to the organization of the curriculum and of bias courses in different types of schools, is the conception held by the educational planners, of the appropriate design of schools for different purposes. This determines the level and type of material resources (number of rooms; proportion of specialist rooms) which are made available to different 'classes' or groups of pupils—for example the intelligent or the dull; boys as distinct from girls; urban or rural children. If the accommodation is not available or is unsuitably or inadequately designed, teachers will find it either difficult or impossible to meet the real, and not the apparent, educational needs of all of their pupils.

Resources—rooms, staff, equipment or money—are needed basically for two separate but interrelated purposes. First, to provide basic education for all pupils at a good minimum standard. Second, to encourage curricular innovation and the development of the capacities of individuals and of groups.

In all three survey areas, the controls exercised by central government, which limited the design of new schools to the barest minimum of facilities when final sketch schemes were submitted for Ministry approval, caused practical facilities in all types of schools to lag far behind the proposals and principles put forward by all three local education authorities as priorities for development. The main yard-sticks against which schools had to be designed were the standards for School Premises and the Building Codes laid down by the Ministry of Education. They applied primarily to new building, but it was implicit that older schools which did not meet these standards were, therefore, deficient in some respect, bearing in mind the new philosophy of secondary education, embodied in the 1944 Education Act. The minimum teaching area required for secondary pupils under the first three sets of post-war building regulations, however, has actually *decreased* over the years in terms of what can be built within the cost per square metre imposed by the Ministry (on which Chapter V commented). However, at no stage in post-war years have regulations specified the precise manner in which the total teaching area should be subdivided (fortunately) except that in the 1959 Standards for School Premises Regulations, all secondary schools were required to have a hall and gymnasium, a library and 'accommodation for practical instruction' as well as a minimum teaching area per pupil which increased progressively by age (at 14+ and 16+). The 1959 Regulations also prescribed for the first time, 'sufficient and suitable facilities . . . for the storage of apparatus, equipment and materials required for teaching'.[1] The 1962 Building Code issued by the Ministry of Education incorporating the 1959 Regulations and a few later amendments, has remained the yardstick against which LEAs are expected to plan and remodel schools, and against which 'minimum standards' in school must be measured. An important assumption in the 1962 Building Code is the provision of accommodation for a *full* five year secondary course unless specifically not required (para 5, 3.2 to 3.6)—a reversal of the earlier attitude which expected a special case to be made for extra resources to house the Vth year of non-selective schools.

Depressed Demand

Staff seemed conditioned by the level of resources hitherto awarded, or by the allocation given annually by the head. 'We were used to the inevitability of iron-frame desks, old books and cramped rooms', or 'we were discouraged as we came here from pressing for new equip-ment by the old stagers'. Such influence as was traced from staff concerned with changing educational ideas did not always suceed in attracting resources—'the diffuse organization of the admini-stration meant we could rarely pin down the point at which to exert pressure'. The removal of Vth- and VIth-form pupils from non-grammar schools exacerbated this especially in limiting specialized resources. 'It killed any experimentation', or 'There was a lack of stimulus in classes below IQ 100, our staffing margin was eroded, we couldn't afford TV or tape recorders.'

Ten schools rehoused in new buildings recalled a long period of artificially depressed demand pending the millenium or rebuilding. Their annual estimates failed to keep pace with price rises. Typical were poor redecoration, emergency staffing, run-down libraries and paucity of new equipment. 'We deferred constantly under the promise of a new school.' 'The new school was always a year ahead.' 'It seemed a waste to remodel the laboratories for a year or so.' 'Looking back, we worked on a very low attainment ceiling.' A school in an area of acute social need, commented that, before it was reorganized, 'we had too little for any real development but too much to qualify for educational priority'. All of these 10 schools found that the appointment of a new head and/or the move to new buildings, broke the cycle of depressed demand. 'It seemed worth pressing for new books for the new courses.' 'The head kept asking what we wanted.' 'The advisers offered us special allowances.' 'Success bred success, it was worth the gamble of planning a new course, that the equipment would really arrive.' One frequent comment from staff in all three areas however, supported the suggestion that a principle of 'to him who hath shall be given' was widespread. 'No one seems to tell a *new* school to make do', and 'Unaccountably the new schools seem to acquire all the extra allowances.'

In those schools or areas where the level of resources and the incidence of demand was seriously depressed, no form of school organization seemed strong enough to encourage participation by teachers in schools in influencing the supply of books, equipment or new specialist facilities. Where, however, the appointment of a new head or a new chief officer radically altered the level of resources and the climate of potential influence, the reverse principle operated quite frequently.

Demand Releases Resources

A number of heads were able to illustrate their success and that of individual heads of departments in divering resources to meet curricular needs—new or existing. A not untypical comment was 'good staff acquire what they need—poor staff can waste their money'. Almost all schools in Nottingham and Northumberland could quote examples of lively or new heads of departments who diverted resources towards their subjects by strong pressures exerted through staffroom politics or directly at the head.

Evidence both from the schools surveyed and from committee records and reports, however, reveals the interesting limitation of impact of innovatory techniques and ideas stemming from teachers' subject associations (The Modern Language Association, the Association for Technical Education in Schools, the Science Masters/ Mistresses Associations) or from national bodies like the Schools Council, to improve or even affect the level and type of curricular resources in 90 per cent of the schools in the survey areas. There was little noticeable impact on the growth rate of *overall expenditure* on equipment and apparatus (beyond price rises and increased rolls) in any of the survey areas either from the Newsom or Crowther reports or from the spate of Schools' Council reports. Innovation in these circumstances in one subject, may largely be at the expense of, not in addition to, maintenance of standards in another. Yet teacher-demand according to the evidence of the survey areas, has increased, in that in 1968 more schools involved teachers in decision-making and more committees sought teacher opinion. One is led again to the view that demand and resources seem only tenuously related.

Implicit Demand from Rising Numbers

It will be recalled that *Lincoln's* building programme failed to keep pace with rising numbers in the secondary modern schools but preserved a standard of grammar school places for 25 per cent of the age group. *Nottingham's* early start in achieving a substantial building programme gave a large proportion of the secondary school pupils post-war buildings by 1965. But the Education Committee itself recorded in 1965 concern at the standard of accommodation in its remaining old schools. *Northumberland's* late start left substantial numbers of pupils in all-age schools until 1962 but nevertheless provided new buildings for 50 of its 83 secondary schools by 1965.

Two things become apparent from the survey. First, that there was still a significant number of old schools—up to one-third—which had not yet been replaced. Second, that some *new* schools were themselves quickly deficient in basic resources, to meet the new demands of growing Vth and VIth forms, or rising numbers and of new curricular methods.

Quantity of Accommodation

Of the schools surveyed, (a 31·5 per cent sample in all) 57 per cent were overcrowded in 1968, although secondary rolls had begun to fall, of which most were secondary modern schools and most had fewer than 450 pupils on roll. And most were in the rural areas. Thus, the authorities were not able to meet completely, even the full basic demand of an *adequate* 'roof over head' for each pupil. It would seem that the authorities were right and the Ministry (Department) of Education wrong, in estimating the capital programmes needed to provide basic equality of educational opportunity by providing a 'suitable' school place. In an overcrowded school, some aspect of the curriculum will be either inadequately taught or not offered since the rigid imposition by the Ministry of both cost limits and Building Code standards when local authorities design schools, means that teaching spaces cannot house more pupils than the number allowed for in the design. The 'margin' in new schools has now been eroded by this constant refusal to allow authorities to build to their own specification.

Over half of all schools surveyed had some major deficiency. Most of these were non-grammar schools. Nearly half of the modern and bilateral schools were seriously deficient in facilities for crafts [both in quantity and in quality: see Tables D (v) and (vi) in Appendix D]. Very few schools at all had respectable facilities for the teaching of geography or history. As a result, more had to teach by lecture and demonstration instead of using pupil-centred or integrated approaches.[2] Ten schools had housecraft or handicraft rooms seriously substandard in size or fitted with near-obsolete equipment. One school had to send all first-year girls to a neighbouring town for housecraft. Five schools could not timetable housecraft for CSE without depriving the second or third year of teaching in the subject because the school was one housecraft room short. About half of the schools had either housecraft rooms with wooden (not steel) draining boards, inadequate facilities for laundry and no facilities for child-care work; or handicraft rooms with one lathe too few, poor storage for CSE finished work; or both. Many had restricted layouts which needed to be redesigned to be suitable for CSE Mode III work or for integrated crafts which the school wished to offer.

Quality of Accommodation Resources

All three authorities placed on record at some stage in the early years, that it was their intention to give non-grammar schools either 'parity of esteem' or the same standards of accommodation, or a suitably equivalent standard of building. The tables and reports in Appendix D however suggest that these aims were not achieved.

Science

The main deficiency was for the teaching of science (see Appendix D, table D (iv)). As many as 25 per cent of schools had only one laboratory and therefore could not offer specialist sciences. Eighteen out of 42 had only two laboratories and had therefore either to choose two out of three sciences or to restrict general science in the lower school in order to teach specialist sciences higher up. In 10 schools of five-form entry or more, with two laboratories only, either one-third of the school had no science at all or half had to have less than four periods in order that all could have some. And one girls' grammar school surveyed had no advanced laboratories at all. Almost all schools had some laboratories which were either not fully equipped or lacking one or more services. And 45 per cent of the schools surveyed had seriously substandard laboratories both in size and in quality. A few were in post-war schools, but most in pre-war buildings; and all but one were secondary modern or other non-grammar schools. Evidence from committee minutes suggests that other schools in the survey areas suffered from similar deficiencies, moreover, and this was used by Nottingham and Northumberland as part of a case for a larger minor works allocation.

Reference was made in Chapter II to the incidence of Nuffield-based courses and to the practice in most schools of teaching science to boys and girls separately. In four schools where there were too few laboratories, the boys were timetabled into these for physics and chemistry and the girls were taught biology in general class-rooms. Even small schools of from one- to three-form entry, taught boys and girls separately for science, craft and technical work, tending to base the boys in specialist rooms and girls in general teaching rooms, wherever accommodation was limited.

In one authority, two grammar schools visited had too few advanced laboratories and their basic laboratories were obsolescent in the period 1945 to 1964. None of the grammar schools in that area could afford, before 1964, to equip their older basic laboratories for pupil-centred work, with the result that the teaching of science by demonstration was imposed on the staff by the restricted conditions. One boys' grammar school staff rejected a concept of technical work based on any craft skills, limiting their preparation for engineering, other technological or technical careers, to an academically biased science course in the VIth form. Any practically based technical education would have been impossible in any case to accommodate.

Nineteen schools, all but one of them non-grammar schools, had laboratories which were seriously substandard. Ten had general science rooms with at least one service (water, gas or power) missing except for the demonstration bench. Eighteen had too few water, power or gas points for pupil-centred work. Eight had 'specialist' laboratories (being used for a single science) which lacked the appropriate service—biology or rural science without water; physics without power. Seven had laboratories below the recommended minimum size of 960 square feet. All 19 had layouts which restricted modern teaching methods but which would be costly to redesign. Some of these 19—indeed most—were schools also deficient in the actual number of laboratories, while some of the 23 whose existing laboratories were adequate in themselves, had however only one or two laboratories. It was thus a minority which had *both* enough laboratories and adequately serviced and equipped rooms.

Libraries

This was the most serious general deficiency in almost all schools. Yet books are the oldest of visual aids. Whatever educational technology may bring, it cannot replace the need for books as the core and spring of learning and knowledge. Libraries have, also, over the past 25 years, become 'resource' centres in themselves, in those schools fortunate enough to have space and money to develop them to house films, slides, tapes and other recorded material (files and cuttings) as well as books.

Libraries are especially important to children from poorer homes and from rural areas where even a mobile public library cannot compensate for the more extensive facilities available to children in big cities. The Carnegie UK Trust in 1936 suggested a minimum standard for a secondary school library of from 900—1,200 square feet, with an additional reference library where possible.[3] Its survey of schools revealed 'schools without even a bookcase specifically set aside for library purposes', new schools without libraries in otherwise 'magnificent new buildings' and (forerunner of post-war difficulties) libraries used for class teaching. Fairly predictably,

'The slowest rate of improvement is in some areas where the education finances are heavily burdened, and generally in rural as against urban areas'[4]

In other words, in the growing competition for resources, the library commanded low priority. The Newsom Committee discovered a similar situation however some 30 years later.

'It is now a commonplace that the school library is as essential for work in the humanities (though not only in them) as the laboratory is in science. Like the laboratory, however, it was not included in the schedules of the old elementary schools. One must, therefore, expect to find a good deal of improvisation and a good deal of going without; and so one does.'[5]

Of the schools surveyed by the Newsom Committee, in fact, only

26 per cent had a proper library used exclusively as such, and 13 per cent had a designated library which had, however, to be used for ordinary class teaching. More than one-fifth (21 per cent) had no library room at all, while about two-fifths had improvised libraries made from small classrooms or stockrooms. Most of the areas or districts where fewer of the schools were new (slum areas, mining districts, areas of mixed housing) had failed to develop vigorous policies to remodel old buildings which would have allowed the provision of a dignified environment for study and reference libraries. The influence of the building standards of the Ministry of Education, and of its Bulletins had clearly not permeated the authorities responsible for the schools surveyed by the Newsom Committee, sufficiently to alter the place of the library in their list of priorities.

In the sample survey of schools undertaken by the writer, despite extremely vigorous attempts by *Nottingham* and *Northumberland* at least, to maintain a rolling programme of improvements to library facilities, only a minority of schools (mostly selective schools) had adequate basic accommodation, and almost all considered their library allowance to be totally inadequate in relation to the cost of books and the shorter life of books now (See Table D (vi) of Appendix D). The position may be summarized by a comment from the headmaster of a secondary modern school in one of the survey areas.

'In an authority prone to innovation and experiment, it is easier to get £2,000 for a language laboratory and £20,000 for a field study centre, than enough money to replace old books; because books don't seem to be so important now, except to teachers and children.'

a possible exaggeration; it bears a grain of truth.

Other Deficiencies

Nearly half of the modern and bilateral schools were deficient in either quality or quantity of facilities for crafts. While technical facilities generally in the grammar schools were good (though mainly underused), 14 out of 17 non-grammar schools offering commerce had no special facilities whatever for its teaching. Fifteen out of the 16 schools with deficiencies for the teaching of art were non-grammar schools. Only two grammar out of seven schools had special practical facilities for the teaching of modern languages, two grammar schools had inadequate facilities for the VIth and five grammar schools were overcrowded by over 15 per cent.

It would appear that a number of aims were not achieved and that resources did not match needs. For example, first, non-grammar schools did not achieve even relative parity of esteem in terms of their accommodation. Second, they were especially deficient in practical accommodation which was, by most ideologies current at the time, considered more essential for less able pupils. Third, the lively concern of *Nottingham* and *Northumberland* that standards should be maintained and improved was only partly successful despite the proportionately higher rate of increase in their budget than mere numerical increase in pupil numbers would justify. Readers are reminded that this relates to the period before 1965. Lincoln's position improved dramatically after 1964.

Curricular Resources

A majority of teachers interviewed expressed concern at the anomalies apparent in the allocation of money to schools for equipment, books, stationery and apparatus. (Most were also concerned at the relatively less favourable position of the less able child or the pupils in a small school.) This is one aspect of resource allocation which has been strongly affected in most authorities by demand from two national organizations, the AEC and the Publishers' Association. The capitation schemes operated by local authorities are diverse, and some authorities (but not all) tend to supplement the basic allowance to schools, either with special allocations for curricular experiment from an annual 'pool' controlled by the inspectorate, or by capital loans for the renewal of, say, libraries or housecraft rooms. Although much has been made of the latter in the educational press, in the three survey areas *capital* sums were not a significant element of the budget for school materials. Both *Nottingham* and *Northumberland* spent reasonably generously from *revenue* however on such additional stock as film projectors and other audiovisual aids, and developed specific policies to encourage schools to buy and use new equipment as it became available (the coming of educational television and the use of programmable calculators, for example).

There is however unanimity that demand was not generally met, in the supply of the basic tools of the trade—books, stationery and apparatus. There is some evidence in Chapter VI (Lincoln) of the failure of expenditure to keep up with price rises and this was a factor in all three authorities. There was other evidence in all three areas of inadequate impact of teacher opinion on this issue. Two principles of *implicit demand* have been common to most if not all authorities. First, the need to keep up with price rises and second, the need to maintain a reasonable minimum or average standard. The Association of Education Committees and the Publishers' Association have attempted by *explicit demand* to keep authorities up to standard by issuing recommendations at regular intervals. These two organizations have in their turn, used the annual records of local authority spending prepared by the Institute of Municipal Treasurers and Accountants and the County Treasurers' Association.

Tables VII (a) to (c) of Appendix B give the annual expenditure for furniture and equipment and for books, stationery and apparatus for the three authorities surveyed. The figures should be related to the secondary school population figures in Tables II (b) and II (c).

Mention was made earlier of the practice of many authorities of differentiating between types of schools in awarding allowances for books and equipment. As early as 1954, the AEC undertook a survey together with the School Library Association. In a long and detailed report, the AEC recommended a uniform per capita allowance because

'while there may be arguments justifying a higher allowance for books in grammar schools, for example, there is no doubt that additional moneys are required for practical subjects to a greater extent in other secondary schools.'[6]

The AEC recommended higher allowances for pupils over 15+. Its recommendations related to books, stationery, apparatus and consumable stock and not to such items as projectors, tape recorders, records and films.[7] On the other hand its 1961 report on school libraries recommended a differential annual maintenance grant for the library of

'not less than £400 for a grammar school, not less than £300 for a secondary modern school.'

In 1965, its report recommended again a common standard throughout its scheme, for all types of secondary school. In the reports issued from 1954 to 1961, the life of a text book was assumed to be eight years. By 1965, the AEC estimated a six-year life. There is no evidence that authorities built in to their schemes any deliberate increase in the later years, to allow for more frequent replacement of books, and in fact all schools surveyed in 1968 gave illustrative examples of an incapacity to replace books every five-six years without cutting back other curricular resources drastically.

Table X (1) which follows, shows the actual expenditure on books, stationery and apparatus in the three authorities in the years of the most influential reports of the AEC specifying a desirable level of allowances and expenditure. The basis of calculation varied *between* the authorities but, as far as can be traced, the sums *within* each authority represent the same elements of expenditure in each year quoted. At face value, the expenditure grew at a faster rate than rising numbers alone would justify thus showing an apparent margin for price rises and (or) improvement. Verbal and recorded evidence during the research however suggested that the base levels themselves were too low in most years to relate to assessed needs in each school or indeed in each classroom.[8]

Table X (1)

	YEAR	EXPENDITURE ON BOOKS, STATIONERY AND APPARATUS £	INDEX	TOTAL SECONDARY ROLL	INDEX
Lincoln	1954	8,939	100	3,494	100
	1956	13,299	148	4,411	126
	1961	17,413	195	5,374	154
	1964	not available.			
Nottingham	1954	42,667	100	16,636	100
	1956	54,723	129	18,294	109
	1961	80,195	188	21,311	128
	1964	82,527	193	20,303	121
Northumberland	1954	44,873	100	15,443	100
	1956	55,865	125	18,088	117
	1961	108,637	241	27,366	178
	1964	148,713	330	28,973	188

Note: Since the three authorities' capitation schemes were different, direct comparisons on apparent cost per pupil are misleading. The table illustrates growth and relationship to school rolls only.

This is borne out by a study of the annual reports of the Publishers' Association and by comparison of capitation schemes with those suggested by the AEC. In 1958,[9] all three authorities were below the 'good' standard of the Publishers' Association.

Publishers' Association standards (1958)

	ACTUAL EXPENDITURE ON BSA £	RECOMMENDED 'GOOD' EXPENDITURE RELATED TO SCHOOL POPULATION £
Lincoln	14,609	18,020
Nottingham	61,021	68,655
Northumberland	76,415	79,608

In 1960, *Lincoln* was still below the average standard, *Nottingham* was assessed as 'reasonable' and *Northumberland* as 'good'. Lincoln remained below standard until after 1965, the other two authorities fluctuating after 1960 between reasonable and good by the standards of the Publishers' Association.

One further example will serve to illustrate the apparent difficulty of meeting the price rises caused by the cost of paper. The cost of books rose by 15 per cent from 1958—1959.[10] *Lincoln's* actual expenditure on books, stationery and apparatus rose in that year by only about eight per cent, most of which was accounted for by rising school rolls. Expenditure in *Nottingham* on these items actually fell in that year. But it increased very substantially in *Northumberland,* largely because of the opening of a number of new schools, but also deliberately to take account of price rises. Two of the three authorities could not (or did not) always meet demand from rising prices, on this evidence.

The foregoing would seem to suggest that the concern of the teachers in all three survey areas that curricular demand was not being fully met by the allocation of financial resources, had some foundation. It is the more perturbing in the light of the argument touched on in Chapter II, that money for innovation (allocated to a minority of schools) is in some respects being allocated at the expense of basic standards.

Summary

The implications of this and the evidence in Appendix D are serious. Despite massive apparent rises in educational expenditure, despite vigorous attempts by two out of three local education authorities to build more schools, better schools and to equip them well, evidence was consistent that basic curricular needs were not fully met. Teachers faced acute educational rationing in an apparent world of plenty. Facilities were lacking for external examination work and for pupil-centred methods alike. This must, surely, have had a major impact on the skills and qualifications acquired by the pupils educated in those years. What happened to the school-leavers?

Notes

1 *Standards for School Premises Regulations,* 195, HMSO, paras. 17 and 18. In the survey conducted by the writer, the single deficiency mentioned by every headteacher and every head of department without exception, was lack of or insufficiency of storage for equipment, stock and teaching materials, particularly acute where audio-visual methods, team teaching and CSE Mode III examinations were used.

2 Building Bulletins specify rooms of about 820 sq. ft. with water and power and blackout. See also HEATON, I.R. in an article in *Education* (26.1.62) pp. 164–165 'The plan and layout of the geography room will be a major influence on the kind of geography taught and the methods which a teacher can employ'.

3 Carnegie UK Trust, *Libraries in Secondary Schools,* 1936. p.4. Secondary in 1936 of course meant grammar.

4 op. cit. para. 33.

5 Central Advisory Council (England) *Half our Future,* 1963. p.255.

6 AEC Minutes, September 1954. All three authorities surveyed nevertheless differentiated at that period.

7 Wood and metal, not tools; chemicals and not scientific equipment.

8 Assessed, that is, by teachers. It will be recalled from Chapter VI (Lincoln) that teachers fought consistently to improve the level of spending on books and materials, largely without success.

9 By which time a substantial building programme had been completed in two of the three areas.

10 Evidence from the Publishers' Association and the AEC.

CHAPTER XI
School-Leavers

*'If you want to slip into a round hole, you must make a ball of
yourself; that's where it is.'*

George Eliot (*The Mill on the Floss*)

One important, if unsophisticated, measurement of the secondary
education system is what happens to its pupils when they leave it.
Evidence from earlier chapters describes some of the factors which
influenced the development and progress of secondary education
in the survey areas, in the context of the allocation of resources.
Despite negative controls by central government and some negative
influences from some (but by no means all) local members and
officers, the history of events related so far shows distinct progress
over the 20-year period. New schools were built; all-age schools
were reorganized. Despite price rises affecting all resources (staff,
buildings, allowances) the level of expenditure appeared still to
grow in at least two of the three areas, faster than rising numbers of
pupils and rising costs alone would account for. And some standards
rose generally. With such apparent expansion of educational
opportunity, it is pertinent to ask whether this appeared the better
to equip school leavers for further education, training or skilled
employment. Increased investment in secondary education must
surely have given some cost-benefit to the pupils, authorities and
regions in the form of greater skills, and improved educational
opportunity or employability?

It did not appear necessarily to do so for the majority of pupils.
The direct impact on the education service from industry, locally or
regionally, seemed minimal. An analysis of the destination of school-
leavers in the three areas, casts some further doubt whether the
majority of less able school-leavers did in fact have proportionately
improved opportunities on leaving school by comparison with peers
in earlier years. It should be stressed that it is not necessarily
suggested that suitability for further education or for skilled employment is the only, or even always the major goal of secondary
education. But it is an important and an increasingly relevant one.
And it is measurable as a crude index of trends.

The opportunity of the school-leaver appeared, in fact, to depend very largely on whether the secondary school pupil was in a grammar or non-grammar school, a boy or girl, in a rural or urban school, or a large or a small school. And while opportunities improved steadily and in two areas constantly, for grammar school pupils, the less able child suffered the greater impact of the scarcity of building, staffing and financial resources. This correlates highly in two areas with a continuing high proportion of school-leavers who entered unskilled work.

This difference in basic educational opportunity[1] was touched on in research undertaken by Jean Ross at the Medical Research Unit of LSE as part of a national survey of health and development. In a special report to the 1965 NUT Conference, differences were discussed as between areas with over 25 per cent grammar places (the 'many' areas) and those with fewer (often below 15 per cent and described as the 'few' areas). Under the terms of Jean Ross's definition, Lincoln was a 'many' area and Nottingham and Northumberland were 'few' areas. How far were children educationally handicapped if they lived in areas with few selective places? Among other findings, Jean Ross discovered that there tended to be more shortages of staff in the 'few' areas, that late transfers at 13+ tended to be middle-class children, that more working-class children in the 'few' areas leave school early than elsewhere and that girls in both social classes did as well as boys in the well provided areas, but much less well in areas with few selective places.[2]

How far, in fact, should the education system equate educational opportunity with the manpower needs of the region or the country, in allocating its resources? Are liberal and vocational educational needs mutually exclusive? These matters are touched on elsewhere, and the case made for some direct relationship. Of the three authorities surveyed, *Nottingham* and *Northumberland* appeared conscious of the need to relate the provision of technical education in their schools to the industries in their regions, but *Lincoln* seemed quite unconscious of an identifiable relationship between education and employment at all for less able pupils. On the other hand, more pupils in *Lincoln* than in the other two authorities received a grammar school education, potentially at least offering entry to the higher levels of industry and the professions, than in the other areas.

National, Regional or Local Planning?

Is it desirable for the curriculum and therefore the design of schools for less able pupils, to take into account local or regional employment outlets rather than national needs? Experience of careers officers and head teachers tends to suggest that the more able and motivated (and often older) school-leavers will fairly readily move outside the home area but that progressively, the less able the pupil, the nearer home he or she will wish to work. This is often for good reasons. Less able pupils leave at 15+ or 16+ rather than 18+. The gifted may be going to college or university or to a firm offering training and support; the less able into an unsupported social situation. Nevertheless, whatever the varied reasons, the preference of the less able for work very near home is a fact. It would therefore be unwise to underestimate local influence, when designing, staffing and organizing schools. There is however a reverse danger, that to fail to strike a balance between pupils' general and their directly vocational needs, would make school-leavers vulnerable if later in their adult life they need to move from their home region or district because of unemployment or for example rationalization of the capital plant of a large firm based in several regions.

The University of Newcastle-on-Tyne recently undertook a survey on behalf of the Ministry of Labour, which is highly relevant to this issue and also to the situation in the County of Northumberland.[3] A major finding of the university survey is the high proportion (over half) of respondents who had stayed in the home district, sometimes despite a complete lack of local employment prospects there. The report comments that

'These figures may speak something of the inertia among young people in the North, with equal proportions for both males and females. . . . By others the same figures will be taken to express attachment to the way of life in the North, and both are probably true in part. The high ratio of male stayers in localities where employment prospects are not good is perhaps the most disturbing factor.'[4]

This raises the question of minimum qualifications for mobility of employment and a continuing need for nationally validated measurements of performance such as GCE or its replacement. There is a continuing need also for a curriculum containing all basic elements required by most employers and not a carefully weighted selection of 'appropriate' subjects related to preconceived ideas about the education of the less able or of girls, in particular. For fewer secondary modern leavers in the North East commuted; and the highest proportion of non-migrants from the area was from secondary modern schools.

The survey comments on

'the unevenness of educational and career opportunities according
to type of school. One fifth of grammar school leavers went on to
full-time further education, compared with 10 per cent from the
two technical colleges and a mere 1 per cent from a much larger
secondary modern population. . . . One of the most disturbing
statistics is that no less than two-thirds of the secondary modern
leavers stayed in their home locality, possibly because their education
did not fit them for wider opportunities elsewhere.'[5]

An analysis of Northumberland's school-leavers supports this. In
Lincoln, moreover, all heads interviewed confirmed that leavers other
than those going on to full-time further and higher education were
reluctant or positively unwilling to look beyond the city boundary
for employment. Those in the north of the city would equally
reluctantly look to firms in the south of the city (a 10-minute bus
ride) and this influenced adversely, in their view, the schools' attempts
to widen the IVth-year work.

The Survey Areas

What happened in the survey areas? Did the changing secondary
developments in the three authorities, change the pattern of placement of school leavers?

Lincoln

It has been established that throughout the survey period the
secondary modern schools were discouraged from developing
extended or bias courses, were not staffed or equipped to organize
GCE courses, and that five out of seven were in pre-war buildings, the
remaining two having acquired new premises only in the mid-1950s,
both moreover for a four-year course only. Appendix A comments
briefly on the main employment outlets of the city, predominantly
in fact craft apprenticeships in engineering or building, clerical work
or work in shops. Some changes of emphasis over the years are
recorded, none of which however affected the expressed policy of the
Education Committee to limit practical resources and specialist
teaching in the modern schools.

Non-academic pupils not entering higher education. Three years
after the raising of the school-leaving age and five years after the new
Education Act, the placings made by the Youth Employment
Service were as follows—a not unfamiliar pattern:[6]

Table XI (1): *Lincoln*

WORK	% OF PLACINGS (1950)	
	Boys %	*Girls* %
Apprenticeships—engineering and allied trades.	33·6	—
other craft apprenticeships	31·4	2·0
leading to skilled work	7·0	5·4
clerical	2·3	28·1
shop assistants	—	24·1
semiskilled	6·1	—
domestic	—	8·5
other unskilled	19·6	31·9
	100	100

Although directly comparable figures are not available for 1965, the pattern was very similar except that more girls were placed in clerical work (33 per cent in all) and none in domestic work and about 15 per cent more boys went on to low level courses of further education instead of taking apprenticeships. In the early 1950s, there was keen competition for craft apprenticeships[7] and by 1956, there were more boys seeking opportunities in the electrical trades than places available. But also at this time local industry began to express preferences for 16-year-old leavers[8] and the engineering industries in particular began to ask for minimum qualifications of the examinations of the East Midland Educational Union or even GCE. But the secondary modern schools were not allowed to run courses for external examinations, and had been instructed to transfer pupils at 15+ to the Technical College for one-year courses, aimed at entry to industry at apprenticeship level. The resources at the college, however, were too limited to house all potential school-leavers. Since the two neighbouring counties then offered opportunities to take examinations of the East Midlands Educational Union at 15+, the apprenticeships in the City were offered increasingly to boys from the out-county schools, ruling out most 15+ Lincoln leavers.[9] A gradual increase in recruitment from grammar schools at 16+ further reduced opportunity for the modern school leavers.[10] For example in 1955, 42 per cent of the 16+ leavers from the larger boys' grammar school took apprenticeships in the city and by 1962, 25 per cent were still entering apprenticeships.

The Youth Employment Committee expressed constant concern about this:

'Employers in general were seeking the better type of boy or girl . . .

and this resulted in the boy or girl who had little academic ability being handicapped.'[11]

The cause lay mainly in the limited skills and qualifications held by leavers who had not been able to transfer at 13+ or 15+ to the grammar schools or to the college—

'There was need to make available (in schools) some form of training facilities and an encouragement for them to improve their manual dexterity.'[12]

The preceding section has shown that the schools simply did not have adequate facilities for handicrafts for such training to be possible. The outlets considered 'suitable' for girls were mainly shops and offices. The minutes of the Youth Employment Committee record a constant difficulty in placing girl leavers in the first decade, but an improved position in the 1960s. But

'Very few girls took advantage of the opportunity for further education offered by the technical commercial course (at the college).'[13]

A constant comment by the Youth Employment Committee was that the output from the one-year Technical College courses 'readily found employment' in the jobs which had hitherto gone to leavers direct from secondary modern schools. (Many of these jobs were not highly skilled, nevertheless.)

There is some evidence that the output from individual schools may be related to facilities and staffing. For the only secondary modern school in the city to have facilities for all three craft techniques (wood, metal and technical drawing) and the staff to man them (including a head with an engineering degree) sent 37 per cent of its leavers directly into engineering apprenticeships, and 28 per cent more to the pre-apprenticeship course at the college, while the parallel figures for the other boys' schools which both had very poor practical facilities, were 23 per cent and 5 per cent, and 30 per cent and 10 per cent respectively. On the girls' side, the only secondary modern school with facilities (albeit limited) for pre-commercial work sent substantially more girls to clerical work and to the college, and fewer to factories, than those with no facilities or staff for vocationally biased work of this kind. Similarly, the two boys' and girls' grammar schools with better scientific and technical rooms and higher head of department allowances, regularly sent more leavers to read science and technical subjects at universities

and colleges and more pupils into apprenticeships, than the two
less well equipped and staffed schools.

Grammar/academic pupils. There was no difficulty in placing pupils
in banks and offices at 16+, but other skilled local outlets, for girls
especially, were few.

The performance of the grammar schools and colleges in sending
pupils on to full-time higher and further education can be said quite
substantially to have met an increased demand. The average age
group increased by only about 43 per cent from 1946 to 1965, but
major and senior awards increased as follows:

Table XI (2)

LINCOLN AWARDS TENABLE AT	1946	1965
universities	24	180
teacher training	12	67
senior awards	5	107

Nevertheless, Lincoln's award holders for university and further
education course have been (and still are) substantially below the
regional and national averages for these. Only its teacher training
students represented recruitment at the national average, influenced
no doubt by the presence in the City of a voluntary College of
Education of national standing.

Nottingham

Appendix A (II) gives details of the wide variety of industrial and
commercial outlets in the city. Chapter VI records the development
of the bilateral scheme; the concentration of the capital programme
on new secondary schools in the first post-war decade; and the
gradual transfer of technical studies from secondary technical schools
to bilateral or grammar schools. Selective places increased from
about 12 per cent to about 25 per cent over the 20-year period.

Non-academic school leavers. In 1946, the main shift of emphasis
in the city was from wartime to peacetime products. Jobs in general
engineering and canvas goods declined and the motor and cycle
trade and the making-up (of clothes) and the building industry all
revived and expanded. Over the 20-year period, the placings made by
the Youth Employment Service showed marked fluctuations, some
readily understandable in relation to changing emphases in industries
but others less so. The following table gives some examples, which
indicate the potential danger of linking the curricular content of
courses for older secondary school pupils too directly with local
industrial demands:

Table XI (3): Nottingham

ENTRANTS TO INDUSTRY		INCREASE OR DECREASE ON PRECEDING YEAR				
	1952		1954		1956	
Blouse and robe making	+104	(g)	— 99	(g)	+ 34	(g)
clerical	— 47	(b)				
	+215	(g)	—253	(g)	+ 64	(g)
Shop assistants	+ 96	(g)	— 12	(g)	+ 50	(g)
Mining	+ 12	(b)	+223	(b)	+ 84	(b)
(g=girls b=boys)						

The leavers from the secondary technical schools did however tend to go for the most part into related industries. In 1952, 60 of 96 school-leavers from the Textile technical school went into the textile trades, while of the 89 leavers from the Building technical school, 48 went into craft apprenticeships in the industry, 21 into the offices of builders, surveyors or architects and 14 into engineering.[14] The schools, it will be recalled, were created because of industrial demand, and in the earlier years they met the demand both from industry and from parents and pupils.

The reports and minutes of the Education Committee speak constantly of a 'demand for female labour' in the city which exceeded the supply of school leavers to fill the vacancies, although it is nowhere recorded why the vacant posts in factories and trades were limited to or designed for, girls only. Many head teachers interviewed in 1969, considered the ready availability of jobs for girls discouraged many from staying on for extended courses in non-grammar schools and especially in girls' schools, although by 1965, 14 secondary schools offered commercial subjects. By 1962, the Youth Employment Committee was however commenting that

'Employers wishing to recruit girls as operatives, also complain that comparatively fewer girls are available. This is because more of the able girls stay on to 16 and thus widen the scope of employment opportunities open to them. Other girls transfer to commercial training and find a ready market in the number of clerical jobs which industry is increasingly creating.'

Table XI (4) illustrates the major employment entered by those placed by the Youth Employment Service. This shows both some changes in emphasis, and a marked difference in the pattern for boys and for girls respectively. Well over a third of boys went into craft apprenticeships; few into clerical work, or distributive trades. The textile industry was largely staffed by girls and women. Certain specific responses to demand can be traced. More boys and girls became laboratory assistants as the education service developed its policy of providing laboratory assistance for schools and as the pharmaceutical industry in the city expanded. In the early 1950s an average of from 10—15 boys and about the same number of girls started training for this. By 1965 the figures were 33 boys and 13 girls —possibly, though not necessarily, a reflection of the higher standard of science accommodation in the boys' schools, or of the tendency in the mixed schools for girls to study biology and not physical and chemical sciences. Hairdressing also was a growth industry—hardly represented in 1946, but recruiting between 70 and 90 girls a year by 1965 (but only about 10 boys). A direct result of one school's policy of encouraging girls to take technical subjects (in its well equipped

Table XI (4): Nottingham

EMPLOYMENT	PERCENTAGE OF TOTAL PLACINGS BY THE YOUTH EMPLOYMENT SERVICE							
	1946		1950		1956		1965	
	B %	G %	B %	G %	B %	G %	B %	G %
Engineering (general)	31·8	2·3	20·0	—	20·9	—	25·1	—
Engineering (electrical)	7·3	0·6	8·1	—	6·2	—	13·2	—
Clerical	6·3	22·4	13·0	33·5	8·0	39·0	9·5	32·2
Shop Assistant	2·5	11·4	2·4	8·6	2·9	16·0	5·6	12·2
Making up trade, blouse and robemakers	—	24·0	—	24·0	—	16·3	—	26·0
Hosiery	—	13·3	—	9·0	2·0	2·9	—	6·2
Lace	—	1·4	—	1·8	—	—	—	1·4
Mining	2·3	—	2·4	—	18·7	—	3·2	—
Transport	7·1	—	8·5	—	5·3	—	2·2	—
Building	3·4	—	7·7	—	4·5	—	11·2	—
Packers Warehouses	6·0	8·1	5·7	6·8	6·7	7·8	4·0	6·8
Printing	3·5	1·7	not shown		2·2	2·9	1·7	2·4
Domestic	—	2·3	—	2·5	—	—	—	—
Labourers	5·6	—	3·7	—	7·5	—	7·4	—

Note: The percentages are of placings by the Youth Employment Service, not of total school leavers. Not all employment outlets are represented.

workshops) was the steady recruitment of about 20 girls a year (together with over 250 boys) to electrical work. Table XI (4) is not exhaustive but it does show that of those dealt with by the Youth Employment Service a fairly constant proportion went into unskilled or semiskilled jobs. Transport and mining declined but packers and labourers (i.e. unskilled jobs) still accounted for nearly 12 per cent throughout. More girls went into shops and offices, by 1965, but proportionately no more girls entered apprenticeships.

Grammar school/vocationally motivated leavers. Those going on to further and higher education would not normally have been included in the Youth Employment statistics. Here too, patterns changed. The following tables, extracted from the 1965 annual report of the Nottingham Education Committee, show the increased educational opportunity offered by the expansion of GCE courses generally and of grammar school places in particular, and the increased takeup of higher and further education, which should be related to the school population figures in Appendix B.

Table XI (5): Nottingham—new awards

ENTRANTS	1954–55	1964–65
Universities	57	167
Colleges of Advanced Technology	—	31
Technical Colleges	5	44
other Future Education establishments	22	87
	84	329

Of the degree courses, 102 were science-based and seven arts-based.

One might assume that all Nottingham pupils of advanced ability had been given improved opportunities as a direct result of the greatly increased resources provided for secondary education, and the reorganization of the secondary system. The following table however shows that while the *growth rate* for women holding places at universities was not so far behind that of the men, nearly three times as many men as women went to university in the 1960s—a worsening of the mid-1950s balance when just over twice as many men as women held places. Only part of the increase is accounted for by an increase in the age group.

Table XI (6): *Total number of awards (Nottingham)*

	1954–55	1963–64	1964–65	% INCREASE 1954–64
Universities				
men	124	275	333	168%
women	53	100	120	126%
Totals	177	375	453	
Other establishments of further education				
men	25	148	192	670%
women	19	57	80	320%
Totals	44	205	272	

Award holders at establishments of teacher training showed a slightly different pattern, (more women went to training colleges) but this does not wholly redress the balance.

Table XI (7): *Total awards (teacher training) (Nottingham)*

	1961	1964	% INCREASE
men	76	106	39·5%
women	128	217	69·5%
	204	323	58·3%

These figures reflect the deliberate policy of the Nottingham authority to train more girls to become teachers (see Chapter VI). At other establishments of further education, the differential widens—awards to boys increased by nearly eight times, to girls between four and five times, and the position in 1964 was still that twice as many boys as girls held awards whereas the balance in 1954 was more even. The pattern of the organization of education in the city, and the allocation of resources within that organization, does not appear to have improved the relative position of girls, who benefited less proportionately than the boys. Chapter II commented on some aspects of the assumptions of role identification which influenced the administrators and heads in distributing resources in schools by sex of pupil.

Northumberland

Directly comparable figures are not available for Northumberland because the county education authority did not organize its own Youth Employment Service but used the agency services of the Ministry of Labour. However, the Department of Employment has made available for this research some special material extracted from surveys undertaken by the Department, from which figures can be given for the years 1961 and 1968, the first year being before the full effect of the reorganization of all-age schools took effect and the later year, able to show the effect, if any, of the subsequent developments. Appendix A (III) gives a brief outline of the industry and employment pattern of the area. A dominant factor in Northumberland was the unwillingness of young people to travel more than a few miles for work—the journey from Morpeth to Ashington or Ashington to Alnwick was an insurmountable psychological barrier to the less able school-leaver.

The Northern regional survey in 1961 undertaken by the Department of Employment gave the following destinations of school-leavers for Tyneside and for the remainder of Northumberland. Tyneside in Table XI (8) includes Newcastle County Borough and the urban fringe of the county education authority; the remainder is wholly in the county area.

Table XI (8): *New Entrants into Employment* (1961)

CATEGORY	TYNESIDE		RURAL NORTHUMBERLAND	
	Boys %	Girls %	Boys %	Girls %
1	48·6	4·0	26·0	5·6
2	1·1	1·0	0·8	1·2
3	6·9	36·5	3·2	17·5
4*	8·7	11·4	9·0	11·2
5	34·7	47·1	61·0	64·5
	100	100	100	100

* includes coal mining trainees.
Categories: 1. Apprenticeship to skilled trades
2. Employment leading to professional qualifications
3. Clerical
4. Involving at least 12 months planned training on the job.
5. Other (mainly unskilled)

It will be recalled from Chapter VIII that the central government's stringent control of capital resources delayed the full reorganization of rural all-age schools in the county until the early 1960s. Despite too, the county's vigorous policy of providing for boarding hostels and schools for children from rural areas, and of providing transport to bring children to urban schools or into market towns, the difference in school leaver patterns between Tyneside and the rural area is startling. Nearly twice as many boys on Tyneside entered craft apprenticeships; nearly twice as many boys in the rural areas entered unskilled employment. Twice as many girls on Tyneside as in the rural area entered clerical work; and nearly a fifth more in the rural area entered unskilled employment. And although more girls than boys overall entered clerical work or work involving some training (category 4), more girls than boys entered unskilled work generally.

By 1968, the position for the county of Northumberland (excluding Newcastle County Borough this time) was as shown in the following table:

Table XI (9): *New entrants into employment* (1968)*

Category	Northumberland		Northern Region		Great Britain	
	B %	G %	B %	G %	B %	G %
1	52·4	6·8	47·6	5·7	43·0	7·4
2	1·0	1·9	1·0	2·1	1·2	1·8
3	8·7	35·8	7·3	32·9	8·3	38·9
4 (a)	2·3	2·2	2·7	4·1	8·3	4·7
4 (b)	1·8	10·8	2·6	13·1	5·1	9·7
5	33·8	42·5	38·8	42·3	34·1	37·5
	100	100	100	100	100	100

* categories as for table XI (8) except that category 4 is split to show 12 months on-the-job training (4 (a)) and 4–50 weeks training (4 (b)).

Northumberland, while being above the national average in the number of boy leavers entering apprenticeships (mainly from Tyneside) is well below average for girls and for the rural areas. (See tables XI (8) and XI (10).) The girls in rural areas also had either less skill or less opportunity for entering clerical employment and proportionately more entered unskilled work than from urban areas. This correlates highly with the pattern of (limited) courses for girls in small rural schools. There is a *prima facie* case for questioning whether, in addition to social and geographical factors, the limited courses, accommodation and staffing resources depressed the achievement of pupils in rural or in small schools, and whether differential principles of allocation affected the achievement of girls and of boys. For in a mining town with a large grammar/ technical school and two new out of four small secondary modern schools over half of the boys went into skilled trades but only six per cent of girls; and twice as many girls went into work with no entitlement to training. In a neighbouring market town, almost all girl leavers went into unskilled work with no training, as did twice as many boys as the national and regional averages. The higher proportion of both sexes entering clerical work in the districts near Newcastle is a direct reflection of the need for security expressed by Tynesiders with memories of the 1930s (coinciding with the establishment of the headquarters of the Department of Health and Social Security near Newcastle). But this does not explain the excessive recruitment of girls rather than boys to clerical work, which may be more accurately accounted for by inherited assumptions of greater 'suitability', although most of the schools were coeducational. Table XI (10) which follows gives the main actual destinations of non-academic school leavers.

Table XI (10): *Northumberland. School leavers—contrasting districts* 1968 *Survey —Department of Employment*

District	PERCENTAGE OF LEAVERS Categories					
	1		3		5	
	B %	G %	B %	G %	B %	G %
Mining town	54·9	6·7	6·5	26·1	34·1	63·0
Rural market town	29·3	2·6	6·2	9·2	69·4	82·9
Larger rural town	43·5	15·7	6·2	13·0	44·0	54·0
Rural town	38·0	6·4	5·8	39·5	54·0	50·0
Rural area	39·0	—	4·9	21·3	44·0	48·5
Seaside resort and residential town	62·2	12·9	12·9	37·0	10·1	27·0
Tyneside district	56·0	5·6	10·1	42·7	29·4	40·0
Newcastle fringe	54·2	11·2	14·1	44·6	29·4	42·5
Post-war new council housing district— Newcastle fringe	51·1	4·2	12·3	52·9	32·8	28·0

Note: The percentages are of leavers placed in 1968 by the Department of Employment.

Categories: 1. Apprenticeship to skilled trade or occupation (includes coal-mining trainees)
3. Clerical
5. Mainly unskilled

Grammar/academic leavers. The more able leavers would not be included in these figures. It will be recalled that like Nottingham, *Northumberland* started from a base in 1945 of grammar school places for only 12 per cent of the age group. As an act of policy the authority restricted its selective places to well under 15 per cent during most of the survey period.

Table XI (11): *Total number of major awards* (*Northumberland*)

	1953	1962	ACTUAL INCREASE	% INCREASE %
Universities	421	744	323	77·2
Teacher training	300	434	134	44·5
Other further education	104	262	158	107·0
	825	1,440	615	74·5

When this is related to the growth rate in Northumberland's secondary school population (Table II in Appendix B) which nearly doubled in this period, the figures show that the *proportion* of awards in fact remained more or less constant, and did not grow; unlike Nottingham and Lincoln.[15]

Urban and rural children. Tables XI (8) and XI (10) above illustrate a marked difference in the entry to skilled and unskilled employment by children from urban Tyneside and rural Northumberland. The schools survey undertaken by the writer in 1968 confirmed school by school, that more pupils from rural schools entered unskilled employment and fewer entered employment involving apprenticeships or 12 months on-the-job training, than from urban areas. Head teachers accounted for this in a number of ways. They suggested an inherited prejudice against moving away from home, a distrust of Tyneside, and a degree of social immaturity in their rural children, as three quasi-social factors. Some rural heads admitted to concern about the viability of their schools, their capacity to offer pupils full opportunity for further education and training or entry to skilled employment, while others, in quoting a 10 per cent take-up of further education, transfer to grammar schools and entry to skilled employment, considered this matched the aspirations and potential achievement of rural pupils. From committee records, the survey undertaken by the Department of Employment and the survey of schools undertaken by the writer, evidence emerged that those schools offering only CSE (and in limited subjects) because they were too small, tended to send more pupils proportionately into unskilled work with no training entitlement. Other schools in similar catchment areas which were larger, with a wider range of GCE courses and *proportionately* more specialist facilities tended to transfer more pupils to grammar schools or to further education at 16+ and more pupils to skilled employment.

National Trends

The main industries of the survey areas—engineering in Lincoln and Nottingham, shipbuilding, mining and agriculture and forestry in Northumberland and textiles and clothing in Nottingham, provide further background for correlations disturbing to the maintenance of equal opportunity. Despite enhanced investment in secondary education, the capital plant and staffing resources were not adequate for the 75 per cent less able pupils at any point in the survey period—mainly because of factors beyond the authorities' control. But further training opportunities reinforced the discriminal opportunities. Rural children went into agriculture, forestry, distributive trades from their small school less endowed with extended courses. Urban children went into apprenticeships. Some of Nottingham's industries are traditionally those with low incidence of day release with the outstanding exception of Boots. The following table shows that many leavers entering dominant industries in the survey areas were not likely to be given day release, and least of all girls. The correlation of deprivation is high.

Table XI (12): *Under 18's attending day release* 1965
1965 *Stats of Education, Table* 14

INDUSTRY OF EMPLOYER	NUMBERS RECEIVING RELEASE AS PERCENTAGE OF NUMBERS INSURED 1965		
	M	W	Total
Shipbuilding and marine engineering	53·1	16·6	49·9
Agriculture, forestry and fishing	16·8	6·6	15·3
Mining and quarrying	42·4	8·6	39·9
Food, drink and tobacco	19·2	6·4	11·6
Engineering and electrical	69·6	9·0	44·2
Textiles	15·3	2·3	6·3
Clothing and footwear	15·8	2·3	4·3
Distributive trades	5·9	1·9	3·3

While two out of three survey areas gave more full-value awards than the national average at further education establishments, these were consistently and almost uniformly for lower level work (B and C rather than A1/A2 levels).

Table XI (13): *New awards (1965) per thousand of a single age group*

	UNIVERSITY	FULL VALUE AWARD (FE)	LESSER AWARD (FE)	COLLEGES OF EDUCATION
Lincoln	47·8	46·2	4·6	36·2
Nottingham	38·8	22·1	2·1	31·3
Northumberland	46·8	45·0	38·4	48·7
National average	52·1	36·9	15·5	38·6

Source: Tables X, XI and XIV of 1965–6 List 69 of Department of Education and Science.

Future Developments

The evidence commented on briefly in Chapter II, in the foregoing sections and in Appendix D, raises the question of how far it is possible to try to offer equality of opportunity, to maintain and improve standards and to provide for the country's manpower needs, by attempting to control the level and distribution of resources at secondary level. It would appear that further detailed research is needed on the interrelationships between curricular demand, employment and further education on the one hand, and the allocation of buildings, staff and money on the other, in a particular district or in contrasting areas. Perhaps those major foundations able to sponsor research might more profitably examine such relationships, than continue to use their resources on refining innovations beyond the means of the greater part of the education service.

It would appear that although opportunity increased for more able pupils, the continuing high proportion of pupils entering unskilled work or work with a low entitlement to training, is highly correlated with the poorer standard of resources awarded to the less able, and with the lower level of educational goals considered appropriate for them when designing, staffing and equipping schools. The undoubted other benefits (cultural and social) which post-war secondary education has made *potentially* available to the less able, does not appear fully to have been matched by vocational achievement. Nor, in the light of the increased demands of a technological age for skilled manpower at the lower levels of industry, is there sharp evidence that the secondary education system has adapted very substantially to these apparent new needs.

Notes

1　Highlighted by the low percentage of grammar places in Nottingham and Northumberland and the restricted courses for non-grammar pupils in Lincoln.

2　ROSS, Jean, *The Education and attainment of a national sample of children at Secondary School,* NUT, 1965.

3　HOUSE, J. W., THOMAS, A. D. and WILLIS, K. G. *Where Did the School Leavers Go?* Dept. of Geography, Newcastle on Tyne, 1968.

4　Op. cit. page 6.

5　Op. cit. page 6. Unskilled and semiskilled jobs could in most cases be found within a 10—15 miles radius of home whereas skilled opportunities could not.

6　Lincoln, Annual report 1950 pp.26–28. The figures are mainly for secondary modern schools since the grammar schools did not tend to use the YES much until the late 1960s.

7　Lincoln, Youth Employment Committee (15.9.53) and (30.6.54).

8　Youth Employment Committee (31.5.56).

9　Interview with former Chairman of the Education Committee (5.6.69).

10　Youth Employment Committee (17.10.57).

11　Youth Employment Committee (31.5.62).

12　Youth Employment Committee (7.3.63).

13　Youth Employment Committee (31.5.56). It did not occur to the authority to encourage girls to enter other courses.

14　Nottingham, Annual report 1952.

15　*Education in Northumberland, 1953–58 and 1959–62.*

CHAPTER XII

Conclusion

'*Be not the first by whom the new are tried; Nor yet the last
to lay the old aside.*'

> Pope (*An Essay on Criticism*)

At first sight, the complete dictum as it stands might well apply
appropriately to *Nottingham;* the first clause, however, bringing to
mind *Northumberland's* innovatory tendencies and the last, *Lincoln's*
excessively slow rate of change. Some fundamental questions relating
to the potential impact of demand and to the inequalities inherent in
the uneven distribution of local and central resources have been
examined, including the relationship of resource allocation to
curriculum development and to educational opportunity. It is evident
from the history of events traced through succeeding chapters,
however, that there was no single identifiable pattern of resource
allocation, but a number of recurrent and complex influences whose
relative importance has altered over the years.

Moreover, the patterns which have emerged and the factors which
seem critical in their degree of influence, become more and not less
relevant following local government reorganization. Two out of
three of the survey areas are now relatively markedly worse in their
financial and material 'pool' of resources following the 1974 reorganization compared with their peers elsewhere, than during the
survey period. Inequalities between areas have widened, not
narrowed.

It is important to restate that the research did *not* aim primarily
to evaluate the performance of the local education authorities whose
problems were mainly not of their own making. The local government
service in the period 1945–65 was expected to develop services with a
proportionately diminishing pool of resources in relation to
expansion of demand and the imposition of dichotomous government
directives. The research did, however, set out to establish the facts;
what actually happened to resources, whatever may have been the
implied or stated intentions of the authorities.

It is also suggested that the patterns which emerge are typical of the
plight of most authorities and that the problems and solutions are
relevant to other local education authorities. It would be unfair to
the survey areas to suggest that they were in any way less 'successful',
however that may be measured, because their needs were in many

ways among the most acute facing local authorities during the crucial years of post-war development.

The Emerging Pattern

Certain identifiable strands in the pattern of resource-allocation do emerge from the account of this research project. Firstly, the principle of sensitive matching of local needs suggested by Bleddyn Davies appears more illusory than real, mainly because of financial constraints. Authorities were obliged by both their Finance Committees and by central government to apply the principle of percentage increase on an earlier base year, a principle which may totally ignore the relevance or otherwise of the pattern of last year's spending to this year's policy. The low base year of 1946–47 in fact held back realistic provision for the new post-war needs, while the accidental inheritances from the pre-war years (all-age schools in Northumberland, low grammar percentage in Nottingham, low spending in Lincoln etc.) proved a major constraint perpetuated by annual planning on last year's base.

This element of the pattern was reinforced by the widespread application of discriminal policies based substantially on inherited assumptions few of which were re-examined against new needs or new educational goals. The combination of basic inequality of resources in the 1940s (see Chapters IV and V in particular) and of subsequent discriminal educational planning of 'rationed' building, financial and staffing resources, created a cycle of deprivation which was reinforced over the years. This cycle of deprivation was most evident for secondary modern pupils in small schools in the poorer authorities and notably in the rural areas. In the decade 1945–55, the correlation of non-selective schools, old buildings, lack of extended courses, lower capitation allowances, poorer staffing, overcrowding and lack of viability was consistently high in all three areas. This group of factors led in turn to lower attainment at 15+ or 16+ and correlated with deprivation of the basic qualifications for further and higher education. The relationship between under-provision and under-achievement was consistent and disturbing.

This resultant inequality of educational opportunity was evident at different points in time in all three areas, depending on which area the pupil lived in, whether boy or girl, academically gifted or destined for secondary modern schools, whether in small or large, urban or rural school. Chapters X and XI most strongly illustrate this when read in the light of the history of events in Chapters VI—VIII.

It might be considered that at least two of the three authorities achieved the most that both limited resources and excessive central governmental controls would allow. It is sometimes suggested that the education service must become more cost-effective, and few would dissent from this in principle. But if for example one accepts even in the simplest terms the 'rate of return' approach of Marc Blaug, Peacock and Wiseman and others then in none of the survey areas did the three authorities achieve true potential equality of opportunity for their pupils. Nor did they noticeably relate the allocation of resources to the country's increased need for school-leavers of both sexes with a higher level of skills of all kinds. Except in a few special highly-paid fields of unskilled employment, higher lifetime earnings are strongly and progressively correlated with extended education. The rate of return on additional education from 15—18 is quoted by Blaug as about 13 per cent; and on three years of higher education as a further 14 per cent.[1] This is not counting the non-pecuniary benefits such as job satisfaction, longer holidays etc. But in all three survey areas, the proportion of school-leavers going on to further and higher education was generally below the national average, as were the GCE performances of schools in some districts within the survey areas.

The research described in this book suggests a direct correlation between the low rate of investment in the non-grammar pupils under 16 (poorer school buildings; less generous accommodation and staffing; lower equipment allowances) and their lower achievement on leaving school which is not wholly accounted for by lower ability where the selection rate was as low as 12·0 per cent. There appears to be a similar correlation between lesser facilities offered to girls either in single-sex or in mixed schools, and their lower achievement both in external examinations and on leaving school. One might well turn the cost-effective approach on its head, so to speak, and suggest that if government departments and educational planners invested proportionately as much money, capital plant and staffing resources per head, in the education of (a) girls and (b) the less able, there would be a disproportionately beneficial rate-of-return in the production of more skilled womenpower and manpower, as well as an increased rate of return for more pupils.

Implicit and Explicit Demand

There is also a *prima facia* case for suggesting on the evidence from the three sample authorities, that neither implicit nor explicit demand were significantly influential—a disturbing result.

Implicit demand from *rising numbers* was certainly not met. The building programme at no time matched defined needs for rural reorganization, rising birth rate, increased fifth-formers or overspill from Newcastle. Even in 1968, after 23 years of major building, most schools were seriously overcrowded and the backlog of un-programmed schools was substantial. Implicit demand from *curricular reform* was at best unevenly met and by no means directly in relation to explicit demands from teachers and pupils for better conditions, more money or books, or extended courses. Implicit demand from the *reorganization* of secondary education was im-perfectly met from limited capital and revenue resources, partly because of discriminal inherited assumptions on differential needs, and partly because of the regular governmental controls on capital investment, standards for school building and revenue expansion. Even the specific demands of extended education for non-grammar pupils were hampered by lack of *basic* accommodation as well as of other resources. In two authorities, a basic policy of 'roofs over heads' proved difficult to put into practice, and grammar school places were not forthcoming in the first decade for the appropriate level of need in two out of three areas.

Explicit demand was on the whole only sporadically successful in controlling resources. *Industry's* relationship to the education service seemed tenuous in the extreme. The *teachers' associations* succeeded in achieving part of their demands in terms of national salary levels, notably equal pay, but had too little effect in the local situation for either curricular or development impact to be measurable. Pressure from individual heads and teachers varied in its success. *Governors* (rightly according to some opinions) were ineffective in influencing decisions and resources, but proved a reasonably popular moral support. Some national organizations like the *AEC, Publishers' Association,* and the *Burnham Committee,* had a significant effect on the level and distribution of money for curricular resources and teachers' salaries. There was no discernible influence from *pressure groups* before 1965. *Inspectors* had relatively little impact on major policy or on resources (regrettably perhaps) and the absence of team-government or any form of *quasi* Cabinet-government in each of the three authorities minimized the possible impact of corporate influence from the *professional administrative staff.* Explicit demand from *Education Committee* members, partly as a group but notably as individuals, was an important influence; but even this was subsidiary to such factors as central controls, intractable expenditure and rising numbers of pupils.

There was evidence in all three survey areas of both principles suggested as hypotheses in Chapter I, that lack of resources depresses demand and that dynamic demand releases resources. This was especially marked in relation to capital building programmes and in the allocation of resources to individual schools.

Among the most decisive factors were the philosophy and

experience of each Chief Education Officer, expressed in his own priorities for development and his administrative skills. Equally influential in some instances, was the impact of one or two outstanding individual members of the Education Committee in each area, often a single chairman.

Central and Local Government

The balance of power appears also to have shifted constantly from local to central government over the last 25 years, to the detriment of the local education authorities' capacity to respond to the local needs and demand which Bleddyn Davies highlights in his study and which is part of the *raison d'être* of local government. The inability of all three authorities fully to meet even the basic needs of the rising school population was almost certainly partly because of the inadequate capital building programme awarded, and partly the Ministry of Education's extraordinary insistence on instalment building or on building less than the known need for Vth-form places. Only in Lincoln did demand for capital allocations *not* grossly exceed the level of programme awarded (and that for the wrong reasons). Negative Ministry policy also held back the early development of external examinations in non-grammar schools; while the central government's regular exhortations to local authorities to cut back revenue expenditure,[2] deterred the county boroughs at certain periods from using revenue resources to make good the environmental deficiencies caused by an inadequate building programme.

The capacity of the central government to speak with two voices, became so highly developed as to render largely ineffective the constant pressure from authorities and teachers alike on a number of issues illustrated in this thesis. Only too frequently a dichotomous Ministry of Education issued a policy circular, White Paper or government statement setting new standards for development, only swiftly to follow this by a governmental directive severely to cut back the level of capital investment and the growth rate of revenue resources, by asking authorities to restrict their annual expenditure.

It is not perhaps necessary to recapitulate the evidence of chapter III and elsewhere that party politics were not dominant before 1965. It is important however to underline that it appeared to make no difference whatever whether a Labour or a Conservative government held Westminster, to how far central controls and grants were adapted to meet local needs. Figure 6 and Tables V (1) and (2) illustrate sharply the consistent decline in the capital programme in real terms. Although moreover the cuts imposed by Florence Horsbrugh (in the early 1950s) and Selwyn Lloyd (in the early 1960s)

had disastrous effects on educational building, it was in fact a
Labour government at the end of the survey period which recorded in
the strongly directive Circular 10/65 that

'It would not be realistic for authorities to plan (comprehensive
schemes) on the basis that their individual programmes will be
increased solely to take account of the need to adapt or remodel
existing buildings on a scale which would not have been necessary
but for reorganization. . . . The total cost of a recast programme must
not exceed that already authorized for 1965–66 and 1966–67 . . .'

Authorities recognized that 'plus ça change, plus c'est la même
chose'; or bricks without straw again.

The timing of the main educational directives of the Ministry[3]
should be studied in relation to the proportionate levels and growth
in local education authority spending illustrated in Appendix B.
Careful analysis of the relationship of pupil-numbers, rising prices
and levels of spending suggests that authorities were not in fact able
to carry out fully either national or approved local policies, without
a time lag of about five years (one generation of secondary pupils).

There would also appear to be no direct correlation between the
increase in *government grant* and the increase in *governmental
controls,* except a coincidence in timing. The developments outlined
in Chapters V and IX in particular, suggest that all three authorities
were subjected to precisely the same stringent national controls
although their receipt of government grant differed markedly (as
figures 2, 3 and 4 illustrate). The three main controls (capital
allocations, teachers' salaries and teaching staff quotas) tended to
be justified by the central government for quite other reasons than
'he who pays the piper'. The increased delegation to local authorities
referred to by the Royal Commission on Local Government and by
other eminent spokesmen proved to be illusory. While one would not
wholly disagree with Sir William Hart that

'a local government system which has to rely on no less than 55 per
cent of its net expenditure being defrayed from central taxation, is
in no strong position to adopt heroic attitudes of going it alone'[4]

this is an argument for removing the psychological and inherited
association of grant-aid with control, as much as for a reform of the
rating system, the inelasticity of which is often criticised and is further
confirmed by the data in Chapter IV.

Inequality of Financial Resources
The key factor indeed in accounting for educational inequality was

the financial question which underlay much of the complex pattern of political, educational and philosophical influences. Innately unequal financial resources, or discriminal redistribution on principles not directly related to assessed needs, seemed to override all other factors.

Local authorities determined their growth rates less by consensus than by 'direction', and different sectors of the budget increased at a faster or slower rate to the extent that the Chief Education Officer retained relative autonomy over his power to vary the detail within the total 'ceiling'. The evidence suggests that in all three local education authorities, the Education departments enjoyed reasonable autonomy over the establishment of their own priorities for development. Accordingly, in *Lincoln* the secondary budget developed at a slower rate than the total education revenue expenditure; in Nottingham at a faster rate; and in Northumberland at nearly twice the rate of all education expenditure.[5] This reflected partly the differing priorities of the Chief Education Officers and partly the different bases in 1945 on which the authorities had to build.

'Pure' growth of financial resources was, however, distorted by the increasing level of intractable expenditure. It will have become evident how far the margin for development was eroded by the increased proportion of revenue expenditure taken by teachers' salaries, loan charges, such non-educational factors as maintenance and fuel, light and cleaning, and the maintenance of basic standards for increasing numbers of children. The main differences in the actual proportion of intractable expenditure over the 20 years between the three authorities, arose because of the different rate and level of the completion of new buildings for the secondary sector, which affected later revenue expenditure.

This research project highlights the acute failure of the past and present system of financing local government either adequately to equalize between different areas or to meet differential degrees of local need. Without recapitulating chapter IV, readers are referred back to Figures 2 and 3 which show sources of income in each survey area, Figure 4 which gives the total differential government grants for the education budget and Figure 1 which gives the actual rates levied. Figure 5 then illustrates rateable value per head.

These illustrate together, more sharply than the text or the Appendices on which they are based, how far the financial system exists in almost total dissociation from needs and problems. At first sight a correlation between need and grant appears; for example in Northumberland. But by 1958 all three authorities received the same proportion of their education income from government grants (Figure 4) although their rates levied varied by over twice as much in

Lincoln as in Northumberland (Figure 1) (and although by then, their degrees of assessed need were very varied). This basis of dependance on local rate yield, based in turn on rateable value, perpetuates inequality of resources, and Figure 5 and Appendix C illustrate how Nottingham for example, in least financial need because of its high industrial hereditaments, benefited most from the revaluations.

The reform of local government in 1974 has merely exacerbated this. The report of the Royal Commission in 1966[6] planned quite deliberately, units of local government which continued to reflect the same sharp financial differentials. The Commission's report stated that 'The new authorities will be more nearly equal in resources than local authorities are now'[7] which the following extracted table does not at all support:

Table XII (1): Rateable value per head

	BEFORE REORGANIZATION	AFTER REORGANIZATION (COMMISSION'S PROPOSALS)
Highest	Herts. (£60·2)	Brighton and
	Brighton (£72·3)	W. Sussex (£65·8)
Lowest	West Riding (£28·4)	
	Halifax (£29·16)	Halifax (£28·4)

Note: *Extracted from Table 4 (a) and Annex 4 of the Royal Commission report.

The survey areas under the Royal Commission's proposals would have fared as follows, in each case a worsening of resources.

Table XII (2): Rateable per head

	BEFORE REORGANIZATION	AFTER REORGANIZATION
Lincoln	£36·9	—
Lincoln/Lincs	—	£32·4
Nottingham	£50·3	—
Nottingham/Notts	—	£39·8
Northumberland	£32·7	—
Northumberland	—	£32·1

In practice, however, the position is now even worse in Lincoln-shire and Northumberland, since the government alterations to the

Royal Commission's proposals have given even more of the urban areas of North Lincolnshire and South Northumberland to the Humberside and Tyneside authorities respectively than the Royal Commission proposed, leaving the rural areas financially even more vulnerable; a pattern matched in the Somerset/Avon area.

The report of the Commission that 'we are deeply concerned that the new local government shall be supported by an adequate financial system with sufficient revenues of its own'[8] and of the 1966 Government White Paper that 'the new structure should provide a more promising context for drastic reform of local government finance'[9] fell on deaf ears.

Future developments

It is perhaps important to stress that this research project ended at the year 1965. Since that date many schools have become larger or coeducational, or comprehensive. Since then also some local authorities have begun to examine more closely the principles of cost-analysis, corporate management and dual use of resources.

There is however little hard evidence that these new approaches have necessarily filtered down to the levels at which the inherited assumptions and daily decisions on the allocation of resources are influential. There is, indeed, little indication that a majority of councils or chief officers accept in principle the need for review and reassessment of the entire process of the allocation of resources in relation to the planned application, over a period of years, of an approved and progressive policy of coherent educational development.

It is to be hoped that the new local authorities will sponsor locally-based *research units* linked with their own education services. Probable subjects for early inquiry would include more appropriate and less haphazard methods of financing and applying *curricular innovation* to a wider range of schools without pegging basic standards. A second early need is intensive practical examination of the different relationships of *budgetary planning* over a longer period of years to the formation of new educational policy, and the concurrent maintenance of present standards.

The lack of readily available data in suitable form for the measurement of even crude indices of local authority and of school achievements, is a major problem. Most of the data on which this research is based was carefully collated during a full sabbatical year from a multiplicity of sources; and much of the financial information and the data relating to numbers of pupils in different types and at different levels of secondary education in particular, had to be converted or adjusted before it was readily usable. Further research by local authorities is needed into effective methods of record-keeping and of *monitoring* measurable standards in sectors of the education service and in schools as a guide to a more sensitive allocation of resources to match future assessed needs.

The structure of local government finance is already under review. Within any major reassessment should be included a re-examination of methods of financing the education service (which is still the major element in the local authority budget) in such a way that a wider margin for development and for local authority discretion is achieved. For if it is not and the trends which are traced in this thesis continue unchecked, real decision-making by a local education authority in relation to locally assessed needs may soon cease to be a practical possibility at all.

For above all, future decisions on major policies in secondary education and on the allocation of resources in accordance with changing needs, should take much more account of the demands of those involved in the service than has been the case in the three survey areas in the 20 years reviewed here. Consultative machinery may continue to improve. It is questionable how far explicit and implicit demand from pupils, teachers, industry, groups in society and the changing curriculum, will influence the allocation of resources without major changes in attitudes on the part of the local government service. A major step would be for the new local authorities to re-examine both the practices which they are inheriting and their real relevance to participation in government by all, and not some, who both receive and provide secondary education. This is probably, however, incompatible with the increasing tendency to construct new regional controls between local and central government. The concurrent development of a direct consciousness on the part of the local education authority of the need to assess and monitor standards of educational provision, might perhaps prevent the kind of inequality of educational opportunity from persisting until the turn of the century, which has resulted from the patterns of the first 20 years of post-war development. If the evidence of this research is a guide, it may take a further 20 years to reverse the current trends and to reinstate some sensitive local autonomy based on real desire for equality of educational opportunity.

Notes

1 BLAUG, Marc and others, *Penguin Economics of Education* Vol. I. pp.215–259 and Vol. II, pp.346–359 give a useful summary of the arguments.
2 which stemmed from the Treasury and the Ministry of Housing and Local Government through the Ministry of Education.
3 For example 1947, 1956, 1958, 1959.
4 HART, Sir William, *International Union of Local Authorities Conference* 1968. IULA London 1968.
   Accountability to central government is traditionally vested in the doctrine of ultra vires, the control of borrowing and the controls of capital investment and revenue growth.
5 See Table IV (3).
6 Royal Commission on Local Government in England, 1966–69. Vol. I. Report. Cmnd 4040, HMSO, 1969.
7 ibid, para. 516.
8 ibid, para. 527.
9 Local Government Finance in England and Wales, Cmnd 2923, HMSO, 1966.

BIBLIOGRAPHY

This contains the majority of works consulted in the preparation of this research but is not intended as a comprehensive bibliography about secondary education or the allocation of resources.

I. General

AEC (1957). *The Threat to Education.* London: Councils and Education Press.

ANDERSON, C. (1967). 'Sociological Factors in the Demand for Education', in *Social Objectives in Educational Planning.* Paris: OECD.

BANKS, O. (1955). *Parity and Prestige in English Secondary Education.* London: Routledge and Kegan Paul.

BARON, E. (1810). *The History of Lincoln.*

BLAUG, M. (Ed.) (1968). *Economics of Education, Vols.* 1 *and* 2. Harmondsworth: Penguin.

BLAUG, M. and WOODHALL, M. (1968). 'Productivity trends in British secondary education 1950–63', *Sociology of Education,* **41,** 1 (Winter).

BLAUG, M. (1967). 'Economic Aspects of Vouchers for Education', in *Education, a Framework for Choice.* Paris: IEA.

BRAND, J. A. (1964). 'Ministry control and local autonomy in education', *Political Quarterly.*

BURSCH, C. (1945). 'Providing Appropriate Housing for Schools', in National Society for the Study of Education, *Year Book XLIV,* University of Chicago.

CARNEGIE, UK TRUST (1936). *Libraries in Secondary Schools.* Edinburgh: Constable.

CLASSICAL ASSOCIATION (1967). *Classics in the School Curriculum.*

DALTON, H. (1967). *High Tide and After.* 1945–60. London: Frederick Muller.

DAVIES, B. (1968). *Social Needs and Resources in Local Services.* London: Michael Joseph.

DAVEY, K. J. (1971). 'Local Autonomy and Independent Revenues', *Public Administration,* Spring 1971, Vol. 49.

FABIAN SOCIETY (1949). *The Education Act* 1944, Research Series 90. *Next Steps in Education,* Tract no. 274, June. *Equality for Women,* by Rendel and others, research series 268.

FISHER, N. (1956). 'Fiscal Management in an English LEA', in *The Year Book of Education.* London: Evans.

FLOUD, J. and HALSEY, A. H. (1956). 'Education and Occupation: English Secondary Schools and the Supply of Labour', *The Year Book of Education.* London: Evans.

FLOUD, J. (Ed.) (1955). *Social Class and Educational Opportunity.* London: Heinemann.

GOULD, Sir R. (1956). 'Factors Affecting Teacher's Salaries in England and Wales', in *The Year Book of Education.* London: Evans.

HOUSE, J. W., THOMAS, A. D. and WILLIS, K. G. (1968). *Where Did the School Leavers Go?* Dept. of Geography, University of Newcastle.

IMTA (1956). *Local Expenditure and Exchequer Grants. The form of published accounts of local authorities.*

MACLURE, S. (1968). *Learning Beyond our Means.* London: Councils and Education Press.

National Society for the Study of Education: Year Book 1946. 'Changing Concepts in Educational Administration', University of Chicago Press.

NEWSOM, J. (1948). *The Education of Girls*. London: Faber and Faber.
NUT (1963). *The State of our Schools*.
NUT (1963). *Power in the Education Service*.
NUT (1962). *Investment for National Survival (reprint)*.
NUT (1964). *The Financing of Education*.
NUT (1960). *Willing the Means*.
OECD (1966). *Organizational Problems in Planning Educational Development*. Paris: OECD.
OECD (1966). *School Building Resources and their Effective Use*. Paris: OECD.
PEACOCK, A., GLENNESTER, H. and LAVERS, R. (1968). *Educational Finance*. Edinburgh: Oliver and Boyd.
PEDLEY, R. (1958). 'The Effect of the Size of School, UK', in *The Year Book of Education*. London: Evans.
PHILLIPS, H. M. (1964). *Economic and Social Aspects of Educational Planning*. Paris: UNESCO.
MACKENZIE, G. (1945). 'Developing and Administering the Curriculum and Pupil Services', *National Society for the Study of Education*. *Year Book 45*.
REESE EDWARDS (1960). *The Secondary Technical School*. University of London Press.
ROSS, J. (1965). *The Education and Attainment of a National Sample of Children at Secondary Level*. London: NUT.
SAYERS, R. S. (1967). *A History of Economic Change in England* 1880–1939. London: OUP.
SEEAR, N. (1964). *A Career for Women in Industry?* Edinburgh: Oliver and Boyd.
SCIENCE MASTERS ASSOCIATION *et al.* (1960). *Provision and Maintenance of Laboratories in Grammar Schools*. London: John Murray.
SHARP, Dame E. (1962). 'The future of local government', *Public Administration*, Vol. 40.
TAYLOR, W. (1963). *The Secondary Modern School*. London: Faber and Faber.
TROPP, A. (1957). *The School Teachers*. London: Heinemann.
VAIZEY, J. (1958). *The Costs of Education*. London: Allen and Unwin.
VAIZEY, J. (1962). *The Economics of Education*. London: Faber and Faber.
VAIZEY, J. (1968). *Resources for Education*. London: Allen and Unwin.
WARWICK, D. (1971). *Team Teaching*. University of London Press.
US DEPT. OF HEALTH AND WELFARE. 'An analysis of the Comparative costs and benefits of vocational versus academic education in secondary schools', Pennsylvania State University.
WEA (1932). *The Practical Effects of Education Economy*. London: WEA.
WEA (1968). *Resources and Educational Advance*. WEA.
WOODHAM, J. B. (1956). *Education Rates and the Education and Equalization Grants*. IMTA.
WORLD CONFEDERATION OF ORGANIZATIONS OF THE TEACHING PROFESSION. (1966). *The Role of Teachers' Organizations in Educational Planning*.

II. Government Publications

ROYAL COMMISSION ON TECHNICAL INSTRUCTION (The Samuelson report) (1884).
BOARD OF EDUCATION (1923). *The Differentiation of Curricula between the Sexes in Secondary Schools*.
MINISTRY OF EDUCATION (1946–48). *List 50, Costing Statistics*.
(1947). *The New Secondary Education, Pamphlet 30*.
(1947–63). Annual reports—Education in England and Wales; especially 1947, 1948, 1955, 1960, 1962, 1963.

(1954). *Standards for School Premises,* 1954. (*Also* 1959 *edition*).

(1958). *Secondary Education for All—a New Drive* CMD 604.

(1965). *The School Building Survey,* 1962.

(1961). *Better Opportunities in Technical Education,* CD 1254.

(1972). '*Education: a Framework for Expansion*'.

HMSO. *The Burnham reports on Teachers' salaries.*

(1951). *Local Government Manpower Committee.*

(1948). *Capital Investment in* 1948. Treasury CMD 7268.

(1966–67). *Manpower Training for Industry.* Ninth report of House of Commons Estimates Committee.

(1968). *The Flow into Employment of Scientists, Engineers and Technologists.* (The Swann Committee).

(1969). Royal Commission on Local Government (1966–1969).

CENTRAL ADVISORY COUNCIL FOR EDUCATION (ENGLAND) (1959). *15 to 18.*

(1963). *Half our Future.*

SCHOOLS COUNCIL (1968). Inquiry 1, Young School Leavers.

III. Other Published Sources

Education. (Journal of the Association of Education Committees).

Minutes of the AEC.

Reports of the Publishers Association.

Lincoln. *Education Development Plan.*

Scheme for Further Education.

Corporation Accounts.

Annual Reports of the Education Committee.

Nottingham. *Education Development Plans.*

Scheme for Further Education.

Corporation Accounts.

Annual Reports of the Education Committee.

Northumberland. *Education Development Plans.*

Scheme for Further Education.

County Council Accounts.

Quinquennial Reports of the Education Committee.

I. Lincoln—A Brief Profile

Lincoln is a small cathedral city whose active history dates from Roman times. It is set in a rural county divided for administrative purposes before 1974 into three counties, Lindsey, Kesteven and Holland, and the City of Lincoln. It is the county town and a market town; a centre of heavy engineering lying at the hub of a rather meagre public transport system, in a predominantly agricultural area with (until very recently) little native industry except arable farming and fishing. The city's population grew from 48,784 in 1901 to 69,412 in 1951, but increased only slowly to 77,180 in 1965. The number of houses in the city has risen from 19,003 in 1945–46 to 25,383 in 1965–66, a relatively small increase for post-war years, in comparison with many other Midland cities.

Industry

In the 19th century, the coming of better communications transformed Lincoln from a small, sleepy market town in an agriculturally depressed area (with a below average percentage of elementary school places provided by voluntary effort), to a fairly lively centre for the design and manufacture of agricultural machinery and heavy engineering, which is still its main industry. (About 70 per cent of the boy school-leavers were still entering some form of engineering at various levels as recently as 1965.) The older engineering industries date from the mid-19th century supplemented by a number of smaller industries which have settled in the city in post-war years, among them the manufacture of plastics, electronic components, industrial belting, clothing, paper, flour, animal foods, and potato crisps. It is, however, not without significance that in the last 10–15 years, light industry has increasingly looked to rural Lindsey for sites for development because the city was slow to offer appropriate practical facilities for development, and this has adversely affected both outlets for employment in the city and basic rateable resources.

The Historical Legacy

Inherited attitudes are an important factor locally. It is estimated in the city that about three-quarters of the present population, if not more, are indigenous. Local pride, to the point of near-complacency, is a powerful influence toward inaction. An independence of spirit towards what was happening elsewhere showed itself as early as the 1870s when there was strong resistance from both the city and the Church to the establishment of a School Board, despite a total inadequacy of school places. There had earlier been similar resistance to a railway with the result that the city even now is served only by a branch line. Although Lincoln became one of the first of the new County Boroughs following the 1888 legislation by virtue of its historic position, the Corporation did not acquire responsibility for education until 1902 and therefore lacked an inherited tradition of responsibility for education. There was a School of Science and Art from 1887, however, which was handed over to the Corporation in 1901 and formed the genesis of the present two Colleges (of Technology and of Art). A Lincoln School of Art was founded in 1863, and is now the thriving sub-regional Lincoln College of Art. But the city and indeed the county still have neither university nor polytechnic.

The People

The city is sociologically predominantly working class compared with cities of similar size in the south and west, and has a relatively small middle class element, few intellectual societies and none of the pressure groups which proliferate in the South East and in larger urban cities; for example AASE, a local Fabian group, or regional branches of national organizations. Its domestic architecture is undistinguished (apart from the Roman and mediaeval historic group of buildings) and the housing and 19th century street layout in particular reflect the mainly working class ethos of the inner city. Most of the inner city older housing was built to provide homes for the workers of the 19th century engineering works. The cathedral, the Diocese and the County families impinged very little on the town in the survey years, and the few middle and upper class families of substance appeared to play little part in public affairs.

Local Stability

The city shows an almost excessive stability among its citizens, its workers and its school leavers. There is a general reluctance to move from the city to the county and only very recently indeed has the development of dormitory private housing estates in villages outside the city boundary, which has characterised heavily populated cities elsewhere, reached any significant level around Lincoln. It has not therefore needed to look to the county for sites for overspill housing until the late 1960s, after the survey period. New estates had been contained within the city, built mainly at two periods—the older housing of the 1930–35 period to the north of the city (for which two single-sex secondary modern schools were then built), and the new post-war estates on the outskirts of the city. The size of the post-war

estates merited their own purpose-built primary schools, but could
not justify, of themselves, complete new secondary schools solely to
meet the need arising from new housing. Both the records, and
comments from interviews with education officers and heads, show
that many teaching staff consistently refused to move from the city
even for promotion, and that almost all schools (primary and
secondary) had a staff of whom up to 50 per cent had been at the
same school for 10 years or more. In 1965 there were few schools in
which the proportion of staff who had taught only in Lincoln schools
was below 70 per cent. School-leavers at 15+ and 16+ in Lincoln
will rarely accept employment outside the city, and the few girls who
were persuaded to travel to Bardney to a canning factory or to
Fiskerton to a knitwear factory tended to return to the city to less
skilled work in under a year. University entrants looked predominantly to Midland or Yorkshire universities for places until the
post-Robbins period.

Lincoln people even now express an intense civic pride when
speaking of Lincoln City, and some former teaching staff who
remembered pupil-teacher days of 50 or 60 years ago spoke of an
unbroken tradition of competition from the county area to teach in
the city until relatively recently. The general civic pride weakened,
however, when it came to action. For there was, in the survey period,
no Town Hall or Civic Centre; no concert hall or assembly hall;
and a sparse cultural life until recently. And a consistent and marked
reluctance to underwrite any significant capital programme before
1965. The word most commonly and spontaneously used of the city
by professional staff, teachers, councillors, and individual citizens
alike, was 'complacent'. In justification, it was suggested that very
few people seemed to have lived or worked outside the city for any
length of time and they had therefore no outside yardstick against
which to set their standards, and no direct competition to put them
on their mettle.

Lincoln has identified more readily with the urban East Midlands
than with its agricultural neighbours until recently. It has tended
to look to its nearest large city, Nottingham, both as a cultural and
shopping centre,[1] and for some special services which it cannot
provide, rather than to seek the co-operation of its rural county

---

[1] The connection goes back over 150 years. At the beginning of the 19th century
—'a coach also sets off every morning for Newark and Nottingham from Mr
Smith's at the Monson's Arms, at nine o'clock; and another leaves Nottingham
every morning and arrives about halfpast five the same day, at Lincoln'.
The History of Lincoln printed by A. Stack for E. Bacon, bookseller at Lincoln,
1810.

neighbours in joint planning (with one exception—the expansion of the girls' county grammar school on joint city and county need). It is essentially a town on a domestic scale, finding genuine comfort in tradition, intensely self-loyal and mistrustful of change to a degree which significantly exceeds the common instinctive protective reaction of the average settled community.

The foregoing, it must be stressed, relates strictly to the survey period 1945–65. Major changes in the establishment of chief officers and senior officers, election of new councillors and the impact of the Herbert Commission and of the reorganization of local government, make it likely that the 1970s will be a very different decade for this City. Some changes of attitude have already been evident in the late 1960s, and more will undoubtedly follow.

II. Nottingham—A Brief Profile

Nottingham is now a thriving regional centre of both industrial and cultural interests. Its population grew from 10,000 in 1730 to over 50,000 by 1850 when it became one of the most overcrowded towns in England, and a major centre for the lace, hosiery, and cotton trades. The town boundaries were greatly enlarged in 1877 and it became a city in 1897, by which time a third of all Britain's knitting frames were to be found in the city, together with a lace industry which had acquired a world market. The population in 1897 had risen to 187,000. The need to house the workers and the desperate scramble for industrial sites in the 19th century created a concentration of buildings in the city centre which has presented the modern city with serious, if familiar, planning problems. In particular, the foundations were laid of the tobacco, cycle, pharmaceutical and engineering industries which are still an extremely important influence on the life and development of the city.

Industry
Unlike Lincoln, the city has a very varied collection of local and national industries based in or on the outskirts of Nottingham and therefore equally varied outlets for school leavers. *Boots Pure Drug Co. Ltd.* occupies a 300-acre site to the south, developed in the 1930s when the central site became overcrowded, and which houses not only two pharmaceutical factories and a soap factory, chemical works and laboratories, but the administrative headquarters of the company, and the purpose-built Boots' College of Further Education,

(closed unfortunately by a new management in 1969). Boots is a major employer locally. Nottingham is also the headquarters of *Players Ltd.*, founded in 1823, expanded in the 1890s and in the 1930s when already 5,000 workers were employed. *Raleigh* cycle industry was founded in the city in 1887, moving to new premises in 1896 (employing 850 workers then) and now has a world market. The lace industry, though less important now than in the last century, boasts six firms of significant size of which three date from the early 19th century. Four of the dozen or so *engineering firms* have as one main production element, the manufacture of special machinery for the lace trade (two firms date from 1837) while others combine precision engineering with manufacture of machines for the textile trade. One engineering firm employing 15,000 workers is the largest national producer of iron pipes and pig iron goods. Other engineering firms make boilers, refrigerated plant, business machines and turbines. The textile trade accounts for most of the female labour and demands qualified technicians and technological workers. The hosiery, knitwear, and machine knitting trade dates from 1744 and developed in two main phases—some firms date from the 18th and early 19th century while firms like *Aristoc, Bairnswear,* and *Vedonis* were established there in the period following the first world war. Three firms specialize in nets, three in fabric making (one founded in 1784), and half a dozen in dyeing, bleaching and finishing. In 1962 *Plessey* took over a telecommunications firm founded by a Swedish firm in 1903 as a branch enterprise and has further developed electronic communications as a local and national industry. Other industries include building, printing (six firms), brewing, rose-growing, leather, and furniture making. The employment outlets are therefore varied and demanding.

The Town

Nottingham has a strong civic pride which is supported by a general willingness to spend money on the city's needs. Pre-war council housing estates are well planned and well built and tend to be named after local dignitaries. The city took its housing liabilities seriously well before post-war needs (leading to post-war housing legislation) arose, and its pattern of expenditure reflects this. Nor has the city been afraid to spend money on civic projects. The Council House, built in 1927, is solid and impressive, if a little pompous, although inconveniently designed inside despite an exterior which contributes not a little to the image of the town centre. Typically, the Council House is predominantly for members of the Council as distinct from the administration, which is variously and in-conveniently housed in nearby scattered buildings acquired as gradually as the Council has acquired its growing responsibilities as a result of post-war legislation.

Nottingham is a university town. The University College was opened in 1881 by the City Corporation, and was rehoused in 1928 by the generosity of Sir Jesse Boot. It was granted its charter in 1948. The Regional College of Technology, formerly a technical college, has now (after 1965) become the Trent Polytechnic. In the survey period, the courses at the Regional College of Technology, founded as a technical college in 1945 (administered jointly by Nottingham, Derby and Derbyshire local education authorities), at the College of Art and Design, and at the two Colleges of Further Education have tended to reflect significantly the changing needs of the city and its surrounding industries. Lace, for example, has declined to be overtaken by other textiles; electronics has joined textile engineering; and telecommunications is now an important local industry.

Nottingham is situated in the heart of a viable network of public transport systems; and is serviced by the M1 motorway and a good basic road system. It has little difficulty therefore in recruiting personnel either for the administration or industrially, with the qualification that the city's industries demand a high recruitment of female labour (part-time and full-time), not all of which can be met from local sources. (This insistence on 'female labour' appears to have had a depressive effect on the already low percentage of girls staying at school beyond the school-leaving age.)

Nottingham is the county town, and is in some respects, a focal point for the people of part of the neighbouring county of Derbyshire also, but an undercurrent of rivalry between the City and Nottinghamshire County Council could still be felt, although the two local education authorities have co-operated well on important matters (like the College of Technology). It is a cultural centre as well as an economic one; and it was the City Corporation which built the Nottingham Playhouse.

The People

The city is still predominantly one of working-class origin and the relatively low proportion of professional and non-manual workers which works in the city tends to live in the outlying county area and not in the city itself. Such wealthier or more affluent areas as have remained securely established within the city are not necessarily on the outskirts, and hence schools within less than a mile and a half of each other can have very diverse catchment areas.

The lack of a strong middle-class element within the city has however had the effect of limiting outside pressure on the city council from intellectual pressure groups. There is no local branch of the Association for the Advancement of State Education, and little involvement of the younger groups of political parties, or of local Fabians. On the other hand, industry has had a certain influence not only at employer level, but through Trade Associations, the Chamber of Commerce and one or two highly organized groups of operatives.

III. Northumberland—A Brief Profile

The County of Northumberland extends over 1,276,205 acres in the extreme North East of England, with most of its western and northern county boundary adjoining Scotland. The southern boundary runs parallel with the river Tyne as far as Blaydon and dips south of the Tyne valley to the west. The river Tweed divides Northumberland from Scotland to the north. To the west, the Cheviot Hills and the northern tip of the Pennine range divide the county from Roxburghshire (Scotland) and Cumberland. The western hills rarely fall below 1,300 ft. above sea level and much has been afforested. The Forestry Commission controls 95,000 acres of forest land and 47,000 acres of moorland. Eastwards, the hills fall away to the lowland coastal strip, mainly east of the Great North Road. The county is one of sharp contrasts. Industrial Tyneside and the mid-county collieries give way to scattered, sparsely populated rural areas of small market towns and upland villages in agricultural districts.

Transport is mostly based on two arterial road and rail systems which cut the county in north/south and east/west directions but with only a limited minor network between. The main road systems are the A1 Great North Road (Newcastle to Edinburgh up the eastern strip) and the A69 (Newcastle to Carlisle) in the south of the county. The A697 also cuts northwards through the rural centre of the county; but for the scattered population in the foothills and the north western reaches, and to the north of the main Newcastle/Carlisle route, transport is still a major problem. The rail routes follow much the same paths—a service from Newcastle to Edinburgh and to Carlisle, with reasonable local railways in the south east of the county, but none penetrating into the rural heart of Northumberland north of the southern Carlisle route. Road transport to the region from the south has been improved by the recent opening of the Durham motorway and the Tyne Tunnel—industrially an advantage.

There were two *county boroughs* in the geographical county before 1974, Newcastle-on-Tyne and Tynemouth. There was one *excepted district,* Wallsend-on-Tyne, a municipal borough incorporated in 1901 (boundaries extended in 1910), which accounts for nine of the County's 83 secondary schools and 24 of its primary schools. Two new towns have also been established within the last decade, Killingworth and Cramlington, within 10 miles of Newcastle. They aim to provide not only overspill housing for overpopulated Tyneside, but for expansion of alternative industries for south east Northumberland where coalmining, so long predominant, is declining. The new towns are being developed jointly by the County Council, the local district councils and private enterprise, and not under the aegis of the New Towns Commission.

Industry

In the region memories linger still of the unemployment of the 1920s and 1930s, and both parents and their children are heavily conditioned by past insecurity of employment. The three staple industries of the county are still *coal, agriculture* and *shipbuilding and marine engineering,* although they are all less dominant than hitherto in the regional 'pool' of employment.

The Northumberland *coalfield* was until quite recently producing up to six per cent of the national coal product with a total labour force of about 28,500. The Durham coalfield attracts workers also from the agricultural areas north of the Tyne where employment is difficult. Coal is shipped from the Northumberland ports of Amble (developed for this purpose), Blyth, and the Tyne ports. Coal is a declining industry and in Ashington, Seaton Valley (with a reduction in 10 years from 10 collieries to two), Killingworth, and Bedlington-shire (six coalmines with 6,000 men) the areas are coming to rely increasingly on other industries. Coal is still however a major employment outlet.

Agriculture is dominant in the north and west of the county, from Haltwhistle and Allendale to Wooler and Berwick. Forestry is a main industry where sheep farming is not possible in the heavy forest areas of the Cheviot Hills. The central lowlands and part of the eastern strip produce corn, barley, potatoes, and beet, and the small towns of Morpeth and Ponteland have developed market gardening. There is an experimental agricultural station at Cockle Park, Morpeth. More important is stock farming, mostly sheep and cattle. There are 750 milk producers in the Tyne and Allen valleys. Sheep farming is predominant near Wooler, Glendale and Rothbury, and in the uplands. The *Forestry Commission* produces pitprops for mining and industrial timber as part of its afforestation programme.

Some new forest villages have had to be created for the foresters and their families (for example, near Kielder) and the children either travel long distances to school or live in residential hostels near schools elsewhere in the county in term time.

Tyneside is the largest *ship-repairing* centre in the world, and the second largest shipbuilding centre in the United Kingdom. Tyneside is also a major centre for marine and allied engineering, and an oil and petroleum distribution depot. Iron ore handling plant has been developed on Tyneside, and the docks at Wallsend and Tynemouth have been enlarged to meet expanding trade in industries other than the staple ones of coal and engineering products. Wallsend, Killingworth, Ashington, Prudhoe (North Tyne) and part of the Seaton Valley have been scheduled as redevelopment areas.

Other industries include the old established fishing industry (Amble, Cullercoats, Tynemouth) and newer kinds such as electronics (Bedlingtonshire), manufacture of artificial stone and mineral waters (Newbiggin) and the trading and industrial estates established at Blyth, Berwick and Prudhoe, and at Killingworth and Cramlington new towns as they develop gradually. School-leavers in Longbenton, Killingworth and the Newcastle borders look also to the national headquarters of the Ministry of Social Security at Longbenton for clerical work.

The People

A distinction can be drawn in some respects between Tyneside 'Geordies' and the rural Northumbrians. Both are friendly and warm in their welcome of strangers and in their pride for their county. The farmers and rural workers tend to have perhaps less direct ambition for their children and a more limited horizon than many of their urban neighbours (especially of the mining areas which traditionally value education) though both share a passionate desire for security which derives directly from the depression of the 1930s. The pace is slower in the rural areas, and competition at school and college a little less keen. Despite the general drift from country to town, the less able school leavers are reluctant to leave their home town or district for work elsewhere, even 20 miles away, while the Tynesiders only slightly and more readily travel for apprenticeships or to obtain a technical trade.

Northumbrians are intensely proud of the ancient heritage of the county. They fight to preserve the relics of Hadrian's Wall; while the association of the early church with the Farne Islands (St. Aidan and St. Cuthbert) is recounted with no less readiness than the story of St. Bede's work at Jarrow, just south of the Tyne. More frequently, Geordie pride will ensure that visitors and local young people alike know of the local heroes of the last century; and will tell of George Stephenson of Wylam and Killingworth whose 'Rocket' begat the new railway engines; and of Hedly (Newburn district) who created the 'Puffing Billy'; of Sir Charles Parsons who pioneered the turbine on Tyneside, and of Armstrong, the genius of hydraulics who was a Newcastle boy. It is not without significance that the names of the industrial heroes spring to Geordie tongues more readily than, for example, that of Earl Grey whose Reform Bill and other parliamentary work made him one of the 19th century's greatest men (commemorated in Newcastle by Grey Street, dominated by his memorial statue). Northumbrians never forget that they have produced the chief source of the nation's wealth; nor that they have received less of it than other regions. The area is in a real sense 'the twentieth century with its sleeves rolled up'.

The county has only one real 'dormitory town', Whitley Bay, which is also a holiday resort. While the urban areas elsewhere in the county are either of mixed social classes or predominantly working-class, Whitley Bay has become a centre for the younger professional families and is more comparable demographically with, for example, Hertfordshire or southern towns than with its northern neighbours.

Northumberland, like much of the north, is not the cultural wilderness which some southerners envisage, and the Universities of Newcastle and Durham, for example, play an important part in the region. There are more intellectual and professional groups generally than in the East Midlands; and the Tyneside AASE and the Tyneside Fabians are both relatively strong pressure groups. Community spirit and involvement are strong in both rural Northumberland and on Tyneside, and are fostered by both County and City in a number of ways. The 'county families' and the aristocracy continue to play a serious role in both County Council affairs and in other services, though in some cases more perhaps because of an inherited mantle of responsibility than through personal conviction.

APPENDIX B

List of Tables

Table I: Total city or county population 1946–64

FINANCIAL YEAR	LINCOLN*	NOTTINGHAM†	NORTHUMBERLAND‡
1946–47	65,280	265,090	412,080
1947–48	65,770	283,160	421,847
1948–49	67,870	291,500	431,847
1949–50	68,810	296,900	436,367
1950–51	69,900	301,240	438,307
1951–52	69,412	306,008	439,908
1952–53	69,500	306,600	438,300
1953–54	70,200	310,700	440,600
1954–55	70,730	311,500	445,900
1955–56	70,640	311,500	453,000
1956–57	70,500	312,000	459,800
1957–58	71,570	312,500	463,900
1958–59	72,220	312,600	470,300
1959–60	73,390	313,000	475,000
1960–61	73,730	313,300	482,480
1961–62	77,077	313,760	480,530
1962–63	76,930	312,280	487,170
1963–64	77,440	314,360	491,200
1964–65	77,180	315,050	494,440
% increase 1946–64	18·2%	19·0%	19·9%

* figures provided by City Treasurer
† Registrar General's Estimates
‡ Registrar General's Estimates

Table II (a): Total school population—maintained schools only

SCHOOL YEAR	LINCOLN*	NOTTINGHAM†	NORTHUMBERLAND‡
1946–47	8,781	37,218	51,788
1947–48	9,350	37,721	51,596
1948–49	9,168	40,837	55,065
1949–50	9,605	41,853	56,970
1950–51	9,754	42,980	58,354
1951–52	10,224	44,309	58,701
1952–53	10,612	46,472	60,853
1953–54	10,913	48,289	63,330
1954–55	11,217	48,779	65,250
1955–56	11,564	50,576	67,869
1956–57	12,053	51,318	69,683
1957–58	12,227	51,770	71,752
1958–59	12,512	52,329	73,384
1959–60	12,678	52,108	74,689
1960–61	12,650	52,383	75,654
1961–62	12,674	51,777	76,358
1962–63	12,586	51,218	76,848
1963–64	12,772	51,434	76,980
1964–65	12,643	51,686	78,064
% increase 1946–64	44·0%	37·4%	50·8%

* Source—Annual reports of Education Committee
† Sources—Annual reports of Education Committee and Education Committee minutes
‡ Source—Education Committee minutes

Table II (b): Secondary school population—maintained schools only

SCHOOL YEAR	LINCOLN*	NOTTINGHAM†	NORTHUMBERLAND‡
1946–47	3,096	13,446	10,315
1947–48	3,175	17,159	10,750
1948–49	3,289	17,312	12,997
1949–50	3,328	17,299	13,785
1950–51	3,332	17,342	14,238
1951–52	3,387	17,537	14,237
1952–53	3,423	17,701	14,142
1953–54	3,366	18,022	15,214
1954–55	3,494	16,636	15,443
1955–56	4,054	17,560	16,185
1956–57	4,411	18,294	18,088
1957–58	4,671	19,028	19,299
1958–59	5,144	20,013	20,764
1959–60	5,316	20,711	23,374
1960–61	5,448	20,324	25,907
1961–62	5,374	21,311	27,366
1962–63	5,228	20,510	27,894
1963–64	5,350	20,685	27,993
1964–65	5,230	20,303	28,973
% increase 1946–64	70·5%	51·5%	179·0%

* Source—Annual reports of Education Committee
† Sources—Annual reports of Education Committee and Education Committee minutes
‡ Source—Education Committee minutes

Table II (c): Lincoln. Secondary school population—grammar/modern

SCHOOL YEAR	SECONDARY MODERN	SECONDARY GRAMMAR	TOTAL
1946–47	1,553	1,543	3,096
1947–48	1,698	1,477	3,175
1948–49	1,798	1,491	3,289
1949–50	1,857	1,471	3,328
1950–51	1,869	1,463	3,332
1951–52	1,894	1,493	3,387
1952–53	1,929	1,494	3,423
1953–54	1,857	1,509	3,366
1954–55	1,981	1,513	3,494
1955–56	2,492	1,562	4,054
1956–57	2,762	1,649	4,411
1957–58	2,954	1,717	4,671
1958–59	3,272	1,872	5,144
1959–60	3,258	2,058	5,316
1960–61	3,291	2,157	5,448
1961–62	3,166	2,208	5,374
1962–63	3,019	2,209	5,228
1963–64	3,109	2,241	5,350
1964–65	3,068	2,162	5,230

Table III (a): Lincoln. Annual gross income from all sources—Education service only—expressed as percentage of total education revenue expenditure

YEAR	(A) GOVERNMENT GRANTS %	(B) RATES %	(C) LOCAL MISCELLANEOUS INCOME %
1946–47	42·4	33·0	24·6
1947–48	47·5	34·9	17·6
1948–49	55·6	32·4	12·0
1949–50	55·6	32·0	12·4
1950–51	54·8	32·4	12·8
1951–52	54·9	32·2	12·9
1952–53	55·4	31·6	13·0
1953–54	55·5	32·0	12·5
1954–55	58·2	31·3	10·5
1955–56	58·6	31·4	10·0
1956–57	60·1	30·8	9·1
1957–58	59·0	31·6	9·4
1958–59	58·6	31·9	9·5
1959–60	7·9	——	13·4
1960–61	7·6	*not*	14·5
1961–62	7·2	*known*	15·2
1962–63	7·2	*thereafter*	15·1
1963–64	6·5		16·1
1964–65	7·1		16·1

Notes: Column (a) represents direct income from government grants. The fall in 1959–60 follows the replacement of government percentage grant for education by block grant for all services. It is not possible to separate rate burden from contribution to the education service from block grant after 1958.

Column (c) represents miscellaneous income from fees, parental contributions, rents for leased premises, etc.

Table III (b): Nottingham. Annual gross income from all sources—Education service only—expressed as percentages of total education revenue expenditure

YEAR	(A) GOVERNMENT GRANTS %	(B) RATES %	(C) LOCAL MISCELLANEOUS INCOME %
1946–47	50·1	41·9	8·0
1947–48	50·4	41·1	8·5
1948–49	55·5	36·8	7·7
1949–50	56·1	36·3	7·6
1950–51	55·6	36·2	8·2
1951–52	55·7	36·1	8·2
1952–53	56·0	36·0	8·0
1953–54	56·5	35·8	7·7
1954–55	57·7	35·0	7·3
1955–56	59·1	33·4	7·5
1956–57	59·6	34·2	6·2
1957–58	59·5	34·3	6·2
1958–59	59·4	34·7	5·9
1959–60	8·9	————	9·0
1960–61	10·7	*not*	8·9
1961–62	12·1	*known*	8·9
1962–63	13·6	*thereafter*	9·5
1963–64	13·3		7·1
1964–65	5·6		18·3¶

¶ sic. The next two years stabilize at about 15 per cent.

Notes: Column (a) represents direct income from government grants. The fall in 1959–60 follows the replacement of government percentage grant for education by block grant for all services. It is not possible to separate rate burden from contribution to the education service from general grant after 1958.

Column (c) represents miscellaneous income from fees, parental contributions, rents for leased premises, etc.

Table III (c): Northumberland. Annual gross income from all sources—Education service only—expressed as percentages of total education revenue expenditure

YEAR	(A) GOVERNMENT GRANTS %	(B) RATES %	(C) LOCAL MISCELLANEOUS INCOME %
1946–47	56·4	35·3	8·3
1947–48	57·9	35·0	7·1
1948–49	69·7	22·5	7·8
1949–50	62·9	30·5	6·6
1950–51	62·2	30·5	7·3
1951–52	60·5	31·6	7·9
1952–53	60·5	31·2	8·3
1953–54	59·8	31·8	8·4
1954–55	61·0	31·3	7·7
1955–56	60·3	32·1	7·6
1956–57	61·1	31·3	7·6
1957–58	60·0	32·6	7·4
1958–59	59·7	32·8	7·5
1959–60	8·4	———	7·8
1960–61	8·5	*not*	8·0
1961–62	8·0	*known*	7·0
1962–63	7·7	*thereafter*	6·7
1963–64	7·3		6·2
1964–65	8·0		5·7

Notes: Column (a) represents direct income from government grants. The fall in 1959–60 follows the replacement of government percentage grant for education by block grant for all services. It is not possible to separate rate burden from contribution to the education service from block grant after 1958.

Column (c) represents miscellaneous income from fees, parental contributions, rents for leased premises, etc.

Table IV (a): Lincoln. Education revenue and capital expenditure 1945–65

Year	Total Gross Revenue Expenditure (Education) £	Education Capital Expenditure £	Total £
1946–47	337,491	3,427	340,918
1947–48	385,473	15,567	401,040
1948–49	415,236	28,672	443,908
1949–50	428,358	38,391	466,749
1950–51	443,068	63,412	506,480
1951–52	518,088	92,613	610,701
1952–53	547,101	45,700	592,810
1953–54	570,196	38,964	609,160
1954–55	628,874	70,653	699,527
1955–56	677,937	84,271	762,208
1956–57	792,456	194,785	987,241
1957–58	879,596	136,959	1,016,555
1958–59	945,837	104,437	1,050,274
1959–60	1,032,830	204,415	1,237,245
1960–61	1,115,876	150,201	1,266,077
1961–62	1,278,122	122,100	1,400,222
1962–63	1,468,046	100,015	1,568,061
1963–64	1,606,506	89,843	1,696,349
1964–65	1,779,177	161,763	1,940,940

Source: audited accounts of the Corporation

Table IV (b): Nottingham. Educational revenue and capital expenditure 1945–65

YEAR	TOTAL GROSS REVENUE EXPENDITURE (EDUCATION) £	EDUCATION CAPITAL EXPENDITURE £	TOTAL £
1946–47	1,241,574	27,323	1,268,897
1947–48	1,419,901	64,674	1,484,575
1948–49	1,599,242	242,313	1,841,555
1949–50	1,738,196	453,985	2,192,181
1950–51	1,859,196	438,526	2,297,722
1951–52	2,199,996	534,823	2,734,819
1952–53	2,430,963	934,292	3,365,255
1953–54	2,650,859	774,852	3,425,711
1954–55	2,961,718	881,710	3,843,428
1955–56	3,226,246	884,936	4,111,182
1956–57	3,735,879	925,696	4,661,565
1957–58	4,188,533	1,119,972	5,308,505
1958–59	4,632,664	1,196,628	5,829,292
1959–60	5,386,850	922,077	6,308,927
1960–61	5,772,701	911,771	6,684,472
1961–62	6,196,001	522,028	6,718,029
1962–63	6,873,724	488 199	7 361 923
1963–64	7 349 302	538 869	7 888 171
1964–65	7 933 534	776 308	8 709 842

Source: audited accounts and published Abstracts of the City.

Table IV (c): Northumberland. Education revenue and capital expenditure 1945–65

YEAR	TOTAL GROSS REVENUE EXPENDITURE (EDUCATION) £	EDUCATION CAPITAL EXPENDITURE £	TOTAL £
1946–47	1,729,287	30,493	1,759,780
1947–48	1,896,158	153,687	2,049,845
1948–49	1,896,712	201,698	2,098,410
1949–50	2,328,045	204,022	2,532,067
1950–51	2,426,092	395,902	2,821,994
1951–52	2,949,092	597,445	3,546,537
1952–53	3,196,615	494,187	3,690,802
1953–54	3,431,223	481,430	3,912,653
1954–55	3,931,945	495,754	4,427,699
1955–56	4,376,962	556,699	4,933,661
1956–57	5,225,828	843,147	6,068,975
1957–58	5,904,825	887,673	6,792,498
1958–59	6,513,576	1,149,459	7,663,035
1959–60	7,479,043	1,331,205	8,810,248
1960–61	8,127,429	902,315	9,029,744
1961–62	9,062,529	1,893,254	10,955,783
1962–63	10,458,616	2,204,476	12,663,092
1963–64	11,450,190	1,959,109	13,409,299
1964–65	12,832,092	2,601,783	15,433,875

Source: audited accounts and published Abstracts of the County.

Table V: Comparative growth of gross education revenue expenditure per head of (total) population 1947–65

| YEAR | EXPENDITURE PER HEAD | | |
	Lincoln £	Nottingham £	Northumberland £
1947–48	5·9	5·0	4·5
1948–49	6·1	5·5	4·4
1949–50	6·2	5·9	5·3
1950–51	6·3	6·2	5·5
1951–52	7·5	7·2	6·7
1952–53	7·9	7·9	7·3
1953–54	8·1	8·5	7·8
1954–55	8·9	9·5	8·8
1955–56	9·6	10·4	9·7
1956–57	11·2	12·0	11·4
1957–58	12·3	13·4	12·8
1958–59	13·1	14·8	13·8
1959–60	14·1	17·2	15·7
1960–61	15·1	18·4	16·9
1961–62	16·6	19·7	18·8
1962–63	19·1	21·9	21·5
1963–64	20·8	23·3	23·3
1964–65	23·1	25·2	26·0

Note: The figures represent the total annual gross education revenue expenditure divided by the total city or county population for each year.

Table VI (a): Lincoln. Breakdown of annual gross revenue expenditure on secondary schools 1949–63 (Percentages)

YEAR	TEACHERS' SALARIES		MAINTENANCE		FURNITURE AND EQUIPMENT (INCLUDING LIBRARY)		BOOKS		STATIONERY AND APPARATUS	
	Grammar %	Modern %	Grammar %	Modern %	Grammar %	Modern %	Grammar %	Modern %	Grammar %	Modern %
1949–50	67·88	71·15	6·13	4·12	2·19	2·2	1·88	2·37	4·89	4·95
1950–51	67·87	69·95	7·77	3·02	2·3	2·47	2·08	2·6	3·52	5·24
1951–52	70·36	71·98	5·93	3·58	2·09	1·99	1·72	2·28	4·1	4·55
1952–53	72·79	73·52	4·04	1·72	1·61	1·72	1·62	1·94	3·38	4·48
1953–54	70·05	70·44	5·14	2·91	3·18	2·21	1·77	1·73	3·34	4·44
1954–55	70·85	71·89	5·29	2·36	2·87	2·26	1·86	1·18	3·05	4·31
1955–56	72·23	70·66	4·65	3·02	2·12	2·25	1·7	2·14	2·92	4·29
1956–57	72·71	67·3	4·46	3·35	1·49	1·61	1·74	2·41	2·63	4·23
1957–58	71·70	69·02	4·88	3·08	1·89	1·5	1·82	1·92	2·37	3·97
1958–59	70·45	67·97	5·2	3·97	1·83	1·37	1·26	1·8	2·61	4·1
1959–60	71·61	69·28	4·41	3·48	2·11	2·04	2·14	1·79	2·86	3·31
1960–61	72·49	69·37	4·11	4·12	1·77	1·69	2·04	1·55	2·62	2·99
1961–62	71·48	69·66	5·13	4·03	2·21	1·47	1·8	1·52	2·35	2·96
1962–63	72·44	70·01	4·89	3·51	1·72	1·83	1·35	1·3	2·56	2·57

Notes (1) The figures represent the proportion of the total annual direct expenditure on *respectively* grammar and modern schools, allocated to each subhead;

e.g., in 1949–50, of the total *grammar* expenditure, 67·88 per cent went on teachers' salaries, 6·13 per cent on maintenance, 2·19 per cent on furniture and equipment, etc., while teachers' salaries accounted for 71·15 per cent of the total *modern* expenditure.

(2) The base figures of which these are a breakdown are extracted from audited accounts of the Corporation. They *exclude* transport, loan charges, aid to pupils and inter-authority payments.

Table VI (b): Nottingham. Breakdown of annual gross revenue expenditure on secondary schools 1946–65 (Percentages)

YEAR	TEACHERS' SALARIES %	FURNITURE AND EQUIPMENT %	BOOKS (INCLUDING LIBRARY) %	STATIONERY AND APPARATUS %	MAINTENANCE %
1946–47	77·87	3·88	1·1	1·24	2·81
1947–48	74·16	5·33	1·42	1·47	3·09
1948–49	69·96	5·8	1·67	1·68	5·19
1949–50	66·10	3·87	2·01	4·04	7·42
1950–51	67·32	3·34	1·93	4·13	5·68
1951–52	69·58	3·28	1·8	4·42	4·31
1952–53	69·39	2·86	2·02	4·33	3·98
1953–54	68·65	2·52	2·11	3·77	4·97
1954–55	68·26	2·5	1·94	3·41	5·22
1955–56	66·95	2·36	2·25	3·45	4·47
1956–57	65·14	2·06	1·2	3·16	4·12
1957–58	67·70	1·86	1·95	2·87	3·59
1958–59	66·34	1·75	2·32	2·76	4·42
1959–60	50·29	1·48	1·55	1·9	11·93
1960–61	50·82	1·27	1·71	1·83	11·65
1961–62	51·72	1·2	1·82	1·89	10·84
1962–63	53·0	1·14	1·66	1·72	10·44
1963–64	55·42	1·23	1·76	1·69	7·76
1964–65	56·97	2·18	1·61	1·57	10·53

Notes: (1) The base figures of which these are a breakdown are extracted from audited accounts of the corporation.

(2) Caution must be used in applying the figures. From 1945–46 to 1958–59 inclusive, the total figure for secondary schools of which the sub-heads are a breakdown, *excludes* loan charges, transport, administrative costs, capital from revenue and inter-authority payments. From 1959–60 onwards, all these are *included* in the total.

Table VI (c): Northumberland. Breakdown of annual total gross revenue expenditure on secondary schools, camp schools and hostels 1946–65 (Percentages)

YEAR	TEACHERS' SALARIES %	FURNITURE, APPARATUS AND EQUIPMENT %	BOOKS, STATIONERY AND MATERIALS %	MAINTENANCE %
1946–47	74·37	1·63	3·73	3·66
1947–48	72·56	1·99	4·63	2·99
1948–49	70·08	2·27	4·97	4·62
1949–50	67·52	3·84	5·13	5·73
1950–51	67·67	2·4	4·94	5·76
1951–52	68·27	2·05	4·4	5·89
1952–53	67·78	2·16	5·09	5·73
1953–54	66·5	1·94	4·88	7·0
1954–55	67·03	2·08	5·13	6·2
1955–56	63·46	2·69	4·59	8·03
1956–57	59·8	2·65	4·39	4·43
1957–58	61·13	2·4	4·49	3·98
1958–59	46·86	2·64	3·97	4·66
1959–60	46·60	2·65	4·35	4·38
1960–61	46·5	2·51	3·84	3·59
1961–62	45·6	2·17	3·47	3·74
1962–63	45·79	2·23	3·65	4·24
1963–64	45·34	2·03	3·31	3·12
1964–65	42·36	2·39	3·25	3·84

Notes: (1) The base figures of which these are a breakdown are extracted from the County audited accounts.

(2) Caution must be used in applying the figures. The total from which the breakdown is taken *excludes* loan charges, transport, capital from revenue, administrative costs, fees at direct grant schools, aid to pupils, and inter-authority payments from 1946–47 to 1957–58 inclusive. From 1958–59 onwards these are included in the total secondary expenditure.

(3) The total secondary expenditure includes all residential centres provided for secondary use, including Ford Castle and the field studies and outdoor pursuits centres.

Table VII (a): Lincoln. Gross revenue and expenditure (secondary schools only) on furniture, equipment, books, stationery and apparatus

YEAR	(A) TOTAL DIRECT SECONDARY EXPENDITURE* £	(B) FURNITURE AND EQUIPMENT £	(C) BOOKS, STATIONERY AND APPARATUS £	(D) TOTALS (B) + (C) £	(E) % (D) OF (A) %
1949–50	128,235	2,815	8,311	11,126	8·68
1950–51	131,133	3,119	8,704	11,823	9·02
1951–52	153,631	3,143	9,650	12,793	8·33
1952–53	156,341	2,597	8,851	11,448	7·32
1953–54	162,759	4,457	9,114	13,571	8·34
1954–55	172,750	4,485	8,939	13,424	7·77
1955–56	197,797	4,315	10,851	15,166	7·67
1956–57	240,731	3,737	13,299	17,036	7·08
1957–58	282,582	4,757	14,372	19,129	6·77
1958–59	313,008	4,941	16,288	21,229	6·78
1959–60	349,035	7,240	17,636	24,876	7·13
1960–61	368,463	6,366	16,950	23,316	6·33
1961–62	403,321	7,375	17,413	24,788	6·15
1952–63	448,648	7,968	17,463	25,431	5·67

* Column (a) represents direct gross revenue expenditure on secondary schools alone and *excludes* transport, loan charges, aid to pupils, administration and inter-authority payments.

Note: Directly comparable figures are not available for the years 1945–46 to 1948–49, or after 1963.

Table VII (b): Nottingham. Gross revenue and expenditure (secondary schools only) on furniture, equipment, books, stationery and apparatus

YEAR	(A) TOTAL DIRECT SECONDARY EXPENDITURE* £	(B) FURNITURE AND EQUIPMENT £	(C) BOOKS, STATIONERY, ETC. £	(D) TOTAL (B) + (C) £	(E) % (D) OF (A)
1946–47	357,337	13,874	8,384	22,258	6·23
1947–48	393,639	20,965	11,400	32,365	8·22
1948–49	468,542	27,212	15,731	42,943	9·17
1949–50	524,638	20,297	31,764	52,061	9·92
1950–51	532,056	17,773	32,260	50,033	9·40
1951–52	631,711	20,722	39,326	60,048	9·51
1952–53	681,497	19,499	43,313	62,812	9·22
1953–54	720,007	18,132	42,329	60,461	8·40
1954–55	796,509	19,978	42,667	62,645	7·86
1955–56	854,861	20,190	48,671	68,861	8·05
1956–57	1,021,054	21,040	54,723	75,763	7·42
1957–58	1,170,961	21,747	56,487	78,234	6·68
1958–59	1,320,245	23,059	67,093	90,152	6·83
1959–60	1,924,574	28,499	66,373	94,872	4·93
1960–61	2,051,820	26,117	72,555	98,673	4·81
1961–62	2,159,137	26,003	80,195	106,198	4·92
1962–63	2,355,570	26,922	79,531	106,453	4·52
1963–64	2,424,866	29,989	83,602	113,591	4·68
1964–65	2,590,007	56,354	82,527	138,881	5·36

Notes: * Up to 1958–59 inclusive, column (a) *excludes* loan charges, administration, transport, capital from revenue and adjustments with other LEAs.

From 1959–60, it includes all these.

Source—Audited accounts of the City.

Table VII (c): Northumberland. Gross revenue and expenditure (secondary schools only) on furniture, equipment, books, stationery and apparatus

YEAR	(A) TOTAL DIRECT SECONDARY EXPENDITURE* £	(B) FURNITURE, APPARATUS AND EQUIPMENT £	(C) BOOKS, STATIONERY AND MATERIALS £	(D) TOTAL (B) + (C) £	(E) % (D) OF (A)
1946–47	363,879	5,927	13,575	19,502	5·36
1947–48	395,468	7,856	18,300	26,156	6·61
1948–49	478,865	10,882	23,970	34,673	7·24
1949–50	533,825	20,487	27,347	47,834	8·97
1950–51	545,289	13,099	26,913	40,012	7·34
1951–52	661,719	13,543	29,149	42,692	6·45
1952–53	728,742	15,755	37,138	52,893	7·26
1953–54	783,472	15,232	38,200	53,432	6·82
1954–55	874,932	18,178	44,873	63,051	7·21
1955–56	1,011,604	27,192	46,406	73,598	7·28
1956–57	1,271,200	33,718	55,865	89,583	7·05
1957–58	1,441,643	34,480	64,672	99,152	6·88
1958–59	2,054,239	54,276	81,649	135,925	6·62
1959–60	2,451,291	64,846	106,712	171,558	7·00
1960–61	2,784,148	70,005	107,046	177,051	6·36
1961–62	3,127,188	67,712	108,637	176,349	5·64
1962–63	3,702,306	82,562	135,151	217,713	5·88
1963–64	4,097,166	83,262	135,531	218,793	5·34
1964–65	4,575,698	109,610	148,713	258,323	5·65

Notes: * Up to 1957–58 column (a) *excludes* loan charges, transport, aid to pupils, capital from revenue, adjustments with other LEAs, medical inspection and administration.

From 1958–59 it *includes* loan charges, transport, adjustments with other LEAs and aids to pupils but not medical inspection, meals or administration.

Source—Audited accounts of the County.

Table VIII: Lincoln. Annual gross revenue expenditure per pupil—maintained secondary schools

YEAR	DIRECT EXPENDITURE	
	Grammar £	*Modern* £
1949–50	46·57	32·7
1950–51	47·85	32·71
1951–52	56·94	37·62
1952–53	56·2	38·24
1953–54	59·29	38·45
1954–55	62·66	42·1
1955–56	67·92	47·97
1956–57	75·92	49·01
1957–58	81·06	53·91
1958–59	83·44	57·46
1959–60	79·53	56·89
1960–61	82·15	58·12
1961–62	88·71	65·52
1962–63	99·94	75·48

The figures have been produced by dividing the total gross annual revenue expenditure on Lincoln grammar and modern schools respectively by the total numbers on roll at the two types of school in each year. They *exclude* expenditure on transport, loan charges, aid to pupils, administrative costs and inter-authority payments.

Source—Audited accounts of the City Corporation.

Table IX: Lincoln. Gross annual revenue expenditure per pupil—maintenance of maintained secondary schools

YEAR	MAINTENANCE OF BUILDINGS AND GROUNDS	
	Grammar £	*Modern* £
1949–50	2·85	1·35
1950–51	3·72	0·99
1951–52	3·38	1·35
1952–53	2·27	0·66
1953–54	3·05	1·12
1954–55	3·32	0·99
1955–56	3·16	1·45
1956–57	3·39	1·64
1957–58	3·96	1·66
1958–59	4·34	2·28
1959–60	3·51	1·98
1960–61	3·37	2·39
1961–62	4·55	2·64
1962–63	4·88	2·65

The figures have been produced by dividing the total maintenance revenue expenditure for each type of school by the number of pupils on roll at grammar and modern schools respectively. They do *not* include *major* capital projects which are shown elsewhere.

Source—Audited accounts of the Corporation.

Table X: Lincoln. Teachers' Salaries—annual expenditure and percentage increase on previous year

YEAR	GROSS REVENUE EXPENDITURE (SECONDARY)			
	Grammar £	% increase on previous year	Modern £	% increase on previous year
1949–50	47,136	—	41,835	—
1950–51	47,770	1·3	42,491	1·6
1951–52	58,621	22·7	50,618	19·1
1952–53	61,078	4·2	53,251	5·2
1953–54	62,054	1·6	52,247	—1·8
1954–55	66,991	8·0	56,215	7·6
1955–56	74,229	10·8	67,147	19·4
1956–57	86,227	16·2	82,195	22·4
1957–58	95,840	11·1	102,774	25·0
1958–59	100,943	5·3	115,362	12·2
1959–60	117,202	16·1	128,427	11·3
1960–61	128,448	9·6	138,683	3·3
1961–62	140,007	9·0	144,508	9·0
1962–63	159,921	14·2	159,534	10·2

Notes: (i) Source for expenditure—annual audited accounts of the Corporation.
(ii) Twenty-five per cent of secondary pupils were admitted to grammar schools and 75 per cent to secondary modern schools.

The Finance of Local Government— A Brief Outline

The finance of local government should be seen in the light of three main factors, the state of the national economy at the time, the richness or poverty of the local authority's area in terms of local rate yield, and the needs of the area (the last two being not necessarily integrally related the one to the other; indeed the relationship can be in inverse ratio since poor areas probably have a high degree of social need).

Local government expenditure has traditionally been financed from three main sources, that is government grants, local rates on property and income raised locally other than by rates (for example rents for council housing, revenue from trading undertakings or fees for evening classes). The method of government grant acts as a direct subsidy without which basic services could not be provided locally. Specific grants can also encourage a particular policy (for example the provision of school meals at the turn of the century; and 30 years later, the continuation of the school building programme to help to create new employment at a time of serious unemployment, with the aid of special building grants). Central government departments can, however, have a negative influence, and at fairly regular intervals the central government has considered it necessary to direct local authorities to cut their level of capital or revenue expenditure (or both) at a time of national economic difficulty.

The Historical Inheritance

Before 1929, the majority of local authority services operated on a percentage grant basis, because the 'assigned revenues' which were given to local authorities after 1888 to help to pay for expanding services proved insufficient to meet the necessary expenditure on the new and growing services which the 20th century brought in its wake. Parliament had also granted relief to the owners of agricultural land with a consequent reduction to local authorities of rate income as a whole. It therefore became necessary to compensate local authorities according to their needs, and a formula was introduced by the Local Governments Act, 1929, which largely abolished the practice of 'assigned revenues',[1] did away with many percentage grants and introduced the first of 'block grants' which were a general subsidy to local authority as a whole and not related to any particular service.

Shortly afterwards however the state of the national economy led the Board of Education to direct local authorities to a series of cuts in expenditure almost as serious as those of the Geddes' axe in the early 1920s. Following the May 1931 Committee on National Expenditure which recommended a 20 per cent cut in teachers' salaries, the Board of Education promptly limited the special percentage building grants which had been instituted two years earlier to help post-Hadow reorganization, to expenditure only for which local authorities were contractually committed before September 1931. The deficiency grant was withdrawn, teachers' salaries were cut by 10 per cent from 1st October 1931 and the grant to local education authorities for wages of administrators and other non-teaching staff were cut. The central education estimates were cut by 10·8 per cent in 1932–33. The result of this was effectively to halt Hadow reorganization in some areas (including Northumberland) and one survey of 102 authorities revealed that 19 authorities suspended reorganization, 47 were seriously held up and 29 were checked.[2]

Post-war Developments

Central government continued to resort to major financial control of local authority expenditure even when the system of grants and revenue had changed beyond recognition after the war. In 1948, a new Local Government Act abolished the 1929 block grant and introduced a new formula for the calculation of education main grant, under which the local education authority received 60 per cent of its *net* expenditure on education plus £6 per pupil, less the product of a rate of 2s. 6d. in the pound. Net expenditure on school meals and milk continued to rank for 100 per cent grant. The two grants together amounted to about 40 per cent of *gross* education expenditure. A rising school population and steadily rising rates accompanied ever increasing revenue expenditure, and two components of the main grant grew more quickly than the general growth rate of education expenditure, with the result that main grant became an increasing proportion of total education expenditure.

The 1948 Act also introduced *Exchequer Equalization Grant* payable only to those local authorities with rateable values per head of population below the national average and based directly on previous actual expenditure of local authorities. Areas with special problems were to receive compensatingly extra grant, if, for example, they had a higher than average ratio of pupils to total population, or an unavoidably higher basic cost per pupil, as for example in the rural 'sparsity' counties whose transport bill was excessively high. Nine counties were given a 'sparsity' weighting, that is an extra element was allowed because of low density of population over an unduly large geographical area, with resultant risk of higher costs per head or lower standards of service, (a risk suggested by, among others, the 1947 Boundary Commission). The EEG was based on a 'weighted' population rather than the actual numerical population, that is an extra allowance was made for the number of pupils under 15, the number of people over 65, and so on. Thus it was partly a 'needs' grant as well as attempting to even out local authority resources. By 1952–53, 54 county councils and 55 county boroughs were receiving EEG. Costs per head were correlated quite highly with an increasing or declining population—the post-war housing pattern of building new housing estates (both local authority estates and private developments) where land could be found, tended to move substantial numbers from towns to outlying county districts. From 1931–1951, population in county boroughs tended to decline, while in counties it often increased. Overall the populations in county boroughs remained fairly static but 33 declined significantly while those of counties tended to increase by an average of 21 per cent. Only nine counties decreased in population.[3] The correlation between declining population and higher costs per head was well established (since there is an irreducible minimum of overhead costs in administration and supportive services below which one cannot fall without failing to maintain full services). Some increases in population were startling, Hertfordshire increasing by 52 per cent from 1931–1951, and Surrey by 42 per cent, while London (the LCC area) declined by 24 per cent, as its population moved out to the Home Counties.[4]

In addition to EEG a further grant, payable under Section 100 of the 1948 Act, compensated local authorities for loss of rates on electricity or transport undertakings. The Section 100 grant was paid in proportion to rateable value, and in county areas was divided between county councils (two-thirds) and rating authorities (one third). In county areas a proportion of EEG was made over to the second tier authorities who were the rating authorities on whom the counties precepted.

Rateable Value and Rates

Two important determinants of local authority income were therefore, first, the total rateable value of the area, (and therefore the rateable value per head); and second, the rate in the pound which the local authority either decided the electorate would accept or it chose to impose. Part III of the 1948 Act took valuation out of the hands of the local authorities and transferred it to national bodies. In 1956 the first post-war revaluation re-rated domestic properties at *pre-war* (1939) values, but set a new value on offices and shops, thus placing such a burden on them that the government had to allow them a 20 per cent rebate from 1st April 1957. Industrial and transport properties paid only one quarter of full rates. The fall in the yield of the penny rate was then such that from 1st April 1959 the government ruled that industrial and transport hereditaments paid one half rates instead of one quarter. The more uniform valuation overall however did improve the rateable value criterion on which EEG was based, especially as non-domestic properties were assessed at current values. There was, however, no guarantee that EEG was actually awarded in rough proportion to local wealth—some of the changes after the 1956 revaluation were quite violent, some county boroughs gaining up to a 5s. 6d. rate and others losing up to a 4s. 6d. rate, while some county councils lost the equivalent of a 7s. 6d. rate and others gained up to a 7s. 0d. rate.

It will be seen that the proportion of domestic to industrial property in a local authority's area would affect seriously its revenue from rate yield. This factor, a matter in some respects of historical or geographical accident, became more acute after the more radical revaluation of 1963 when transport and industrial hereditaments became liable to meet rates in full and domestic properties were reassessed at post-war values. The average penny rate trebled but of course the rate in the pound accordingly fell.

The position in the survey areas is illustrated by the following table:

(a) Increases or decreases as a result of the 1956–57 revaluation

	RV PER HEAD £	% INCREASE AFTER REVALUATION %	RATES IN £ s. d.	% DECREASE AFTER REVALUATION %
Lincoln	7·80⎱ 11·67⎰	+40·9	26. 0.⎱ 19. 0.⎰	—26·7
Nottingham	8·09⎱ 14·21⎰	+75·7	23. 0.⎱ 16. 0.⎰	—30·4
Northumberland	6·05⎱ 9·85⎰	+62·8	16. 3½.⎱ 11. 5½.⎰	—28·4

(The figures represent the year before and the year of revaluation)

(b) Increases or decreases as a result of the 1963–64 revaluation

Lincoln	13·02⎱ 33·13⎰	+158	22. 6.⎱ 10. 2.⎰	—55·0
Nottingham	15·68⎱ 46·12⎰	+193	23. 0.⎱ 7.11.⎰	—65·2
Northumberland	11·40⎱ 29·15⎰	+155	16.10.⎱ 7. 6.⎰	—56

As Appendix A shows, *Lincoln* had relatively little by way of large industry and no substantial commercial undertakings. The city has been, and still is, largely a residential market town with a few large engineering firms. *Nottingham* by contrast has a significant number of large industries and several large commercial undertakings. After the 1963 revaluation although Nottingham's rates in the pound had been marginally higher than Lincoln's from 1960 to 1963 (after years of a consistently lower rate) the revaluation in fact brought Nottingham's annual rate level well below Lincoln's. Nottingham benefited more substantially from the full rating of industrial premises. The basic resources of the two cities were very different. Northumberland's area was extremely uneven, with industrial revenue from those parts of Tyneside in the administrative county but relatively little either industrial or commercial property in the large rural areas and small market towns, and only one 'residential town', Whitley Bay.

The survey undertaken by the Institute of Municipal Treasurers and Accountants in 1956[5] concluded that the award of EEG resulted in genuine equalization—'suffice it to say here that no individual authority can now be handicapped in the development of local services by the shortage of rateable resources',[6] but this overlooks the fundamental fact that EEG only brought the below-average authorities up to a *minimum* level consistent with providing an efficient service. It did not give the margin for development and expansion which the above-average authority could command from its richer rate-yield.

Central and Local Grants

The research for the IMTA report was undertaken in the mid-1950s, and the other main conclusion of the survey was that percentage grants (which again tended to benefit those authorities able or willing to be high spenders) were both more equitable and more efficient than the proposed block grant which was being already mooted in the mid-1950s to replace percentage grants. One major (if specious) argument in favour of block grants, leaving local authorities discretion to distribute them between the different social and supportive services, was the much debated need for greater local authority autonomy. But this pre-supposed an integral relationship between government grant and government controls the precise correlation of which has not yet been proved. In brief, the arguments for percentage grants have been that they are simple, easily intelligible, they stimulate development of local authority services and they take automatic account of rising costs. It is easier to persuade a committee to underwrite a £100,000 project if it can be said at the outset that £60,000 will be met by central government. The fact that the £60,000 still comes from taxation is rarely considered at the time of decision, as that taxation is less directly connected with the local electorate. The main argument against is that—in theory—they involve too much detailed control from central government.

Vaizey and Sheehan[7] show a rise in central government grants thus:

Year	Central government %	Rates %	Fees and endowments %
1920	50	42	8
1938	46	48	6
1955	58	36	6
1965	60*	36*	4*

* estimates.

Norman Fisher gives 49 per cent as borne by local rates in 1938 and 40 per cent in 1953.[8] K. J. Davey quotes both France and Japan in his argument that there is no universal correlation between central control and dependence on grants. French local government is traditionally highly regulated, and 'local' only in a decentralized sense. (Autonomy is a quality not commended by French government.) Yet in 1948 the communes derived only 12 per cent of current revenue, from the state, and the départements only 34 per cent.[9]

The IMTA erroneously concluded that the percentage grant had come to stay,[10] but in 1958 there was in fact a further radical change when a general government 'block grant' replaced former specific grants for education, children's care, health, fire and other services. This general grant was assessed on a national basis and became influenced in due course by the changes in the level of expenditure by local authorities on services previously subsidised specifically. Thus the percentage grant to the *local education authority* was replaced by the inclusion of an element in the general grant to the *local authority*, of an amount which, although it was related to such factors as previous spending on the education service and to numbers of school-children was not specifically or proportionately linked. The local authority could use as much or as little of the block grant as it chose, to subsidize its education services. Since other factors (for example the number of people over 65) were also taken into account, education was pitched directly into a local battle of priorities in social services, from which its percentage grant had tended to shield it hitherto.

The EEG was in turn replaced by Rate Deficiency Grant to any local authority whose product of a penny rate was less than average for the size of area, the 'average' rate yield being calculated in the same proportion to the product of a penny rate for the country as a whole, as the population of the town or county bore to the total population of England and Wales. The aim of the RDG was also therefore to bring the local rate product to the national average, but by a different method from EEG.

While the percentage grant related directly to actual net expenditure, general grant was prescribed by the Minister of Housing and Local Government for two or three years in advance, and therefore did not take immediate account of inflation or the rising cost of intractable expenditure (on for example, salaries of teachers or manual workers whose pay awards were fixed nationally and not locally). Retrospective adjustment was made only with reluctance and depended largely on the skill or special expertise of the local Treasurer. The supposed greater freedom from central control proved largely illusory because central control of capital investment remained and indeed increased, and because control through regulations of central government departments was directly linked to policy decisions and not to financial considerations. The total sum to be made available for general grant was to be settled by the Chancellor of the Exchequer and the Minister of Housing and Local Government, bore no direct relationship to local authority expenditure, and ignored different levels of cost between local authorities.[11] General grant was divided into 'basic grant', based on population and on school population, and 'supplementary grant' based on such factors as density of population, road mileage, number of old people etc.

In theory, if a local authority failed to achieve or maintain 'reasonable standards' in the provision of main grant services the appropriate Minister could report to Parliament recommending a reduction of grant which would however almost certainly have involved a formal resolution of the House of Commons. In practice, controls exercised by the various central government departments were not aimed at assessing 'reasonable standards', which would indeed be difficult to define at a time when for example the percentage of places for a grammar school education, which might be used as a criterion, varied between local authorities from eight per cent to 34 per cent of the relevant age group; and the percentage of those staying for a fifth year of education varied equally. To pursue assessment of local authority performance moreover beyond these crude criteria, to some form of assessment either of work in establishments of of use of manpower is a step no Minister to date has shown any desire or capacity to take.

After some years it became necessary for the government to yield to pressure from the AEC and the local authority associations and to increase the total amount of general grant available, to take account of known price rises due to come. The general grant in 1961–62 for example was increased to a national figure of 467 million (from 454 million) to take account of price and salary rises including the recent Burnham award for teachers, and a further increase took place in 1962–63.[12]

School meals and school milk continued to rank for 100 per cent grant from the central government however, subject to detailed central control of unit costs. Some expenditure was met from a national 'pool' to which all local education authorities subscribed according to the size of their population and school population, and to which they then charged all expenditure for teacher training, advanced technical education and the costs of educating pupils not belonging to the area of any authority.

Accounting

Lincoln and Nottingham were rating authorities, but Northumberland was not, since a county *precepts* on the urban and rural districts and non-county boroughs in its area. Each rating authority must by law keep one rate fund termed 'the general rate fund'.[13] If the general rate fund is more than sufficient to meet the immediate purposes for which it is needed, the surplus may be applied under the direction of the council for the improvement of the borough and for the benefit of its citizens.[14] In practice county councils have a rate fund into which all receipts from precepts are paid, both general county rates (for the whole area and for services for all) and special county rates (for example precepts for maintenance of magistrates' courts).

The surplus from general rates, which some authorities deliberately raise, can, however, be paid into special capital accounts built up over the years to finance yearly programmes involving recurrent capital expenditure too costly to finance directly from revenue account. Two Acts of Parliament (in 1953 and 1959) specifically encouraged local authorities and local education authorities to set up specific extra capital funds with a limit set to the level of annual payments, at one stage the product of an annual 3d. rate. *Nottingham* built up two such accounts. Neither Lincoln nor Northumberland felt able to do so, but while it was in fact discussed at officer level only in the county, in the mid 1950s, the proposal never reached Committee. The idea did not occur to Lincoln at all and the city still works without specific capital funds for education 'rolling programmes' of repair, renewal and re-equipping.

The very heavy capital expenditure involved in the education building programme meant that local authorities had to borrow the capital sums needed to finance the new schools needed, and the loan charges on these sums have become an increasingly heavy debt to be met each year from *revenue* account, i.e. out of annual rates. Until 1953 local authorities were in general allowed only to borrow from the Public Works Loan Board, but after this the Board could lend only if local authorities were unable to borrow from elsewhere.

Notes

1 The last remnant of the system is the retention by county and county borough councils of the duties collected on guns, game licences and dogs.
2 *The Practical Effects of Education Economy,* WEA, 1932.
3 *Local Expenditure and Exchequer Grants,* IMTA, 1956.
4 Proportion was also important. 'It is significant that all the boroughs incurring high expenditure on education have an above-average number of pupils in relation to their populations'. op. cit. p.86.
5 *Local Expenditure and Exchequer Grants,* IMTA, 1956.
6 Ibid. p.21.
7 VAIZEY, J. and SHEEHAN, J. *Resources for Education,* Unwin University Books. pp.27–28.
8 FISHER, N. 'Fiscal Management in an English local education authority', *The Year Book of Education* 1956. pp.357–8.
9 DAVEY, K. J. 'Local Autonomy and Independent Revenues', *Public Administration,* Spring 1971, vol.49, page 48.
10 'Nor, in our assessment, is its dominant position likely to be seriously disturbed in the foreseeable future'. op. cit.
11 For the main case put at the time against block grants, see *The Threat to Education,* Association of Education Committees. Opposition to the abolition of percentage grants was an issue which united the teachers' unions, the AEC, the General Council of the TUC, the Executive Committee of the County Councils Association, the WEA and many other powerful bodies—to no avail, however.
12 *Education* (23.2.62). p.582.
13 Rating and Valuation Act 1925, Section 10.
14 Local Government Act 1933, Section 185.

Sources, Method and Schools Survey

Sources
These are divided into written, oral (by interview) and evidence from visits to schools and colleges.

Written
Local sources were mainly committee and sub-committee records, and unpublished material on for example school accommodation, staffing and building programmes. Official City and County Guides gave useful background on industrial and social aspects of each area while organizations such as the AEC, NUT, Ministry of Labour, Economic Planning Council, provided special material on request. National written sources also include all circulars and memoranda issued by the Ministry of Education during the period 1945–65 and published governmental reports.

The evidence for all three areas gained from Committee records is based on full examination of the minutes for the complete 20-year period in every case and not a sample check of certain dates. This was considered essential to continuity, to check that decisions recorded were not later reversed, and to make sure that unforeseen factors or influences were not overlooked. The dangers of a sample check on minutes using only the index as a guide are even more marked in areas like Nottingham where the political strength was marginal and Councils changed in political colour regularly changing policies accordingly by implication.

Written local authority sources included:

(i) Minutes of the Education Committee, Secondary Education, Sites and Buildings, Finance and General Purposes Sub-Committees and Youth Employment Committees; Consultative Committee minutes for the sporadic periods when the committees met. In addition, County Council and City Council minutes were checked for specific subjects.

(ii) Minutes of County School governors for Lincoln City for the full period, for special information not available elsewhere.

(iii) Corporation and County Council accounts (capital and revenue) for each year from 1945–6 to 1964–5 (to establish, for example, how money was allocated, and how much came from central and from local sources).

Interviews

This early study led to the formation of a number of major questions the answers to which were likely to lie not only in written records but in the memories and attitudes of councillors, officers, heads and other local agencies affected. All existing (and some retired) administrative staff who were concerned with secondary education and/or with major policy generally in each area during the 20-year period, have therefore been interviewed (including heads of sections and senior clerks as well as Assistant Education Officers and their senior professional colleagues). Where necessary senior staff in the Treasurers' departments have also been interviewed, and grateful acknowledgement is made to those who not only explained financial policies but accounted for apparent ambiguities and discrepancies which can arise where the method of recording expenditure has been altered from year to year, or differs from that of other authorities. Evidence on the role of committees and councillors and on the possible contribution or otherwise of party politics, has been collected from a wide variety of sources including interviews with leading existing and retired Councillors in each area, especially those who had held major office within the period in question (not necessarily only those serving on the Education Committee and subcommittees). In Northumberland, councillors were deliberately chosen from both rural areas (Hexham, Berwick, Lynemouth) and urban areas (Wallsend, Tyneside). Representatives of teachers' organizations and, where they exist, of specific pressure groups, have been interviewed in each area, and it also proved possible to interview a limited number of specialists such as HMIs, the secretary of the AEC, representatives of the Association for Technical Education in Schools.

School Visits

The views of practising teachers are important, both as an alternative view of the history and development of secondary education and of the role of committees and officers in local decision-making in each area on the one hand; and as informed comment in general on the relationship of resources to school organization, courses, curriculum and standards. One underlying theme of this research is an underestimation of teachers' problems in meeting new educational needs and the demands of existing syllabuses, with decreasing resources. Visits were therefore made to a 29 per cent sample of secondary schools in Nottingham, 26·5 per cent in Northumberland and to nine out of 12 of the Lincoln secondary schools, representing a 31·5 per cent sample overall. In visiting each school, care was taken to ask a specific range of basic common questions in a loosely-structured interview as well as to seek informed comment on specific aspects either of local policies, or of the allocation of resources to schools or within the specific school. In all cases, head teachers spoke freely, gave up a full morning, afternoon or day, and encouraged other members of staff to speak with similar freedom. Many took trouble to prepare special information on pupil options in the upper school, placement of leavers or on matters of local interest.

Because of their potential 'explicit demand', representatives of the teachers' organizations have also been consulted in each area, with interesting results. Two main areas of discussion were chosen. First, how far they (a) aimed at and (b) succeeded in influencing policy and the distribution of resources locally, and second, how far they considered resource allocation to have affected the development of secondary education in their areas.

Necessarily, research which depends on evidence from interviews as well as from recorded facts and the interpretation of the latter, is likely to rely more heavily on judgement that some scientific research, or than that type of educational research which is based, for example, on more objectively controlled psychological testing or motor reactions of pupils. Some of the oral evidence itself relies for its validity or otherwise on the professional judgement of the person interviewed as well as on the judgement of the interviewer. On the other hand it is for the interviewer to judge the people as well as the accuracy of their memories and the soundness of their opinions. An interesting and impressive outcome of the collation of evidence from councillors, officers and heads in each area, is the general unanimity, despite vivid differences of phraseology and outlook, on the factors which were or were not important in each locality, and on the actual history of the developments.

Survey of Secondary Schools (1968–69)

The visits were paid to a sample of secondary schools in each area for a number of reasons. It should be emphasized, however, that most visits took no longer than one full day and that it was in no way the purpose of the school visits to analyse in depth the character and performance of the schools or to evaluate their quality of education—as distinct from the quality, quantity and allocation of their resources. To have attempted to evaluate the education provided was neither directly appropriate nor possible in the time available. Nor was it intended to compare schools of similar types one with another, except in the context of the allocation of resources and of the effect, if any, of this.

The survey had four main purposes. First, it was considered

necessary to check at first hand, a sample of the standard and quantity of accommodation and other resources; and to relate them both to the apparent policy of the authority over the 20-year period, and to the general availability of resources. Did the authorities carry out their intentions, in fact? Did the accommodation relate to the needs of pupils and of local industry? What was the actual effect of the allocation of capital resources? Second, it seemed highly desirable to seek a cross section of teacher-opinion on whether demand had released resources or whether lack of resources had depressed demand. Similarly, the views of teachers are important in relating curricular needs to the level and type of resources allocated to the schools. The visits were therefore a valuable source of 'feedback'. Third, it was important that in accounting for why and how the policies of the authorities developed in allocating resources and in shaping development plans, head teachers' views were sought as well as those of officers and members of the authorities. Fourth, the views of teachers were sought on the role, or potential role, of governors, teachers' organizations, industry and pressure groups.

On the question of obtaining information from heads and teachers in schools, each head was asked whether he or she would have preferred an 'objective' questionnaire to a personal visit taking up a whole day of their time. Of the 42 schools visited, all heads were unanimous in preferring a full visit and rejecting a questionnaire, their views being briefly summarized as follows:

(a) A questionnaire is no more objective than two-way personal discussion since the answers are in either case subjective, while it was suggested that a questionnaire rarely succeeds in translating the real aim of the research to the head.

(b) It is easier to show or explain differences or variations in accommodation standards, school organization, use of staff, etc., at the school than to attempt to describe them on paper, while difficult local questions or discussion of governors or administration can be dealt with in personal conversation, in a way which it might be inappropriate to commit to paper. In interview heads felt they had an opportunity to gauge the knowledge, understanding and responsibility of the research worker, and answer accordingly in greater or lesser detail and with appropriate frankness.

(c) Questionnaires do not moreover allow for follow-up questions arising from the exchange of ideas.

(d) Heads would willingly devote a full day to a visitor showing an obvious interest in the school as a school, but they resented abstract paperwork. Most commented that they would tend either to ignore yet another questionnaire or to answer it in a 10-minute break, probably superficially.

To these the writer would add an important rider. There is no substitute for the exercise of a degree of personal judgement on, for example, such aspects as common standards between types of schools. One research worker visiting 42 schools has a more valid hope of applying a comparable standard, than by assessing the material supplied by 42 heads replying in isolation to written questions. One head's estimate of a generous allowance or good science laboratories may be regarded as inadequate by another. One head's estimate of the practical use of governors may be more soundly based on shrewd reflection than another's.

The Sample

The schools included in the survey were chosen so far as possible to reflect the variety of provision in each area. They include grammar, technical, bilateral, comprehensive and modern schools. They include boys', girls' and mixed schools. The smallest was one-form entry, the largest 10-form entry. By far the majority (*as at* 1965) were from two- to five-form entry which reflected the average size of the schools in each area as a whole, as they had been planned by the authorities.[1] Analyses, by type and sex of school of the total number of schools and of the schools surveyed, appear in tables D (i) and D (ii) which follow. The sample represents 31·5 per cent of all secondary schools in the three areas. Nine schools out of 12 were visited in *Lincoln* (75 per cent) because the town is so small that a lesser sample would not have provided both grammar and modern schools and both old and new buildings; and for other reasons it was necessary to visit all six county secondary modern schools. Eleven schools out of 38 were visited in *Nottingham* (29 per cent) including its only comprehensive school. Twenty-two schools out of 83 were visited in *Northumberland* (26·5 per cent) including the only two technical schools; and including very small rural schools, schools in market towns, on housing estates, and on Tyneside. Visits were in fact also paid to a number of other schools but not in the context of the survey.

The schedules in Appendix E show that Lincoln rebuilt one grammar school, built two new modern schools, and enlarged three grammar and one modern school. *Nottingham* built six new grammar schools in the period 1948–66, enlarged a seventh, and built one new comprehensive school and 21 new non-grammar schools as well as adapting others. *Northumberland* built 10 new grammar schools, two new technical schools and 38 new modern schools in the survey period.

1 But since 1965, all three authorities have reorganized their schools and many schools are now much larger.

Sample survey of secondary schools. Distribution and type of schools visited

CODE	TYPE OF SCHOOL AND ORGANIZATION	DESIGN FORM ENTRY AND DATE OF MAIN BUILDING	CATCHMENT AREA
NORTHUMBERLAND			
1	Grammar Mixed	4 (1956)	Council housing estate—overspill from Newcastle
2	Grammar (technical bias)	5 (1960)	Small mining town
3	Grammar Mixed	4 (1959) (now 5)	Campus in rural area on Tyneside fringe
4	Grammar Mixed	5 (1962)	Middle-class seaside resort
5	Modern Mixed	1 (1960)	Isolated rural community in South Tyne Valley
6	Modern Mixed	4 (Mid-1930s)	Small country town near coastal strip
7	Modern Mixed	3/4 (1963)	Small mining town
8	Modern Mixed	2 (1960)	Suburb on the border of Newcastle city—centre of private housing estate
9	Modern Mixed	4 (1958)	New council estate in Tyneside Wallsend
10	Modern Mixed	3 (1960)	Very small town in isolated rural area between Newcastle and Carlisle
11	Technical Mixed	3 (1962)	Rural area in west of County, South Tyne
12	Modern Mixed	3 (1931)	Country town near junction of South and North Tyne
13	Modern Mixed	3 (1959)	Small country town
14	Modern Mixed	3 (1931)	Ditto.
15	Modern Mixed	4 (1963) (now 5/6)	Very recent council overspill estate north west of Newcastle
16	(Voluntary) Modern Mixed	2 (1964)	Village in rural area on borders of forest in Coquetdale
17	(Voluntary) Modern Mixed	4 (1964)	Council estate and Killingworth new town

NORTHUMBERLAND (continued)

18	Modern boys	4 (1954)	Overspill housing estate on northern borders of Newcastle—early post-war
19	Modern girls	4 (1954)	
20	Modern Mixed	3 (1959)	Campus in rural area on Tyneside fringe
21	Technical Mixed	4/5 (1960)	Dense urban area by Tyne estuary
22	Modern Mixed	4/5 (1956)	Middle-class seaside resort

LINCOLN

23	Grammar Boys	3 (1968)	Mostly south of the City
24	Grammar Girls	3 (1893)	North of City
25	Modern Girls	4 (1957)	South of City, including new housing estates
26	Modern Girls	2 (1936)	1930s housing estate and urban centre of City
27	Modern Boys	2 (1932)	West of the City—older housing
28	Modern Boys	4 (1903)	Urban City centre
29	Modern Girls	3 (1929, 1934)	Centre and north of City— old terraced housing
30	Modern Boys	2 (1936)	1930s housing estate and urban centre of City
31	(Voluntary) Modern Mixed	2 (1956)	Whole City

NOTTINGHAM

32	Grammar Boys	5 (1955, extended 1964)	About half of City but mainly local council estates
33	Grammar Mixed	4 (1893 + science wing 1960)	South of City—partly a depressed area
34	Bilateral Girls	5/6 (1957)	Extreme north—strong local community. On outskirts but near a poorer urban district
35	Modern Mixed	4 (1930s)	Slum area near City centre
36	Bilateral Mixed	8 (1966)	Poor area east of City— school took in three old schools on opening. Some new housing

NOTTINGHAM (continued)

37	Comprehensive Boys	10 (1958)	Post-war housing estates in self-contained area south of City
38/39	Bilateral Mixed	6 (formerly 2 x 3) Main building 1952. Annexe pre-war. New extensions being designed	Very old area with very little new housing at all. Working class district
40	Bilateral Mixed	6 (1955)	Borders of better middle class area of City. Some older council housing
41/42	Bilateral Mixed	4 (formerly 2 x 2) (1930s)	1930s housing estate, spacious and well planned

Table D (i): Total maintained secondary schools in the survey areas, by type and sex (1965)

B=Boys; G=Girls; M=Mixed

	LINCOLN	NOTTINGHAM	NORTHUMBERLAND	TOTAL
Grammar				
B	2	2	2	6
G	2	3	5	10
M	—	3	9	12
Technical *Bilateral* *Comprehensive*				
B	—	2	—	2
G	—	3	—	3
M	—	12	2	14
Modern				
B	3	4	5	12
G	3	4	5	12
M	2	5	55	62
Totals	12	38	83	133

Summary	B	G	M	*Total*
Total schools	20	25	88	133
Schools surveyed	9	8	25	42

Table D (ii): Analysis of schools surveyed by the writer in 1968/69, by type and sex of schools

B=Boys; G=Girls; M=Mixed

	LINCOLN	NOTTINGHAM	NORTHUMBERLAND	TOTAL
Grammar				
B	1	1	—	2
G	1	—	—	1
M	—	1	4	5
Technical				
Bilateral				
Comprehensive				
B	—	1	—	1
G	—	1	—	1
M	—	2	2	4
Modern				
B	3	2	1	6
G	3	2	1	6
M	1	1	14	16
Totals	9	11	22	42
% of total schools in Table D (i)	75%	29%	26·5%	31·5%

Notes: The organization of the schools is shown as at 1965. In Nottingham, four single sex modern schools were reorganized between 1965 and 1968 as two mixed bilateral schools. The survey examined the accommodation, resources and organization as at 1965, and they are therefore shown here as single sex modern schools although in the code list they are entered as mixed bilateral schools (codes 38/39 and 41/42).

Table D (iii): Schools Survey 1968/69. *Schools deficient in basic classrooms or form bases*

Note: For each missing classroom, a class had to be based on a specialist room (e.g. science, housecraft, library or hall) for general teaching thus limiting its specialist use.

Total schools—24 out of 42 = 57%

(a) Type

	B	G	M	TOTAL
Grammar/technical	1	1	3	5
Modern/Bilateral	3	4	12	19
Total	4	5	15	24

of whom over half were short of more than 3 rooms.

(b) Size

	2/3 FORM ENTRY	4 FORM ENTRY AND OVER	TOTAL
Grammar/technical	2	3	5
Modern/bilateral	15	4	19
Total	17	7	24

Note: In calculating the adequacy of accommodation a form base is needed for each group of 30 pupils (i.e. a four-form entry five-year school needs 20) with half as many more specialist rooms overall.

Table D (iv): Schools Survey 1968/69. *Analysis of science accommodation basic provision*

(*a*) *Schools with at least* 3 '*O*' *level laboratories and for grammar and technical schools, enough advanced laboratories*

	B	G	M	TOTAL
Grammar	2	—	5	7
Technical	—	—	2	2
Modern/other	—	—	4	4
Sub-total	2	—	11	13

(These schools were adequate)

(*b*) *Girls' grammar school with no advanced laboratories:*   1

(*c*) *Schools with only one laboratory (secondary modern)*

SIZE	B	G	M	
One-, two- and three-form entry	2	5	3	10

(*d*) *Schools with only two laboratories (secondary modern)*

SIZE	B	G	M	
Two-form entry	2	—	—	2
Three-form entry	1	—	5	6
Four/five-form entry	1	1	6	8
Five/six-form entry	—	1	1	2
Total	4	2	12	18

Total schools: 42

Table D (v): Deficiencies in handicraft and housecraft accommodation (non-grammar schools)

(a) Many schools had too few craft spaces for the number on roll. Five modern schools had only one handicraft room, usually woodwork. Thirteen non-grammar schools had no facilities for technical drawing, which was timetabled in an ordinary classroom. Eleven non-grammar schools had no facilities for needlework, using ordinary classrooms without sinks, fitting bays or adequate space for machine tables. (Craft facilities in all but one grammar schools were adequate; and underused in all but one.)

(b) Most mixed schools had an imbalance of provision of which the following sample is typical:

SCHOOL	WOOD	METAL	TECH. DRAWING	HOUSECRAFT	NEEDLEWORK
5 f.e. mixed grammar	1	2	1	2	1
3 f.e. mixed modern	2	2	—	1	—
3 f.e. mixed technical	1	1	1	1	1
3 f.e. mixed modern	1	1	1	1	—
3 f.e. mixed technical	2	2	1	2	2
4 f.e. mixed modern	1	2	1	2	2
	8	10	5	9	6

Thus crafts appealing predominantly to boys were given substantially more accommodation than those appealing to girls, when authorities designed or adapted schools.

Table D (vi): Schools Survey 1968/69. Semi-specialist rooms—Accommodation

---

(a) Libraries

Only 21 schools out of 42 had libraries of the minimum size recommended in the 1934 Carnegie report and in postwar building bulletins (Building Bulletin 2 suggests 960 square feet as a minimum). Four schools had no library at all. One school had built a library from parental funds. One school used a former secretary's office and another a former store. Six schools had libraries (for over 400 pupils) of less than 400 square feet. Five schools had to use libraries as classrooms because of overcrowding.

(b) Music

Only five schools out of 42 had purpose designed music rooms or suitable rooms of adequate size in which to teach either groups or individual work.

(c) Geography

Only 12 schools out of 42 had geography rooms of 700 square feet or above, with water, and suitable furniture and space. The remainder either shared a multi purpose room or used standard classrooms thus severely restricting teaching methods.

(d) History

Only six non-grammar schools had purpose designed or adapted history rooms suitable for child-centred learning.

(e) Commerce

Of the 17 schools offering commerce or typing only three had a larger room than a standard classroom, suitably designed and equipped. The remainder used ordinary 500 square feet classrooms, limiting availability to a half class, and cramping teaching method.

(f) Art

Sixteen schools had fewer art teaching spaces then necessary for the number on roll. Thirteen schools had art rooms either totally inadequate in size or not suitably equipped.

(g) Needlework

More than half of the schools taught needlework in ordinary classrooms of 480 square feet, (to half-classes) without sinks, mirrors, fitting bays or adequate storage or demonstration tables. The siting of the rooms was rarely related to the housecraft provision.

Table D (vii): Schools Survey (1968–69). School allowances

Head teachers and heads of departments were asked questions about differential allowances. The answers are briefly summarized below.

(*i*) *Grammar school pupils need more money than non-academic children.*

All modern and about half of the grammar/selective teachers interviewed disagreed in principle with this. About half of all teachers supported a differential allowance for the sciences.

(*ii*) *Older pupils need more money than younger pupils.*

All staffs consulted had reservations about this except VIth form teachers. About 65 per cent produced evidence for supplementary allowances in the year of transfers in the survey areas from 11–12, and for IIIrd year remedial work.

(*iii*) *Boys need more money/resources than girls.*

Only about 10 per cent of staff interviewed supported this in theory, but a majority of schools differentiated in practice when the destination of the allowances was identified.

(*iv*) *Curricular innovation—should LEA's finance this or should it be financed by the Department of Education and Science?*

Opinions were sharply divided on this. Most teachers in schools with experimental allowances preferred their main subsidies to come from local authorities, but teachers in (mainly non-grammar) schools without major project work or special allowances tended to disapprove of the pegging of basic standards to meet local costs of experimental innovation for a minority of schools. About three-quarters of all teachers were not satisfied with the present method of funding new approaches to teaching. About 60 per cent of secondary modern teachers interviewed wanted the same level of special allowance for new projects incorporating new techniques or approaches, as is awarded to 'recognised' Schools Council projects. About 80 per cent of all head teachers interviewed would prefer to see longer periods of 'feedback' before substantial sums are disbursed by local authorities for innovation.

(*v*) *Allowances are adequate for both replacement and development.*

Between 80 per cent and 90 per cent of all heads and heads of departments interviewed, produced evidence that school allowances were inadequate for both maintenance and renewal and curricular development. About half chose to innovate so far as possible and cut back on renewal of basic equipment and books; but half maintained existing standards and held back the introduction of new schemes. Fifteen schools (out of 42) were prevented from introducing team teaching, integrated courses and Mode III CSE because of inadequate resources.

(*vi*) *Virement*

Only about a quarter of heads favoured block allocations in the school budget with power of virement. Threequarters thought pressure for individual subjects more effective.

Table D (viii): Schools survey 1968/69. The role of the governors

---

(a) *What part do your governors play? Do they influence either major decisions, or the resources available to the school? Do they change things?*

Thirty-five out of 42 head teachers said their governors were ineffective. Twenty-seven considered them a complete waste of time, administration and money. Eight heads thought governors should no longer be political appointments. Four heads said 'they don't even visit'. Six heads said 'not a ha'porth of difference'.

One head commented 'it is inconceivable that the governors would not support my view' but added that she got things done because of her relationship with her chief officer and not through her governors. Another commented 'a good head can flannel his governors anyway, so why bother?' Another—'In no circumstances would I allow lay governors to overrule my professional judgement'.

Of the seven who thought governors had had an effect on their school only one included an effect on resources. This was a technical school—the governors had helped to acquire and conserve land for the school's use. 'Their technical advice was useful'. Three heads were from voluntary schools, and thought their governors had more power. Three quoted instances of a decision for which the governors fought. These three were asked 'What would have happened if you had had no governors, like your primary schools which have no managers? What would the chief officer/committee have done?' All three considered that the decision would have been unchanged. One head thought it directly wrong that governors should attempt to influence the allocation of resources.

(b) *Do the governors have a community role? Do you prefer to keep them?*

Fifteen heads thought governors were 'a good moral support to a school'. One head in a rural town used them to place his school-leavers. Another commented—'they take a real and personal interest in our school'. A third said 'I don't want to be governed. But if I had had a School Community Committee, we wouldn't have started on this new estate with only two small shops, no community centre, no clubs, no play area and no Youth Block . . .'. A number said 'governors are nice to have around'.

Table D (ix): *Schools survey (1968). External examination courses (1965) by size and type of school*

Schools	GCE Only	GCE/CSE	GCE/CSE/Northern Counties Technical Education Certificate	CSE Only	None*	Total
Grammar (3—5 form entry)	2	6	—	—	—	8
Technical	—	1	1	—	—	2
Other non-grammar (1—3 form entry)	—	7	1	5	5	18
Other non-grammar (4 form entry and over)	—	11	1	—	2	14
Total	2	25	3	5	7	42

* in the survey period. All seven offered some examination work in 1968.

APPENDIX E

Table E (i): Major building programmes authorized by the Ministry/Department of Education and Science

YEAR	PRIMARY AND SECONDARY £000	FURTHER EDUCATION £000	SPECIAL SCHOOLS £000	TEACHER TRAINING £000	TOTAL ALLOCATION £000
1945–47	28,038	—	—	—	28,038
1947–49	9,453	2,911	446	1,161	13,972
1949–50	55,045	8,720	648	1,466	65,879
1950–51	46,440	6,990	931	782	55,143
1951–52	14,169	3,957	258	1,171	19,195
1952–53	45,642	4,064	1,059	997	51,762
1953–54	45,937	4,064	1,089	1,093	52,183
1954–55	48,286	4,897	1,808	1,401	56,392
1955–56	79,590	8,178	1,392	2,081	91,241
1956–57	73,751	13,899	2,239	1,484	91,193
1957–58	24,474	19,157	599	360	44,590
1958–59	50,121	16,788	1,683	929	69,521
1959–60	41,294	20,800	1,862	493	64,449
1960–61	78,427	8,532	3,172	934	91,065
1961–62	81,659	15,357	2,924	1,030	100,070
1962–63	71,013	19,105	3,482	1,611	95,211
1963–64	55,535	19,200	3,000	1,060	78,795
1964–65	53,259	20,007	4,230	307	77,803
Between 1958 and 1963 there were in addition four special Teacher Training expansion programmes totalling				50,718	50,718
Total:					1,197,220

Source: Building Intelligence Team of the Department of Education and Science.

Table E (ii): Lincoln. Secondary school major building programmes approved by the Ministry of Education (1945—1965)

YEAR	SCHOOL	ORIGINAL ESTIMATED COST £	COMMENT
1954–55	New RC secondary mixed modern (150 places)	50,000	Replacement of existing all-age school. No net gain in places.
1955–56	Boultham Moor girls' modern (480 places)	155,342	Replacement of Sincil Girls' School which closed in 1958 with a roll of 563, the girls transferring to the new school. No net gain in places.
1956–57	St. Giles modern mixed	28,000 revised to 42,000	Separation of mixed school for 500 into separate boys' and girls' schools of 250 each.
1956–57	Christ's Hospital High girls' grammar	29,000	Completion of the extension from two- to three-form entry.
1956–57	Lincoln boys' grammar	30,000 approx.	Extensions from two- to three-form entry.
1959–60	South Park High girls' grammar	50,500	Extensions from two- to three-form entry. No extra places for children from the City. Places provided for Lindsey children from the county area.
1960–61	Boultham Moor modern girls, phase II	52,740	Second instalment— 120 extra places.
1961–62	S.S. Peter & Paul RC modern mixed, phase II	56,258	Second instalment— 150 extra places.
1965–66	City School boys' grammar	250,113	No extra places— replacement of existing three-form entry grammar school. (Second phase for VIth form in 1964–68, £41,500).
		£715,953	

Table E (iii): Nottingham. Secondary school major building programmes—approved by the Ministry of Education (1945—1966)

YEAR	SCHOOL	TYPE	PLACES	PRELIMINARY ESTIMATED COST £
1948	Bestwood	Modern	2 halls	20,000
1949	William Sharp I	Modern	400	144,935
1948–49	Glaisdale	Modern	640	160,000 ⎫
	Padstow	Modern	480	199,790 ⎬
	Manvers	Modern	480	190,000 ⎭
			Total	549,790
1951–52	High Pavement Phase I ⎱	Grammar	Ultimate 550	50,000 ⎫
	Farnborough	Modern	680	200,060 ⎬
	Wollaton (1)		680 ⎱	
	Wollaton (2)		680 ⎰	420,780
			Total	670,840 ⎭

Farnborough and Wollaton schools were subsequently deferred

Revised

1952–53	High Pavement II	Grammar	—	152,040 ⎫
	Farnborough	Modern	600	181,338 ⎪
	Margaret Glen Bott ⎱	Modern	600	186,336 ⎬
	William Sharp ⎰ (Phase II)	Modern	80	55,000 ⎭
			Total	524,674

But £367,674 was carried over from previous year.

1953–54	Greenwood	Modern	600	192,000 ⎫
	Peveril	Modern	600	192,000 ⎬
	Roland Green	Modern	600	192,000 ⎭
			Total	576,000
1954–55	Charnwood	Modern	600	192,000 ⎱
	Bilborough	Grammar	550	172,425 ⎰
			Total	364,425
1955–56	William Derbyshire	Modern	600	153,000 ⎫
	Clifton No. 3	Modern	680	192,000 ⎬
	Clifton Hall	Grammar	360	128,000 ⎭
			Total	473,300

Year	School	Type	Places	Preliminary Estimated Cost
1956–57	Sherwood	Modern	450	151,604 ⎫
	Corpus Christi RC	Modern	300	92,240 ⎬
	Fairham I	Comprehensive	1100	351,981 ⎭
			Total	595,825
1957–58	Fernwood	Modern	450	151,604 ⎫
1958–59	Fairham II	Comprehensive	450	119,800 ⎬
	Mundella (science)	Grammar	—	61,500 ⎭
			Total	181,300
1959–60	None (Both projects transferred to later programmes)			
1960–61	St. Catherines RC	Grammar	360	123,420
	Guilford I & II	Bilateral	1200	306,935
	St. Bernadettes RC	Modern	450 (only 150 extra places)	144,036
			Total	574,391
1961–62	Elliott Durham I	Bilateral	540	187,170 ⎫
	Claremont I & II Remodelling	Modern	—	69,192 ⎬
			Total	256,362
1962–63	Padstow II	Bilateral	200	85,639
	Elliott Durham II	Bilateral	600	193,146
	High Pavement III (extensions) (VIth form)	Grammar	100	33,412
			Total	312,197
1963–64	Bishop Dunn RC	Modern	300	161,086
1964–65	Padstow III Completion	Modern	?	43,594
	Bilborough	Grammar	90	51,570
			Total	95,164
1965–66	None			—
1966–67	Forest Fields (new)	Grammar	550	270,358
	Bluecoat CE	Grammar	350	177,331
			Total	447,689

Table E (iv): Northumberland. Secondary school projects—major building programmes approved by the Ministry of Education (1946—1965)

Year	School	Form Entry	Preliminary Cost £
1946	Amble modern	2 f.e.	38,982
	Bellingham modern	2 f.e.	122,636
		Total	161,028
1949	Longbenton (SB) and (SG) modern.	3 f.e.⎫ 3 f.e.⎭	343,570
	Blyth modern	2 f.e. less one classroom	120,000
		Total	463,570

Approved but later deferred by the Ministry

	Wooler modern	2 f.e. less one classroom ⎫	—
	Longbenton technical	3 f.e. ⎭	—
1950	Wooler Glendale modern	2 f.e.	100,515

Approved but later deferred by Ministry

	Longbenton technical	3 f.e. ⎫	—
	Newburn modern	3 f.e. ⎬	—
	Seaton Burn modern	3 f.e. ⎭	—
1951–52	Seaton Burn modern	3 f.e.	128,640
	Prudhoe (but deferred until 1956 in practice by LEA)	3 f.e.	128,640
		Total	257,280

Approved but later deferred by Ministry

	Newburn	3 f.e.	—
1952–53	Newburn (cut to 2 f.e. and reinstated as 3 f.e. after negotiations)	3 f.e.	128,640
1953–54	Whitley Bay modern	3 f.e.	164,619
	Longbenton (SB) and (SG)—extensions	1 f.e. ⎫ 1 f.e. ⎭	129,360
	Walbottle (East) modern	3 f.e.	158,940
		Total	452,919

Year	School	Form Entry	Preliminary Cost £
1954–55	Belington Westridge modern	2 f.e. plus 2 classrooms	99,000 instalment
		revised on negotiation to 3 f.e.	170,410
After deputation to Minister	George Stephenson grammar		141,069
	Whitley Bay Valley Gardens modern	3 f.e.	164,619
	Hexham hostel for boys		8,910
		Total	485,008
1955–56	Prudhoe modern	3 f.e.	167,954
	Wallsend Hadrian modern	3 f.e.	184,475
	Walbottle grammar phase I	2 f.e.	112,200
	Tweedmouth modern	2 f.e.	136,701
	Morpeth ⎫ Chantry ⎬ modern ⎭	2 f.e. plus one classroom	143,968
	North Sunderland modern	1 f.e.	58,130
	Alnwick modern ⎰	2 f.e. less 2 classrooms	88,700 ⎱
		revised after negotiations, to remodelling of old school to become 4 f.e.	142,038
	Ponteland (voluntary) modern	2 f.e. plus one classroom	103,150
		Total	1,048,616

YEAR	SCHOOL	FORM ENTRY	PRELIMINARY COST £
1956–57	Walbottle grammar phase II	2 f.e.	118,483
	Walbottle (West) modern	3 f.e.	148,890
	Alnwick RC St. Mary's modern	1 f.e. revised to	49,368 ⎱ 61,066 ⎰
	Wallsend Technical	4 f.e.	223,800
	Corbridge modern	2 f.e. less 2 classrooms	93,456
	Belford modern	1 f.e.	49,368
	Gosforth East Modern	2 f.e. instalment of 4 f.e.	106,145
	Ashington Grammar phase I	3 f.e.	177,725
	Allendale modern +hostel	1 f.e. revised to	59,368 ⎱ 82,445 ⎰
		Total	913,378
1957–58	Haltwhistle modern	3 f.e. less 2 classrooms, revised to 2 f.e. plus 2 classrooms	150,233 ⎫ revised to ⎬ 111,425 ⎭
	Alnwick, Duke's grammar	1 f.e. remodelling	53,250
	St. Josephs RC Killingworth modern	3 f.e.	148,104
		Total	312,779
1958–59	Seahouses modern	1 f.e.	48,620
	Haydon Bridge Technical	2 f.e. plus one classroom instalment of 3 f.e.	108,785
		Total	157,405

Year	School	Form Entry	Perliminary Cost £
1959–60	Gosforth grammar	3 f.e. instalment of 4 f.e.	186,011
	Newbiggin Hall Cheviot modern	3 f.e.	148,104
	Blyth Technical	3 f.e.	220,719 (later withdrawn)
	Whitley Bay Grammar phase I	4 f.e.	482,862
		Total	1,037,696
1960–61	Hexham Queen Elizabeth grammar	3 f.e.	298,205
	Bedlington St. Benet Biscops RC modern	2 f.e.	127,653
	Newbiggin by the Sea modern	4 f.e.	297,383
	Guide Post modern	3 f.e.	217,156
	Ashington Bothal modern	3 f.e.	267,972
	Lemington, Claremont modern	3 f.e.	213,497
		Total	1,421,866
1961–62	Rothbury Tomlinson's CE modern	1 f.e.	112,272
	Blyth grammar school phase I	5 f.e.	281,205
	South Broomhill modern	2 f.e. plus one classroom	175,723
	Dudley modern	3 f.e. less 2 classrooms	211,658
	Prudhoe stage II		36,518
		Tota	817,376

Year	School	Form Entry	Preliminary Cost £
1962–63	West Denton,	2 f.e. less	172,853
	St. Aidans RC modern	2 classrooms	
	Astley modern	5 f.e. less 2 classrooms	322,715
	Alnwick, Duchess's grammar	—	219,999
	Ashington grammar, phase II	2 f.e.	135,416
		Total	850,983
1963–64	Whitley Bay RC grammar	—	291,555
	Morpeth King Edward grammar (boys)	3 f.e.	612,318
	Morpeth grammar (girls)	3 f.e.	
		Total	903,873
1964–65	Berwick grammar/ technical	2 f.e.	138,127
	Ashington, St. Benedicts RC modern	1 f.e. + 2 classrooms	109,794
	Wallsend Deneside modern	4 f.e.	382,513
	Willington Quay modern	4 f.e.	382,513
	Alnwick,Dukes— extensions	—	69,223
		Total	1,082,170
1965–66	Ponteland grammar	2 f.e. +75 VIth instalment of 4 f.e. +120 VIth	186,990
	Cramlington grammar	3 f.e. +90 VIth instalment of 4 f.e. +120 VIth	228,279
	North Killingworth modern	3 f.e. instalment of 4 f.e.	230,786
		Total	646,055

INDEX